FILMMAKER 365

"IT'S NOT A JOB IT'S A LIFESTYLE"

Part 2: *July - December*

365 FILMMAKING AND VIDEO PRODUCTION TIPS, TRICKS & TECHNIQUES

CR PRODUCTION MUSIC.COM

July 1st

10 Things to Know About Starting a Production Company

Starting a production company isn't easy. Here's what you need to know to get started successfully.

Let's go ahead and repeat what we said up top, because it's a hard truth: **Starting a production company isn't easy.** It's a lot of hard work. But if you dedicate yourself to it, then you can make it happen. I learned a thing or two after starting a production company of my own in 2013. So let me share some advice I was given when starting out. Hopefully these ten points will help you as much as they helped me.

1. Have an Idea of What You Want to Do

This can be the hardest step in the entire process – but it doesn't have to be. You should know going into all of this what you want to do, whether that be films, commercial, industrial, etc. If you don't? Now is the time to figure it out. It's also beneficial to write out your short term and long term goals. Identify your strengths and see how you can build your company around them. Just be sure to have all of this in place before you **begin the process of developing your company.**

2. Research What Others Have Done Well and Not So Well

Now that you know what you want to do, you'll need to do a lot of research. This is key. If you are doing commercial or industrial work, then you need to **research your local area and gauge who else is doing this same type of work.** Use a site like ProductionHUB to help aid in your research. Pay attention to the services and fees that other companies provide and charge. If you can find this information, then you can **find ways to compete in the market.**

If you're going into film, then you need to really research areas of the industry that fit your talents. You may be an incredibly skilled artist and could offer pre-visualization services. Maybe you're great at promotions and could offer film marketing. Look at other **successful production companies in your field** and read how they got started. Use this information as a road map.

3. Be Creative with Your Name

Creating the name for your **production company** is key — this will eventually become your brand. So make it good and make it something relevance to you. For instance, Steven Spielberg's production company is Amblin Entertainment, whose name came from Steven's very first completed film *Amblin*. Or you could go another route and use part of your name like Ridley Scott did for his production company Scott Free. Just be creative and **make sure your company stands out.**

Here's a great article from Ian Mohr of GQ that gives you insight on *How to Name Your Hollywood Production Company.* There's some great humor here — and a lot of truth.

4. Research and Make Sure Everything is Legal

Once you have your name hammered out, you need to begin looking ahead. One thing you need to be aware of is that you're eventually going to want to **trademark the name.** Now this doesn't sound like a big deal, **but it is.** For example, years ago I applied for a trademark for my **production company**. However, another company had a name close to what I had created. They were also using the same classification code I was applying for. Because of this, I was not awarded the trademark and had to start all over.

Be very creative with your name and then check that name against the USPTO trademark database. Scour the internet for already established companies. You'll eventually want to contact an attorney who works with trademark law. They can do a comprehensive search and help you **file for your trademark.** Just be aware that a trademark filing will run you $2000 or more when all is said and done.

5. Decide What Type of Company You'll Be

We know what you want to do with your company. We know the name. **But now what type of company are you going to be?** Confused? It's okay, I was too when the question was posed to me. You want to decide early on if you need to be a DBA, LLC, C-Corp, S-Corp, etc.

This decision is going to affect the cost of filing to do business. It will also affect your tax filings as well. Check out this information from the Small Business Administration.

Sole Proprietorship: *"A sole proprietorship is the simplest and most common structure chosen to start a business. It is an unincorporated business owned and run by one individual with no distinction between the business and you, the owner."*

LLC (Limited Liability Company): *"A limited liability company is a hybrid type of legal structure that provides the limited liability features of a corporation and the tax efficiencies and operational flexibility of a partnership. The "owners" of an LLC are referred to as "members." Depending on the state, the members can consist of a single individual (one owner), two or more individuals, corporations or other LLCs."*

Cooperative: *"A cooperative is a business or organization owned by and operated for the benefit of those using its services. Profits and earnings generated by the cooperative are distributed among the members, also known as user-owners."*

C Corp (Corporation): *"A corporation (sometimes referred to as a C corporation) is an independent legal entity owned by shareholders. This means that the corporation itself, not the shareholders that own it, is held legally liable for the actions and debts the business incurs."*

S Corp (Corporation): *"An S corporation (sometimes referred to as an S Corp) is a special type of corporation created through an IRS tax election. An eligible domestic corporation can avoid double taxation (once to the corporation and again to the shareholders) by electing to be treated as an S corporation."*

Partnership: *"A partnership is a single business where two or more people share ownership. Each partner contributes to all aspects of the business, including money, property, labor or skill. In return, each partner shares in the profits and losses of the business."*

6. Find a Certified Public Accountant

Now that you have your name and your structure, you'll need to **find someone to help you navigate the world of accounting for your business.** This is not something you want to do yourself. **Hire a Certified Public Accountant.** A good CPA will not only help you figure out what will be required of you when tax season comes around, but they can help you set a realistic strategy for your business as well.

With all of this said, don't just pick the first CPA that you find. Go in and sit with them and talk with them. Find out if they are the right fit for you. Research them online and look for reviews from others who have used their services. You're going to be working very closely with your CPA, **so find the one that is right for you and your company.**

Try using the CPA Directory to get started, or just Google CPAs in your area.

7. Create Your Business Plan

Every business needs a plan. A **production company** is no different. This is the time when you want to take the short and long term goals you set for yourself and turn them into a business plan. Get really detailed and try to map out your path for the next three to five years. Give the **description of your production company, what area of the industry it will focus on, and who will be running it.**

Also, include all of the research and market analysis you did in the beginning that helped you determine what type of **production company** you'll be. A business plan is a must have for any business and it's a great way to gauge your progress and keep that progress on track.

8. Consult an Attorney

Once you get rolling and want to take it to the next level, **you're going to need representation.** While this shouldn't be one of the last things you do, it usually is the costliest, so it tends to get put off for as long as possible. Don't wait too long to consult with and find an attorney to represent you — at some point you are going to need them. **Better to have them in place early than too late.**

Just like the CPA and Trademark Lawyer, take your time meeting and researching attorneys. You want someone who is going to work hard for you. One way to **find a good corporate or company attorney** is to talk to people you know in the industry. Gauge their recommendations and then go from there.

Check out this really good article from Entrepreneur.com on *How to Hire an Attorney.*

9. Secure Start-up Capital

Next to creating the name of your company, the hardest thing to do is to **secure start-up capital for your company.** If you're working in commercial and industrial, you'll need a certain level of equipment — which means you'll need money. I've never been a fan of taking out loans, but I've seen some people do this and capitalize on it to start a really successful business.

For film production companies, there are all sorts of venture capitalists out there looking for ways to expand their portfolio. One of the good things about being in film is that pre-production is usually going to be the cheapest part of the process. With that said, you might be able to float this part of the project and get something together that can **impress potential investors.** Just be sure to have a well-developed presentation before you go into these meetings. If you can show that you have the skill and development to pull this off, then you should be able to **secure some sort of funding for your film.**

10. Get Out There and Spread Your Name

The biggest part about our business and this industry is **networking.** You really can't ever talk too much about your project and your **production company.** But in order to maximize your visibility, make sure **you have a presence online.** Start with a website for your company, then start looking at social media like Facebook and Twitter. Then jump to the next level of social media that exists specifically for film professionals like Creative District and Stage 32.

July 2nd

8 Questions to Ask Yourself When Deciding on a Script

Have you written or received a script for your next project? Here are eight questions to ask before moving into production.

There is a tremendous amount of scripts written every year. Conservative estimates began at 30,000-50,000 scripts, and that's only including those filed with the **Writers Guild of America** (WGAe & WGAw). If scripts filed for copyright are included, the number can easily go up to 100,000.

With all those scripts floating around, it must be easy to find your next project — right? Wrong. According to the latest Scoggins Report, only **90 specs were sold in 2014**. Up until March 2015, only 26 specs have been sold.

So what does all this mean to you as a filmmaker? If you find a script that you can get behind 100%, then you have found a very rare story. Here are some questions to ask before you get your film moving.

1. Why Do I Want to Tell This Story?

It seems like an easy question, but it really isn't. When it comes to deciding on a project, you must be willing to give your whole life to seeing it through. That means you need to be emotionally involved with every character. You need to know every little detail in order to make this project a reality.

If you don' think you need to know every character, just look at D.B. Weiss and David Benioff, the showrunners of *Game of Thrones*. The duo actually got the green-light for the show when an HBO executive saw Benioff working out in the gym while reading his annotated copy of his *Game of Thrones* book. That's the type of dedication a project requires.

2. Why Am I the Best Person to Tell This Story?

You cannot only dedicate yourself to a script, but you also have to believe in yourself. If you don't feel like you have the ability to see a project through to its completion the way it should be done, then you'll begin to question your own abilities. **Don't be afraid to walk away from a project if you don't believe in yourself.** A bad film can destroy your mentality.

If you do believe in yourself, don't just rely on your skill. Really push yourself to do something you've never done before. This is a chance to not only hone your skills, but to create a project that you can cherish forever. You need to believe that you are the perfect person for this job, and that no one could ever do it better.

3. What Is My Emotional Connection to This Script?

As mentioned in the first question, you need to become emotionally involved with every character. You also need to become **emotionally attached to the story** itself. What is the true meaning of the film? What do you want your audience to take away after the credits start rolling?

This was something incredibly challenging for director Pete Docter as he was re-working his film about emotions, *Inside Out*.

I'll tell you a story: there was a dark point about three years into the making of the film. The pressure was mounting. We were approaching a screening and I went for a walk the weekend before, going, "Shoot, it's just not working. What if I just quit and move to Mexico — what would I miss the most?" And I thought, well, my friends. But then I thought, the people I really feel close to are the people that, yeah, I've felt happiness with, but also they are people that I've been pissed off at, and scared for. The subject matter I'm dealing with in this movie is the key to relationships. So I got electrified, went back, talked to the guys, we rewrote the script, and that was a major turning point in the film. [Wired] (Pete Docter)

4. Am I Willing to Dedicate Months or Years to This Project?

Is the story so great that you are willing to dedicate yourself to the project for years? **You don't know what obstacles await**, and your production could be halted. Are you willing to wait to make this film?

For a great recent example, let's look at director George Miller. His 2015 film *Mad Max: Fury Road* received rave reviews, and the film was heralded as an all-around spectacular action film. You may not know that the film was stuck in "development hell" for 20 years. Miller reacquired the rights to Mad Max in 1995. It took three more years until he had his story in place.

He was set to start filming in 2001, and then the events of September 11th postponed the project. Then turmoil in Namibia, the location of the shoot, postponed the project further. Principal photography didn't begin until July 2012.

5. How Long Is the Final Product?

Is this a **full length feature or a short film**? That is one of the first things you need to decided. If it's still very early in your career, making any film over 30 minutes in length can be an incredibly daunting task. The length of the film will also help determine the length of production. You have to take into account the budget and time you have to make this project. From there you can decide the length you want to aim for.

If you can't afford the project, can you make another version? If you are unable to make the full length feature, try making it a short film first. Short films have successfully turned into features. Look at *Bottle Rocket*, or last year's **Best Motion Picture Oscar Nominee**, *Whiplash*.

Director/Writer Damien Chazelle was unable to secure funding for his film *Whiplash*. He pulled one of the most prominent scenes from the film and turned it into a short. His goal was to submit the short film to film festivals in hopes of securing the funding for the feature. The short film was so powerful and well done, he not only secured funding, the short won **Best Short Film** at Sundance. The next year, the **feature was nominated for five Oscars**, winning three of them.

6. When and Where Is the Film Set?

The setting of your film is a huge factor. Do you have the budget to shoot an epic in the desert? Is the film a period piece? If so, go ahead and hand over your budget to costumes. Are you able to turn this script into a film you can actually shoot now? The best thing you can do as a filmmaker is **embrace your limits.**

The 2004 film *Primer* is a perfect example. Not only did the film have a limited budget (approximately $7000), the script called for time travel. The story and science behind it was so sound, the story actually carried the film. With some creative thinking, nearly the entire film was shot in a storage unit. A perfect example of embracing you limits and working with your budget.

7. How Many Actors and Crew Members Will the Project Need?

Now that you have looked at the story itself, what about the practical necessities for bringing the story to life? How many characters do you need to cast? How big of a crew do you need? **These are major factors.** Not only do you need to know how many people you need, you need to know how much each of them will get paid.

Will you be able to afford costumes, or even food for the set? Are you still going to have enough left over for your camera, lights, and gear? This leads us to our next point.

8. Can You Afford to Make This Film?

As any filmmaker can tell you, **making a film is incredibly expensive**. Every project presents even more expenses you never accounted for. This is why many projects require multiple studios collaborating to make a film. Trying to take on a whole project alone is nearly impossible.

Even if you can't afford it now, you may be able to afford it later. We've presented many examples already with making short films first, or even waiting for years.

After all of this, you still face your decision to move forward with this project or not. If you have not been swayed at all, and you mind is still set on a project, get to it. Start making the film. Just know challenges will arise, but handling problems is the greatest skill a director can have.

July 3rd

Effective Pre-Production: Collaboration Between the Cinematographer and Editor

Although the cinematographer and editor work in different phases of projects, by collaborating early, their synched efforts will result in a better final film.

It doesn't matter if you're shooting a $250 million blockbuster or a micro-budget short, filmmaking is a collaborative art form. Directors rely on their crew and must coordinate the efforts of each person, in particular the department heads, in order to see their vision to fruition.

Two of these key personnel on any movie are the **cinematographer** and **editor**. Let's get the basics out of the way first, and look at what each of these positions does. If you're more of an industry vet jump down to the next section, "Planning the Shots".

Cinematographers and Film Editors

The cinematographer, also known as the director of photography (D.P.), is responsible for photographing the motion picture and overseeing the camera crew and lighting team. On low-budget films, the D.P. might be the sole person responsible for lighting and may also act as the camera operator. The cinematographer's primary responsibility occurs during the principal photography stage of production, but they must also spend a great deal of effort during prep and may even oversee the color grading during post production.

The editor, on the other hand, mostly works during post-production by **taking the shot footage and making decisions on how to best put the project together**. During principal photography, the editor's main responsibility is to organize the dailies and sync the sound. On larger productions, you'll have an entire team of people handling picture edit, sound and color grading, but on smaller films, you may have a single person responsible for all of the post-production. The final product is in the hands of the editor.

It seems that these two critical jobs would not overlap—the D.P. shoots and the editor takes the footage and turns it into a movie. However, the one phase where they should collaborate is pre-production, which Alfred Hitchcock considered to be the most important stage of filmmaking.

Some low budget filmmakers prefer to do one or both of these jobs in addition to directing, as it saves money and resources and is often perceived as preserving the director's vision. However, it is better to have different people serve as the D.P. and editor. The D.P. will carry out the director's wishes with lighting schemes and angles, but can also offer a second set of eyes to make sure all of the technical aspects of the shots are completed while the director focuses on the overall picture, including talent, art direction, continuity, etc. An editor brings in objectivity to post-production and can "kill the darlings" — cutting shots and scenes that the director can't bear to part with but need to go for the sake of the film.

Planning the Shots

During pre-production, the D.P. must work with the director to know what style of filmmaking they should use in the making of their movie, as well as how to plan the day-to-day activities. The D.P. will know how long certain shots will take to set up and can schedule accordingly. But where does the editor fit into this?

If the editor participates with developing the shot list, he or she will have a clear understanding of what to expect upon delivery of the footage. Oftentimes the editor sees the footage for the first time while watching the dailies and then must make sense of all the disparate images they receive. However, if the editor participates in pre-production, then he or she has a clear sense of what the director wants in the final film.

Editors are storytellers, but from a technical end. They know how the pieces fit together to effectively communicate dramatic and emotional expression to the audience, as well as determining proper pacing of the story. **All films will benefit if the editor is involved in the early stages of planning**, working with the cinematographer so that both are on the same page about how the director wants the story to unfold visually.

Traditionally, the shots are planned by the director through developing a shot list and then commissioning storyboards to illustrate those shots. Storyboards are made either by hand-drawing them, using computer-aided programs like FrameForge 3D or taking still photographs to replicate what will be shot on set. **Both the D.P. and the editor can add their expertise during the storyboarding** stage to ensure the proper footage is acquired during principal photography.

Correcting Problems in Advance

One of the biggest problems facing filmmakers is whether or not the footage they shoot will actually cut well together. A lot rides on this, including consistent performance from the actors and continuity of props, costumes, hair and makeup, actor placement, etc. The director of photography needs to worry about camera placement and gathering appropriate footage that the editor can use.

For instance, the camera crew has to adhere to the 180 degree rule, otherwise editing becomes much more difficult. The D.P. and camera operator should be aware of this, yet mistakes are constantly made that require the editor to "fix it in post." With the editor's help in pre-production, shots can be properly planned to avoid these types of situations. While it's easy for the D.P. to pass off problems to the editor to handle after photography is completed, doing so can create problems that are detrimental to the finished film. You don't want to have to salvage a scene through clumsy editing. It's better to have the scene play out naturally without any distracting edits that pull the audience out of the story.

Additionally, **an editor can identify other potential editing problems ahead of time and suggest supplementary ideas** for coverage. For instance, if the director is planning an extended take, an editor can see opportunities for alternate shots to cut to in case the extended take doesn't work. The editor can also point out places where insert shots and cutaways can be used for the best effect.

Getting the Right Look

The director of photography works hard to create a specific look for the film by choosing angles, lenses and lighting schemes. Not only does the lighting provide illumination for the actors, but it also creates a mood through brightness level, direction of the light and color—all of which, to varying degrees, can be altered in post-production. During pre-production, t**he D.P. should communicate his or her intentions to the editor** who can then plan out how to approach the final color correction and grading.

Another person, other than the picture editor, may be the one responsible for performing the color correction and grading after the picture lock is complete, but the editor will probably oversee this process (especially in lower budget projects). **The editor and D.P. should collaborate on what color design would be best for the film**. Also, the editor can discuss what tools he has available, which will allow the D.P. to use the proper settings on the camera to effectively capture the image in the best way for use in the post-production programs.

Successful Collaboration

The director needs to act as a ringmaster in coordinating the efforts of all the various departments, especially cinematography and editorial. These department heads need to be brought in as early as possible to prep the film and work out any potential problems, provide a unified effort toward the completion of the movie and to support each other with their duties and responsibilities. Your film and your audience will appreciate it.

July 4th

The 3 Most Important Tasks for A Director During Pre-Production

Most directors believe the majority of their work is done on set or in the editing room. In reality, just as much of the director's job is performed during pre-production.

On-set work is the bread and butter of most directors. While it can be stressful, there's no substitute for the energy gained working on set with a great team and talented actors. That said, in order to get the best possible results on set (and in post), **adequate pre-production work must be done.**

So before you jump into your next film, make sure that you're focusing enough on these **three critical tasks that all directors are responsible for:**

1. Refine the Script

Whether you've written the script yourself or are **working with a writer**, it's ultimately your responsibility to ensure its shootable by the time you step on set. There will always be other cooks in the kitchen (namely producers) giving you valuable notes and feedback, but **it's up to you to know what else your script needs.**

Your producers are going to give you notes that come from an important — but different — angle than you're coming from. They'll likely focus on logistical elements, commercial viability, and other factors that don't necessarily pertain to the overall creative vision. No one is going to do that part for you, so if you drop the ball, then **any undesired results ultimately fall on you.**

2. Rehearse Your Actors

Most productions are run on very tight schedules, and with your story hinging on the quality of your actor's performances, it's crucial that you **set aside enough time to rehearse with them.** If you fail to do so, you'll end up spending too much time on set working through the scenes with your actors, and may risk losing important shots or coverage due to a lack of time.

On the same note, you also need to know when you're over-rehearsing your actors. The worst thing for a performer is for the material to become stale to them, so always be sure to **find a good balance in the prep work** that you do with your talent.

Maintain Your Shot List

Probably your **most important tool on set as a director** is your shot list. It's the blueprint for your shoot and the 'to-do' list that you can continually reference as things inevitably become chaotic throughout the day. Directors often neglect to create a detailed shot list and ultimately **pay the price when they get to the editing room.**

The last thing you want is to start cutting your footage only to realize you missed an important **insert, cutaway, transition, or reaction shot** and can't complete your scene. That will mean you either need to cut around it (which will likely yield poor results), or reshoot it — **which won't be an easy conversation to have with your producer.**

July 5th

5 Top Habits Shared by Successful Directors

Great directors are not all cut from the same cloth, but the most successful of them share these five habits.

With more film and TV content being produced right now than ever before, **the demand for directorial talent is greater than ever.** Unfortunately, though, most aspiring directors are never able to break into the industry in the way that they want to — despite the fact that they are technically and creatively qualified. The reality is that **going to film school and owning a camera simply isn't enough.** Everyone wants to direct, so when the competition is steep, you need to step up your game.

In my opinion, finding success as a director has just as much to do with your habits **off set** as it does with your skills **on set.** It goes without saying that you need to **understand the fundamentals of directing, set etiquette, post-production, etc.** before finding professional success as a director. But that's only 50% of the battle. The other half is everything that happens when you aren't on set or in the editing room. It happens during your everyday life.

With that in mind, here are five habits that all successful directors share:

1. They Never Stop Learning.

Filmmakers who understand that **there's always more to learn** are the wisest and often the most successful. An inflated ego can be the ultimate downfall of a director (especially early on), and one of the side effects of an ego problem is an unwillingness to develop your craft further. Everyone is born with some degree of natural talent, but it's how we hone that talent and develop it that grooms us for long term success.

Film school is all well and good (and certainly is a good starting point for some), but as it relates to this point — it's not enough. You need to constantly strive to absorb more information at all times. Watch as many films as possible, attend lectures, pick the brain of your DP, learn new software, do everything that you can possibly imagine to know the business inside and out.

The more insight you have, **the more value you have as a director**… And it will show very obviously in your work.

2. They Read.

Every successful director I've ever met **is also an avid reader.** This applies equally to fiction and non-fiction. Reading fiction allows your brain to absorb stories in a very different way than watching a movie would, and it can inspire new techniques or storytelling ideas that you may have never considered.

Nonfiction on the other hand (specifically newspaper articles or biographies) can spark specific ideas for stories and details that simply wouldn't otherwise exist. Take Breaking Bad for example. The creator (Vince Gilligan) has mentioned on several occasions that the inspiration for the show came from a small newspaper article he came across while casually reading the paper one day.

3. They Network.

Unfortunately show business is still a business, and **succeeding in any business requires networking.** This can be a big challenge for a lot of directors who might be more introverted and less willing to socialize and network with their peers. The harsh reality though is that **networking is one of the biggest keys to success as a director** — and even if you don't like to do it, you're going to need to learn to.

You can have the best idea in the world, but if you don't have any friends or colleagues that are willing to let you pitch it to them, it's not going to go anywhere. Maybe you could go out on your own and attempt to produce something by yourself, but you'll still be far behind with regards to festivals and distributors which also could come along with great networking.

It's not that you need to be the life of the party, but if you make an effort to go to festivals, conferences, and other creative events, you'll be amazed at some of the great people you'll meet.

Being able to send someone a script over e-mail and saying **"We met last week at ____"** will go a lot further than approaching them with no pre-existing relationship.

4. They Exercise.

Numerous studies have confirmed that **exercise is one of the best ways to spark creativity.** After a long run or a workout at the gym, your brain is rewired to an extent (for lack of a scientific term), and is at an optimal point for creative thinking. Personally speaking, when I'm active I tend to have ideas that are constantly flowing out of me, but when I'm not I can start to get writers block.

This is something that is universally true of people, yet so many directors don't want to get off the couch and start moving. Exercise may seem unrelated to filmmaking and therefore may not be your priority, but it's a lifestyle choice that affects all areas of your productivity – **including your creative drive.** Many of the greatest writers and directors that I've ever worked with have told me that some of their best ideas came to them when running on a treadmill, or out for a hike – and that certainly came as no surprise.

5. They Have Exceptional Work Ethic.

If your work ethic is questionable, **you will have a short shelf life in the world of filmmaking.** Filmmaking is like a sport that is extremely competitive… There are thousands of other aspiring directors out there that will fight day and night to get the job, producer, financing, or opportunity that you might be after too. If you want to succeed, you need to outwork them on every level.

This notion applies to every step in the process: **development, pre-production, production, post, and distribution.** You will have many chances to mess up an opportunity for yourself at every phase, but staying on top of things and having a great work ethic is the only way to ensure that you don't drop the ball. The idea of working 16 hours a day and not taking a break for 2 years (or more) to get your film made might not sound all that enticing, **but if you're not willing to put in that work then someone else will.**

July 6th

4 Mistakes Nearly Every Director Makes on Set

Experienced film directors understand how difficult it can be to complete a feature. Here are four mistakes that can make the task even harder.

On a film set, anything that can go wrong **will** go wrong. No matter how much you prepare, plan, and scrutinize every last detail before you get to set, something will always go wrong. But even though you may never be able to make your film set a place that is completely worry-free, you can at the very least take some measures to ensure that the best creative result is achieved.

Below, I've outlined **four common mistakes that you need to avoid as a director** in order to achieve that best possible end result:

1. They Surround Themselves with the Wrong People

Nothing kills a film project faster than a poorly constructed crew that's responsible for executing the exceptionally complicated task of making a film. Unfortunately, most indie film directors tend to overlook the importance of **bringing the right people onto their project**, and ultimately pay the price later on.

This is especially true in the case of **micro-budget films** where projects come together quickly and options feel very limited. Due to issues like limited funding and lack of experience, independent directors often sacrifice elements of their film in the areas of casting and crew members by hiring whoever is readily available and able to work for next to nothing.

It isn't uncommon for directors to downright settle in these departments just for the sake of **cheap or free labor**, which is one of the most fatal mistakes that can be made. If you do not collaborate with a cast and crew that shares your vision, passion, and enthusiasm for the project, your experience on set and the results you yield will be utterly disappointing.

In the end, you need to rely on your team to bring your vision to life, as you alone will never be able to do it all yourself. Make sure you build a team that can remain **positive and enthusiastic** through thick and thin (and are, of course, qualified for their respective positions) and you'll be off to a great start.

2. They Don't Own the Creative Vision

While working with an inexperienced crew can be detrimental to a film (as we've gone over above), working with an experienced crew can be just as challenging – especially when the director is new to the game. Often, indie film directors end up **working with crew members that have been on far more sets than they have** and start to feel insecure about their role on set and their vision as a whole. This can lead them to allow others to make critical decisions for them on set, and in the end their original vision for the film becomes stifled and muted.

No matter what your experience level, as the film's director it is your responsibility to **lead and inspire** your cast and crew all the way from pre-production to post-production. It is also your responsibility to yourself and to the film, to keep your vision alive and fight for it – even if your producer/DP/crew is suggesting that you go in a different direction.

Ultimately, if you don't take this position, your lack of vision will leave your cast and crew feeling uninspired – and believing that they are working on an insignificant project. Perhaps even worse, you'll be left with a **watered down final product** that you'll be profoundly unhappy with and that your audience may not connect with.

Vision is the art of seeing things invisible. - **Jonathan Swift**

Remember, it's your story to tell and it must be told from your point of view. Mistakes are inevitable and it's perfectly okay to take notes from others (more on that in the next point), but it's crucial that you own your creative choices for the better of the project.

3. They Don't Listen to Others

As we discussed above, taking in too many opinions and losing your own vision is an issue that many directors are challenged with, but the opposite situation can be just as problematic. Many film directors go into their projects with a unilateral vision that leaves no room for **creative collaborators** to contribute whatsoever. They seem to forget that film is a collaborative medium and that (even though they need to maintain their vision throughout the process) it is okay to hear out the suggestions of others.

Many film directors will joke that they don't care where a good idea comes from, as long as they get credit for it. And, with all joking aside, I would argue that the most experienced directors are also those that are the most willing to **listen to suggestions from the rest of their team.** This may seem contradictory to the second point on this list, but it really goes hand in hand with it. **It's all about balance.**

As the director, you want to be the filter that takes in ideas and decides which of those ideas is in line with your vision. You don't simply want to take every idea thrown at you, or take none at all – So always remember to keep an open mind and a **maintain a confidence in the story** that you are telling.

4. They Save the Most Important Scenes for the End of the Day

It always baffles me when directors choose to shoot the most important scenes of any given shoot day at the end of the day. Understandably, directors often feel that they want to **break in their cast and crew**, or warm up a bit themselves before jumping into the really important material – but I would argue that this is a very bad approach for a number of reasons.

For starters, anyone that's ever been on a film set knows that no matter how well planned your shooting schedule is, **things will almost always take longer than you anticipate.** The last thing you want is to feel rushed at the end of the day when you're shooting your most important scene. But even if things are running perfectly on schedule (which of course is almost never the case!), your cast and crew are not necessarily going to be performing at their peak after **12 (or more) hours on set**. If it's important for you to warm up your cast, crew, and yourself before getting into an important scene, then by all means go for it. Just opt to schedule that scene in the middle of the day, rather than at the end.

July 7th

What All Producers Need to Understand About Working with Directors

For a film to truly succeed, its lead producer must understand how to effectively collaborate with the film's auteur. Unfortunately, no two directors are exactly alike.

The **producer/director relationship** can arguably make or break a great film. A talented **director** needs a dedicated **producer** to help bring their vision to life, and that **producer** needs to be working with a **director** that they truly believe in. But really, having a complimentary working relationship is just the tip of the iceberg. There are so many complexities involved with the creation of any film. For a great **producer** to achieve the best possible final product, they absolutely need to adhere to these guidelines:

1. Understand Your Role as a Support System

Unfortunately, it's quite common for **producers** to neglect one of their most crucial tasks – to ultimately support the **director** to the point where they're performing at the top of their game. A great **lead producer** is far more than just someone who pulls together the crew and keeps the schedule running on time. A truly great **producer** will always be able to get the best creative work possible out of their **directors** by being honest with them, supporting their decisions, and pushing them (even when the going gets tough) to finish each stage of the film to the best of their abilities.

As a **producer**, I'd argue that your role is partly that of a psychologist: you need to understand what your **director** needs in order to maximize their potential, which will ultimately benefit the entire production by leaps and bounds.

2. Don't Try to Direct

Some of the worst collaborations I've ever had with **producers** were with individuals that didn't know their roles. The most effective **producers** understand that they're there to bring someone else's vision to life, and not to interfere with that vision. That's not to say that a **producer** shouldn't have a vision of their own, but rather that their vision needs to be focused in a different place.

The vision of the **producer** should be big picture oriented. Above and beyond production and post, they need to be able to see the path to success with the film – including distribution, marketing, and countless other elements. When too much emphasis is placed on trying to do the **director's job** for them, ultimately everyone loses.

3. Picking the Right Director Is Paramount

To use a music analogy, finding the right **director** to collaborate with is just like finding the right bandmate. You need to work with someone who you respect, can tolerate for months on end, and who you trust immensely. It isn't enough to just work with a **director** because they have some clout and you think they can open some doors for you with regards to talent, financing, or otherwise.

Fostering a positive collaboration between yourself and your **director** starts with finding the right person to work with. Someone whose style you understand and respect. Someone whose personality gels well with yours. And someone who's willing to work through the rough patches with you. If you don't choose your **director** wisely, you won't be able to see eye to eye on most things, and the film will very likely falter as a result.

July 8th

Learn the Art of Hollywood Storytelling

Polish your script and learn the secrets of Hollywood storytelling from three professional story consultants.

I recently stumbled onto this vast archive of interviews with filmmakers who work in positions that you don't often get access to. There are interviews (broken up into handily titled sections) with storyboard artists, script consultants, production managers, focus pullers, compositors, and many more. Unfortunately for me, as a non-Swedish speaker, most of the interviews are in the participant's native language, which I believe is Swedish!

That said, I've pulled out this **trio of interviews with three professional story consultants and script doctors**, all speaking in English, who have great insight to share on improving your storytelling and filmmaking abilities.

Script and Story Consultants

Chris Soth, Michael Hauge and Linda Seger are all story consultants. This means they've been called in to help filmmakers like Will Smith on *I Am Legend, Hancock,* and *The Karate Kid*, or Ron Howard on (apparently) every one of his movies since *Apollo 13,* to help restructure the film and ensure the character arcs and motivations are working as well as they can.

"Story is the most important thing, everything comes after. and if you're serious about being a filmmaker, and that means being serious about being a storyteller you have to understand structure." – Chris Soth

Linda Segar's bestselling book *How to Make a Good Script Great*, is personally **endorsed by Ron Howard,** and after working on over 2000 scripts and a 30+ year career, she certainly knows her stuff. In this video, Linda shares her thoughts on **the best way to make it as a writer,** which sadly, involves no short cuts.

Writers write. you need to get writing and you need to get a number of scripts written. Rarely do you sell your first script. Sometimes in the US people say you need to write at least five scripts, and spend at least five years learning the craft. And then maybe, you'll sell it, or get an agent or have something happen with it… it's learning the art in yourself and bringing that out and learning the craft.

Michael Hauge, who can be found on Story Mastery.com, shares some **elementary advice for the things writers need to do to write their first script well.**

One of the things I recommend that writers do, that sometimes are either too obvious, or writers don't think of it. Number one, you gotta read screenplays. I encouter a lot of people who hire me to consultant on their screenplay and pay a lot of money to do that, and I'll say 'Well how many scripts have you read.' and they'll say 'Well, I've read three.' And it's like, you can't possibly master a craft when you've only seen three examples of it being done.

A fantastic resource for script writers (that gives you over **four hundred examples of different ways of approaching screenwriting elements**) is the Mentorless series of script breakdowns, How Did They Write That. Essentially you can see how the writer achieved various things from introducing a character, or writing an action scene, or a phone call, or a description of a character and much more.

It's a brilliant way to quickly **see how numerous professional screenwriters approach the task in their own style**.

The Art of the Storyboard

As an added bonus, there is also this extended interview with storyboard artist Giuseppe Cristiano on how he approaches **his storyboard art work and craft**. In this first video you get a tour of the tools Cristiano likes to work with and pick up this handy tip…

You'll notice that I use a red pencil [for the initial sketch], and that's something that you use in animation, so that you can do your clean up in pen, and scan them in you can remove the red pencil [digitally].

July 9th

Honing Your Craft: Find Your Voice as a Director

A big issue that plagues some indie filmmakers is their lack of identity. **Many independent films can end up feeling like a parody of someone else's work, ultimately leading them to be flops both commercially and critically.**

If you watch enough movies, you should be able to tell the work of Aronofsky from Spielberg simply based on their directorial style and **the trademarks that they leave on each scene.**

These are filmmakers that spent decades honing their craft and understanding what they wanted to say and how they wanted to say it. They found their voices long ago, and ultimately their work has become extremely identifiable as a result. If you (as a director) want to get the most out of yourself creatively, one of the most important things you can do is develop your directing style so that your work can speak for itself.

While it might take a long time to get where you want to go (creatively-speaking), in this post we'll explore three powerful steps you can take to **find your voice as a director.**

1. Watch More Movies

One of the biggest red flags of a director that hasn't found their own voice is when their taste in movies is all over the place. Don't get me wrong – there's nothing wrong with binge watching movies across every genre; I truly believe you can learn something from any movie no matter how far off from your own taste it may be.

But if you simply like watching movies, but aren't particularly drawn to one genre, director, or style – then that may be the first sign you haven't found your vision or style as an artist.

If this sounds like you, I would recommend watching loads of movies (I'm talking 1 – 2 a day on average) for as long as you can. Completely saturate yourself in films and after a short while some of them will get stuck with you. There will be those films that nag at you, that you want to go back and watch, or that inspire you to make something yourself.

Chances are, whatever films are drawing you back to them will be in a similar genre or will deal with similar subject matter – and that may very well be the first step in identifying the films that you are best suited too direct and **that you really want to make.**

2. Understand How to Tell a Story with No Dialogue

Everyone wants to be the next Tarantino or Sorkin. A lot of indie films these days are busting at the seams with heavy dialogue, yet there is often no substance to what is on the screen – not to mention there is no distinct style in the way the dialogue is being delivered.

While you might be more inclined to direct heavily dialogue-driven films (and may be a great dialogue writer too), you need to challenge yourself to tell stories without dialogue if you want to maximize your talent. This may seem counterintuitive, as your strength may be as a writer, but the fact of the matter is you aren't doing yourself any favors as a director by resting on your laurels as a writer.

If you really want to develop your directorial style, trying shooting a test scene or a short film with little to no dialogue at all. Once you've mastered that, and you go back to your heavily scripted material, your work will improve dramatically.

Imagine a musician that isn't very good at playing guitar, but can write great songs. This person would always be held back by the fact that they can't express their art form to the fullest, much in the same way that a director is held back when they don't know how to direct with images.

Just remember, filmmaking is a visual medium. And as the adage goes – show, don't tell. It's in the subtleties of camera movement, framing, and other visual choices that your directing style will really come out, so be sure to embrace that as much as you can.

3. Tap into Your Music Taste

There are a lot of similarities between film and music, in my opinion at least, and it's no coincidence that the type of music that filmmakers love is often in the same vain as the films that they create. Take Tarantino for instance.

It would be hard to deny that his musical influence isn't obviously put front and center in so many of his films, and as a result the tone and style of his movies are **largely centered around his taste in music.**

The Tarantino example might be the most obvious, but the same could be said for nearly any auteur that has really found their voice. It's why Spielberg has worked with the same composer (John Williams) for so long and why Fincher has stayed with Trent Reznor and Atticus Ross after hitting it off with them creatively several films back.

So for these reasons amongst others, I would argue that a big part of developing your style as a director is understanding your taste in music. **After all, 50% (or more) of the viewing experience of a movie is dependent on the audio, and the music more so than any other element of the process guides the viewers emotional experience.**

And by the way, if you aren't a big music fan, that doesn't mean you can't find your voice. Perhaps your style is simply best served with sound design or natural backgrounds as opposed to a traditional score. Whatever the case may be, understand yourself on a creative level (musically speaking) as it is very much related to who you are as a storyteller.

July 10th

Why All Directors Need to Take Up Acting

Indie film directors today have largely become more concerned with gear, effects, and post-production than with story and acting, which is one reason so many indie films fail to have any success. While the technical side of filmmaking is critical in today's filmmaking environment, it is raw performance that will always be what captivates audiences most.

It's interesting to look at how many high budget blockbuster films have completely failed over the last few years, and how many small independent films have done better than ever. While there are many factors that contribute to this situation, I would suggest that the largest of them is the lack of emphasis on story, character, and most importantly performance. Not all blockbuster films are flops, and they certainly aren't all bad. It's interesting though to recognize that big blockbuster hits like Chris Nolan's Batman films, had a heavy emphasis on character and performance, and ultimately those elements helped to elevate and compliment the technical and visual aspects of the film.

You might think that it's only on the large scale blockbuster films where these issues occur, and where performance has become a lost art. But truthfully, I see it happening more than ever in independent film today which is likely a direct result of the easy access to equipment and knowledge. **Just about anybody can pick up a camera today, learn how to set it up on YouTube and then go out and shoot something that looks half decent.** But that certainly doesn't mean their film will be strong or that the most important ingredient will have been delivered on – the performance.

It goes without saying that for a film to be successful a certain level of quality must be there in terms of production value, and of course story as well. But I would argue that performance is the single most important element for any given film, and unfortunately as I mentioned above – probably the most overlooked element too. **Films with flawed scripts, but great performances can still be successful** – take a look at *August Osage County* for an example of this dynamic. That film had some problem areas in regards to the script and structure (it really was better suited for the format of a stage play), but exceptionally strong performances by the cast helped to make it an enjoyable and memorable film. On the other hand, films with fantastic scripts and poor acting are destined to be flops. It is the actors and their performances that represent the words on the page, so unfortunately no matter how good those words are, without great actors to deliver them they are going to fall flat.

This may seem obvious, but unfortunately for many filmmakers today it isn't. **Most independent directors that I talk with don't know the difference between Meissner and Method.** They don't understand what an actor needs to warm up, how they need to be spoken to on set, and what tools they use to get into character. Without these pieces of critical knowledge, it's really impossible to communicate with an actor in the best way possible and to get the most accurate performance from them. The good news is, you don't need to be an expert on acting to understand how actors think – you just need to take some initiative and interest in their craft.

I've taken a number of acting classes and they have been undeniably the best assets for me as a director, and far more beneficial than anything I've ever learned with regards to blocking, cinematography, or screen direction. Earlier on in my career I fell into the trap at least once or twice, of focusing so heavily on the wrong aspects of my productions, and ultimately they were not up to par in my mind because of the lack of attention to performance.

In the early days of cinema, a director's job was simply to direct actors. That was it. The DP shot the film, the editor edited the film, and a writer wrote the film. Today, many directors (myself included) do all of these things (and then some) because of the accessibility to technology and the shift in production from a technical perspective. This is all well and good – in fact, I personally love being very hands on with my film work and shooting/writing/editing much of it myself, but never at the expense of performance. **If I ever feel that the amount of time or effort that I am putting into any given facet of the production is taking away from time that I could spend with my actors, I will have someone else fill in for me.** There is a certain hierarchy in my mind to my approach on set, and at the very top of that pyramid is performance. If I can successfully direct my actors and focus on the cinematography at the same time, I may go ahead and do that. But the moment that I am focusing too much on camera and not enough on talent, it starts to show on screen.

My suggestion to any aspiring directors out there, is to simply learn how to act. Take a class here or there and just understand the basics of the craft. You don't need to be an expert, but you do need to understand the fundamental principles that drive the people that are ultimately representing your film – the actors. While everyone else is struggling to get a bit more resolution out of their cameras, or learning how to use a new piece of editing software, you will be jumping by leaps and bounds by actually focusing on directing – something that many directors no longer do.

July 11th

The Benefits of Storyboarding Your Next Film

Storyboarding is a commonly overlooked part of the indie filmmaking process. Here are some ways that your production can benefit from storyboarding.

While it may be true that storyboarding is not necessarily a mandatory part of a filmmaker's process, **there is a reason why most major feature films still storyboard every last shot.**

Storyboards not only let you and your collaborators "see" the totality of your film while in production, but they also help you get there in the first place by **helping you sell your ideas more effectively** to potential investors, producers, etc. When you consider all of **the benefits of storyboarding**, it will be hard to justify ever producing another film without properly storyboarding again.

Why You Need to be Using Storyboards

The greatest incentive for storyboarding is simply the fact that storyboard will help you make a much stronger film by **allowing you to visualize your movie before it's even made.** This is essentially your chance to create a blueprint for your film that will help you identify any potential problem areas or missed opportunities while you still have a chance to fix them.

Technically speaking, you can include as much or as little detail as you want when storyboarding, **as long as the ideas are accurately conveyed.** By the time you get to post, your editor will be thanking you, as the film will have coverage in all the right places, proper transitional moments, and a slicker aesthetic.

You Don't Need to Be an Artist or Designer

It's a huge misconception that storyboarding requires that you have the ability to draw/illustrate professionally. That's not at all to diminish the role of the storyboard artist, as they are truly **masters of their craft and will inevitably deliver the best results**... But if you can't afford a storyboard artist or need to do it yourself, **that's perfectly okay.**

As an independent filmmaker, no one really needs to see your storyboards outside of you and your team, and once again, as long as your idea is conveyed that's really all that matters. If you choose to storyboard by hand, your illustrations can be **as simple as geometric shapes** used to illustrate props/staging and **stick figures** for your characters. Or to make things even easier, you can use any of the vast number of storyboarding programs available to download on your computer, tablet or phone.

Storyboards Strengthen Your Vision

Your screenplay is the backbone of your film, but no matter how beautifully written it may be, **it will never translate exactly as you might be picturing it to film.** There's a pretty common saying among directors: If your final film looks even 70% of the way you thought it would, you did your job really well. From my experience, storyboards play a huge part in getting to that 70%, as they help you to visualize your project in a way that is not otherwise possible.

The last thing you want is to get to set and realize that something about your shoot isn't congruent with the script. Storyboarding will help you nip those issues in the bud, and **keep your vision alive.**

The Basics of Storyboarding

Having now gone over some of the **perks of storyboarding**, I want to very briefly break down the basics of storyboarding your film for those of you that have never done it.

Generally speaking, for every illustration (or storyboard) you create, there are five types of shots to choose from: **master, long, medium, close-up, and extreme close-up.** Sound familiar? Once you've decided on which of the 5 shot types you want to go with for any given shot, **you'll want to illustrate camera movement.**

To depict a panning or tilting shot, where the camera either moves sideways or up and down, you'll want to create two frames to indicate where the camera will start and where it will wind up. From there, **you can use arrows moving in both directions in order to portray movement.** To illustrate a tracking shot, (which involves moving the entire camera in order to follow your continuously moving subject), you simply draw an arrow on the frame – indicating camera placement – **and point it in the direction the camera will be moving in.**

You can also illustrate zooming, which only involves a lens and no camera movement at all. To show zooming in (moving closer to the subject) and zooming out (moving away from the subject, taking in more of the scene in its entirety), you'll have two frames on your storyboard, and depending on which direction the zoom is going in, **you'll either have arrows moving toward the interior frame or out toward the exterior frame.**

These are some of the basics of creating a storyboard, and as you can probably gather it's pretty easy to pick up. **Just remember how critical storyboards are to the filmmaking process**, and at the very least, understand some general rules/technique associated with creating them so that you can ensure they get done properly.

July 12th

Tips for Being an Awesome Production Coordinator

To succeed as a production coordinator, you need the patience of a director, the organizational skills of an assistant director, and the knowledge of a producer. No problem, right?

Thriving under pressure, being able to multi-task, and playing well with others are just a few of the necessary skills that you need to succeed as a production coordinator. It's a demanding job and certainly not a perfect fit for everyone, but for those that work well in this type of environment and are heavily self-motivated, working as a production coordinator can be an **excellent career move.**

It's the natural progression away from PAing and into ADing, and eventually producing. If you're considering a career move and think you're up for the challenge (or already work in this demanding position), these tips will make your life easier both on set and off.

1. Communicate Impeccably and Lead Your Team

Communication and the ability to take charge and lead are two of the most critical qualities for you to have as a PC. Throughout every phase of the filmmaking process (and especially during pre-production and production), **you are the point of contact for most (or all) of the crew** - and that is a massive responsibility to have.

Having likely come from a PA background, you may be accustomed to feeling like you should simply do your job, stay quiet, and get out of the way. But this mentality needs to change drastically as you step into this new position, as your role is now more in line with that of a producer than it is a production assistant. And just like a great producer – **communication and leadership are key.**

2. Stay Organized and Stay Ahead

Your ability to organize and stay a step ahead of things is what you were hired for above all else, so make sure to prioritize these aspects of your job. It's often assumed that producers do most of the dirty work on and off set, but in reality **it's often the production coordinators doing a lot of the heavy lifting – even if they aren't getting credit for it.**

The bottom line: **Organization is key**. Even the slightest organizational misstep can lead to disaster during production. Take a look at this call sheet. See all those blank fields? If you're the production coordinator, it's up to you to fill them in accurately. A single typo that places a talent's call time later than it should be could ruin an entire day on set and cost the production thousands of dollars in overtime and/or reshooting expenses.

There is an infinite amount of issues that could arise as a result of **poor organizational skills**, so always be sure to stay detail oriented and triple check everything you do before sending it out to the team – otherwise you could be out of a job.

3. Know your Role

A production team is naturally set up as a hierarchy, and it's crucial that you know exactly where you stand in the **chain of command**. Although I mentioned earlier that being a production coordinator in many ways is like being a producer, you still need to make sure those lines aren't blurred. Many production coordinators make the mistake of overstepping their boundaries during production as they grow to realize their importance on set.

As production coordinator, you report directly to the production manager, while also taking the lead on overseeing the production assistants and assistant production coordinators. For those of you that have already worked in this capacity, you understand that there's a lot of juggling involved to do this well, and you are often required to wear many hats.

There are times when you need to take on roles that are outside of your usual production coordinator responsibilities, and that is perfectly okay as long as you are being guided to do so. In other words, if you need to handle something that the production manager is passing off to you, that's great – just **don't overstep your boundaries** and do it before it's asked of you or it will reflect very poorly on your set etiquette.

Final Thoughts

Not everyone is cut out for the role of production coordinator. It is a **demanding, high-pressure job** that requires a very particular set of skills, namely the ability to execute tasks with just the right balance of patience and tenacity. Over and above a concrete knowledge of film production from A to Z, you must be a great communicator and leader, remain ahead of schedule and completely organized at all times, and understand the boundaries of the role in which you work. This can sound like a difficult position to fill, and truthfully it is a big challenge for many. But if you're willing to stick with it and make yourself a productive member of the team, things start getting easier **very quickly**.

July 13th

How Micromanaging Your Indie Film Set Could Ruin Your Project

Many amateur directors decide to write and direct their first film before they have had much on set experience in other roles. This method must be approached with caution – particularly with regards to how the cast and crew is treated on set.

A film set can be a very dynamic place – at times it is exhilarating and inspiring while at other times it can be frustrating and tense. **Although film is undeniably a very collaborative medium and there are so many moving parts that need to work together to bring an idea to**

life, the director is still the captain of that ship. And as a director, you really need to understand your responsibility in this unique structure and how your behavior will not only affect how your cast and crew feels during your shoot, but also how your final product comes out as a result of their attitude.

Your job is to inspire and instigate in a positive way, not to create difficult and uncomfortable situations for the rest of your team. **Many first time directors are very unsure of themselves.** They don't quite know what they want to say yet, or how to say it. When challenged on set, or a new perspective is shared from one of the cast or crew – it's very common for a first time director to become standoff-ish and defensive. They often feel (even if they don't consciously realize it), that they have something to prove. Even if an idea is presented to them that could make their film better, they will reject it in order to protect their own ego and so that they can stand their ground in front of the others on set. This mentality really couldn't be more toxic for a film set. Not only do some fantastic ideas get swept under the rug, but everyone on set starts to feel uncomfortable and uninspired…and it can become a vicious cycle.

It's important to remember that **as a director your job at its core is translate the way that you see the world (or see the story) onto the screen.** You are a filter. If someone has a great idea and you choose not to use it because it isn't in line with the perspective that you take on the subject matter – that is completely valid. But if you are simply throwing a way a good idea that someone presents you (that was in fact in line with your initial vision), then you're going to have problems.

A common misconception about high level feature film directors is that they are dictators. While there are certainly a few notable examples of famous directors that have thrown temper tantrums on set, or are known for blasting their cast and crew, these are the exception not the rule.

Seasoned directors that have been telling stories for years are confident in their own vision. They understand that if a good idea is presented to them it is their duty as a director to at the very least consider it. They also know how to politely turn away ideas that might not work for their vision of the film in a way that is not offensive to the rest of the crew. **They truly act as the ultimate filter, making sure that only the strongest ideas that are most in line with their vision come**

through, and value the opinions of others. Granted, few if any directors want every crew member running up to them with their two cents every two seconds, but that's why professional directors hire professional crew members that understand their role – just like the director should.

Probably the most detrimental thing that a director can do in regards to micro-managing is to over direct their actors. Amateur directors often have this false vision of what it means to be a director. They think that they need to literally direct every last step that their actors make, and every last line of dialogue. In my opinion, **the best directors are those that trust their actors, and only hire actors that they know will inherently fulfill their vision.** They give their actors breathing room and allow them to try different ideas, and even fail at times, if it means that they get to the best end result.

The most obvious sign of a first-time director is when he/she starts to coach an actor on how to say a specific word or a line. In my opinion this is a huge no-no and is probably the fastest way to ensure that the actor will never want to work with that director again. **Most good actors have been training for years (or possibly most of their lives) to understand the complexities of performance, so it is extremely insulting to them when the direction that they are being given is so trivial.** It makes them feel that the director doesn't have any trust in them, and ultimately that causes them to lose trust in their director. This is not a good place to be.

I want to point out after stating what I did above, that directors do of course still need to direct. They are not simply there to be passive onlookers that only are inspired by the ideas of others. They need a clear cut vision and they need to communicate that vision with everyone on the cast and crew – that way when new ideas are shared with the director, they are in line with his/her vision.

I really like to think of directing as instigating situations. Directors should cause conflict and energy by strategically setting up scenes, getting their characters into the right headspace, and making sure the crew is on their toes. That's where great films live and breathe. That's when actors have room to explore and the cast maintains their passion and focus even after a 16-hour day on set. And ultimately, that's how the best movies are made.

July 14th

Art of Pre-Production: Concept Art

Go along for the ride as a leading concept artist brings an incredible story to life.

Whether a film is based on an existing story/franchise or conceived from a wholly original concept, the film's 'world' and characters need to be fully developed before shooting ever begins. The script provides the backbone for the story, while **concept art** can set the stage for the look.

This design process can begin as early as the treatment stage, but usually begins once the script is complete. Once the script is set and pre-production begins, directors often hire artists to develop the visual feeling of the film.

The use of concept art is two-fold. It is used as an **asset for the pitch** – the process of selling the initial movie to a production company. It's second use is for prepping the other production departments. For instance, giving the costume and set design team a direction for their work, as well as giving the visual effects staff direction during production and post-production.

Feng Zhu is a concept artist who has lead art development for game companies like *EA*, *NCSoft*, *Epic Games*, *Sony* and *Microsoft*. He has also worked alongside Hollywood film directors *Steven Spielberg*, *James Cameron*, *Michael Bay*, *Luc Besson* and worked closely with *George Lucas* for development on *Star Wars Episode III: Revenge of the Sith*. Feng now has his own design school *FZDesign* where he trains artists for the professional world of concept art and design.

July 15th

Create Explosive Action in Your Next Film with a DIY Air Cannon

Learn how to make great practical explosion effects with a DIY air cannon. It's safe for your cast and crew — and the results are impressive!

Have you ever wondered how they get those great **explosion effects** in films? They look so real. This was a question I was pondering myself as I began working on my next film.

As we went into pre-production, we looked at the Civil War battle sequence on our shot list. We knew that there were going to be several **6lb non-lethal cannons** involved in that sequence. The question staring us in the face was: how do we go about filming a sequence with this type of **practical effect**? And how do we do it in a way that doesn't endanger our actors and stuntmen? Well, there are three important things that we discovered we needed to do... **research, prep and placement**. Let's go through each one of these together.

1. Research is key.

On any film, if you want it to be successful, you need to be successful at research. The first step for any action sequence is to **look at how you want to film the scene.** I've always found it extremely helpful to look at what worked well in the past. With this in mind my crew and I looked at many different war films from over the years and saw how **some shots worked and some did not.** The three final films that we set aside as concrete inspiration for storyboarding were the films Glory, Saving Private Ryan, and Paths of Glory.

During the Civil War, cannons would often be aimed at the tree line above the opposing side. Upon impact, **large quantities of debris** would rain down on the soldiers below. They would also volley mortar rounds either straight ahead or in an arcing fashion, which would give you the debris explosion on the ground.

Finally, we looked at how Saving Private Ryan's Omaha beach sequence was shot. Spielberg used a shoulder rig to place the audience right into the chaos. He also employed the use of a **45 to 90-degree shutter angle** to cut down motion blur and make the imagery crisp. Again, the use of air cannons and barrels in the earth were used to **replicate explosions on the beach.**

2. Prep for your scene.

Now that you know how you want your scene to look and feel, and you have your storyboards or shot list ready to go, let's prep for the sequence. We had the good fortune of being able to contact **pyrotechnic professionals** who showed us how to make these explosions happen on the cheap. You can do this just as easily as we did. Here's what you're going to need:

- 3″ Pressure-rated PVC pipe (This is crucial!)
- 3″ Pressure-rated end cap
- 2 reducers
- Sprinkler valve
- Bushings
- Pipe nipples
- PVC cement
- Tire valve
- Pressure gauge
- Detonator
- Empty 2 liter soda bottle
- Gaff tape
- Tire pump or air compressor

3. Know your placement.

Now that you have your **air cannon** built, you'll want to stuff the soda bottle with debris. Remember not to put things like rocks or sticks into the bottle. With the debris moving out at a high rate of speed, the projectiles can **seriously** injure someone. Instead, use dead leaves, dirt, flour, and cut up sponges painted to look like rocks or large pieces of dirt. You want your crew, your actors, and your stuntmen as safe as possible.

Now, don't place the **air cannons** just anywhere. Make sure you strategically place them around the scene that you've developed. The best thing I've learned from talking to other filmmakers is to rehearse the sequence several times with your actors, **marking where the explosions will happen.**

July 16th

Considerations for Shooting in Abandoned Locations

Videographers love taking their cameras and drones into beautifully eerie places. Want to try it? Here's what to consider before shooting in abandoned locations.

The key to **shooting in abandoned locations** is **packing lightly**. Odds are, you will be out in a very open location **without any power** or any other resources. You probably **won't have signal on your cell phone** either.

Also, **having permission to shoot in these locations is advised**. You should also let other people know where you are going, just in case anything happens.

Here are a few considerations for shooting abandoned locations:

- Carry everything in a backpack.
- Pack plenty of batteries.
- Bring a flashlight and/or headlamp.
- Have some wet pads or a cleaning cloth to clean yourself and your gear.
- If you are in a radioactive zone, make sure you have a Geiger counter.
- Carry a designated GPS Tracker (not your phone) to mark you location, so friends can check in with you.

Now that you've got that down, check out what these videographers were able to pull off with a small amount of gear.

Chernobyl

Director of Photography Danny Cooke travelled into the radioactive wasteland that is Chernobyl. In April of 1986, an explosion and fire at the Chernobyl Nuclear Power Plant caused radioactive particles to spread all over the western USSR and into Europe.

Cooke shot the **piece for a CBS News** segment on 60 Minutes with a **Canon 7D and DJI Phantom 2 with GoPro3+.**

During my stay, I met so many amazing people, one of whom was my guide Yevgen, also known as a 'Stalker'. We spent the week together exploring Chernobyl and the nearby abandoned city of Pripyat. There was something serene, yet highly disturbing about this place. Time has stood still and there are memories of past happenings floating around us. **Armed with a camera and a dosimeter geiger counter I explored.**

Fukushima

The Chernobyl incident is one of two nuclear incidents categorized as a **Level 7 Event** by the International Nuclear Event Scale. The other being the 2011 disaster in Fukushima.

In March of 2011, an earthquake in Tōhoku caused a tsunami, which in turn caused an **equipment failure at the Fukushima I Power Plant.** The famous Japanese cherry blossom trees in Tokioma now line abandoned streets.

Sheffield Ski Village

The United Kingdoms' Sheffield Ski Village closed down in April of 2012 after an arsonist set fire to the property. When the ski village was open, the it was home to some of the UK's best freestyle skiers.

After the ski village had been abandoned, a few skiers returned for a dry run on the charred remains. The video was shot by Fleye and Extreme Cams.

Rhyolite

Rhyolite is an abandoned mining town in Nevada. The ghost town was once home to many gold seekers and miners during the gold rush. Many residents worked in the Montgomery Shoshone Mine. After the richest ore was exhausted, production fell significantly and it was closed in 1911. By 1920, the city was completely abandoned.

July 17th

How to Make Corporate Videos More Cinematic

Who said corporate videos have to be boring? Engage your audience by taking a more cinematic approach to corporate videos.

A lot of people glaze over immediately when they hear the words **corporate video**. It's understandable. A lot of **corporate videos** are exceptionally bland and lifeless. But that doesn't have to be the case. To ensure your client's video breaks through the boredom barrier, you need to add **cinematic quality** to the production. Let's look at a few tips that can help make your next **corporate video project** stand above the rest.

1. Shoot RAW at 24 Frames Per Second

For the best possible image, don't compress it by using a codec. Instead, **capture it using RAW**. This will give you much more **flexibility in post** with your image. Also, **use 24fps instead of 30fps**, as all major motion pictures are shot using 24fps. By utilizing these two basic settings right out of the gate, you're putting yourself in a great position to **capture cinematic footage** before you even start rolling.

2. Add Dynamic Movement to Your Shots

"Dynamic" is certainly not a word that most people associate with **corporate videos**. Utilizing camera movement is a fantastic way to transform a **drab promotional piece** into a **dynamic marketing tool**. This can be done by using a dolly, steadicam, dolly, crane, jib, or even a drone. The key is to have **motivation for your movement**.

3. Make Use of Shallow Depth of Field

By adding movement, we're able to ramp up the cinematic style of the video. Another way to do this: using **shallow depth of field**. Think back to all of the films you've watched. What's one component of those films that you can easily pick out? It's those moments where you get a shallow depth of field shot. You can't capture this effectively with a wide angle lens, so you'll need to utilize a prime or telephoto lens.

4. Utilize Dynamic Lighting

As any good cinematographer can tell you, **dynamic lighting is the key to capturing a truly cinematic image**. While the concept of lighting can seem a little overwhelming, it's really a lot simpler than you think. You don't need to be a certified lighting expert or have a massive budget to capture great lighting... just get your hands on some LEDs. You'll be able to create some **amazing moods and tones** for your next shoot.

5. Add a Cinematic Color Grade

Now that you're filming in RAW, using 24fps, and adding dynamic movement and lighting, there's really only one more thing to do in order to give your **corporate video** a cinematic flare — **color correction and grading**. Utilize such assets as Magic Bullet from Red Giant or take the time to learn simple grading techniques in DaVinci Resolve. Any of these options will help turn your client's **corporate video** into a **cinematic work of art**.

6. Make it Sound Cinematic

One key ingredient to any video production is the **musical score**. Music (or the lack there of) can **make or break your video**, so you should spend time looking at resources like CR Production Music.com to find the right sound for your client's video. Having a solid soundtrack underneath a **corporate video** can help **set the mood and tone**. This will definitely help keep your audience engaged.

July 18th

Leading a Revolution: Studios Producing Virtual Reality Films

As VR rigs continue advanced testing, there's been a shift from video game development to interactive virtual reality films. These are the studios leading that charge.

Originally intended as a gaming device, the **Oculus Rift** continues to evolve into a world-changing technology. Other companies are also experimenting with virtual reality, like **Google** with **Cardboard** and **Jump**. Even **Samsung** has teamed with Oculus to create **Gear VR** for their **Milk VR** platform.

Now, these tech giants are turning to filmmakers to create original content. **The problem is – no one has ever done this before.** How can you tell a story in a 360 degree room? Does the story even need a script? Here are how some filmmakers are breaking ground in the world of virtual reality films.

Oculus Story Studio

It should come as no surprise that the company leading the virtual reality charge is also the forerunner for developing VR films. A few months after Facebook's acquisition of Oculus, the VR company announced the newly formed Story Studio. **The goal of the studio was to determine what was possible for VR filmmaking, and then share that knowledge with the world.**

Even more incredible than sharing their discoveries is the person leading the **Story Studio**. Oculus hired Saschka Unseld, a 6 year veteran of Pixar Animation Studios. Unseld was a layout artist on several Pixar features, and gained notoriety for directing the Pixar short film *The Blue Umbrella*.

Since becoming the creative director, Unseld has been able to enjoy not having a set budget. **It's his responsibility to explore and learn everything possible.** In doing so, they developed a slate of five films to be released in 2015. The goal was to create drastically different projects to determine what type of story is needed for a VR project.

The first film, *Lost*, was focused on magic and wonder. The film was released in January of 2015. It told the story of a giant robot who was searching for his hand. The film takes place in a dark forest, and the team soon learned that a VR film could be far more frightening that they imagined.

The Forrest engulfed the viewer, which could truly terrify a person. **It was apparent that there was a massive power and responsibility to VR filmmaking.** Their VR film could actually traumatize a person.

Story Studio's second feature would depart the darkness of their first film and focus on humor in a brighter environment. Originally titled *Kabloom*, the film about a hedgehog on his birthday would evolve into the movie *Henry*. Henry the hedgehog only wants to hug people, but others are terrified to hug him. The main character was so adorable, the audience watching literally wanted to reach out and hug him as the story moved on.

Released in July 2015, *Henry* was such a success that it has become the most talked about feature throughout tech sites. The film also made the team realize that the audience will question if there is a set story of not. **They become so attached to the character, they wondered if the character was actually responding to them.**

The film was also played on the Unreal Engine. Unlike any video game currently using the engine, *Henry* really pushed the game engine's capabilities. The multiple Pixar vets behind *Henry* were thrilled, as it was similar to the technical boundaries pushed by the first *Toy Story* film.

Currently the studio is working on their third film, *Bullfighter*. The film aims to put the audience in the ring with a charging bull. We are bound to hear about the exhilarating and terrifying experience soon.

Industrial Light & Magic

Leave it to the magicians at **Industrial Light & Magic** to take things to another level. **ILM** actually has an entire department dedicated to researching the use of VR. The Verge was recently let into the **ILM** VR lab, and what they saw was absolutely incredible. Not only are they working on interactive worlds with dinosaurs and Star Wars characters, they are already using VR practically.

For the first Star Wars anthology film, *Rogue One*, the VR team built a **fully interactive digital set**. This allowed director Gareth Edwards to put on VR glasses and literally walk the set before the practical set is built. He could decide on any changes he wants to make, move buildings or trees, and he can even plot out camera angles and movement.

If VR cinema never takes off, it will certainly become a pre-production tool at the least.

Samsung Milk VR: Gear Indie

When Samsung decided to offer **Gear VR** for owners of the Note 4, it only made sense to use the technology **Oculus** was creating. Users could attach the Note 4 phone to a **Gear VR** rig to experience the incredible world of virtual reality. Now that the gear was available, **Samsung** needed content.

Samsung launched **Milk VR**, a service providing free 360-degree experience for **Gear VR** users. They are now seeking even more content. Samsung made a short VR video called *The Recruit*. They also signed David Alpert, executive producer of *The Walking Dead*, to create an original VR series.

The company also started a new channel called **Gear Indie**. The channel is a **Milk VR** exclusive that showcases short films from independent filmmakers. The added bonus is the fact that the channel will issue a series of challenges for filmmakers to earn rewards.

Challenges will require contestants to figure out technical problems or how to handle storytelling. **Gear Indie** also established a mentorship program for these independent filmmakers to meet and collaborate with prominent members in the VR community.

Google Cardboard & Google Jump

In an attempt to open Virtual Reality up to the masses, **Google** released Cardboard. The device is literally a cardboard box turned into VR headset. Users can either purchase a **Cardboard** box, or download the instructions to build their own. Then they simply insert their smart phone into the box. Boom! Instant VR.

Google also released **Jump,** an open source platform that uses **16 GoPro** cameras to shoot VR environments. The cameras capture a 360-degree environment. Users can then upload their videos to **YouTube**, which now supports 360-degree videos.

Vrse

Vrse is a VR production company headed by Chris Milk. What sets **Vrse** apart are the partnerships with Vice News and Annapurna Pictures. At the Sundance Film Festival, **Vrse** released *Vice News VR: Millions March NYC 2014.* It's claimed the be the first 360-degree VR news broadcast. **Vrse** also released the documentary *Clouds Over Sidra*, the story of a 12-year-old girl in a Syrian refugee camp.

July 19th

2 Dream Gear Loadouts for Documentary Filmmaking

You're a documentary filmmaker and you've just been handed a blank check. What kind of gear loadout should you put together? Here are a couple of options.

Because of the rise of digital technology, documentary filmmakers have access to higher-end equipment like never before. We've already covered one-man-band documentary loadouts — but what about **dream gear loadouts** for **hybrid and traditional documentaries**? Let's take a look at two options.

Dream Gear Loadout: Hybrid Documentaries

This loadout is geared toward **hybrid documentary productions** like *America: The Story of Us, Making a Murder, The Visit: An Alien Encounter,* and *The Imposter*. We'll start with the **base camera** and add accessories from there. Remember: We're throwing budgetary concerns to the wind and looking for the best available options.

EPIC-M DRAGON MONOCHROME CANON PACKAGE: $35,950

EVERYTHING ELSE YOU NEED TO START FILMING:

- REDMAG 1.8" SSD (x4): $495 ea.
- RED Station REDMAG: $250
- 7" RED Touch LCD: $2,950
- DSMC2 RED EVF w/ Mount: $4,150

- VF Cables (x2): $220 ea.
- RED Quick Release Platform: $600
- RED V-Lock Module: $595
- IDX Endura Elite: $572
- IDX VL-2Plus Charger: $299
- Miller Compass 12 Solo Tripod: $2,332
- Zacuto Cine EVF Recoil: $1,200
- ARRI Matte Box: $2700
- Zeiss CP.2 Prime Lens Kit: $10,775
- Zeiss CZ.2 28-80 Zoom Lens: $19,900
- Zeiss CZ.2 70-200 Zoom Lens: $19,900

TOTAL COST: $100,000+

Dream Gear Loadout: Traditional Documentaries

This **traditional documentary** dream gear loadout is going to be considerably less expensive than the hybrid version. We're loosely basing this loadout on the gear used by cinematographer Nick Higgins to film the documentary mini-series, *O.J.: Made in America*. You can read more about the production in this interview with HD Video Pro.

Canon C300 Mark II (Body): $15,999

EVERYTHING ELSE YOU NEED TO START FILMING:

- SanDisk Extreme PRO CFast 2.0 Memory Card (x2): $369 ea.
- SanDisk CFast Extreme Pro: $50
- Zacuto Gratical Eye: $1950
- SmallHD LED Kit: $1399
- Redrock Micro Rig: $550
- ARRI Matte Box: $2700

- Miller Compass 12 Solo Tripod: $2,332
- IDX Endura Elite: $572 ea.
- IDX VL-2Plus Charger: $299
- Canon CN-E 50mm T1.3: $4,650
- Zeiss 35mm CP.2 Prime: $3,990
- Zeiss 85mm CP.2 Prime: $3,990
- Canon 28-300 F2.8: $2,450

TOTAL COST: $41,000

July 20th

3 Creative Ways to Use a Ladder on Set

Step up your video production skills with three camera rigs constructed from ladders.

Some people seem to think that anything that isn't officially called "film gear" is some sort of DIY approach to filmmaking. Nothing could be further from the truth.

Billion-dollar blockbusters still use simple pieces of equipment like apple boxes. Another often-used tool is the ladder. Ladders aren't only used for hanging lights or set pieces. **Here are three ways a ladder can take your footage to the next level.** *Last ladder pun, I promise.*

Ladder Camera: The Super Tripod

Sometimes a tripod won't be tall enough for certain shots. One of the most commonly used techniques is **turning a ladder into a tripod**. (Yes, I know a ladder has four legs and not three.) To pull this off, you'll want use a stepladder.

The most popular ladders are the Werner stepladders that have a **HolsterTop®**. Not only can the HolsterTop® store your tools, it's perfect for mounting a tripod head.

Look for a HolsterTop® ladder with a hole in the middle. This is normally used to hold a hammer, but in this case you will use it to lock the tripod head in place.

Just **attach the tripod fluid head to a ball mount** and rest the ball mount in the ladder's HolsterTop® hole. There are other options as well, like using a Ladder Cam mount, but I find the ball mount to be the most practical and easy to set up.

The ladder camera tripod is perfect for capturing high-angle shots. It's also great for capturing nice wide shots from above. There's also a much added benefit over raising a tripod — your operator can just stand on the ladder and work the camera.

Ladder Dolly/Ladder Slider

If you don't have a slider of your own, or you need a longer dolly track on a tight budget, try using a ladder. For this setup, you're going to need a **straight ladder**. An extension ladder could also work, but you can't extend it — so you're just adding weight to all your gear.

The actual ladder dolly setup is up to user preference or budget. Some crews make their own sliding platforms using a flat surface, some track wheels or skateboard wheels, and a tripod.

There are also professional systems designed to work with ladders. The Hague D10 featured above is a skater dolly that rolls on any smooth surface. It can even turn and swivel. If you would prefer something that is fixed to the ladder, there are options like the CamTram System from AbelCine.

Finally, you can go ladder crazy by placing your ladder on ladders. Check out this tutorial from George Dean on building your own ladder dolly. George even rigged up a system that allows him to move the platform by using a power drill.

Ladder Platform (Only for Advanced and Crazy Users)

Photographer and Videographer Corey Rich was offered a chance to show off the Nikon D5 when the camera was first released. He decided to follow various extreme athletes, which meant he too would have to go to extremes to capture footage.

Some of these setups definitely would not meet the OSHA ladder safety guidelines. If you're going to be using a ladder in any way it wasn't designed for, you must be aware of all potential risks. Keep every shoot safe. Take **plenty of precautions in your setup.**

July 21st
3 Lo-Fi Techniques for Better Camera Stabilization

Nail your shot without an expensive gimbal! Check out these three easy camera stabilization tips that won't bust your budget.

Camera stabilization devices like the Movi and Steadicam are able to deliver a truly unique look that can't easily be replicated. The techniques I've outlined below are by no means intended to replace **proper camera stabilization systems,** but rather provide an alternative when you can't afford to buy or rent a stabilizer. So, without further ado, here are three quick and easy lo-fi/DIY techniques for getting stable shots.

Lo-Fi: Use Your Monopod in a New Way

While **monopods** are probably used more often by photographers than they are by filmmakers, they undeniably offer one of the best solutions when it comes down to **stabilizing your image** in specific instances. In many ultra-low budget shooting situations, productions are unable to even use a tripod for a number reasons. When shooting guerrilla-style, a tripod would draw too much attention. In other situations, having to reposition the tripod for every setup would slow down the shoot too much if a lot of coverage needs to be done in a short period of time.

Monopods are an excellent solution to both of these problems, as they allow for camera stability that's nearly as solid as a tripod, but with the **flexibility of shooting handheld.** What's more important for this post, however, is not just *why* you might use a monopod, **but *how* you could use it.**

If you need to cover a tracking shot of two actors walking down a street, **you can use the monopod much like a glide cam**, by gripping it from the bottom and tracking with your actors. This will give you a far more stable shot when compared to attempting to track them using a handheld or shoulder rig. It will also allow you to reposition for **easy close-ups and coverage** once they stop moving.

Very Lo-Fi: The String Trick

The 'String Trick' is a very old image stabilization technique that has been used in photography for decades. It can be applied to any camera and costs you virtually nothing. The technique is intended to reduce camera shake and micro-jitters when doing handheld work and can replace either the monopod or a shoulder rig if you're on a super tight budget.

All you need to do is get **a piece of strong string** (like fishing line) that's long enough to reach from your toes to your head. Attach one end of the string to a **1/4″ screw** (that will connect to the **tripod mount** on the bottom of your camera) and attach the other end to **a large metal washer.** Here's how it's done, courtesy of Cobbler Video.

You could really use anything in place of the washer, as long as it's durable and large enough that you can step on it. When filming, you simply step on the metal washer and hold the camera up to your eye so that **the string pulls tightly and keeps the camera in place.** This trick greatly **reduces camera shake** and, while it may be an *extremely* low-fi solution, it actually works quite well.

As Lo-Fi as It Gets: Elbows In

This simple physical technique will also cost you nothing to learn, but might take a bit of practice to get just right. There are many ways you can **use your body to reduce camera shake**, but perhaps my favorite technique is called "Elbows in". This is a very simple handheld shooting technique: **Simply pull your elbows together and into your body** (while gripping the camera body with your hands) and **breathe slowly and steadily** for the duration of your shot.

It's amazing how much this body formation can **reduce shake and micro-jitters when shooting handheld.** You might feel a bit awkward shooting this way, but your shots will look far better in the end. Much like the string trick, I use this technique when s**hooting guerilla-style**, as it helps to keep the amount of gear on me at any given time to a minimum.

July 22nd

3 Reasons Why Gimbal Based Stabilizers Aren't Always the Best Choice

When Freefly Cinema announced the Movi just a year and a half ago, filmmakers everywhere rejoiced. But now that it's been out in the field for a while (along with dozens of knock offs), many shooters are finding it to be more of a speciality item.

I have been fortunate to have used the Movi a number of times (as well as several other gimbal based stabilizers), and I've been able to achieve fantastic results with it – even with no formal training whatsoever. It's an incredibly innovative product and one of the most powerful tools that we as filmmakers have access to today, but I am not alone in feeling that Gimbal based stabilizers aren't always the best stabilization choice.

When the first promo videos of the Movi were released last year, it truly seemed that this device could do it all. It could theoretically be used to replace just about any type of stabilization system – from a tripod to a jib and everything in between. In many respects, it can replace a lot of traditional stabilization systems…but that doesn't mean that it's *always* better suited than its more traditional counterparts.

They Can Only Be Held for So Long

Before I ever actually operated a Movi myself, I had not even considered the fact that since the system isn't attached to any sort of vest (like a Steadicam) it can become extremely tiresome to hold. This is especially true when you have a heavier camera such as a RED Epic set up on it. For those of you that have never operated a Movi yourself, imagine holding out your arms straight for ten minutes… It would get pretty tiring right? Now imagine adding 10 to 20 lbs. of weight to the equation and things get even more difficult.

I can tell you from personal experience that on any professional set that I've been on (where we've had a Movi or Ronin and a substantial camera setup on it), our operator was unable to successfully hold the setup for more than a few minutes at a time. This severely limits the way that the device can be used as it doesn't allow for long takes and requires more time in between takes for the operator to recover. **The solution to this problem is to rig the stabilizer up to an Easy Rig (which takes a lot of the weight off of your arms), but then the movement of the Movi is limited heavily and the purpose of having a gimbal based stabilizer is largely diminished.**

They Require Multiple Operators

Many filmmakers were excited that the Movi would free us up creatively. If we wanted to try out a completely new type of shot that was never possible before, now the Movi would allow us to get there. That certainly is still true, and I am by no means opposed to the Movi as there are certain circumstances where it works beautifully. However, when considering the notion that it frees you up creatively, you also need to consider that it restricts you in other ways – namely crew requirements.

In order to really operate a Movi properly you need at least two specific crew members, and potentially three at times. There is the Movi operator, the focus puller, and potentially a third crew member who is responsible for planning and tilting the device via a remote control (if you don't choose to use it in single operator mode). This means that even though from a technical level it may be possible to accomplish the shot that you're after, you may now need to hire a couple more crew members to make that happen. And while the same argument can be made about other stabilization systems that require additional crew members (such as a dolly grip for a traditional dolly), the specific crew members you need for Movi operation is often more specifically skilled.

They Can Be Overused Easily

Many productions that make use of a Movi fall into the dangerous trap of overusing it simply because they can. Much like shooting handheld, working with any gimbal based stabilizer doesn't always challenge you to get the most purposeful shots, as you could theoretically leave the camera on it for your entire shoot and make every last shot a Movi shot – even if that's not what's best for the scene or sequence. In some rare cases, shooting an entire project on a Movi actually could be a good thing. For instance, maybe you're shooting something that calls for a very specific and fluid movement throughout, and the Movi is the best tool for it. I would argue though, that more often than not if it's used from A to Z on an entire shoot, the unique effect of the camera movement can get lost due to overuse.

When you need to spend time setting up a dolly or a steadicam, you have no choice but to be especially careful about the choices that you are making. We all know the effects of camera movement on the viewers' interpretation of a film, which is why it is so important for those movements to be purposeful. A great film will often make use of many types of camera movement in order to evoke different emotions, and unfortunately when using the Movi it is fairly common to fall into the trap of shooting everything that way, and losing sight of some of the more traditional methods of making a film. That doesn't mean it has to happen, but simply that it can.

Final Thoughts

After reading this article you might think that I'm not a fan of the Movi, but that really couldn't be farther from the truth. **I love what Freefly has done and truly believe that gimbal based stabilizers are the future of stabilization in many respects.** With that said, there is still a time and a place for them to be used and they aren't always the best solution – nor is any stabilization system for that matter. If you are shooting on a larger scale production and can afford a couple of crew members that are dedicated to operating/controlling the Movi, then you are in a good place, especially when you know when and where to use it. Just make sure that whenever you make use of a Movi, it is the right choice for your story.

July 23rd
3 Tips You Must Know Before Shooting a Multicam Production

Multicam productions have become more popular than ever, thanks to the extremely low cost of camera gear and easy integration into video editing apps. Even still, many producers attempting multicam for the first time aren't able to get it right.

While the thought of setting up a multicam shoot can be daunting to producers/directors who have never done it before, knowing how to do it right has some massive benefits. Not only do multicam setups help keep time on-set to a minimum (and therefore also keep the budget down too), but they can also provide creative freedoms that aren't otherwise offered by single camera environments. For instance, if you are directing a comedy and want to allow your actors to improvise, a multicam setup would be ideal so that you can catch all of the spontaneity, while also having enough coverage to cut together the scene cohesively in post.

Whether you're interested in **shooting multicam** as a means to keep your budget down, to give you actors more freedom, or you simply have no other choice – this article will go over a few considerations for getting started with multicam shooting.

Camera Placement

The very first thing you need to address with your multicam set up is **the placement of your cameras themselves**. I have seen some huge mistakes made with regards to camera placement in low-budget multicam situations, and the end result always ends up looking sub-par.

If you want to achieve professional level results with your shoot, **you need to make sure that you are optimizing your coverage**. In other words, if you are shooting a scene with two actors and you have 3 cameras on them – you probably want a close up on each actor, and then a wide/medium master shot. This may sound obvious, but you probably wouldn't believe some of the poorly executed camera placements that I've seen over the years. For instance, in a situation like the example above, I have seen setups where the director wanted all three cameras roaming (as opposed to locked off on each of the different actors) and ultimately it defeated the purpose of shooting with a 3 camera setup. As you might imagine, when it got time to edit the scene it was extremely difficult for the filmmakers to cut together all three angles as they often were too similar looking to intercut. This doesn't mean you can't get creative with your multicam setups, but rather that you **make sure you are never doubling up on coverage**, regardless of the creative choices that are made.

Lighting

The manner in which you and/or your DP approach your lighting setup also needs to change drastically from what you may be used to in single camera situations. When shooting with one camera, your setup naturally only matters for the particular angle and take that you are executing, and when you go in for coverage you can make small adjustments to your lights (such as walking in a key or fill) as needed. **With multi-camera lighting though, everything changes.**

The easiest way to get the look that you're after while maintaining visual consistency is by **setting up your lights much in the same way that a stage plays or a sitcom is set up**. To clarify – I'm not suggesting that you make creative choices that will make your final product look like a play or sitcom, but rather that you make rigging and logistical choices in that same way. For example, lighting from above (by rigging lights to a ceiling or grid) would be hugely preferable over lighting using traditional stands. The reason of course being that when rigged to the ceiling, the lights are completely out of the way and you can shoot in nearly any direction that you want. Lighting your set this way will inevitably take more time up front – so **be prepared for some extra time pre-lighting**, but in the end it will completely balance out as you will save loads of time once you start rolling.

Matching The Cameras

Amongst the most common and problematic issue that arises on multicam setups (particularly on low budget indie films) are mismatched cameras. In many instances, small productions don't want to rent two or three identical cameras, so they mix and match various cameras that they have access to in order to supplement their multicamera setup. While this can be done and in some circumstances you can get away with it, **I would highly advise against mixing cameras whenever possible.** In an ideal world, you want every camera to be the exact make and model, or at the very least the same brand. For example, a Canon 5D MK II and a Canon 7D will match a lot better than a 7D and a Lumix GH4 since Canon and Lumix use completely different firmware and color science.

Even if you are shooting on identical cameras, you still need to be extremely diligent when it comes to your settings (camera profiles, shutter angle, white balance, etc.) as **any slight difference in your camera settings can cause some big headaches in post**. And unless you are a professional colorist, or have it in your budget to hire one, you'll want to avoid making any mistakes in post that can cost you some serious time and money down the road.

Final Thoughts

Shooting multicam isn't right for every project, but when time is of the essence and budgets are low, it can be a fantastic way to save money and allow you to move quickly without sacrificing quality. In order to do it right, you need to place your cameras strategically, have a rock solid lighting setup, and make sure that you are using cameras that match as closely as possible. Also, be prepared to spend some extra time up front on rigging/pre-lighting days, and know that investing your time in prep will help you immensely once principal photography commences.

July 24th
5 Awesome Filmmaking Hacks

These filmmaking hacks are a great way to get epic footage while not breaking the bank.

When you're shooting a video, there are a lot of different pieces of equipment that you need to remember. It's not uncommon to bring dozens of pieces of equipment to your set. But if you forget an important piece of gear, you can still get good results with a few hacks. Here are a few of our favorite filmmaking hacks.

1. Zip Tie Follow Focus

Things You'll Need: Zip Tie, Rubber Band

When it comes to smooth focusing, nothing can quite match a follow focus... but for a few small pieces of plastic and metal, a follow focus can cost a pretty penny. It's not uncommon to see a follow focus north of $500. So what are you to do? Well, one quick hack that you can use is to simply use a zip tie and a rubber band around your focus ring. It looks like this:

2. Tripod Glidecam

Things You'll Need: A Tripod

When it comes to shooting cinematic footage, stabilization is the name of the game. Unfortunately, stabilizers can be super expensive. So instead of spending hundreds of dollars on a specific rig, you could always use your handy-dandy tripod as a makeshift steadicam. Sometimes simply giving your camera a little more weight and changing the center of balance is all you need to do, and a tripod can pull off the trick. After you shoot the footage, you can then move it into your NLE and stabilize it even more.

3. Lamp Light

Things You'll Need: A Lamp and Possibly a Lamp Shade

Film lights are crazy expensive, but if you're working on a budget you don't necessarily need to get 'production' lights to get good lighting results. You can easily use various lamps and bulbs laying around your house to adequately light, if you know what bulbs to choose. The easiest thing to do is to simply go with Tungsten Balanced (orange) bulbs and a simple diffuser. To diffuse the light, you should use a white lamp shade. A few common household lamp choices are either china balls or the rectangular lamps found at simple home furnishing stores like Ikea.

4. Shower Curtain Diffusion

Things You'll Need: A Shower Curtain, A Stand, and Clamps

Diffused light is often praised because of its versatility. Luckily, it's incredibly easy to make any light softer if you simply go grab the shower curtain out of your bathroom. Using a simple stand and a curtain or sheet, you can easily diffuse harsh lighting and create soft, flattering light.

5. Car Dolly

Things You'll Need: A Car

While you'd certainly be hard-pressed to fit a car into an indoor location, if you happen to be shooting outdoors, a car can be a smooth way to track alongside your subjects. Cars can be great for tracking or dollying. Plus, if you're downscaling 4K footage to HD, you can stabilize your car-dolly clips to get ultra-smooth footage.

This staff-picked video from Vimeo shows us a few of the creative possibilities of using a car on a production. In the video, the hosts outline a few further ways that you can use a car for filmmaking beyond simply tracking and dollying.

July 25th
13 Products You Wish You Had in Your Video Editing Suite

Top of the line computers, a library of cutting-edge visual effects and some of the most ergonomic furniture ever created…check out this roundup of dream video editing gear!

Imagine if you could afford all of the leading post-production tools for your own personal edit suite.

What's on your dream gear list?

If money was not an issue, THIS is how we'd deck out an edit suite!

Computing, Storage & Displays

Apple Mac Pro 12-Core Dual 2.93GHz

$9,749 - This Apple tower from proMAX was customized specifically with the video editor in mind. 64GB of RAM make it a beast at processing and a great workstation for the Avid, Premiere or FCPX editor. Imagine blazing fast edit sessions on this CPU!

Eizo ColorEdge 27" Monitor

Approx $3200 - This high-end broadcast monitor from Eizo was designed for color grading and non-linear editing. Significant features include a digital device emulator (see how your image would look on an iPad for instance), self-calibration settings and 10-bit simultaneous display. Pretty awesome.

Apple LED Cinema Displays (x2)

$1,998 - These 27" Cinema Displays from Apple provide a crystal clear image and ton of screen real estate for your photo and video projects. They're not cheap, but they pair well with the Apple CPU and they've got a really wide viewing angle.

AJA Io Express

$995 - The AJA Io Express is a powerful video input/output device that's designed for monitoring and mastering. Designed to work with Avid, FCP and Adobe Creative Suite, the Io is capable of handling a variety of HD/SD video outputs and conversions. Little box – tons of options.

Audio Monitoring

Genelec 1038B (x2)

$16,478 - If you want the top in post-production audio monitoring, these refrence speakers from Genelec fit the bill. Priced at over $8,000 A PIECE, these three-way active monitors provide accurate audio reproduction. An added bonus for editors: they are magnetically shielded for use near video monitors.

Genelec 7271A Subwoofer

$6,129 - $7k may seem like a ton for good bass, but pair this awesome subwoofer with the Genelec speakers and you've got an unparraled audio setup for your editing suite.

Edit Suite Furniture

Martin and Ziegler Ergo Duet 68

$3995 - This may be the perfect video editing desk. The Ergo Duet comes complete with a monitor bridge (that can accommodate two computer monitors PLUS a reference monitor). Sitting all day can be draining, so instead reduce fatigue by activating the electronic height adjustment. Goes from true sit down to all-out standing desk in a matter of seconds.

Herman Miller Embody Chair

Approx $1400 - This chair actually claims to "boost creativity" by keeping your body in motion. The Embody moves and adapts to your body's position, improving oxygen and blood flow. This chair is a dream in day-long edit sessions.

Editing Accessories

Wacom Intuos5

$229-789 - Take your editing to new heights with this big pen tablet from Wacom. Whether you're working in an NLE, touching up images in Photoshop or creating graphics in After Effects, a pen tablet will likely speed up your workflow. Editors that use them regularly tend to swear by them.

Bella Corporation Pro Series Editing Keyboard

$139.95 - This keyboard is designed specifically for the video editor, with speciality keys, a task light and even an integrated jog shuttle. Bella makes a specific keyboard for FCP7, FCPx, Vegas and Media Composer. We're adding this one to the list for it's productivity increasing powers!

Color Correction and Effects

DaVinci Resolve with Control Surface

$29,999 - The Resolve software my come in at just under $1,000 but if you're REALLY serious about color correction you're going to want the full DaVincivi Resolve Control Surface! The surface has been designed with the pro colorist in mind and takes advantage of all the color correction tools that Resolve has to offer.

GenArts Sapphire

$600-$5,000 - Sapphire is arguably the premiere visual effects plug-in for video editing, so no doubt it made this "dream" list. Used in such films as X-Men, Lord of the Rings and the Matrix, Sapphire offers over 220 highly customizable effects. The price for the package is dependent on the NLE or motion graphics application you use it with.

Magic Bullet Suite

$799 - Give your video it's own distinct look with this awesome plug-in pack from Red Giant Software. The suite includes all 9 of the Magic Bullet stand-alone applications including Mojo, Colorista and Looks. This made our list because it's a full-featured toolset that's great for giving any project a sleek high-end look.

What dream gear would YOU want?

July 26th
Affordable Gimbals for Light Cameras

3-axis gimbals are wildly versatile filmmaking tools, offering stable footage and the ability to create movements that would usually require extra gear.

While **gimbals** have certainly become more affordable, with more conservative options such as the DJI Ronin M, they are still fairly expensive for the average video enthusiast or blossoming professional. Over the past year, however, a plethora of affordable **gimbals** have been released.

While these were primarily limited to GoPros and built-in cameras, Filmpower changed this when they released their compact gimbal for light DSLRs and mirrorless cameras, the Nebula 4000, in January. The Nebula 4000 was the first to enter the sub-$1000 **gimbal** market, and while it was relatively well-received, it was still flawed.

Since then, two more distinct **gimbal** models have been released: The **Pilotfly H1+** and the **Came-TV Single**. These two **gimbals**, while slightly more expensive than the Nebula, bring significantly more to the table in terms of features, practicality, and general product quality.

Let's take a look into these two new **gimbals**, how they have improved upon the aging Nebula, and how they hold up against one another. Before we dive into that, here are the respective prices of each **gimbal** for reference:

1. Nebula 4000 – 699.00 USD
2. Pilotfly H1+ – 791.10 USD
3. Came-TV Single – 988.00 USD

The Nebula 4000

The **Nebula 4000** is an 8-bit **gimbal** that supports cameras up to 2.1 pounds and uses one sensor. Its frame is lightweight, simple, and small, making it very portable and great for small cameras that don't necessarily need something larger.

Beyond these fundamental features found in the Nebula 4000, the **Pilotfly H1+** and **Came-TV Single** have a number of important differences. They tend to provide nearly identical footage in terms of stability, but they really stand apart in terms of ease of use and more situationally-specific features.

The New Gimbles on the Block

The **Pilotfly H1+** and **Came-TV Single** both push compact **gimbal** technology much further. To start, they both include dual sensors as opposed to one, which improve accuracy and responsiveness. In addition, both **gimbals** are 32-bit, providing additional processing power and more precise tuning.

They also feature larger frames and larger motors, allowing for larger and slightly heavier camera bodies. This obviously comes with the disadvantage of holding bulkier, heavier equipment, but in the end you can choose which direction to go depending on how large and heavy your camera is.

Lastly, while customer service isn't an improvement in terms of performance, it is important. Filmpower (The creator of the Nebula 4000) has a rather poor reputation in regards to their customer service, but luckily both Pilotfly and Came-TV have been commended for theirs. Lastly, the Pilotfly is only $100 more than the Nebula, which is a rather small price difference considering the many ways it outperforms the Nebula.

1. Pilotfly H1+

- **Pros:** Price, Customizable PID Profiles, PID Profile Presets, Low Profile Design, Light, No Exposed Cables, Supports Inverted Mode, Supports 2.6 pounds, Control Via Bluetooth
- **Cons:** Balance Requires PID Tuning, App Only Available on Android, No Encoders, Case Off, Single Axis Joystick, 2 Hour Battery Life, Non-Removable Battery, Requires Hex Tool (included)

Let's begin with the cheaper of the two options. Pilotfly's H1+ stands out the most in its customization and versatility. You can adjust and fine-tune your PID (Proportional, Integral, Derivative) settings to your heart's content.

PID settings adjust the three motors to achieve the best balance for a particular camera and lens combination. Pilotfly has provided a plethora of common camera and lens presets to allow a quick-and-easy setup for your specific camera. **These can be adjusted using a Mac, PC, or an Android smart phone.**

Using the Android app also allows you to control your **gimbal** orientation wirelessly via bluetooth. Bear in mind the Android app is rather hard to find information on, and is actually called SimpleBGC. An app has not yet been released for iPhone users, but hopefully that will change in the future.

The H1+ supports Inverted Mode as well, which allows you to hold the device upside down for convenience or extra low shots. The Came-TV Single does not support inverted mode, and limits you to holding it in the traditional vertical way.

The physical design of this **gimbal** is notable too. Unlike with the Came-TV Single, there are no loose wires to fear, and the device is generally much smoother and less bulky than the Single. Its low-profile build is a bit more appealing, as it makes the device more compact and less flashy. The H1+ reportedly supports up to 2.6 pounds as well, making it the strongest of these **gimbals**.

2. Came-TV Single

- **Pros:** Fast Setup, Encoders, Auto-orientation, Up to 10 Hour Battery Life, 18650 Batteries, Quick Release Plate, No Tools Required, Larger Camera Support, Heavy Duty Case
- **Cons:** Price, No Inverted Mode, Bulky Design, No PID Customization, Exposed Cables, Heavy, Supports 2.2 Pounds

Now let's look at the Came-TV Single. The general consensus seems to be that the Single is the better of these two **gimbals** – but is it justifiable at nearly $200 more than the Pilotfly? Well, that really depends on how important its unique features are to you.

The Came-TV certainly brings **gimbal** technology the furthest within $1000 (though just barely), mostly through its use of encoders. Encoders are a common component in robotics that provide a number of benefits to motor performance. Among these are less de-sync and skips, less power consumption, increased precision, and more motor torque. Encoders are part of what make the Came-TV wonderfully simple to set up.

The biggest selling point of the Single is its charming simplicity. The Single requires no in-software calibration, and will balance itself almost instantly. Thanks to its encoders, you can actually reset the orientation of your camera by simply physically forcing the camera to a new orientation for a few seconds, at which point the **gimbal** will automatically adjust.

Came-TV also improved upon Pilotfly's design by implementing a 2-axis joystick instead of a 1-axis one.

This allows simultaneous pitch and yaw adjustments without having to toggle between the two. Pilotfly's Android app alleviates this by allowing the same functionality, but again, requires further set-up before shooting.

While this **gimbal** is great for quick setups, unfortunately Came-TV has also prevented users from customizing PID settings on their own. They insist that it is unnecessary, but unfortunately in the event that you want to make minor adjustments to your calibration, you will be unable to do so with the Single.

While the Single is rather bulky and rugged in comparison to the H1+, this comes with its advantages. For one, its frame is larger than that of the H1+, allowing it to support larger cameras. Its built-in quick release plate is a nice addition as well. The H1+ and Nebula both require the use of a hex tool for balancing, whereas the Single has removed this hassle and instead replaced it with simple screws that require little fine-tuning.

The larger nature of the device warrants the nice, heavy-duty hard case that it includes, compared to the *adequate* soft bag that comes with the H1+.

Lastly, the Single excels in its battery type and life. The Pilotfly H1+ will run for a respectable two hours or so, but it is dwarfed by the 9-10 hour battery life of the Came-TV Single.

Additionally, the Came-TV runs on generic 18650 batteries, which are both cheap and easy to acquire. Pilotfly uses a proprietary, non-removable battery, limiting usage to just a couple of hours at a time. Pilotfly does offer an external battery, but this is still disappointing when compared to the stellar efficiency of the Single.

Conclusion

In conclusion, **both the Pilotfly H1+ and Came-TV Single** are blessings to the video production community, offering very impressive, cinematic footage with little effort.

If you don't mind going the extra financial mile to save time down the road, the Came-TV Single is the way to go. However, if you like having maximum control (especially wireless) over your equipment, can't live without inverted mode, or just want something a bit easier to carry, you'll want to go with the Pilotfly H1+.

Regarding the Nebula 4000, it's still a great tool, but it's best for those whose foremost concern is either budget or size, considering how outdated the technology is quickly becoming.

July 27th

Best Lenses for Corporate Video Interviews

Corporate video demands a certain look and approach. Let's take a good look at the best lenses for corporate video interviews.

As videographers and filmmakers, we have to be keenly aware of what the day's production requires in terms of gear. This is especially true for interviews and the lenses used to capture them, no matter if the project is narrative, commercial or industrial.

The difference between a documentary interview for a narrative film and a **corporate interview** is minimal at best. With this said, most documentary filmmakers and videographers run a two camera setup. However, you may not be able to do that, so we'll be sure to go through an easy solution for a single camera setup before we go into the lens options for a two camera setup.

Before we get started, let's look at this example of solid **corporate interview** composition that comes from an Apple **corporate video**.

Single Camera Setup

For single camera setups, you can do one of two things. The first being that you use one single prime lens, probably a 50mm Prime lens. Your second option, and potentially best option, would be to use a zoom lens like the Canon 70-200mm. Now, both options will require quality lighting of the subject and framing, but beyond that, let's look at why we picked these two lenses.

50mm Prime

No lens can simulate the human eye better than the 50mm Prime. When you're regulated to just one camera, and you want to make sure that the interview you're capturing looks fantastic, you'll need to use a 50mm lens.

This particular lens will offer you the best options in terms of sharpness of the image. If you set your camera up correctly, you'll get a shot with great depth of field. Also remember you can move your camera closer or further away from your subject in order to capture varying compositions.

- Canon 50mm – $329
- Rokinon 50mm – $399
- Zeiss 50mm – $625

70-200mm Zoom

If you don't have the space needed to move your camera between closer and farther away from the subject, then you'll want to utilize a zoom lens. For this we suggest a Canon 70-200mm, but know there are other quality options out there. By using this zoom lens, you can frame your wider shot by setting the lens to 70mm. Then, when you need to go close-up, you make that adjustment by moving closer to toward 200mm. This option can be a time saver, and you'll find that, for interviews, a zoom lens like the 70-200mm looks fantastic.

Canon 70-200mm – $1999
Canon 24-70mm – $1799

Two Camera Setup

Most professionals prefer a two camera setup. When running two cameras, what you'll usually find is that A Camera will remain on the sticks as a static shot, while B Camera can either be on sticks, on a slider, or on a Steadicam. The B Camera lets you capture additional dynamic information, such a hands moving while the subject is talking or getting in close to frame their eyes. Let's look at two different lens pairings for the two camera setup.

Two Prime Lenses

The first pairing is pretty straight forward; you use two prime lenses. Many times you'll see videographers or documentary filmmakers use a combination of a 50mm and an 85mm Prime lens. What happens here is that A Camera gets the 50mm to capture that great looking master shot, then you supplement this by using the 85mm Prime with B Camera to capture much tighter shot.

B Camera then usually becomes the camera of movement. By using the 85mm and adjusting our camera setting correctly, we can capture nice dolly shots or tracking shots that will have a parallax effect.

Rokinon Cine Prime Kit – $2,099
Zeiss Prime Kit – $6,063
Canon Cinema Prime Kit – $13,950

Using a Prime and a Zoom

For the second pairing, we'll just take the two main options for the single camera setup and combine them together. So, in this case, we'll again run the 50mm lens on A Camera, but now we'll place a zoom lens like the 70-200mm on B Camera. Essentially what we are doing is exactly what we did above with the two Prime lens pairing — but by using a zoom lens, B Camera has a ton of flexibility in terms of framing.

- Zeiss 50mm - $625
- Canon 70-200mm - $1999

Any of the lens setups above will work for your next **corporate video interview**, just be sure to do whatever is comfortable. Above all else, your interview is the most important, so be sure to capture it as best you can with what you have.

July 28th

Buying Tips: Tripods for Video

Don't cheap out on your camera support! Investing in a quality tripod and fluid head is a smart decision for the future expansion, performance and safety of your gear.

Build quality in a tripod has a huge impact on the final image, for both filmmakers and still photographers.

Inexpensive tripods are often shoddily constructed, made from aluminum or a similar, thin metal. This flimsy construction makes the tripod prone to breaking and doesn't provide strong stabilization. Conversely, investing in a more expensive, but higher quality tripod, will provide a more stable image, a longer product lifespan and additional peace of mind when you go to shoot. Are you in the market for a new tripod? Make the following considerations…

Avoid Center Columns

Tripods with height adjustable center columns introduce a lot of vibration and instability to your camera rig. There's a reason professional quality tripods don't have center columns: the engineering will not provide enough stability. If you're looking for adding height, **go with a tripod that has longer legs.**

Avoid Aluminum, Stick with Carbon Fiber

Aluminum tripods are usually much more prone to vibrations than tripods constructed of carbon fiber. **Aluminum has a longer dampening time,** meaning vibrations are much more prevalent – traveling easily throughout the tripod.

Carbon fiber has a much shorter dampening time, containing and minimizing vibrations with every camera movement or bump of the tripod. Although lightweight tripods tend to cost more, they do not necessarily perform better. That being said, many professional tripods are made from carbon fiber, which is considerably lightweight. **A tripod with better dampening times will produce a professional looking result** with minimal hassle.

Load Capacity

Every tripod will have a maximum load capacity, ranging from 7-10 lbs. for cheaper models and upwards of 50 lbs. for higher-end types. This is where a little planning can go a long way. Selecting the right tripod for your needs (and future needs) is key to your tripod investment.

Factor in the weight of your camera combined with weight from any other equipment that will be rigged onto your tripod. As previously stated, it is best to account for the future when that time comes to add more equipment (and weight) to the tripod. A teleprompter, monitors, lights, field recorders and microphones all add weight. **Never plan to be at or near your tripod's load capacity.** If you have a 20 lb. rig, a tripod rated at 30 lbs. will obviously perform better (and safer) than one loaded to capacity.

Head & Bowl Mount

Not all tripods come with a fluid head. **It's important to use a quality head with the appropriate counter-balance and weight load.** Tripods that use **bowl systems** are the **most widely used by professionals** because it's easy to level and balance a fluid head in a pinch to get that perfect shot.

July 29th
Essential Gear for Product Videos

Shooting a professional product video is surprisingly easy — if you have the right gear. Here's everything you need.

While many professional videographers shoot **product videos** in super boring and ugly rooms, you don't want your finished video to look anything short of perfect. Let's take a look at some of **the most important gear to bring to any product video shoot.**

1. Reflectors

The most important item to have on a **product video** shoot is a 5-in-1 reflector. Reflectors serve as multi-tools on set because they can do a number of different jobs, including:

- **diffusing light**
- **reflecting light**
- **flagging light**
- **absorbing light**

- **makeshift backgrounds**

Reflectors allow you to **shape the way your product looks on camera.** There are a lot of DIY reflector tutorials out there, but all of them are impractical. Reflectors are inexpensive enough (around $15) that there's really nothing to prevent you from buying your own.

2. C-Stands

C-Stands are especially important when shooting **product videos**. Even more than most commercial work, a **product video** will require subtle changes in lighting; you might need to add additional reflectors or even a backlight to your subject. Between holding up the background, lights, and reflectors, it's not uncommon to need six or more C-Stands on a **product video shoot**. Make sure you have plenty when you arrive on set.

3. Soft Box

There's a time and a place for harsh lighting. **Product videos** are not the time nor the place. If you do a lot of product photography, **owning a soft box is a must**. A soft box makes it a lot easier for you to light your scene; it will soften shadows, eliminating visual distractions. My favorite thing to do is **place two soft boxes around my subject** (one to the left. one to the right) and then add in smaller lights to stylize the scene.

4. Macro Lens

A macro lens has a very short minimum focus distance that allows you to get *really* close to your subject. As you can imagine, this is imperative if you are **shooting a product video**. The most popular macro lens on the market is a 100mm f/2.8. This lens, found across multiple brands, is perfect for **shooting small objects.**

While not technically a macro lens, if your subject is a little larger you should use a **50mm prime**. This will allow you to get wide and not distort your subject in the camera. And, frankly… you really should have a 50mm prime in your lens bag anyways.

5. Tripod

The importance of a good tripod can't be overstated. While you'll typically find the best luck with a **fluid head tripod**, you don't have to spend hundreds of dollars to get a decent set of sticks. There are a lot of good, affordable tripod options out there, if you just take the time to do your homework. One of my favorite brands is Magnus. While their tripods will only last about three to five years, they are super smooth, especially when you consider that they're friction head.

6. External Monitor

Details are everything in filmmaking and video production. This is especially true for **product videos**. On a narrative set, you might be able to get by with a focus that's slightly off. But if your focus is even a *little* off on a **product video shoot**, you're going to have to reshoot. This is why an external monitor is super important. An external monitor will allow you to see your finished footage the way your audience will see it. Good external recorders will allow you to see your focus points and find any overexposed areas.

7. Backgrounds: Paper > Cloth

Nine times out of ten, your background for a **product video** will be either solid white or solid black. Normally when you're shooting a video with a solid background, you want any distracting background creases or wrinkles to be minimized. This is especially important for **product videos**. Any distracting background blemishes will distract the viewers from the actual product being featured.

I recommend **using rolls of paper rather than cloth** when working with solid backgrounds. Paper rolls are consistently smooth and solid, perfect for product videos. Plus, if you accidentally stain the paper, you can just cut it off and roll out some more.

Fun Fact: If you want your product videos to have a little reflectivity, place a solid piece of glass down over your table top.

8. Gaff Tape

Okay, so maybe gaff tape doesn't necessarily fall into the 'gear' category, but it's still an incredibly useful tool on any film or video set. Gaff tape, as you can imagine, can serve many different roles on set. It can hold down loose background pieces, keep your products steady, set actor marks, hold reflectors steady, and much more.

While you will have to fork over a little extra cash to get gaff tape over other kinds of tape, it's absolutely worth it. Gaff tape doesn't leave residue behind.

9. Lazy Susan

If you've ever eaten at a fancy Chinese restaurant, then you probably have experience with a Lazy Susan. In a nutshell, a Lazy Susan is a small tabletop that spins in circles. If your **product photography** requires you to shoot all 360 degrees of the featured product, this is a must — especially when you can't move your camera all the way around your subject without getting lights and crew members in the shot.

All you really need to do is place a piece of solid-colored poster board over a Lazy Susan, tape it down, and then have a crew member (or yourself) give it a spin. It's actually pretty easy to use and the results look fantastic.

10. Slider

Good **product commercials** have one thing in common: movement. It doesn't matter how good your lighting is, if the footage is boring, nobody is going to want to watch it. The slightest movements will go a long way when shooting **product videos**. This is where a slider comes into play. When coupled with a decent rotating head, a slider can add a lot of visual interest to an otherwise boring video.

11. Wood Panels (Fake Wood Table)

Typically, when you see **product videos** with 'hipster' table tops, the table top isn't actually real. It's typically a wooden panel that's been put together to simulate a real table. This helps with storage space and allows you to light the scene more easily.

All you really need to do is get a few pieces of plywood and an assortment of wood stain. Simply stain one side one color and the other side another color. Now you have two different table tops without having to store two different tables. Of course, this method doesn't work if you need the actual table legs in the shot. But for most shooting scenarios, this set up will work great.

July 30th
Expensive Hollywood Camera Gear

Let's take a look at some of the most expensive pieces of camera gear in the world and find out if they're worth their exorbitant price tags.

Film gear is never cheap, as most filmmakers and video producers know all too well. Early in your career, you'll buy a few pieces of gear that will allow you to complete projects and **get your reel together**. Then, when you find some success, you'll begin adding crew members and working with a production team. At this point in your career, **you'll be renting your gear.**

If you're fortunate enough to work within the studio system, then you'll see a level of drool-worthy, astronomically priced gear that very few filmmakers ever will. Just for kicks, let's daydream about working with some of **the most expensive gear in the world.**

Panavision Film Cameras

Camera: $120,000+ (rumored)
Lenses: $500,000 for full set (35, 40, 50, 60, 75, and 100mm)

We'll start things off with quite possibly the **coolest A and B cameras in the world**, which were nicknamed "Death Star" and "Millennium Falcon." These two cameras were developed by

Panavision specifically for director J.J. Abrams and cinematographer Dan Mindel, who used them to capture the latest installment of the Star Wars franchise, The Force Awakens.

Panavision also worked with Mindel and first assistant Serge Nofield to develop **custom anamorphic lenses**, now known as the Retro C Series, just for the film. These lenses helped capture images much like those captured by the lenses used on 1977's Star Wars. With these cameras and lenses being custom built, we're looking at a total price tag in the hundreds of thousands of dollars. Of course, for studios the size of Lucasfilm and Disney, this probably wasn't too big of a budget hit.

IMAX Camera

Rental: $12,000 – $16,000 (per week)
Purchase: $500,000+

In the 1950s and 60s, directors, producers, and cinematographers wanted to introduce large formats to the public, so multi-projector setups like Cinerama, VistaVision and CinemaScope were born. However, filmmakers William C. Shaw, Graeme Ferguson, Robert Kerr, and Roman Kroitor wanted a **single projector/camera setup for large formats**, so they introduced the world to IMAX.

IMAX cameras are being used consistently on major motion pictures such as The Dark Knight and Interstellar. To get your hands on one of these bad boys, you'll need to have a budget of **up to $16,000 a week just for the camera rental**. To purchase one, you're looking at just north of half a million, which makes the IMAX camera one of the most expensive cameras in the world.

Phantom Flex4K

Rental: $10,500 (weekly)
Purchase: $100,000 – $200,000 (depending on configuration)

Vision Research began developing and manufacturing high-speed cameras back in 1992. With a line of cameras called the Phantom series, **of which the Phantom Flex4K is the crown jewel,** Vision Research has seen its products used extensively for live sports broadcasting and wildlife programming.

Pictorvision Camera Array

Rental: unknown
Purchase: $250,000 – $350,000 (estimated)

When it comes to camera arrays, there's probably no company out there putting together rigs quite like Pictorvision. Their Eclipse Camera Array was used recently for 2015's Jupiter Ascending, as the VFX team needed high-resolution background plates through downtown Chicago.

The Eclipse array consists of six RED EPICS that can capture a 140-degree horizontal and 60-degree vertical image at 12K resolution. The cameras rest inside a gimbal system that can be mounted to a crane or helicopter. The entire setup is run by a seventh RED EPIC which is essentially used as the controller.

With a single RED EPIC going for roughly $24,000 – $30,000, you can easily determine that the price tag for this piece of equipment is, well… **it ain't cheap.**

ARRI ALEXA 65

Rental: unknown
Purchase: $150,000+ (body only)

The ARRI ALEXA is the go-to camera for big-time filmmakers all over the world. One of the reasons this line of cameras is used above most others is the fact that it comes closer than any other digital camera to **replicating the look and feel of film stock.**

In 2015, ARRI introduced its newest camera — the ALEXA 65. Currently, this camera is only available as a rental. Because of this, only major Hollywood productions have been able to use it. One particular film that utilized this camera to perfection was The Revenant, shot by Emmanuel Lubezki.

Leica APO-Telyt-R 1600mm

Rental: don't get your hopes up
Purchase: $2,064,500

There's "expensive," like the gear listed above. And then there's **Leica's APO-Telyt-R 1:5.6/1600mm telephoto lens**, priced at a cool two million bucks and custom-made for Sheikh Saud Bin Mohammed Al-Thani of Qatar. Your only chance of getting anywhere near this piece of equipment is to view the prototype on display in the German factory where it was made.

July 31st

Freelance Video: Keep a Client from Doing It Themselves

In the world of freelance video, some clients will insist they don't need you. Here's what to say to keep yourself in the game.

Every so often, you're going to run up against a client who decides to **"do it themselves."** Because equipment is cheaper and more accessible than it has ever been, people get the idea that production is cheap and easy. However, they are not accounting for **variables like quality, skill, or equipment overhead.**

Here are a few things **freelance video artists** can discuss with a client who insists that they can keep their production in-house.

Talking Point #1: The quality of their marketing video reflects directly on their customer's perception of the quality of their product or service.

This means that if it looks like they **cut corners to make a cheap video with a low production quality**, it will appear to their customer that they **cut corners and offer a cheap, low quality product.** And because of the pervasiveness of it, we've been exposed to enough quality video that we've come to expect it. Even the people trying to get their projects funded on Kickstarter know that you have to have an awesome video if you want people to invest in your product.

Luckily, if they have anyone in that company invested in the brand, they can help be your advocate for this. Ugly video is not only ineffective; **it can be harmful to sales.**

Talking Point #2: They won't do it cheaper by keeping it in-house.

They are thinking, "I'm already paying this person, I'll just have them do it." Nine times out of ten, it seems that the employee they pick to do this work is **fresh out of college and assumed to be tech-savvy** (this is seldom the case, by the way).

A business owner is always going to be thinking about the bottom line and that's what is motivating them to not hire you — but they may not be thinking about **lost productivity and the cost associated with that.** You may have to remind them that **producing a video is not as simple and pointing the camera and turning it on.** Will their employee understand how to use the camera (even at a very basic level), light the subject, capture usable audio, and then edit the footage? Or what about techniques to actually make the footage look good, how to color it in post, or add animations and effects?

Seven Pictures, of Hollywood, CA, notes the benefits of an independent production company over an internal solution.

Video production companies come with a staff of other creators that help in the creative process to make these quality videos. Between cinematographers, editors, professional lighting crews, and hair and makeup artists, an independent production company employs these creatives, thus getting you the best rates and best professionals tailored specifically to your project.

Remind them that there are a lot of **pieces to production they are likely not even aware of** and the time it takes to learn all of these skills (let alone master them) is significant. If they account for all the hours of lost productivity involved in letting their own people do it, you are going to be able to create it at a lower cost to them and be able to turn it around significantly quicker.

Talking Point #3: They will not get a good ROI on equipment.

I've seen this happen again and again: a company will buy a nice video camera thinking that's all they need. They then try to use it a few times and, because they are not using a operator that actually knows how to work the camera (and because they are missing the dozens of others things that go into making quality video), **they give up**. The camera gets stuffed in a closet, and they end up needing to outsource their video anyway.

By letting you source and provide the equipment, they don't have to bear the burden of owning those depreciating assets. If they choose to do it themselves, they'll have to spend *some* money on equipment and when they start comparing that cost to your fee, **it will quickly become clear that they're really not saving anything.** Mark Suszko of Creative Cow mentions demonstrating your value over the sunk cost of an equipment purchase.

The market is over-saturated with talent right now so you can hire great talent with complete gear for cheap. Why duplicate that in the office, only to let it sit around 4 out of 5 days depreciating, not being used? The P/L ratio on any internal communications division, no matter how large or small, is always running, always being examined. You need to show added value for existing every day, and minimize costs without a return on the investment. Make yourself the executive producer and director/editor, and hire out the other jobs as needed.

They also don't have to worry about researching the best equipment and making buying decisions. As knowledgeable **members of the industry**, we have a significant head-start at, not only knowing the benefits of different brands and different models, but also what everything is. There are a lot of different kinds of gear and it takes time to understand what they would need.

Unless they are really going to **invest in a production team** that can be consistently doing work using said equipment, it will be **under-utilized and likely forgotten.** Instead of throwing money at something that won't give them any return on their investment, **they should throw it at you, right?**

The Bottom Line

They will invest in video production with you **if can trust that they can get a better product and a better value from you.** It will benefit them to transfer the burden of production to you and it allow them to concentrate on what they do best.

August 1ˢᵗ

Freelance Video: Keep a Client from Doing It Themselves

In the world of freelance video, some clients will insist they don't need you. Here's what to say to keep yourself in the game.

Every so often, you're going to run up against a client who decides to **"do it themselves."** Because equipment is cheaper and more accessible than it has ever been, people get the idea that production is cheap and easy. However, they are not accounting for **variables like quality, skill, or equipment overhead.**

Here are a few things **freelance video artists** can discuss with a client who insists that they can keep their production in-house.

Talking Point #1: The quality of their marketing video reflects directly on their customer's perception of the quality of their product or service.

This means that if it looks like they **cut corners to make a cheap video with a low production quality**, it will appear to their customer that they **cut corners and offer a cheap, low quality product.** And because of the pervasiveness of it, we've been exposed to enough quality video that we've come to expect it. Even the people trying to get their projects funded on Kickstarter know that you have to have an awesome video if you want people to invest in your product.

Luckily, if they have anyone in that company invested in the brand, they can help be your advocate for this. Ugly video is not only ineffective; **it can be harmful to sales.**

Talking Point #2: They won't do it cheaper by keeping it in-house.

They are thinking, "I'm already paying this person, I'll just have them do it." Nine times out of ten, it seems that the employee they pick to do this work is **fresh out of college and assumed to be tech-savvy** (this is seldom the case, by the way).

A business owner is always going to be thinking about the bottom line and that's what is motivating them to not hire you — but they may not be thinking about **lost productivity and the** cost associated with that. You may have to remind them that **producing a video is not as simple and pointing the camera and turning it on.** Will their employee understand how to use the camera (even at a very basic level), light the subject, capture usable audio, and then edit the footage? Or what about techniques to actually make the footage look good, how to color it in post, or add animations and effects?

Seven Pictures, of Hollywood, CA, notes the benefits of an independent production company over an internal solution.

Video production companies come with a staff of other creators that help in the creative process to make these quality videos. Between cinematographers, editors, professional lighting crews, and hair and makeup artists, an independent production company employs these creatives, thus getting you the best rates and best professionals tailored specifically to your project.

Remind them that there are a lot of **pieces to production they are likely not even aware of** and the time it takes to learn all of these skills (let alone master them) is significant. If they account for all the hours of lost productivity involved in letting their own people do it, you are going to be able to create it at a lower cost to them and be able to turn it around significantly quicker.

Talking Point #3: They will not get a good ROI on equipment.

I've seen this happen again and again: a company will buy a nice video camera thinking that's all they need. They then try to use it a few times and, because they are not using a operator that actually knows how to work the camera (and because they are missing the dozens of others things that go into making quality video), **they give up.** The camera gets stuffed in a closet, and they end up needing to outsource their video anyway.

By letting you source and provide the equipment, they don't have to bear the burden of owning those depreciating assets. If they choose to do it themselves, they'll have to spend *some* money on equipment and when they start comparing that cost to your fee, **it will quickly become clear that they're really not saving anything.** Mark Suszko of Creative Cow mentions demonstrating your value over the sunk cost of an equipment purchase.

The market is over-saturated with talent right now so you can hire great talent with complete gear for cheap. Why duplicate that in the office, only to let it sit around 4 out of 5 days depreciating, not being used? The P/L ratio on any internal communications division, no matter how large or small, is always running, always being examined. You need to show added value for existing every day, and minimize costs without a return on the investment. Make yourself the executive producer and director/editor, and hire out the other jobs as needed.

They also don't have to worry about researching the best equipment and making buying decisions. As knowledgeable **members of the industry**, we have a significant head-start at, not only knowing the benefits of different brands and different models, but also what everything is. There are a lot of different kinds of gear and it takes time to understand what they would need.

Unless they are really going to **invest in a production team** that can be consistently doing work using said equipment, it will be **under-utilized and likely forgotten.** Instead of throwing money at something that won't give them any return on their investment, **they should throw it at you, right?**

The Bottom Line

They will invest in video production with you **if can trust that they can get a better product and a better value from you.** It will benefit them to transfer the burden of production to you and it allow them to concentrate on what they do best.

August 2nd

How the iPhone is Changing Modern Videography

It's been nearly 10 years since the iPhone first hit shelves. The drastic improvements to the device's camera are nothing short of remarkable.

As camera manufacturers struggle to bring **higher video resolution and dynamic range** to their gear, Apple has seemingly been pushing micro-camera technology to extraordinary lengths. And they aren't alone… Samsung and other manufacturers have been bringing 4K to cell phones for years.

Now that you have these insane resolutions in your pocket, it's easy to see how you can **use an iPhone on set**. We've covered turning old iPhones into wireless microphones, and even commercials shot on the iPhone. The camera has practical uses as a crash cam or additional camera on set, but what about productions using *only* the **iPhone**?

The film *Tangerine* made headlines at Sundance, as the **film was shot using three iPhone 5s cameras**. The independent feature even reached a limited release in theaters. The entire film was produced with the iPhones, Final Cut Pro, and DaVinci Resolve.

Of course, *Tangerine* is far from the only film to use iPhones. There's an entire film festival solely dedicated to featuring movies shot on the iPhone.

Countless music videos have been shot on **iPhones**. This beautiful music video for *Dark Waves* by Robot Koch and Delhia de France was **shot on the iPhone 6s Plus**.

Last year, a Swiss TV station switched the whole staff to shooting on iPhones with selfie sticks. In September, RYOT news released this piece on a citizen living in the slums of Haiti. It was also **shot on the iPhone 6s Plus**.

RYOT also released a behind-the-scenes look at the shoot, giving a glimpse at the camera cage that allowed them to **use SLR lenses with the iPhone**. They also used a variety of stabilizers, and even **attached the iPhone to a DJI Phantom drone**.

If you think you need a stabilizer or drone to pull of **great footage with an iPhone**, then just take a look at this video from Nicolas Vuignier. Using an **iPhone 6 attached to a string rig** he built himself, Vuignier took to the ski slope to create this *Centriphone* video.

Apple knows how great the **iPhone 6 camera** is, which is why they've featured many of the best videos shot by regular users. As with the *Dark Waves* music video, using an underwater case can give you stunning images.

The **iPhone** even captures quality video at high speeds.

You can even simply setup an **iPhone** to capture a quick time-lapse.

One of the best parts of always having the camera on you is the ability to pull the **iPhone** out of your pocket when you see something amazing happening around you.

But perhaps the *most* spectacular feature is the **iPhone's slow-motion capability** — which has captured so much great material.

August 3rd
Know Your Gear: The Steadicam

Steadicams offer a wide variety of feature and pricing options. So, which one is right for you?

Since it's introduction in the the mid-1970's the Steadicam has been a great way to stabilize cameras. However, over the last two decades we've have seen steadicam stabilization hardware evolve into many different forms to handle specific challenges. In the following post we're going to examine some of the top Steadicams on the market, explore a few affordable options, and learn how steadicams work.

Invented in 1975 by cameraman Garrett Brown, the steadicam allows camera operators to recreate steady camera movement without the dolly setup. It's first introduction to Hollywood came with its use in the film Bound For Glory (1976). Since then countless filmmakers have used the Steadicam, most notably Stanley Kubrick for his film The Shining (1980) and George Lucas in Return of the Jedi (1983) for the speeder bike chase sequence.

Nearly 40 years since its introduction the Steadicam has become an affordable tool for both studios and independent filmmakers alike. With the introduction of DSLRs and GoPro cameras the Steadicam has grown more compact and lighter. We'll run through the heavy duty studio style rigs as well as the lighter rigs for independents and the price points for each.

For Steadicam options we'll look at two companies Tiffen, owners of the Steadicam brand, and Glidecam Industries.

TIFFEN:

Tiffen's high end line is led by the **Ultra 2,** a complete rig for any professional camera system (13-70 lbs. camera capacity). The Clipper and Shadow series are half the price (non-motorized), but offer the high-end features needed for feature film production. From there the product line goes down significantly in price, all the way down to GoPro and iPhone stabilizers.

Ultra 2 – Complete Rig ($66,000)

Clipper 324 – Non-Motorized System ($36,000)

Shadow Series – Basic Non-Motorized System ($35,000)

Zephyr – Standard Hi-Def System ($10,000)

Tango – Zephyr Only System ($8,000)

Scout – Standard Hi-Def System ($5,500)

Pilot – HD/SDI System Standard Vest ($4,000)

Merlin2 – Merlin Arm/Vest Kit ($1,000)

Solo – Standard Solo System ($500)

Smoothee – Standard Smoothee (GoPro, iPhone) ($149)

Curve – Stabilizer for GoPro Series ($100)

GLIDECAM:

For the last twenty years, Glidecam has offered a variety of camera support systems, from the professional level X series rigs, down to the lightweight support of the XR series.

X-45 - 25-45lbs Vest Support System ($19,000)

X-30 - 15-30lbs Vest Support System ($17,000)

X-20 - 10-20lbs Vest Support System ($6000)

X-10 - 4-10lbs Vest Support System ($2499)

Smooth Shooter - Vest Support System ($1500)

HD-4000 - 3.3lbs Hand-Held System ($649)

HD-2000 - 2.5lbs Hand-Held System ($549)

HD-1000 - 1.9lbs Hand-Held System ($449)

XR-4000 - Hand-Held System for Camcorders ($329)

XR-2000 - Hand-Held System for DSLRs ($289)

XR-1000 - Hand-Held System for Smaller Cameras ($199)

iGlide – Standard Hand-Held System ($149)

(Glidecam Prices Listed on Product Pages)

August 4th
The Camera RZR is an Insane Mobile Video Crane

This new beast is part camera crane, part off-road vehicle – designed specifically for shooting in extreme environments.

To show off the powerful capabilities of a new snowmobile it's best to head out to the 'backcountry', far from roads or civilization. With a large scale camera crew, this task would often require hours of travel time and cumbersome sleds to transport equipment. Now, enter in the **Camera RZR**, an all-terrain vehicle designed to make this type of shooting infinitely more accessible. Gearheads and camera geeks will love this…

We've seen cameras mounted to cars, trucks and boats before, but this is a new one...**a snowmobile with a full scale camera crane** mounted on top. In a joint collaboration by "The Factory, a commercial production company and The Ultimate Arm, the film industry's premiere provider of live action gyrostabilizer camera arm technology", the **Camera RZR** is designed to navigate treacherous terrain and extreme weather. It was recently created to shoot the 2015 Polaris snowmobile advertising campaign:

Although much of the available specs on the rig detail the technical aspects of the vehicle (and not the camera equipment) we know the crew outfitted the crane with a RED camera and Phantom (for slow motion shots). The release notes, "the **Camera RZR** serves as a fully capable crane able to rise 20+ ft. above the trail, creating overhead shots, whip pans, and grand, sweeping reveals."

August 5th
The Perfect Gear for One-Man Corporate Video Shoots

When you've got to go it alone, the right gear can make a big difference. Here's what you need to pull off top-notch one-man corporate video shoots.

There are any number of issues that can arise when working a corporate video job without a crew, but the right gear can make a big difference in the end. Let's look at exactly what you need to pull off **one-man corporate video shoots**.

Camera Setup

When producing corporate videos on your own, you need to choose a camera loadout that's easy to set up and break down. You'll be moving from place to place in order to get the interview you need, plus the coverage for that interview. For this, a good ol' **tripod and camera** will do just fine.

Corporate videos have a reputation for being bland and lifeless, but this mindset is changing. YouTube and similar sites have increased the audience for all manner of content, including corporate video. Because of this, corporate videos are becoming more cinematic. That means you'll need to invest in a cinema camera and top-quality lenses. You'll find some suggestions below.

1. Blackmagic USRA Mini 4K (Body Only): $2995
2. Zeiss 50mm Prime Lens: $4499
3. Lexar C-Fast 128GB Card: $506
4. Benro Aero 4 Tripod Kit: $259

If you're looking for options beyond the Blackmagic URSA Mini 4K, then check out the Canon C300 Mark II, Sony FS5, and RED SCARLET.

Sound Setup

With your camera setup in place, you need to ensure that you can capture professional audio to go with your imagery. Since you're a one-man band, you'll probably want to get a **shotgun mic** that you can mount and connect directly to the camera. Additionally, you'll need a **lavalier microphone** to capture clear and crisp interview sections. If you only have one audio input to the camera, a **field recorder** certainly wouldn't be a bad addition to your gear. Below is a rundown of audio gear you'll need.

1. Rode NTG-1 Shotgun Mic: $250
2. Lectrosonics Lavalier Mic: $150
3. Zoom H6 Field Recorder: $349
4. Sennheiser HD 280 Pro Headphones: $99.95
5. SanDisk 32GB Ultra SDHC Card: $12.28

Accessories

With your camera and audio setups worked out, it's time to turn your attention to some **additional tools** that can help make the overall production easier on you.

You'll obviously need some solid **lighting**. Beyond that, you'll want to invest in some **c-stands** to hold up tools so you don't have to. You can also look at purchasing a **slider**, **Steadicam**, or **3-axis gimbal** for smoother moving shots. Just remember: all of this is secondary to your camera and audio setup.

1. Kessler Timelapse Slider: $995.99
2. Genaray Spectro LED: $284.95 ea.
3. Impact Light Stand: $44.99 ea.
4. Glidecam HD 4000: $499.99
5. DJI Ronin 3 Axis Gimbal: $2039.99

August 6th

The Video Gear I Can't Travel Without

If you're new to the road and traveling internationally anytime soon, here are some recommendations on how to master the art of packing light.

In our globalized and mobilized world, it's easier than ever to **shoot high-quality video** in some of the world's most remote places. But just as much as we have the world at our fingertips, we also have a mountain of gear that we assume we need to make our projects shine. Spare your back and your luggage fines by **taking a more practical and thoughtful approach to shooting remote.**

Below you will find a comprehensive **packing list for video pros**, as well as a few tips to streamline your ultra-sleek and incognito camera package.

The Packing List

Travel-Friendly Camera Body

Sony a7S ($2,998), Canon 5D Mark III ($2,599), or a Canon C300 ($11,999) or C100 ($2,499) are a few of my top recommendations for the most quality per square inch of camera.

Prime Lens Kit

If you prefer the look of primes like me, make space for a basic set of four. I always run with **24mm**, **35mm**, **50mm** and **85mm** kit. The Zeiss CP.2 ($3,990) is my first pick and Rokinons ($1,996) are my budget backup.

Zoom Lenses

When there's no time to be switching between lenses, I make sure to always have **two zooms**. The Canon EF 24-105 mm ($999) and Canon EF 70-200 mm (above, $1,999) are what usually make it into my bag.

Spare Camera Batteries

Do **not** skimp here. You'll need lots of juice if you're away from power sources for long periods of time. And don't forget plenty of **spare chargers** as well, so you can knock out your nightly recharge in one punch.

Power Strips

Make sure you have the **correct outlet style and wattage**. Here is a list of what is compatible by country.

On-Camera Shotgun Mic

The Rode VideoMic Pro (above, $199.95) or the Sony XLR-K2M XLR Adapter Kit with Microphone ($598) if you're shooting on the a7S. A perk to shooting on the Sony a7S with the Sony XLR Adapter is that you have an **extra XLR input** for your lavs or your shotgun. Same perk applies to the c100 or c300, which have XLR inputs built into the camera.

Lavaliers

I have worked most frequently with Seinheisser Lavs ($679). I usually travel with a minimum of **three sets of transmitters and receivers** to cover my interview subjects and the translator.

Shotgun Mic and Boom Pole

I work most frequently with a Sennheiser MKE 600 (329.95) and a boom pole. **Don't forget your XLR cable** as well!

Video Tripod

The Sachtler Ace ($621) is a travel-friendly size. I also recommend all your baseplates between all your support be **seamless**. Keep this in mind when picking out your gear. This makes it easier to move quickly between each support system.

Small Slider

The Duzi Slider (above, $439) might not give a ton of range, but it's super lightweight and compact and will at least give you a little extra **clean movement in your shots** without weighing you down. If you're on a larger budget, check out the latest lightweight slider that's changing the game: Rhino Slider ($500).

Simple Handheld Rig

Say goodbye to your shoulder rig with the ten-pound counterweight. Strip it down to something with a plastic cage, rods and a follow focus. I throw a baseplate on the bottom of my rig and it lives on my camera and I just **snap the whole rig into a monopod, sticks, or a slider** when shooting documentary style.

Glidecam

If you absolutely need **something a bit more stable for tracking shots**, throw a Glidecam ($469) into your checked bag.

Monopods

These Manfrotto Monopods ($279.88) are my best friend when **shooting international documentaries**.

Small Reflector

Raya makes a great 5-in-1 Reflector ($23.95) for a fair price. And it comes with its own carrying bag!

Filtration

A good **Variable ND** like the one Tiffen ($129.95) makes will save you time and space. Toss in a Polarizer ($93.90) and some step-up rings to sync all your lens diameters to the same size (for ease and speed when moving your filters between lenses) and you're golden.

Panel Lights

Pair a panel light ($159.95) with a GorillaPod, some gaff tape, and your reflector and you can give a pop to any scene.

Carry-On Bag

LowePro Roller x200 ($284.19) is my favorite **roller board camera bag**. If the airlines hassles you about overhead space, you pop the main compartment of the bag out into a backpack and check the shell. This has saved me from having to send expensive gear rattling down into the bottom of the plane many times.

Large Checked Bag

I recommend a bag by someone like Tenba ($599.95) versus the popular Pelican Case. It's **more discreet** and calls less attention to itself, while still providing great protection.

Shooting Bag

I toss a Think Tank Sling ($99.75) into my Tenba to carry my **lenses**, **filters**, **cards**, and **spare batteries** once on the ground shooting.

Accessories

Let us not forget our **roll of gaff tape**, **spare batteries** (AA, AAA, 9V, etc), **clamps**, **GorillaPods**, a small **tool kit** with your necessary **flat head and allen wrenches**, etc. Most of these items do better in your checked bag.

Laptop

Make sure all necessary updates are complete and **all needed software is downloaded**, incase Wi-Fi is spotty where you're shooting.

3x Portable Hardrives

Lacie Rugged Hardrives ($139) are compact and their name says it all. I always backup my footage between three drives every night and **spread the drives between people and bags when traveling.**

This is a package that has **worked great for me across several continents**. I was able to capture competitive documentary footage in India, Cambodia, and all across Africa **with this exact kit**.

August 7th
Three Tips for Lighting Product Shots On a White Backdrop

Shooting product shots on a seamless white backdrop calls for a very specific approach to lighting. Here are some tips on how to get it right next time you're in the studio.

Many cinematographers and shooters mistakenly assume that shooting product shots is simple. They often feel that, because they're effectively shooting a still object, they'll be able to get good results with their eyes closed — even if they have little or no experience in that realm.

The reality, of course, is that lighting product shots is as complex as anything else. Each product will have its own unique challenges and needs to be approached as its own entity. At the same time, there are some universal principles that come into play when shooting just about any type of product.

If you regularly shoot commercial content, there's a very good chance at some point you're going to need to step up to the plate and deliver clean product shots. Here are some crucial lighting tips to take into account when you get there.

1. Always Use Soft Lighting

Commercial and product photography is all about beauty, and we all know that soft light is far more conducive to a beauty shot than hard light. This is true across the board, whether you're shooting products or talent.

While there may be some exceptions to this rule (depending on the type of product you're shooting), **you're almost always better off using soft light sources.** This will not only help you get more pleasing results on the product itself, but will also help you control the spill on the white background, which can save you a lot of time on set.

2. Use Flat Lighting if Necessary

If you come from a cinematic background, you probably have it drilled into your head that you should never light a scene so that it appears flat. Film is all about finding pockets of light and shadows to add dramatic effect, and flat lighting of course does the exact opposite of that.

With products however, you generally aren't trying to dramatize anything. You're almost always trying to **capture the most realistic and neutral version of the product** that you can, and in order to achieve that end result, flat lighting may be critical.

I typically recommend lighting your product shots very **evenly with one source directly in front or overhead** (depending on your product) and two additional sources — **one on each side of your background.** This will help you to not only achieve a very flat look, but also will help you to avoid shadows, which can become problematic when working with certain types of material.

3. Know When to Backlight

There are many scenarios where a backlight isn't necessary when shooting products on a white seamless, but in some cases a backlight can actually be very helpful. **For instance, if you're shooting a light-colored product against white (or a transparent/clear product) and needs it to stand out more obviously, backlighting is a great solution.**

That said, you need to be careful with how and where you place your backlight to maintain the consistency of a polished, neutral look. A singular backlight placed above and behind the product is usually an optimal location, as placing your backlight off to one side or another might throw off the symmetry.

August 8th
How to Use a Third Camera on Interview Shoots

When shooting professional interviews, a one or two camera setup is usually the norm. However, if you have the resources, a third camera can bring an extra dynamic to your productions. Here's how.

Most filmmakers are familiar with standard **A-cam and B-cam setups for interviews**. If you've shot an interview with **only one camera**, you know how tricky it can be to work with the footage without having a different shot or angle to cut between. While it requires additional resources and management, **a second camera opens lots of additional coverage opportunities**.

However, **if you have the resources** to use a third camera (and have an additional shooter to utilize), **a third camera can be a huge help.** Assuming your tripod, the A-cam and B-cam, you can have the C-cam on a **shoulder mount or move between setups** (tripods, sliders, etc....) with an eye for creative filler shots.

From your third angle, you can get a handful of other **creative shots to use in your edit that you normally wouldn't be able to try or risk**. Feel free to **get creative or use some of your own go-tos**, but here are a few suggestions.

Rack in and Out of Focus

If you're operating solo, **you may need to conduct the interview** with your whole focus. However, if you have a **producer or interviewer** to help, but need to manage the cameras yourself, you can **set the A-cam and B-cams on tripods for steady shots**. (Be sure to allow for enough **depth of field in case the subject moves forward and backward** while talking.)

This should free you up to operate a **third free-motion camera** where you can take liberties like working with some **in and out of focus tricks**. When done at the right times, a nice focus rack can **add emphasis to your edit**.

Extreme Wide Shots

I'm a fan of including production elements (**lights, other cameras, crew, green screen edges, etc....**), but a wide shot that is **significantly different from your A-cam or B-cam shots** is a great way to add **depth and impress magnitude**. Unless you have the room to **physically move much further away**, you should be able to make do with a **wide-angle or fisheye lens** to get all the space you'd like into the shot.

Extreme Close-Ups

Conversely from an **extreme wide-angle shot**, a third camera can also be used to get those **extreme close-ups** you would never risk shooting with an **A-cam or B-cam position**. Again, if your space is limited because you don't want to encroach on your other shots, using a **telephoto lens is a good way to get a nice close-up** to help emphasize points in the interview. From the close-up, you have lots of options to shoot depending on **what the story of the video dictates**. A few suggestions:

- Faces

- Eyes
- Mouth talking
- Hands
- Legs
- Clothing
- Jewelry

Profile Shot

While not a practical shot for a two-camera setup, **a profile shot of the subject against a flat background can be a great insert in your edit** that you don't usually get to capture. Set at a **90-degree angle against your A-cam**, a profile angle can vary from a **full-body wide shot to a close-up on your subject**. The flat angle can help build a theme by **framing the subject squarely against a background** — which will bring us to our next point.

Use the Background

Like the points above state, **using a third camera gives you a chance to be a little more thematic and objective** in how you shoot your interview. You even have the option of setting up a shot **where the subject is no longer the sole focus**. If the background of the interview plays thematically into your story, **you can frame up your subject to be overshadowed by what is behind him or her**. This can be done in several ways to pull the viewer's attention away through **focus, light levels, exposure, or creating a silhouette**.

August 9th

3 Hacks for Shooting Without a Focus Puller

Cinematographers on low-budget indie films are often required to operate their camera while also pulling focus. Here are some hacks to make this situation less frustrating.

The role of a **focus puller** is critical on nearly any professional set. The skills required to accurately pull focus in challenging situations are independent of the skill set required by the cinematographer, though there is some crossover.

Even if a DP also happens to be fantastic at **pulling focus**, they are often busy with the camera and keeping an eye on lighting. In these instances, a dedicated 1st AC can make a world of difference on set.

All that said, there are many situations where DPs need to fly solo these days, which can lead to frustration when they are unable to deliver the desired creative results. In my opinion, the frustration usually stems from **attempting to act as both DP and 1st AC**, as opposed to setting up the shots in a way that allow for a single operator/focus puller.

Below are my 3 hacks for working without a dedicated 1st AC.

Attach a string to your talent to maintain your distance when tracking.

Tracking shots are one of the most common shooting challenges when there's no focus puller on the crew. When following an actor, it can be extremely difficult to keep your shot in focus, as the talent will always be walking at a slightly different speed than you.

As you can imagine, this is a nightmare when it comes to **pulling focus**. Because, unless you're shooting with a very high F-stop, leaving nearly the entire image in focus, your talent will drift in and out of the focus plane every few steps.

Attempting to pull focus yourself when shooting like this is usually a terrible idea, since by the time you move your focus to compensate for the talent's movement, you've already lost them again.

Instead of trying to pull focus, **you can eliminate the issue entirely by ensuring that your talent is always the exact same distance from the camera**. One of the easiest – and cheapest - ways to do this is mind-blowing in its DIY simplicity: Attach a string to yourself. Attach the other end of the string to your talent.

You would usually do this by tying it around your belt or waist, and would have the length of the string be the exact distance that you need to be from your talent for the framing to be right. This effectively allows you to walk in a way that will always keep your talent the perfect distance from you, as you are essentially tethered together. It's an extremely low-fi solution, but it works every time.

Always use peaking & never use markers.

Using **marks on a follow focus is one of the fundamentals of pulling focus** for a 1st AC. But when you're pulling focus yourself, you need to learn to throw that out the window entirely.

Even if your shot is locked off on a tripod and you're simply pulling focus between two characters on alternating lines, you still shouldn't be diverting your vision to the follow focus for too long, if at all, as it will inevitably take you away from the monitor.

If one of the actors moves in a way that is slightly different from the blocking, you may very well miss it if you aren't 100% visually focused on the monitor at all times.

For this reason, **I always recommend using focus peaking whenever possible**. Peaking is often used by 1st ACs to lock in their focus marks, and sometimes is then turned off so the DP can see the image without the strange effects of the peaking on the monitor.

When shooting by yourself though, it's critical that you learn to **constantly shoot with focus peaking on**, and rely on it solely, as it's truly the only way you can achieve critical focus without taking your eyes off of the monitor.

Avoid unnecessary pulls.

When you're used to working with a focus puller, you might tend to take them for granted and simply assume that every shot needs a focus pull. In reality though, there are loads of scenes/set-ups that don't require focus pulls at all.

If you can get away with shooting a wide shot at infinity (and it still works for your story) then go for it. Or if you want to use selective focus to isolate a character in a scene, intentionally avoiding pulling focus to their scene partner, that could be a great technique too – as long as it serves the story well.

I'm by no means suggesting you do this strictly out of necessity or laziness, however I am suggesting that you **stop yourself before each shot and really ask whether or not you need to be pulling focus.**

There have been a few really great films in recent years that have implemented this technique in memorable ways. Two examples worth sharing are *Upstream Color* and the recently released *Still Alice*. Both of these films make use of shots where the blocking is designed in a way that allows the characters to walk in and out of the focal plane, as opposed to having the focus following their movement.

It's a really fascinating technique and certainly one that worked beautifully in the films mentioned. Check out the technique as showcased in the very first shot of the *Upstream Color* trailer.

Hopefully these tips can alleviate some of on-set stress that comes with shooting without a focus puller.

August 10th
5 Tips for Shooting a Period Piece on a Shoestring Budget

Period pieces are usually out of reach for low-budget filmmakers, but these five tips will open up the possibility of setting your story in a different era.

It's tempting for many **filmmakers to write scripts** that take place in a completely different time period. After all, **period pieces** open up so many possibilities for telling new stories that just wouldn't be relevant or possible when set in modern times. Unfortunately, many of these same filmmakers are hit with a big wake-up call when it comes time to actually produce their film, as they realize just how expensive it's going to be.

When you're **crafting a period piece**, everything is more expensive. Not only do your hard costs skyrocket (wardrobe, locations, set dec, etc.), but a lot more time and effort is needed in other areas of the production as well. During pre-production for example, you (and probably your art director/production designer) will need to thoroughly **research the time period** in which your film is set in so that you can portray it accurately.

Even in post-production, things can get tricky. Depending on how good or bad your locations were, you may need to do set extensions, or other **VFX work** to help sell the setting that you're trying to emulate. Not to mention, more extensive and specific color correction is often required to really help craft the feel of your world.

With all that said, there are ways to **make great period pieces even when dealing with limited budgets**. Your options certainly won't be as extensive as they would be if you were working with Hollywood-level funds, but that doesn't mean it's not doable. If you're willing to take into account the five tips outlined below, you might just be on your way to making your next period piece.

1. Choose Simple Locations

The look of your film will ultimately be determined by the locations that you choose. If you choose the right locations, your work is going to be a lot easier both on set and off. However, if you make less than desirable choices, you might not be able to pull off the look you're going for and **the entire project could fall short.**

My rule of thumb with locations on low-budget period pieces is to **always go simple**. If you're shooting an exterior shot at the beach, on a farm, or in the forest, chances are there isn't a whole lot of set dec that will need to be done. The same can be said about **a vintage home or train station** (that hasn't been restored). These are just a few examples of course, but the point is that you need to look for locations that work for you 'as is'. Chances are you don't have the budget (or research) behind your project to create something from scratch, so look for locations with **no discernible giveaways of modern times**, and you're off to a good start.

2. Get Your Wardrobe Sponsored

Wardrobe is one of the best ways to add production value and realism to your period piece. At the same time it can be very costly. Vintage wardrobe items can be really rare and hard to find, and naturally the price can be prohibitive for many filmmakers. That said, if you're willing to knock on some doors, **you might just get it for free.**

If you team up with the right stylist, they may just be able to work some miracles for you. Typically, stylists have relationships with brands and can pull some really amazing options for you, usually at no cost (since the items are loaned). Rather than spending your wardrobe budget on actual items, **invest in a good stylist** and it can pay off big time. Here's a quick video that features Paco Delgado (the costume designer from 2012's Les Misérables) discussing period piece costuming

3. Props Are Everything

Without some key props, you won't be able to create a **realistic world** to set your film in. The good news is that you don't necessarily need a lot of props, but just a few key props that can become focal points. For example, if you have the budget to rent a vintage car for a couple of days and can use it to capture all of your driving scenes, your **production value** just went up immensely. Much like the wardrobe solution above, you don't always need to spend an arm and a leg for props. The car example might be somewhat costly, but many other **vintage props** can be bought or rented for very little if you're willing to do some digging around.

4. The Right Music is Critical

Your locations, wardrobe, and props will get you most of the way there when it comes to production, but **post is really where it all comes together.** One of the easiest, most effective, and inexpensive ways to add to the realism of your period piece is through the use of **great, authentic music.** By licensing some period specific music (not just for the score, but also for background music, radios in the scene, etc.) you can really help to shape the tone of your film and compliment all of the visuals.

5. Learn How to Color Grade

Color grading can be a very expensive part of your process, and in many cases should be left to a professional. With that said, if you have a knack for color and are willing to do some of the legwork yourself, you can make a huge impact of the visual feel of your film with color alone. In the same way music will add a layer of **period-specific polish** to your film, so will the color. Whether you're doing something obvious (like black and white) or more specific (like a 60's technicolor look), the color grade will truly bring all of the elements of your **period piece** together and will inevitably make it feel far more authentic.

August 11th
9 Tips for Shooting Cinematic Footage

Looking to give your footage a high-budget cinematic look? Check out these tips.

There's a lot more that goes into getting a **cinematic image** than simply buying the right camera. From pre-production to post, every aspect of the filmmaking process works together to create a beautiful end film. Let's take a look at a few ways to **create beautiful cinematic footage.**

1. Storyboard

Storyboarding is one of the most overlooked yet vital aspects of filmmaking. While you may not be able to **storyboard** for every project (like, say a documentary), you should always be **storyboarding** for a narrative film. **Storyboarding** allows you to get the ideas from your head onto paper so you can share them with the rest of the crew.

Even if you think you have an incredibly clear vision for your film in your head, you will inevitably run into a point on set where your original creative vision is getting a little fuzzy under pressure. Take time to **storyboard** each shot before you arrive on set. You don't have to be the best artist in the world. Just jot down composition notes as best you can.

2. Shoot 24fps

Almost all modern film is shot in **24 fps**, however the default for most modern video cameras is 30fps. So if you want to make your footage look more cinematic, you need to be shooting in **24fps**. Most modern cameras allow you to at least change between 30fps and **24fps**. If you want to shoot slow motion footage, you could shoot at even higher frame rates like 60fps or 120fps and slow it down to **24fps** when you edit.

3. Shallow Depth of Field

There's very few things as noticeably cinematic as a **shallow depth of field**. If you're not already familiar with the term, **depth of field** refers to the portion of the frame that is in focus. A camera like an iPhone has a very wide **depth of field**, meaning it's very hard to get a background out of focus. A DSLR style camera can get an out-of-focus background very easily.

If you're determined to get the most cinematic footage possible on a budget, you should definitely look into using a DSLR or mirrorless photographic-style camera instead of a camcorder.

4. Don't Zoom

Zooming is great for shooting a high school football game, **not so much for shooting a film**. There are very few cases of zooming in modern cinema. Don't believe me? Watch your favorite film and look for the number of times they zoom.

Unless you're watching an Edgar Wright film, it's unlikely that you'll find any zooming shots. Instead filmmakers typically use a technique called dollying in which they will physically move the entire camera towards the subject. The result is a much more natural movement that is pleasing to the eye.

5. High Dynamic Range

Dynamic range refers to your camera's ability to simultaneously record both bright and dark areas simultaneously. To illustrate the point, think about **terrible local news footage**. In most of their footage you'll likely see a reporter standing under direct sunlight with a sky that is completely white. This is incredibly distracting and it will look terrible to an audience in a theater. Now contrast that with the footage from *The Revenant* trailer where you can see details in the clouds and in the ground at the same time.

Back in the day (5 years ago), cameras with **high dynamic ranges** were very expensive. But with recent advancements in technology, notably from Blackmagic Design, you can now get beautifully balanced images for an affordable price.

6. Shoot in RAW

You've probably already heard of a term called **codec**. Essentially, a **codec** is the way in which your camera packages up your video before it gives it to the computer. Some **codecs** squish your video files to make them smaller, while others allow for more information and are subsequently larger in size. However, if you want to get the best image possible, you don't want to use a **codec** at all. Instead you should shoot in a format called **RAW**.

RAW files are essentially the raw pixel information straight from the camera to the card. Instead of the camera compressing the video image, it will record all of the data to a card. This will result in some pretty large file sizes, but you will have greater control over the color of your video when you jump into your editing software.

7. Dramatic Lighting

Lighting is not as scary as it sounds. While you could certainly spend your entire career trying to understand the subtle nuances asserted with **cinematic lighting**, it doesn't necessarily take an expert to **create decent lighting**. All you really need is a 5-in-1 reflector and a cheap LED light. Less is more when it comes to **lighting a cinematic image**.

8. Prime Lenses

If you want to make your footage (and photographs, for that matter) look 4x better, go out and buy a **prime lens**. Sure, a **prime lens** doesn't quite give you the flexibility of shooting on a zoom lens, but you probably won't be using that zoom feature anyways (remember #4). **Prime lenses** tend to be sharper, better in low light, and capable of producing a more shallow depth of field.

Prime lenses can be incredibly expensive (like in the $100K range) but they can also be incredibly cheap. At $100, Canon's 50mm f/1.8 is a great place to start. If that's still too much, you can always convert an old prime lens using an adapter.

9. Color Grade

It can be easy to simply want to export your project once you get done editing, but if you want your footage to look really cinematic, you should **color correct and grade all of your footage** before hitting that export button. There are people who spend their entire careers **color grading** footage, so don't think this process is easy. Luckily, there are a lot of really easy resources out there for **creating cinematic color grades** very quickly.

Most notably is Magic Bullet from Red Giant. Using their drag and drop **color grading** presets, you can very quickly give your footage a stylized look. If your budget is slim, there are also a lot of good free color grading presets out there.

August 12th
14 Tips for Shooting Live Stage Events

Thinking about shooting a live event? Here are 14 things you need to remember.

For videographers, a **live event** can be an exhilarating experience that pushes you outside of your creative comfort bubble… but if you're not careful, a seemingly insignificant technical error can ruin the entire video. Don't let this happen to you! Here are 14 tips for **shooting your next big live event.**

Quick Note: This article will focus on an "in-camera" video style, not using a switcher or live-directing.

1. Pick a Style

Before you shoot a **live stage event**, do some research into what you want the look and feel of your video to be like.

TED-itional Tripod

Ideal for: Lectures, Church Services, Conferences

While they may be the most popular lecture series in the world, TED talks are surprisingly simple when it comes to shooting style. Most TED talks consist of a few cameras on tripods with a master camera. It's all pretty stationary, which is not a bad thing.

Mixed Shoot

Ideal for: Plays, Concerts, Award Shows

Most modern **live events** consist of a mixture of tripods, shoulder rigs, cranes, and sliders. These events can become incredibly complicated to edit in post (or direct live). But when done well, a **mixed-camera shoot** can bring a lot of life to an otherwise boring event.

Cinematic Highlight Video

Ideal for: Weddings, Festivals, Expos

Sometimes your client will only want a **"highlight reel"** of the live event and not the entire event itself. This is your opportunity as videographer/filmmaker to show off your cinematography skills. Good event highlight videos will feature complex movements. It's also more common to see highlight videos shot on DSLRs instead of more traditional video cameras.

This article will focus mainly on the traditional and mixed camera style of **live event** videography. If you shoot a lot of highlight videos,

2. Tap into a Sound Board

When it comes to **shooting live events**, you will absolutely need to record audio from a soundboard. No matter how good your on-camera mic setup is, it won't be good enough quality to use. For this reason, you'll need to invest in an external audio recorder. The key is to get an audio recording device that can record signal from an XLR or 1/4" audio output and run on batteries. Something like a Zoom H4N or Tascam DR-40 should do the trick.

In addition to the actual recording device, you'll need to buy the various accessories that are necessary for **recording great audio**. Don't be cheap when it comes to accessories. Cheap cables are often unreliable.

3. Monitor Your Audio

You will need to have someone **monitor the audio during the event** to make sure there are no problems. While the audio may sound fine coming out of the main speakers, there's a chance that the audio engineer might not have given you the best mix into your external recorder. As such, it's vital that you **monitor your audio** for peaking, distortion, and bad audio.

4. Go Multi-camera

If you're recording a live event, **you have to use more than one camera.** A multi-camera setup will make your entire video more engaging and make it seem much more professional. Moreover, you'll be covered in case one of your cameras goes out.

Every event you shoot should have at least one master camera that will remain virtually stationary the entire time, just in case something happens to one of your other cameras. It's usually best to let the person manning the master camera be the same person **monitoring the audio feed.**

5. No Handheld Footage

Because of the extreme distances between you and the subject, handheld footage is a bad idea when shooting live events. Instead, try using either a stationary tripod or a shoulder rig to help keep your footage steady.

Your decision to record with either a tripod, shoulder rig, or slider is entirely dependent on the style in which you will be shooting the event. If the event is more formal (plays, lectures, conferences) you will probably **want to go tripod.** If it's more casual (concerts, award ceremonies) you might **want to have a shoulder rig.**

6. Don't Ever Stop Recording

Assuming you have your master camera on a tripod in the back of the auditorium, you will probably be manning a secondary camera that is more mobile. Whatever you do **DO NOT** stop recording during the event. If you stop recording, you are going to have a syncing nightmare when you sit down in post. Sure software like PluralEyes may make syncing easier, but it's still unnecessary if you simply keep recording.

7. Try to Use "Real" Video Cameras

DSLRs may be good options for some controlled events like weddings, but if you're going to be shooting a live *stage* event, you should **consider using a professional video camera.** This is mostly due to their flexibility when it comes to focal length and their ability to record long durations without stopping.

If you simply must shoot on a DSLR, do your research. Some modern DSLRs will stop recording after a certain duration which can have disastrous consequences. DSLRs are also pretty difficult to keep steady while zooming, focusing, and tracking a subject.

8. White Balance

DO NOT set your white balance to automatic when shooting a live stage event. If you're shooting on more than one camera, you'll be in for a horrible surprise when you sit down to edit your footage and discover that the white balance on one camera is completely different than the other. Even if the stage lights change color dramatically during the event, it's much more ideal to set a white balance keyframe in your post-production software.

9. Zoom Sparingly

There are very few instances in professional video production where zooming is a good idea. When it comes to **shooting live events**, you may be tempted to zoom in and out a lot to compensate for the changes on stage, but try to avoid this. It's far better to simply cut to your master shot, zoom in or out, then cut back to your close shot. It does, however, all depend on the style in which you are going for.

10. Plug in Your Camera

Needless to say, **changing your batteries during a live event is a bad thing**, if not an impossibility. If possible, plug in your camera into a wall outlet. This will require a little pre-planning on your part. The best thing you can do is buy a long black extension cable (50+ feet) and gaff tape the cable down so nobody trips.

11. B-Roll

While you're **shooting a live event**, try to get some b-roll of the crowd watching the event. Even if you don't think you'll use the footage, b-roll may save your life if you have to add in a cut in post. B-roll can also **give some context to your video** and make scene transitions easier.

12. Turn Autofocus Off

Using autofocus during live events may seem like a good idea in theory, but cameras are notoriously bad at focusing on subjects under stage lights. If you leave your autofocus on, you'll find **your focus pulsing in and out** every time your subject moves.

It is especially important to turn off the autofocus on your master camera. In my own experience, I've had unattended master cameras remain out of focus after the stage lights come on, rendering my footage useless.

Side note: Focusing by hand makes the event more fun to shoot.

13. Manual Exposure

If you try to **record a live stage event** on an automatic exposure setting, you will likely end up with incredibly blown out images. This is because your camera automatically exposes to split the difference between the light and dark parts of your scene.

Instead, you should expose by hand. **Don't look at the waveforms, look at your subject.** Your histogram will lie to you during a live event. In order to expose well you'll need to arrive early to get your camera settings right before the pre-show lights dim.

14. Show up Early

No matter what the event is, you should always show up early so that you will be prepared once the event starts. Here are a few things you should do before the show starts:

- **Talk the the audio person about tapping into the sound board.**
- **Ask the director about details regarding the event and if there are any surprises you should know about.**
- **Reserve your shooting locations.**
- **Set your camera's exposure to match the stage lights.**
- **Tape down any cables.**
- **Hide your gear in the sound booth or backstage.**
- **Talk to your crew about shooting style.**

Shooting live stage events is an art form and it can be more challenging than making a film. Once you get a formula down, **shooting live events** will become much easier every time you do it.

August 13th
Get Moving with Dolly Systems Under $500

Adding dolly movement to a film or video can really enhance your project. Let's take a look at some dolly options that come in under $500.

When you need movement in your work, a **dolly system** is a great asset to have in order to get those smooth motions. The only problem is most **dolly systems** can be extremely expensive. Let's take a look at four options that won't break the bank.

1. DIY Tripod Dolly Shot

This method is for those who just don't have the money to spend on *any* **dolly system**, but need to capture a quality dolly shot. The process is pretty simple and can be accomplished with a standard tripod. Mount your camera to the tripod and reduce the length of one of the legs, allowing the other two legs to work as pivots while keeping the tilt of the camera straight. If you're in a pinch with little to no money, this will get the job done.

2. Tripod Dolly System

Another way to capture a smooth dolly shot is by using a tripod **dolly system**. This system showcases a platform for your tripod to rest on, while the wheels underneath allow you to move it across a smooth surface. Options for this type of dolly aren't too expensive.

- Davis & Sanford - $179
- Manfrotto - $319

3. Table Top Dolly System

Another very inexpensive solution for capturing a dolly shot is using a table top dolly. These small **dolly systems** allow users to mount a DSLR camera to a small plate that rests on wheels. This type of **dolly system** comes in really handy if you're ever doing interviews and have access to a flat surface.

While you have your main camera on a tripod capturing a static master image, you can place a secondary camera on the table top dolly in order to get cutaway footage. It's a cheap solution and very effective. If you've paid attention to camera tech on Kickstarter, then you would have seen a really interesting table-top-style **dolly system** called the Hercules by Rollocam.

- ALM Mini – $67
- ePhotoInc – $100
- Hercules – TBD

4. Dolly Slider

The last **dolly system** option is the slider. For many filmmakers and videographers, sliders can be extremely effective during narrative, commercial, or industrial work. Sliders are pretty robust, and many times will require more than one person to operate. Just be aware that sliders can range anywhere from $100 to roughly $1000 depending on the length and brand. However, once you use a slider, you'll find that you can capture some amazing Dutch or angle shots for your next project.

- Benro - $250
- Kessler – $450
- Glidecam – $500

No matter your budget, you can add a really nice professional element to your visual work with dolly shots. This will not only make your work more impressive to fellow professionals, but it will keep your customers or producers coming back with more work.

August 14th
How to Salvage Overexposed Footage

You've overexposed your shot. Now what? Thankfully, all is not lost. Use these techniques to salvage overexposed footage.

When you've accidentally **overexposed a shot**, you'll likely want to try to find ways to correct it. Unfortunately, it's just not that simple. In fact, it's not so much about *correcting* an overexposed shot, but how to **salvage** it.

As soon as your **whites are sitting at the top of the waveform monitor** making a straight line, that detail has been lost — and you're not getting it back. Overexposure is, for the most part, **incurable for digital footage**. With film (celluloid), it overexposes with more of a beautiful aesthetic. The light shifts between the different layers of emulsion which can cause a soft glow to overexposed film.

The difference between an **overexposed image** in comparison with an **underexposed clip** is when a sensor is **overexposed** to the point that **all RGB channels are maxed out**, the particular area of the image contains no data whatsoever. You can try and lower the highlights, but it's not going to bring back any detail. It will, however, give you a gray spot within that area. If your scene is **unreasonably overexposed**, well, there's no fixing it I'm afraid to say; **you either reshoot or scrap the scene**.

However, if you find that there's a particular small spot in your scene where the highlights are clipped, there may be a few things you can do to **make the scene look a little better**.

Add Color to The Overexposed Area

In the first take of the shot below, I had stupidly exposed for the actor while he was in the **shade** instead of his end point which was **directly in the line of the sun**.

When he stepped into his final position, there was an area on his cheek which was **overexposed**. Admittedly, it could be worse. Nonetheless, as you can see from the **waveform monitor** below, I lost a small bit of detail within his cheeks. When he is still in motion, the overexposed area is very noticeable.

To limit the amount of highlights in the overexposed area, you can **add color** to somewhat hide the damage. You do this by doing the following: First, you need to **bring the highlights down** so you can add saturation to the image. Around 85/90 percent white value should be okay. As you can see in the waveform monitor below, there's a straight horizontal line towards the top of the graph. This represents that there are some highlights that have been clipped.

Next, using the qualifier while in the HSL window, **isolate the blown-out highlights**, and then **drag the highlight color control** to a section that is equivalent in color to the area, next to the blown-out highlights.

You may need to **lower the highlight control** and possibly **increase/decrease the saturation** of the patched area to make it blend in better with the surrounding area. With this, as seen below, your overexposed area should look a lot better.

Add a Haze to the Highlights

In the introduction, I mentioned the halation that can occur with **overexposed film**. You can mimic that effect with **digital footage** to ease the visual stress of having overexposed patches.

First and foremost, you need to **bring down the overexposed highlights** into the legal region. You need that white line at the top of the waveform monitor to fall around the **85-95 mark**.

Next, like adding the color to the area, you need to **isolate the overblown area** using the luma control of the HSL qualifier. However, this time, **extend the key to a slightly larger area** than you did in the method above. In DaVinci Resolve, you have the option of blurring the area you've just isolated. You want to increase this according to your image. The more you blur, the more of a haze you will get.

You then want to **raise the midtones/gamma control** to that layer/node you've just adjusted. The result should give you somewhat of a glow, similar to the way celluloid film glows when overexposed.

With the first method, we tried to **mask the overblown highlights**. With the second approach, we used the overblown area on his cheeks to our advantage and **gave the image a soft glow**. It's actually smoothed the actor's skin out quite nicely.

You've probably noticed that these aren't fixes that will completely repair an overexposed area. It's incredibly hard to set overblown highlights. However, it's important to note that keeping certain elements — such as windows — in balance is a creative aesthetic. Some choose to blow out their windows, while other filmmakers will go to great lengths to keep their windows balanced.

There are some highlights which might not be worth preserving because they occur **naturally,** such as a sun glint on the side of a chrome motorbike handle. As long as these highlights are legalized, you'll be ok to proceed with the image.

August 15th
How to Shoot Cinematic Footage with a Drone

Drones are capable of filming much more than landscapes. Here are some tips to help you capture great cinematic footage and performances.

There are tons of drone videos online, but many of these suffer from the same problems… shaky shots or excessive fisheye footage. Here are some tips to get much more cinematic footage out of your drone.

1. Plan Each Shot Well Before Takeoff

The average consumer drone battery life is around 13-18 minutes. By the time you go airborne and check your camera settings, you may already be down to **10 minutes of actual flight time.**

It's really important to **plan your shots before taking off**. Know your starting point, and where your next waypoint is. If there are actors in the scene, be sure to go over the shot in detail. Let them know exactly where they need to be and when.

If you are planning a very complex shoot, be sure to have **plenty of extra batteries** and a charging station handy.

2. Pick the Right Camera and Gimbal

While a majority of the public thinks every drone uses a GoPro, this couldn't be further from the truth. Nearly every quadcopter manufacturer has added their own camera or given you the ability to add your own to customize your drone's camera.

Depending on the type of drone, you may have an array of cameras to choose from. DJI offers the Zenmuse Gimbal for a dozen different cameras. With the FreeFly Alta, you can add a 15 lb camera to the top or bottom of the drone.

Just remember: the lighter the better. With more weight, your battery life won't last nearly as long.

3. Fly Slowly

Now that drones have become much more agile and precise in their movements, pilots tend to move the aircraft very quickly. Though it can create some cool shots, overall it's best to take your time while in the air.

Subtle movements will playback more powerfully among audience members. Too much movement and speed will also give you very shaky footage.

4. Shoot in Reverse

While this isn't an option for every shot, shooting in reverse can help you capture shots much faster. This is great when you are running low on battery. If you are focusing on a specific building or location, start up close to the object, then move away.

Not only is it easier to reverse the footage in post, it's a lot safer than flying up close to a person or crashing into the building.

5. Use Two Operators

While many of these drones are designed for one person to fly and shoot, having a designated pilot and a cameraman will make a shoot much smoother. Each can focus on their own specific tasks.

In my personal experience, having a cameraman operate while I pilot not only helps us shoot faster, but we can also collaborate and come up with better shots. I may notice a specific path I can follow, or the cameraman may take note of a great shot they are getting in the viewfinder.

August 16th

How to Shoot Video Testimonials

Testimony videos are a great way to humanize a video. Let's take a look at how to shoot effective testimonial videos.

If you're considering shooting a **testimonial video** for your brand or simply want to get better at your interview skills, then you've come to the right place. Whether you're shooting the video for a church or for a business, these quick tips will cover everything you need to know to shoot a **great video testimonial**.

Testimonial Styles

There is one very important question to ask when creating a testimonial video: **scripted or non-scripted?**

Scripted Testimonials

- **Perfect for:** Professional Business Videos, Promotional Pieces, Product Releases, Brand Videos
- **Pros:** Control Over Script, Easier for Beginners, Easier to Edit
- **Cons:** Less "Authentic"

For most testimony videos, a **scripted video is the way to go.** This is because most of your subjects are not experts when it comes to talking in front of a camera. For this reason, you'll probably want to set up some sort of teleprompter off to the side of the camera. I will usually just use a laptop, but you can use an iPad or even paper if you are having issues with glare.

The other option would be to have your subject memorize the script then recite each line to the camera individually. This can be a very authentic way of presenting scripted work, but it will always take longer than simply reading off of a teleprompter. There is also the issue of vocal fluctuations. When you have a scripted work, it can be easy for the subject's voice to bounce around as they get exhausted, frustrated, or excited — especially if they are inexperienced on camera. If you don't keep an eye on pacing on set, you might end up with some very strange pacing issues that will need to be worked out in post.

Perhaps the most popular scripted videos right now are Apple's product videos.

Interview Testimonials

- **Perfect for:** Church/Charity Videos, Organic Business Testimonials, Documentaries
- **Pros:** Authenticity, Organic Answers, Better for Great On-Camera Personalities
- **Cons:** Less "Professional," Less Script Control

The second option when shooting **video testimonials** is to ask your subject questions and simply have them answer them on the spot. This will by no means generate the most professional video possible, but it will be very authentic which could be an important selling point depending on your brand.

When I have to shoot **interview testimonial videos**, I will typically email the questions to the interviewee before the day of the shoot. That way the interviewee can get somewhat prepared before they arrive on set.

In this interview-style testimonial, Kate King is simply answering a series of questions that the interviewer is asking her. You'll notice how the answers are not quite as polished as the Apple commercial, but there is an extra level of authenticity.

No matter which style you prefer to use, it's always a great idea to have an outline of what you want your finished piece to look like before you arrive on set. This can be as detailed as a full script or as small as some simple notes. Remember, no matter what video you are creating, **you are always trying to tell a story.**

Gear Considerations

You can shoot great **video testimonies** with very little gear, but it all depends on what you want your finished video to look like. If you are going to be incorporating cinematic b-roll, you don't want your footage to look like it was shot on an iPhone. In the same way, it's not always necessary to use an ARRI to capture epic cinematic interview footage if your b-roll was shot using a cheap camcorder.

When it comes to recording good video testimonies, **the biggest consideration should be audio.** Take time to pick a great location for audio. Avoid echos, air conditioners, and high-traffic areas. No matter what type of interview you are shooting, you want to use an off-camera mic. If you're the only person recording the footage, you might want to use a wireless lav that you can simply run straight into the camera. Or if you have some help, it's usually best to use a boom mic, as it will not be seen in the shot like a lav mic.

When it comes to shooting an interview, there is really no bad camera to choose, just be sure to check out your camera's limitations before you hit record. Some cameras (especially DSLRs) can only record for a short amount of time before stopping. Needless to say, this can be a very bad thing if your camera goes out during an emotional interview.

Camera Setup Ideas

An interview shoot is typically very simple, so it's really best to not overthink it. Simply pick a style before you show up on set.

Two-Camera Setup

Overview: one Master Shot with Prime Lens, one Roaming Camera with Zoom Lens

The most popular setup is the two-camera testimonial style. When you record with two cameras, you can seamlessly edit two clips together by simply switching to the other angle. Most two-camera setups feature a master shot on a tripod and a roaming camera that will shoot multiple camera angles during the shoot. Depending on your shoot, the roaming camera can stay in virtually the same location or it can move around dramatically.

The biggest consideration would be to make sure the roaming camera is significantly different than the master shot, as you can get some very weird cuts if the shot is too similar. For more on that check out the 30 degree rule in filmmaking.

One-Camera 'High-Resolution' Setup

Overview: one Camera on Tripod in 4K

The other option when recording a video testimonial is to record on a single camera in a high-resolution format and then crop in to simulate a second camera angle. While this isn't ideal, it can make the video a little more exciting than simply having the same shot the entire time. This is great if your finished video will be in HD, but it won't work if it's in 4K.

This example (shot on a GH4) shows how this technique could be used.

One-Camera 'Low-Resolution' Setup

Overview: one HD Camera on Tripod with B-Roll Transitions

If you have plenty of b-roll footage, or simply want to shoot quickly, you can use a single HD camera setup. The concept is simple... just place b-roll footage over the transition points and the entire video will feel like a one-shot video. For smaller in-house videos, this setup should work perfectly.

This video shares some quick insight into how you might use a single camera to shoot a good interview or testimonial. I recommend checking out the full course on Lynda.com if you want to learn more.

Music

When it comes to shooting video testimonials, **music is just as important as the footage**. Music will tell your audience how to feel about the words the subject is saying. The music should match the tone of your video. Here on CR Production Music.com, we have **thousands of tracks** that can match any video testimonial style. From sad production music to upbeat corporate tracks, if you need the perfect song, I recommend checking out our **curated collection of music**.

Graphics

One amateur mistake that you should avoid is making your graphics too complicated or stylized. Having bright flashy graphics may work in some cases, but simple text is the way to go for most situations. Due to their flexibility and legibility, sans-serif fonts are the best for videos. A graphics pack will typically include lower thirds and title graphics that will help elevate your video's quality.

Additional Video Testimony Tips

1. Ask your interviewee a few warm-up questions to get them comfortable in front of the camera.
2. Shoot the important stuff multiple times, just in case.
3. Ask your subject to repeat the question back in their answer. For example: Q: What is your favorite color? A: My favorite color is blue.
4. Keep lighting simple: You can usually get by with a soft-box or simple reflector.
5. Don't be afraid to ask your subject to repeat something. It's better to spend a few extra minutes re-recording a question than to have to come back and shoot again.

August 17th
Important Cameras of Cinematic History

These game-changing cameras changed the face of cinema, one frame at a time.

After roughly a century of cinema, we've seen countless looks appear on screen as a result of countless camera variations, each with their own pros and cons. Among so many types of cameras throughout **film history**, few have stood out. With the transition from **film to digital** currently in its final stages, now is a good time to look back at some of the most iconic or **game-changing cameras** in movie history.

1. Bell & Howell 2709 Standard 35MM

In the early 20th century, **one of the biggest faults in camera technology** was a **lack of standardization.** Manufacturers had yet to establish a universal film size that could be played back at any theater, but **Bell & Howell changed this** when they **decided to only manufacture**

their various camera and projection **technology** according to a **35mm film width** format. By standardizing their already popular equipment, they **standardized the entire motion picture industry.**

The **2709 Standard 35mm** was arguably their **most historically significant model**, as **prior** to its existence **cameras were built with wood and leather.** After filmmakers **Martin and Osa Johnson lost their camera to termites and mildew** in Africa, Bell & Howell released the **first ever all metal movie camera**, the 2709 Standard. By **1919, almost all Hollywood productions were using Bell & Howell** equipment.

2. Bolex H16

While the Bolex H16 **didn't quite provide** a level of **image quality comparable** to many on this list, it was nevertheless **very important in film history.** Bolex chose to take a **step forward in the consumer industry** by giving **more people** the **opportunity** to experiment with the medium.

Eventually **one of the best-selling cameras** of its time, this **consumer-level 16mm** camera was a **choice tool for the young Steven Spielberg**, and was a blessing for many other aspiring filmmakers that were looking for something **reliable and versatile, yet still cinematic.** Arguably the equivalent of the modern day DSLR, the H16 offered a stellar picture at a reasonable price.

3. Super Panavision 70/Ultra Panavision 70 Systems

The Super Panavision 70 is among the more recognizable names on this list, having provided some of the **definitive cinematic experiences** in movie history. One of the **quintessential 70mm systems**, this **spherical lens-based** camera system **brought you classics such as** *West Side Story, Lawrence of Arabia,* and *2001: A Space Odyssey.*

Boasting a simply **massive image size** that still **exceeds that of most digital movies today**, the Super Panavision 70 **brought forth a sense of true scope** and wonder synonymous with films such as Kubrick's *2001*. This camera's anamorphic counterpart, the **Ultra Panavision 70,** is similarly recognized, and actually saw a recent resurrection for Quentin Tarantino's western, *The Hateful Eight*.

4. Sony HDW-F900

The now industry-standard **digital format** is not as old as it may seem; at the turn of the century, the Sony HDW-F900 **ushered in the digital era** with the first (well known) all-digital production, *Once Upon a Time in Mexico*.

George Lucas worked with Sony to develop this camera for his upcoming *Star Wars Episode II: Attack of the Clones*, but first **showed it to director Robert Rodriguez**, who would become the first to utilize it. Offering a **resolution of only 1920X1080** that had to be cropped down to 1920X817 for widescreen, this camera **showed that digital had a long way to go** before surpassing the quality that film offered. With that being said, it also showed that digital was at least potentially viable in the future.

5. RED ONE

If the Sony HDW-F900 highlighted the weaknesses of digital filmmaking, the RED ONE **highlighted its strengths. Oakley owner Jim Jannard founded RED Cinema in 2005**, and completed the company's first camera, the **RED ONE, in 2007**.

The ONE was **designed to revolutionize digital cinema**, and did just that, as the **first ever 4K-capable camera**. Also offering **high frame rates and surprisingly impressive low-light performance**, the RED ONE made the digital platform seem a viable one for the first time. Since then, RED has excelled with many newer models that are constantly pushing the limits of what one can do on a budget.

6. IMAX

IMAX **premiered to audiences is in the early 1970s**, with a showing of *Tiger Child* **in Osaka, Japan**, and later, its first permanent installation in Toronto, Canada. Yielding an **unforeseen film size three times larger than that of standard 70mm**, IMAX is **roughly the digital** equivalent of a 12K image. Unfortunately, the size of the film stock **limited the running time of an IMAX feature**, and they are therefore **mostly** used to show **documentaries** in museums and the like.

As technology has progressed, **a number of Hollywood productions have made it** to IMAX screens, the first being *Apollo 13*. 6 years later, *The Dark Knight* was the **first ever mainstream feature** to actually **shoot** parts of the film **with an IMAX camera**. A handful of later films have used IMAX cameras, with *The Dark Knight Rises* holding a record of 72 minutes of IMAX footage. *Star Wars: The Force Awakens* is one of the more recent examples of brief IMAX use, featuring it during the Millennium Falcon chase scene on Jakku. The upcoming *Avengers: Infinity War* will be the first ever full-length feature shot entirely in IMAX.

7. ARRI ALEXA

The **ARRI ALEXA has become the final nail in the coffin for film**. When ARRI, an established name and frontrunner of Hollywood film, made the transition to digital cinematography, it arguably marked the **true start of the digital era**. Up until 2010, digital movies were becoming increasingly prevalent, but still didn't dominate all facets of the industry. Sony and RED were both excelling in digital cinema, but the ALEXA soon overcame them both to become by far the most common platform for digital shooting.

The ALEXA took digital to the point of exceeding most of the capabilities of film, even **convincing acclaimed cinematographer and film lover Roger Deakins** to make the switch and **declare digital the future**. With the stunning possibilities that the new **ALEXA 65** showcased in *The Revenant*, it's now more clear than ever that times are changing.

The history of film has seen so many variations of camera technology that have almost all contributed something to the industry, but these cameras were able to stand out with true innovation that impacted cinema forever.

August 18th
Protect Your Camera from Dirt with Simple Household Items

Here's how to protect your camera from dirt, dust, and sand with inexpensive items you've got sitting around the house.

David Fincher once said, "If I do my job right in prep, I always feel like the shooting should be boring." It's an excellent statement to embody. If every shoot could be 'boring' because it has been so well prepped, then a lot more fantastic films would be getting made every year. Unfortunately, that's not the case for many filmmakers, and as you descend the ladder from professional budget to no-budget, you will have less chance of a dull shoot as more things are going to go wrong.

Preparation in filmmaking is half the battle. The beauty of working on a soundstage or inside is that you will likely have control of everything. When filming outside, that isn't always the case — especially when it comes to dealing with the wind in a dusty or sandy environment.

A pinch of dust isn't going to do much other than cause a smear on your images, and it will be an annoyance rather than a certified problem. Dust can quickly be removed in post-production, and physically with a lens pen and the sensor cleaning application found on most DSLRs. Sand and dirt, however, can have a much more detrimental and long-lasting effect on your camera. It can degrade the efficiency of the mechanics, it can scratch your lens, and worst of all, the sensor. **A sensor clean isn't going to rid you of a scratch.** It will be back to the repair house if you encounter that dilemma.

Six years ago I once had sand find its way into the middle of my variable ND filter, and to this day, **I can still hear the sand grind against the filter.**

In the perfect circumstance, you would have housing to protect your gear, whether it be **a designated cover or case** or even underwater housing (underwater housing works perfectly in sandy conditions). Regrettably, you might be in a circumstance where you do not have professionally designed protective gear available to you, and will have to make do with what you have.

If you ever find yourself in a situation where the sand is starting to blow, or you need to place the camera down into the dirt for a specific shot, this easy-to-follow DIY hack is an excellent way to protect your DSLR. The items needed are more than likely always going to be found on a set, whether it be a no-budget or professional shoot.

You will need a sandwich bag or a plastic bag, a cable tie/elastic band/tape, and screw-on filter. There is no preference for the filter you use, as long as it is cheap and replaceable.

Step 1

Take the sandwich bag and place the camera inside. You want the zip or the tied end to be on top of your camera so you can see the LCD screen and control panel.

Step 2

Very carefully pinch a hole on the front side, and pull it apart just enough so the front of the lens can fit through. **You want this gap to be snug.** Using the cable tie (or tape), close the hole tight.

Step 3

Place a **UV filter or protective filter** onto the front to better protect the lens.

Step 4

Shoot away in the dirty/sandy location.

An optional precaution to take: wrap electrical tape around the lens-to-camera connection.

This useful tip cost next to nothing. Although it will limit your function at the control panel (and ultimately devalue all of the work of the camera designers), it will stop dirt and sand from entering your camera. It's recommended to set your camera settings before placing it into the bag because of the limited functionality, especially with touchscreen LCDs. If you're aware of a shoot taking place in a sandy location, perhaps look into acquiring professional housing. **The above method does have drawbacks and should be used when you have nothing else available.**

August 19th
Set the Mood with a Silhouette

The perfect silhouette can immerse audiences into a story without ever revealing too much information.

Silhouettes have been a huge part of cinema, but **telling stories with shadows** is nothing new. You can go all the way back to the Han Dynasty of China (between 206 B.C. and 220 A.D.) to find some of the earliest records of shadow puppets. This ancient form of storytelling and entertainment has **captured audiences for centuries**.

Many directors and cinematographers have made legendary film sequences using silhouettes. Here's a look at how silhouettes can be used to create suspense, a feeling of isolation, or a romanticized view of the world.

The Suspenseful Silhouettes of Alfred Hitchcock

Perhaps the most prominent use of silhouettes come from the noir films of the 1940s and 50s. The French term *film noir* literally translates to **black film** or **dark movie**. Those Hollywood noir films were actually heavily influenced by the German Expressionism of the 1910s to 1930s. German silent cinema of that era was decades ahead of Hollywood.

The Babelsberg Studio, located just outside of Berlin, is one of the oldest film studios in the world. The studio began producing films in 1912, and was home to countless projects like Fritz Lang's classic *Metropolis*. In 1924, Babelsberg collaborated with the UK studio Gainsborough Pictures on the film *The Blackguard*. That film was the first by Gainsborough to be produced abroad. To work on the film, they sent over assistant director and art director Alfred Hitchcock.

German expressionism would be a huge part of Hitchcock's signature style on countless films. The director's use of silhouettes helped him earn the moniker *The Master of Suspense*.

He frequently used the technique to **focus the audience on a threat.** In 1941's *Suspicion*, Hitchcock used a silhouette of actor Cary Grant carrying a glass of milk.

Cinematographer Harry Stradling Sr. worked with Hitchcock to create this eerie image, which makes the audience wonder if the glass of milk is poisoned. This sequences cuts to a scene of Grant pressuring his co-star Joan Fontaine to drink the milk. Without the silhouette, the scene wouldn't be nearly as ominous.

This particular Hitchcock silhouette pays homage to the 1922 German film *Nosferatu*, which featured the vampire Count Orlock creeping up a staircase.

You can't mention Hitchcock's use of the silhouette without mentioning the legendary shower scene in *Psycho*. The entire sequence **disguises the murderer** in silhouette, failing to give the audience a real glimpse of the attacker.

The shower sequence was storyboarded by Saul Bass, who was tasked with capturing screenwriter Joseph Stefano's notes that stated the scene should give:

The Isolated Silhouettes of Roger Deakins

Cinematographer Roger Deakins could have an entire masterclass written just on his use of silhouettes. Many of his films feature at least one silhouette. When it comes to choosing when to use a silhouette, Deakins admits it comes down to instincts.

Most of he choices I make are instinctive, so I can't really give you a reason for when I shoot a silhouette shot. Obviously, it comes from the script and the scene, but a silhouette can be used for a romantic moment as much as it can be used for something more sinister. - Roger Deakins

Deciding on the shot also comes down to the the circumstances of a character's situation. More often that not, **isolation is a key factor** in Deakins' silhouettes.

A silhouette could signify isolation and loneliness or it could signify a threat. Context is key. – Roger Deakins

Isolation doesn't only mean that the character is alone. The feeling of loneliness can be portrayed with the right framing. In the below still from *Jarhead*, notice there are actually several Marines in the shot, but only one stands out by himself.

Deakins pulled off a similar shot in *Sicario*, however this time the audiences feels the isolation as they walk alongside Emily Blunt. Blunt plays an outside agent caught up in an operation against a drug cartel — an operation that the others want her being no part of.

The Romantic Silhouettes of Steven Spielberg

Like Deakins mentioned before, silhouettes can also be used to romanticize a moment. This isn't merely referring to romantic relationships, but as a way a **presenting images in an idealized way.**

Steven Spielberg is a director known for using silhouettes in a variety of situations. The blockbuster master used silhouettes to terrify people out of the water in *Jaws*.

Spielberg whisked audiences to magical heights with his famous lunar flyby in *E.T. the Extra-Terrestrial*. The silhouette was so instantly iconic, it became the director's signature; the image now represents his production company, Amblin Entertainment.

He made us feel the brutal heat of the desert sun in *Raiders of the Lost Ark*.

Spielberg even took audiences far across enemy lines in *Saving Private Ryan,* accentuating the impossible task of finding one unknown man among many armies.

An examination of Spielberg's work alone showcases the silhouette's ability to transcend storytelling. His silhouettes evoke so much more than the image presents on screen. So many of his silhouettes have become iconic film images in their own right, proving the silhouette can not only set a mood — but define an entire film.

As a cinematographer, you have many options when using a silhouette. You can easily use the technique to romanticize a moment or accentuate action. You can terrify audiences by building suspense or feel the isolation of a character.

August 20th
Shooting Night Exteriors on a Budget

The nighttime exterior shot is one of the greatest challenges for filmmakers on a budget. This filmmaking tip will make lighting your scene a lot easier.

Nighttime exteriors typically require a ton of powerful lights (and generators) to illuminate your scene, which naturally poses a problem if your budget is limited. This is especially the case for wide shots where there is such an expansive area that needs to be lit. It doesn't matter how fast your lenses are or how sensitive your low-light camera may be, there is no substitute for **great lighting techniques** when trying to capture a cinematic look.

That said, one of the best and most effective tricks of the trade in this type of situation is very simple: **water.** For years' filmmakers, have been using water on streets, sidewalks, asphalts, etc. to create a more reflective surface. By **evenly spraying the concrete surfaces** in your shot, you're able to brighten up your scene *drastically*.

You might be wondering if this technique will make it seem as if it's raining in your scene, however if done right, this will never be an issue. In fact, some of the biggest feature films use this very same method on set to do exactly what I've described above – Not because their budgets can't accommodate proper lighting, but more so because they prefer the aesthetic of the **shiny street at night.**

If you're working on a tight budget, then it's essential that you're able to **think outside the box.** It can be a waste of time to think about how to get more lights on set or how to come up with the money for such a thing. Instead, you should think about **how to make the lights you already have *more* effective.** In situations like the one I've described in this article; the problem is not necessarily solved by shooting with the most light sensitive camera. You may just need a trick or two up your sleeve.

August 21st

The Art of the Freeze Frame

Learn how to use the simple effect of the freeze frame to hold your image on screen and in the minds of your viewer.

What Is a Freeze Frame?

A **freeze frame** halts the perceived movement in your image, effectively converting it to a **still shot** reminiscent of a photograph. **Freeze frames** are self-reflexive, so they call attention to the **filmmaking process** and to the **filmmaker,** but they are invaluable in **adding emphasis,** covering up for **lack of footage,** or creating a **note of ambiguity.**

In the days of shooting with film, the selected shot was optically reprinted to achieve the effect. With digital technologies, freezing your image has become as easy as tapping a few keys — so the real question becomes **how and when** should you use the **freeze frame?**

Ways to Use It

Freeze frames can be used at the beginning and throughout your movie. It's all a matter of setting the stylistic tone of your work. For example, you may want to give your title card a little extra punch as Soderbergh did in his 1998 film, *Out of Sight (*via Universal).

Soderbergh continues his playful use of the **freeze frame** during the opening act of *Out of Sight* as a transitional device and as a way to introduce a new character (another great place to use **freeze frames** early in a film, especially if you are running voice over on your soundtrack). In his film, *Election,* Alexander Payne uses **freeze frames** during his character introductions for a comedic effect.

Martin Scorsese uses the **freeze frame** to great effect in films like *Goodfellas, The Departed,* and *The Aviator,* as you can see in this video compilation of Scorsese's editing techniques. Justin Morrow includes **freeze frames** as one of Martin Scorsese's influential editing techniques in this article.

Freeze Frame as an Ending

It seems that the most common —and memorable — use of the **freeze frame** is at the end of films. Employed in this manner, the **freeze frame** can be a way to avoid showing **gruesome details of a character's demise** and instead leave your viewers with a note of **romance** and **ambiguity**. Though many of these endings are the stuff of legend, **this is your official spoiler alert.**

Instead of seeing the titular characters from *Thelma and Louise* (via MGM), plummet to the bottom of the Grand Canyon, we are left with their car hanging in mid-air, seemingly defying gravity as the two characters hang above a chasm representative of their situation both as **outlaws** and as **rebellious women** in a male-dominated world.

Another famous use of the **freeze frame** as a substitute for a bloody finale can be found in *Butch Cassidy and the Sundance Kid* (via 20th Century Fox). When the two main characters are trapped and outgunned, **they confront their fate head on.**

The **freeze frame** can present an opportunity to halt — and highlight — the atrocity of violence, as seen in the final frame of *Gallipoli* (1981). The splotch of blood on the main character's chest echoes a shot early in the film when the same character races through the red ribbon of a finish line.

One of the most famous **freeze frame** endings occurs in François Truffaut's French New Wave classic, *The 400 Blows*. Although the final **freeze frame** does not suggest a violent death for the main character, Antoine Doinel, the image creates uncertainty, ambiguity, and concern for the life of Antoine.

It's not uncommon to use a **freeze frame** of the main character as a backdrop for conveying story information that happens after the plot of the film. *Animal House* (1978) uses this technique to a comic end, but the approach can have a more serious tone, as evidenced by the final **freeze frame** in *Bloodsport* (1988).

While we're considering Jean-Claude Van Damme's involvement in the **freeze frame** ending, let's not forget this classic pose from *Street Fighter* (1994).

The **freeze frame** isn't immune to parody, as made evident in the ending of *Police Squad!* (via Paramount and ABC).

The **freeze frame** ending gives a moment of **pause** and **consideration** for your audience. Everything that preceded the final, frozen instant can take on additional dramatic weight and helps in the transformation of a seemingly ordinary film ending into a **mythic one**.

August 22nd
The Downside of Multi-Cam Shoots

Considering going multi-cam for your next film? Here are some filmmaking tips regarding multi-cam shoots that you absolutely need to consider.

At one point, multi-cam productions were synonymous with television, **but lately they have become quite popular for film projects too.** The benefits of shooting multi-cam are pretty self-explanatory. If you were to shoot a scene with three cameras instead of one, you could theoretically complete that scene in much less time.

You might have a single camera locked off on a wide shot and the other two cameras covering close-ups, which essentially allows you to eliminate your coverage – **other than maybe some insert shots here and there.**

In most cases, shooting with **a multi-cam setup is more about efficiency than art.** A production that is severely limited on time will sometimes opt to shoot this way as it can help them move far more quickly, which of course is why sitcoms or other quick turnaround programming has been shot this way for years. But in some cases, multi-cam can be used as a creative tool as well.

For example, if you're shooting a comedy with lots of improv, it would be very freeing for the actors to be able to perform in a multi-cam environment, since every take could be different and

continuity wouldn't be an issue. Even still, I would say that the vast majority of feature films are better off sticking with a single camera setup for a few key reasons. Here's why:

1. It Can Slow You Down

We all like to believe that a multi-camera shoot will speed up our process on set, **but in some cases it can actually slow us down.** Unlike television, where sets are pre-lit and cameras are more or less stationary, films call for a different and unique setup every single time. In other words, **once you actually start rolling you start to save a lot of time.** But the setup and preparation you need to do before each shot or scene will take longer.

Assuming you are working with three cameras, your set up time has just increased dramatically. Instead of one camera needing to be prepped, built, and set up for the first shot – **now three cameras need to be up and running simultaneously.** And even though you will have more crew to help set up the additional cameras, it is still going to take longer. The DP is still going to want to check each camera, and any inconsistencies between the shots will need to be dealt with before rolling.

So always remember that multi-cam isn't always going to be a time saver. If you are shooting with the same lighting/camera setup in a single location for a long time, it absolutely will speed you up. But if you need to move your locations often, **it can actually work against you.**

2. Multi-Cam Can Cost You More

We've already gone over how multi-camera setups don't always save you time, and the same notion applies to money. Following up on the previous point, if your shoot ends up taking almost as long as it would have were you to shoot with a single camera, **the overall cost of your production will be much higher.**

Instead of renting (or purchasing) one camera/lens package, **now you have rented three.** Rather than having a single DP who might also be able to operate the camera, you're likely going to need the DP to stay off of the cameras and hire more crew to handle the operation. Depending on the type of cameras your shooting on and the logistics of the production, that might mean you need an operator and 1st AC (at minimum) on each camera.

On a three camera setup, that would mean that there are minimally seven crew members dedicated solely to those three cameras. Conversely, if this was a single camera shoot with the DP as an operator, those seven crew members get cut down to two.

The bottom line is **that there is a threshold at which multi-cam productions no longer save you money.** There is no general rule that more cameras = faster and cheaper. You need to assess the unique needs of your production and decide for yourself whether or not it actually will save you money to shoot on more than one camera.

3. Your Lighting is More Limited

For me, this point is the biggest factor in why I rarely (if ever) shoot multi-cam.

Like many DPs and filmmakers, **I am someone that likes to be very specific with my lighting setup from shot to shot.** Even on the most basic scene where I am lighting a conversation between two people at a dinner table, I will adjust the lighting when moving in for closeups. For example, I might have an overhead key light that is lighting both characters on the master angle. But then when i go in for coverage, **I will tweak the direction and placement of that light just enough so that it creates a better key for the close up.**

Unfortunately when shooting multi-cam, **this isn't an option.** Instead, you need to find some sort of middle ground with the lighting that will work for both the wide shot and the closeup. This can be done, and you can certainly get great results using this approach – but I do find it a bit creatively limiting. Not to mention, your entire approach to lighting the scene needs to be different, since your lights can't be as close for the closeup shots (or the would of course be in the frame on the wide shot). Again, this doesn't mean you can't do it well – **but it's something to consider if you don't like working this way.**

In Summary

Multi-camera shoots can be hugely beneficial, **but only under the right circumstances.** Never assume that they are a one stop solution that will allow you to speed up your shoot or save money, as that will only be the case in certain instances. Make sure to assess the specific needs of your production. If you feel that multi-cam can work for you, then go for it. Just remember that there may be some **creative limitations you need to work around along the way.**

August 23rd

The Middle Ground: Ideal Shooting Conditions for Post Production

It's important for production personnel to know how footage should best be readied for video editing and color grading. In this post, we share actionable tips for optimizing your shoots for post.

When your crew is aware of the following production fundamentals it will lead to less headaches down the line. It will also optimize other stops in the pipeline including, but not limited to, the color grading stage.

Most of my best grading work has resulted from being handed a great starting point from production, where I can work freely with the image, not correct shooting errors. Let's discuss the elements that produce an optimal canvas from which to accomplish beautiful grades.

A Neutral Look

Unless you're going for an extreme look, the best place to position the image is in a place I call "the middle ground." Colorists prefer for the image to sit in a neutral space so the image can be swung wherever the client desires. **Placing an extreme look on the footage while in production can tie everyone's hands**, especially the colorist. For instance, if you shoot everything with a blue wash, there will be limits to how warm the image can become. Depending on the shooting medium, the footage may only be able to withstand a certain amount of tweaking before artifacts become noticeable.

Log Mode, If Possible

The RED, Alexa, and other camera models have the ability to shoot or later convert to a logarithmic ('log' for short) mode. **Low-contrast log images may look ugly because they're so flat, but they're actually the best place for a colorist to start.** In log mode, the largest range of data has been captured by the camera, allowing the colorist to grade with the most freedom.

Log images can be treated with a Look Up Table (LUT) to recreate the look everyone saw on set with the ability to utilize the raw data underneath. Many LUTs are preinstalled in Resolve for use in these workflows.

HDRx: Icing on the Cake

RED footage can be a bit unwieldy, but it's a boon in post. On a recent RED job, the camera clipped out the highlights of the image, and the client wanted to bring them back. I lowered the clip's ISO in the metadata to return the highlight information to the image. This would've been impossible on another format with no access to the metadata.

It's even better if HDRx mode is sustainable through your workflow. Using HDRx allows you to combine several additional stops of latitude on top of your original exposure, protecting your highlights against bright shooting days.

LUTs for Post

I wish I received LUTs from set more frequently. Aside from working with log images, **LUTs can be used to transmit a stylized look from the creative team, leaving less guesswork in the session.** LUTs are non-destructive and serve as a visual reference to dial in looks in-line with the client's intent. There exists a world of nuance in the typical commercial directive of "brighten the image and make the colors pop." Saturation amounts, the balance of cool versus warm, and amount of contrast are just several matters that require a fine attention to detail. LUTs can provide insight into the client's vision for the look.

Invest in Glass

I would almost rather have a good lens on a lower-end camera than a bad lens on a great camera. While the image acquisition medium is important, the image is filtered first and foremost by the lens, and **if you're not working with a decent lens you'll hit a ceiling in terms of what you can achieve**.

When video on DSLRs became prominent a few years ago, projects arrived in my color suite shot with the standard lens bundled with the camera all the time. The quality was lacking on the majority of these projects, but I remember a well-budgeted commercial that shot on DSLR. The director of photography opted to spend money on quality primes. The results were clear. While the camera was shooting to a compressed format which limited my ability to grade, the overall image came out looking better due to the production team's lensing choices.

Subject is in Focus

This might seem like an obvious one, but in session I'm asked to sharpen blurry footage all the time. Remember to **keep checking your focus as setups change**. Even in a controlled interview environment, the subject can move a couple of inches and leave the depth of field sweet spot. Digital sharpening can help, but in a blurry shot the information is just not there, and artificial sharpening will never, ever look as good as having razor-sharp focus.

Visual References

Colorists appreciate visual references, like stills taken from print or web. **Previous spot campaigns can help continue brand consistency throughout campaigns**. Visuals serve as a talking point between the colorist and the creatives to determine what can and cannot be achieved. Some clients admit it's difficult for them to speak the language of color, but most know what they like and what they don't. For these clients stills are effective tools to express what they're going for.

Following these steps will better ensure that your next project is completed as close to your creative vision as possible. It's far better to grade with creative freedom than to be stuck fixing production mistakes, isn't it?

August 24th

The Negatives of Shooting on Film

The debate over film versus digital will rage on well into the future, but let's take a look at some of the emerging negatives of shooting on film.

You've probably read the following at least a hundred times: the advances of digital technology have finally caught up with film and may soon surpass it. Yes, the advances in digital filmmaking are nothing short of amazing. In less than a decade, small and independent films have gone from **1080p to 4k**, and now 6K and 8K cameras are legitimate options for small budgets.

Major blockbuster films and your local video house even use some of the same production cameras from RED. That is why so many of the biggest blockbusters have turned to shooting on **large-format film like 65mm, 70mm, and IMAX**. They are trying to stay ahead. Major studios are also the testing ground for new digital cameras. Marvel's *Guardians of the Galaxy Vol. 2* will be shooting on the **RED 8K Weapon**, a camera that is not yet available.

Choosing film over digital comes down to options like director's preference or the type of movie. There has been a major shift between classic cinematic tales and the VFX heavy films that completely rely on digital effects. Here's a look at the negatives of shooting on film.

Cost (One Feature vs Multiple Films)

There are a few things we need to first take into account. **Are you looking at immediate cost or long-term cost?** Are you buying gear or renting? Are you spending the entire budget on this one project, or are you hoping to keep your gear for the foreseeable future?

If you are only taking into consideration the cost of one feature, you'll find that **film is not that much more expensive than digital.** The biggest difference will come down to crew experience. If you have a very experienced camera crew, you shouldn't have any problem shooting film. If the crew is inexperienced, expect a few of those film rolls to be worthless. You'll need a couple thousand extra feet of film stock in case your dailies come back and the footage isn't useable.

Film requires an incredible amount of detail to camera settings. There is no deleting the file and reshooting.

With digital, you can keep using the same memory card over and over again. Depending on the type of card, you can even keep using it after a camera upgrade. With film, you can keep using the same magazine, but you need a new film reel every time. The **benefit of digital is the longevity of the memory cards**, which you can keep using on future projects.

For new **16mm film**, you're looking at **$200 for 400 feet of film**. For **35mm** it will be closer to **$870 for 1000 feet**. That's eleven minutes worth of recording. You can also get a **recan of 16mm for around $100 – $150** or **35mm for $400**. Recans are film rolls that were loaded into a magazine but never used. You can also go cheap and buy short ends, which are partial rolls left over from other shoots. **Short ends cost about $0.25 per foot**, or $100 for 400 feet of 16mm. Don't forget the **cost of processing**, which is around $0.15 – $0.20 a foot.

Like mentioned earlier, eleven minutes for an experienced crew is not a problem. However, compare that to a high-end CF card which costs around **$50 for a 64GB**. 64GB at 4K is a little more than an hour of footage.

Now you may be questioning some math here. **How does $200 for eleven minutes compare to $50 for almost an hour and a half of footage?** You have to remember that the film itself is an archive that can be rescanned. With a memory card you will also need a hard drive which will be another couple hundred dollars. Also depending on the type of camera, you may need an adapter for the memory card. For a RED camera, you'll need to buy a CF card module, which by itself costs $500.

With film, all of the cost is in the camera, film stock, and processing. With digital, the cost is in the camera, memory card, storage, and backups. What does all this mean toward the negatives of film? This still depends on your project. **For film, all of your cost goes into one production. With digital, you can spread the cost over several films** and keep using the same memory and storage.

Processing

Processing your film should be your biggest concern. It doesn't matter if you shot immaculate footage, that film can be destroyed and lost forever if not processed correctly.

The biggest problem with processing is the lack of labs. So many processing labs have closed their doors during the digital boom. That means there are **only a few labs that have an experienced staff to properly handle your film.** Just because there's a new lab in your area doesn't mean everyone working there knows what they're doing.

And it's not just the labs themselves. There has also been **a decrease in the quality of film stock.** Kodak nearly shut their doors until there was a revival of major films shot on film. A few cinematographers have since come out to say that some of the stock from the various film companies isn't up to the same standards of years past.

One of the most outspoken cinematographers on the issue is the critically acclaimed director of photography Roger Deakins. He had this to say after shooting *Hail, Caesar!*

We did have some problems. We had some stock issues and stuff like that, which was really disconcerting. And I've heard that's happened to a lot of people lately, you know, stock and lab problems. That's unnerving. I mean I never really remember having those kind of problems before. But it makes me nervous now. I don't want to do that again, frankly. I don't think the infrastructure's there. - Variety

That's not the only thing Deakins has criticized. There are also **issues with the processing of dailies.** Film reels must be sent to the lab to be processed and then sent back to set to be viewed by the director. With so many lab closures, films are dependent on the nearest processing lab. The feature *Unbroken* was shot in Australia.

There was no lab in Australia by then. All the labs had closed down. So we would have been shipping film across the world and that was just not going to be — you know, it's stressful. It takes two or three days to get a report. That's stressful. – HitFix

As I say, just the technical problems with film, I'm sorry, it's over. - Variety

Deakins certainly thinks film has died, but that doesn't mean it will go without a fight. Directors like Christopher Nolan and Quentin Tarantino aim to keep the format alive, but after them – who knows.

August 25th
Tips for Shooting Behind-the-Scenes Video

Prepare yourself to shoot behind-the-scenes videos and mini-docs with these easy to remember tips.

Productions move fast. Chances are no matter the scale of production you are tasked with covering, everyone on set will be moving quickly. A thorough **behind-the-scenes video** encompasses everything entertaining about production. The talent joking around, the director revealing their stress levels, producers running around barking orders, all the unscripted madness — **and it's your job to capture all of it**. This might seem daunting, but here are a few things I have learned about in my time shooting behind-the-scenes videos.

Always Be Ready to Shoot

Due to the lack of structure or set narrative to your assignment, anything could happen. Part of the beauty of **behind-the-scenes footage** is the naturalistic element to the whole thing. Viewers want to see how people around the production are actually acting. No lines, no script. In order to effectively capture these moments, you must always be on your toes looking for the worthy moment.

Because of the "on your toes" nature of shoot, make sure your camera bag, battery charger, and **gear you have brought with you to set is in a secure place** in case you need to leave the designated area to shoot somewhere else.

Know Which Areas You Can Access

If possible, you should do your best to scout a location or take a look at a set the day before shooting. Having spacial awareness can only benefit you and everyone around you come time to shoot. Knowing good points to shoot and areas to access will not only help you be more efficient with your time, you'll **know exactly where you can or cannot physically get to**.

One of the things I would look for was a remote open area to setup a camera and tripod – or at least mount a GoPro. This let me **set up for a quick timelapse** to capture some awesome B-roll.

Shoot as Much As Possible

Even if what you're capturing seems mundane and unusable, keep shooting. **Behind-the-scenes footage** doesn't have to look like Roger Deakins shot it. The raw aspects of the footage are what make it great. Don't be afraid to get creative – **the bigger variety in shots the better chance you'll have at shooting an effective video**. Speaking of different kinds of shots, the more B-roll you can capture the easier it will be later on to match/hide audio (if in fact you are using audio). Film everything.

Don't Be Timid

Without a doubt the event or production you're covering will have extended periods of down time. Conversations between the cast and crew are bound to happen. This is your time to jump in and capture it. However, the key to capturing natural dialogue between two people is for them to not feel as if they're being filmed. If they are clearly uncomfortable, shooting from behind works as well.

The more footage you can give to the editor the better. Establishing a relationship with your subjects is important as well, letting everyone know what you are there to do and your intentions with the footage. The goal is for everyone on set to appear as comfortable as possible.

Know the Camera You Are Using

Due to the unpredictable nature of capturing **behind-the-scenes footage**, working with a camera you are familiar with is key. Moving in and out of lit areas, buildings, and rooms, can prove difficult when trying to capture usable footage. Adjusting to the changing light, switching to photography, changing lenses, attaching or detaching shoulder mounts – all of this can prove to be very stressful if you aren't completely confident with the gear you're using.

If a production provides a new camera or gear for you to use, make sure you take time to get familiar with the equipment prior to shooting. Look for some pocket camera guides and watch some YouTube tutorials to help you get up to speed.

August 26th

Why Big Budget Films are Shooting in Australia

Why are so many major blockbuster films shooting in Australia? Incentives. Giant cash-back incentives.

With blockbuster films now having absolutely insane budgets, many states and countries are trying to get in on the business. With all the success, New Zealand has had over the past decade, Australia is now making moves to lure big studio productions in a big way. Where New Zealand landed all of James Cameron's *Avatar* sequels, Australia is now making huge deals with major companies like Disney – luring multiple large franchises.

Production in Australia

The Australian Government created the **Australian Screen Production Incentive** as a means to bring all stages of film production to Australia. The main target is feature films over 60 minutes in length. This includes live action, documentary, and animated films. There are also incentives for television production as well.

Originally, films could get up to a 16.5% tax rebate for any foreign production company. In 2011, Australia moved to compete with New Zealand (particularly the power house WETA Digital became) by increasing tax incentives to **30% back for post production, digital, and visual effects (PDV)**. This helped them secure several animated sequences for Warner Bros. *The Lego Movie*.

At the same time, the government announced a **$230 million national arts policy called Creative Australia**. The fund was created after Australia secured production for Twentieth Century Fox's production of X-Men franchise film *The Wolverine*. The new Creative Australia fund was used to begin negotiations with Disney, in hopes to secure *20,000 Leagues Under the Sea: Captain Nemo*.

The Disney film failed to meet deadlines and has since remained "in development." However, Disney seemed determined to shoot in Australia for the incentives. They renegotiated the deal to shoot *Pirates of the Caribbean: Dead Men Tell No Tales*. The fifth *Pirates* film received the $19 million tax incentive, which was less than Disney was seeking.

Disney was considering filming in Mexico, where the water tank used in *Titanic* was located. This meant that regional agencies in Australia would have to help make up the difference. Queensland stepped in, securing production work at the water tanks at Village Roadshow Studios on the Gold Coast.

Now Australia has announced new incentives, offering up to **a staggering 40% Producer Offset on feature films**. Apparently Warner Bros., 20th Century Fox, and Disney were pleased with their deals, and are excited about the new incentives. **All studios have returned to Australia for multiple productions**.

Current Australian productions include *X-Men: Apocalypse* and *Alien* for 20th Century Fox, *Thor: Ragnarok* for Disney and Marvel, as well as *The Lego Movie Sequel* and *Lego Batman* for Warner Bros.

Australian Production Incentives

The new Australia tax incentives provides a **40% Producer Offset for Feature Films, 30% PDV Offset, 20% Producer Offset for Television, and a 16.5% Location Offset.** Compare that to popular places in the US, like Georgia – whose tax incentives max out at 30%.

There is no cap or sunset clause on the incentives, and they are a cash rebate paid to the producer. The Australian incentives can be combined with state, territory, and local government incentives as well.

The Location Offset requires the film to be shot in Australia, and the Television Offset may require at least two episodes must be shot. However, the **PDV Offset is available for worldwide productions**, as long as a significant portion of post-production work is done in Australia.

The Producer Offset offers **40% for theatrically released feature films**. This includes documentary, animation and IMAX films. Films must meet minimum format lengths and requirements for broadcast and/or distribution. The must also demonstrates Significant Australian Content, which examines the subject matter, locations, nationalities of key personnel, and production expenditure.

Applicants for an offset must be an Australian company, or a non-resident company with a permanent establishment in Australia. For eligibility and terms, visit both Aus Film and Screen Australia.

August 27th

Video Gear for Traveling Road Warriors and Frequent Flyers

Do you frequently travel with your camera? Here are a few pieces of must-have support video gear for traveling video pros.

Even seasoned traveling videographers and filmmakers can get stressed out when it comes time to pack up their gear. Check out this checklist of essential video gear for shooters on the move, plus some rules and tricks for getting through security faster.

Power

Depending on your location, you may not have access to electricity while you are shooting. Make sure you're charged up and have plenty of batteries before arriving. Also, traveling with batteries is a *huge* pain in airports. You need to carry-on all of your batteries. **Don't put batteries in your checked luggage** unless you want dogs sniffing your bags before a SWAT team destroys it.

You need to know each batteries wattage as well. As long as each individual battery is under 100 Watts, then you shouldn't have any problems in the airport. Passengers are only allowed to carry 2 batteries that are over 100 Watts. Also, make it a habit to put some gaff tape over the connection points. It puts security at ease, and will helpfully help you get through checkpoints faster.

Don't forget that you will also need to charge all those batteries when you make it back to a hotel. Be sure to bring **battery chargers** and **surge protectors**. If necessary, bring quality **travel adapters, car chargers**, and/or **portable usb chargers** for your phone and laptop.

If you find yourself low on power in the middle of nowhere, you may have to get creative. Check out this video from Tim Johnson at Whitespace Films. He figured out a way to use his Canon LP-E6 batteries to power his Sony a7s.

Memory

Wait. So the first two things on a travel list are batteries and memory cards? **YES! You will need a lot of them.** It's always better to have too many **memory cards** rather than not enough. If the cost of memory cards is a factor, then invest in a portable hard drive or *at least* some thumb drives. You'll definitely want an **external hard drive that does not need power**. Just keep in mind that if you are constantly dumping footage in the middle of nowhere, **your laptop battery will die.** *Are you starting to see the vicious cycle here?*

Don't forget that you will also need a **memory card reader**. You'll also want the **cables** to connect your card reader and hard drive as well. Bring an extra cable or two. They can get damaged or just stop working. If you are dumping footage straight to your **laptop**, you'll certainly want to remember your **laptop charger**.

Light

Light kits are actually a hot topic among travelers. Some swear by packing them, and some tell you to rent on location instead. I fall in the middle category. If you are going somewhere that you can easily rent a light kit, it's usually the better option. If you are traveling to remote areas without plumbing, you may have a hard time finding a rental house.

I found the easiest thing to take are **cheap video lights.** If they get damaged in transport, it's not a big deal. You can grab **a cheap $30 video light** and get by. It's also a good idea to pack a **flashlight** or **headlamp**. A headlamp will help you search for gear in dark locations — and (if you are in a pinch) you can use that as a video light. Combine a cheap $30 light, a flashlight, and a cell phone, and you have the cheapest three point lighting system. Hey… if it works, it works.

Don't forget that lights need batteries. *VICIOUS CYCLE!*

Stabilization

Any videographer should know how important it is to have stable footage. **Having stable footage while traveling becomes a real challenge.** You're most likely trying to pack as lightly as possible. You don't want to carry around too much gear if you are hiking up mountains. Heck, I don't even like trying to get all my gear to my car in the driveway. Compact is key.

The type of shoot you're on will determine what you need to bring. I am a big fan of **monopods** for travelers. They are so much easier to work with than just about anything else. If you are going to need a **slider**, then a monopod won't cut it. I frequently use the travel size Kessler Stealth slider when I am abroad. It's small enough to fit in my check bag, and I can carry it around pretty easily on location. If you are using a slider, you will also need to grab a **travel tripod**. Be sure that it can support the weight of the camera, lens, and slider. *(Author's Note: I am not sponsored by Kessler. I just give them my money.)*

A **Glidecam** is another option to stabilize your footage. Glidecams come apart fairly easily and are easy to pack. The difficult part is knowing how many counter weights you need to pack for you camera. You'll really start to question yourself for carrying actual weights around in your bag. MoVI and Ronin are other choices as well, but I find that they don't travel very well. They're fantastic tools, but not the best for long distance.

Cleaning Kit

When I say cleaning kit, I don't mean just for your camera. Yes, you will need **microfiber wipes, sensor wipes, cleaning solution,** a **brush,** and a **dust blower.** Go ahead a grab a nifty little cleaning kit like this one from Giottos.

On top of camera cleaning kit, don't forget a **first aid kit** too. Don't go for the cheap kind with bandages that slide right off. Invest in a decent quality kit, one that has **alcohol wipes.** You'll never know when you'll get a cut or roll an ankle. True story: I once partially dislocated my kneecap when traveling for a shoot. I got checked out and then hobbled my way to a drug store to buy pain pills and a knee brace. I spent the next day hopping around while shooting. Now my first aid kit always includes **aspirin** and a **compression wrap.**

While on the topic of cleaning, don't forget to pack **toilet paper** if you are going to a very remote location. You can even use it in the airport instead of relying on the so called paper that their bathrooms offer. In very remote locations, you'll also want **bug spray** and **sunscreen.**

Bags

Finding the right bags and cases for traveling is going to be a trial and error process. It's different for every person. The one thing I can certainly say is this: rolling bags are great for checked items and to get things to a hotel room. Other than that, they will be a curse. **A rolling bag should never be your primary bag.** Find yourself a quality backpack that you can wear all day long.

Another thing to consider is your location. If you will be in a big city, thieves are on the lookout for camera bags and gear. **Sometimes it's best to use an inconspicuous hiking backpack.** One that can still store the gear you need. You don't always have to have a lens placed safely in a foam cube. You can wrap it in a t-shirt and be just fine.

Messenger bags are great for when you don't have to carry much gear at once. That's why they are so popular amongst photographers who only need a camera, lens, and maybe a tripod. But if you are hiking long distances, do yourself a favor and properly balance your weight with a backpack. That audio equipment, laptop, and all the extra gear will take its toll on your body as you get tired.

Bonus: Waterproof Jacket

A rain jacket is *always* handy. Obviously it's great for rain, but you can also use it to cover up your gear. If the sun is beating down on you and you can't see your monitor or screen, you can use a rain jacket to make a monitor hood. When packing for travel, always think of multiple uses for everything you have. Then you will save yourself the trouble of packing too much.

August 28th
Traits of a Good Film Crew

Picking the right film crew isn't hard if you know what to look for. In this post, we share a few tips to aid in the success of your film project.

Sometimes the most difficult part of making a film is finding the right people to make it with you. There is a reason why professional filmmakers get paid so much money to do their job, **they are worth it.** However, even if your budget is nonexistent there are a few qualities to look for in a crew member that will help you **sort out the good apples from the bad.**

A good crew member...

- Helps solve problems on set.
- Improves morale on set by complementing **instead of complaining**.
- Is concerned with making the film as great as possible even if it means shooting late.
- Is more concerned with making a film than getting lunch, eating snacks, taking breaks.
- Is able to admit when he/she has made a mistake.
- Will offer help to other crew members once their work is complete.
- Is concerned with the success of the entire team rather than getting praise for themselves.

A bad crew member...

- Complains outwardly about long working days and early mornings.
- **Shows up late** to call times and blames it on traffic and phone alarms.
- Criticizes the decisions made by the director or producer in front of other crew members.
- Brings down the moral on the entire set.
- Only does things when he/she is told to do them.
- Misses pre-production meetings.
- **Wants to receive praise for everything** they do.

Based on that criteria do you think you are a good crew member or a bad crew member? **Are you a good crew leader?**

How to Assemble an Awesome Crew

Now you may be asking, "Where do I find these good crew members?" Well, the answer to that question is not as simple as going to FindaFreeCrew.com and selecting people...you're going to have to put in some leg-work.

Finding a good crew always begins with good networking. As any good filmmaker will tell you, one of the most powerful tools you can have is networking skills. This means as a filmmaker you should be spending time with other filmmakers. Once you have a network asking for help isn't as difficult.

Build Excitement

It is very important to hire people who are **excited** about your project. A crew that isn't excited about a project will be very difficult to motivate and subsequently will not create a good finished product.

You can build excitement through interacting and tagging crew members on social media, inviting crew members to brainstorming sessions and highlighting crew members on the film's website. On the same note, crew members who are **eager to gain work experience** will probably be more reliable than those who are simply trying to make money.

If your budget is low it might also be helpful to ask crew members with access to **good equipment** to be a part of your shoot. This might save you precious money that would have been spent somewhere else. This is definitely where your developed relationship will have to come into play. There's nothing worse than having an audio person volunteer to help bring equipment then not show up. Not only would you be out a crew member you would also **not be able to shoot your film**.

Set Expectations

The line between a good crew member and a bad crew member can sometimes be blurred under poor leadership. It is your duty as a director/producer to **communicate exactly what you expect** from your crew every step of the way.

Expect good work but **be patient with crew members** if they don't have a lot of experience. Never boss people around especially when they are helping you for free. Nothing screams amateur than a director who is impatient and rude to his crew.

Give a schedule to everyone on set so they will know what to expect. In my own experience I've found that a **checklist** with each step of the production process increases the morale and buy-in of every crew member.

Be sure to maintain relationships with your crew after a project has been shot and make everyone feel involved during every phase of production. This will give your crew a greater sense of ownership and will keep them motivated to help you on **future projects**.

August 29th
5 Products for Audio Editing Under $50

Deck out your video editing bay with these audio-related products — all available for under 50 bucks!

Discover five products that can improve your audio editing without breaking the bank. What inexpensive gadgets do you use in your edit suite?

1. Powermate USB

The Griffin Powermate is a multifunction controller that not only looks amazing in your edit suite, it also can serve a multitude of functions. Use the Powermate as a volume control or jog wheel in your video editing timeline. **The controller comes in two flavors, Bluetooth and USB.** The Bluetooth version costs twice as much as the USB version, and many users have actually reported having a better experience with the wired model. At around $25 USD, it's an inexpensive tool to potentially speed up your audio and video editing workflow.

2. Bluetooth Headphones

Most quality Bluetooth headphones extend well over the $100 USD range. That's why we were surprised to hear about the new LX-10 from EditorsKeys (a company that specializes in shortcut keyboards for video editors). Currently retailing for $49.99 USD, the LX-10 offers ten hours of playback on a single charge. They sent us a loaner to review and we put it through the paces...

The line-in function is useful, enabling the headphones to work as a traditional wired version when Bluetooth isn't available. The metal body is also a nice touch... the set feels substantial and able to withstand being tossed in a bag for editing-on-the-go.

Arguably, that's where the strength lies with this pair of headphones... **I can see this as the perfect set for video editing on the road.** The sound is clear, but the top end does seem to get lost in the mids and the bass is a bit over powerful. The ergonomics are 'middle of the road'... while the earpieces are comfortable, the overall fit is a bit on the tight side.

That said, for the price, this is a respectable pair of headphones. You may find other wireless Bluetooth models in this lower price range, but for the battery time and overall quality, this is a solid choice under $50.

3. Blue Snowball

Having a simple USB microphone in your edit suite is essential for recording 'scratch track' audio. Are you waiting on a final voiceover recording from voice talent? Do you need to test out the timing of narration? Having a mic handy makes it simple to record directly into your video editing application.

For nearly a decade, the Blue Snowball mic has been a great USB option (it's the mic we use for on-the-fly recordings). The Snowball iCE offers much of the same functionality as the regular Snowball, has a built-in desk stand, and is available for less than $50. **The vintage stylings are a nice touch too.**

4. Blue Icicle

While we're on the topic of microphones, it's worth mentioning another product by Blue, the Icicle. This XLR to USB converter is a simple interface option for recording audio from *any* traditional microphone into your computer. Audio quality is 44.1 kHz / 16-bit and the unit is phantom powered — an external power source isn't necessary.

5. Acoustic Panels

Upgrade the sound of your edit suite with acoustical wall tiles. A quality pair of foam panels can actually be purchased for less than $50 USD. Not only will the acoustic profile of your space be better for recording audio, **it will also improve sound playback by minimizing reflection and reverb.**

August 30th
5 Tips for Planning Your Audio in Pre-Production

Capturing great audio begins before hitting 'record'.

Having low quality audio in your film or video is a quick way to lose credibility in the eyes of your audience. Instead of simply taking audio into consideration once you get on-set, you should be preparing to make your audio amazing before production begins. In the following post, we will take a look at 5 ways you can plan out your audio approach during pre-production.

1. Go Scouting

Parking garages are notorious for being acoustic nightmares. Location scouting is one of the most important aspects of the pre-production process. As a filmmaker, you probably have already developed an eye for finding good locations, but it is equally important to develop an ear. **Keep the acoustics of your location in mind.** Does your voice echo loudly in the room? Is it in a highly-populated area? Along with the room acoustics you need to be able to control other audio related factors like the air-conditioner or a humming refrigerator. **What ambient noises can you anticipate?** If you're shooting in a large building you might not be able to turn off the air conditioner using a thermostat on a wall, so for this reason it is important to have a location contact that can help answer your location related questions. You should also be mindful of things like proximity to airports, fire stations and bus routes, as these things might not be heard during location scouting but can definitely be picked up by your microphones. It's also important to look around and see if there are any construction projects going on, a setback that can be disastrous for location sound. You don't want to be surprised by ambient noises once you get on set.

2. What Does the Shot Demand?

Top-notch wardrobe has the ability to add a greater since of believability to your film, but when picking your character's clothing it's important to consider audio. For example, silk clothing is notorious for being difficult to mic, so instead you might consider using a boom instead of a lavalier mic. You may even want to change the wardrobe to accommodate.

That chase scene may be cool, but how are you going to mic it? It's also important to think about the action in your scene before you arrive on set. Will the actors be walking and talking? If so, will their backs be to the camera while they are talking? How much are they going to move? Asking these questions before shooting may also speed up your production time. Instead of showing up on-set and deciding what mics to use, make an educated decision before you arrive. In order to do this you will need to **have your audio person involved in the pre-production process.** This admittedly adds another layer of complexity to the whole process but it definitely pays off in the end.

3. Invest

Indie productions are notorious for having incredibly bad audio. It doesn't matter if your image is immaculate…if the audio is bad your audience isn't buying it. If you're serious about your project it's important to **invest in quality audio equipment**. Online rental houses like BorrowLenses, LensRentals.com and LensProtoGo all offer microphone and audio gear at affordable prices. If you're needing the equipment for an extended period of time, inquire about a discount off of the normal pricing. Good audio investments don't end once the shoot is wrapped. It is equally important to invest in your audio during post-production. Instead of using low quality music, spending a fortune for original composition, or using copyrighted commercial tracks (which could put you in legal hot water), consider high quality production music. CR Production Music.com has thousands of handpicked tracks from professional composers at affordable pricing.

4. Hire a Professional Boom Operator/Sound Mixer

Sites like Mandy.com and ProductionHub are great resources for locating audio specialists in your area. This is a key crew member, so don't fall for letting a friend or family member be your on-set audio person. Oftentimes filmmakers and video pros get caught up in the visuals of the production and the audio takes a back seat. Capturing audio on-set is more than just holding a boom pole. Professional sound recordists will have experience using field mixers, know the proper ways to mic talent, and can work in tandem with the director of photography.

5. Make a Plan

Making a detailed plan is imperative for streamlining the production process. If you are creating storyboards before you shoot (you should be!) take the audio into consideration during this process. The audio recorder and video editor will be appreciative when you hand them a detailed storyboard with audio notes. Always **schedule time to record natural sound while you are on-location**. Picking up several minutes of nat sound from every location is important for preventing choppy audio in post. Be sure to **record additional nat sound every time the audio environment changes** (for instance, if an A/C unit kicks on). This is really important for preventing choppy audio in post. Will you use a boom or a lav? Which shots will you ADR (if any)? What sound effects will you need to enhance the action? Will you need an external recorder, will audio be recorded into camera, or both? These are all important questions to answer before the camera rolls. Good luck!

August 31st

10 Audio Accessories Under $100

Only have a small amount of money left in your budget for audio accessories? No problem. Check out all this great sound gear that's available to you for under $100!

As filmmakers, we're quick to make sure we've got all of the camera accessories we need... but what about sound gear? Let's continue down that path in a more budget-minded fashion with this list of ten must-have audio accessories for under $100.

Note: the links below are just examples of where you can purchase this filmmaking gear. These are not sponsored or affiliate links. We encourage you to make your purchases at your favorite gear store!

1. Tascam DR-05 Portable Recorder
Price: $99.99

The Tascam DR-05 is a great option as a **field recorder** for the price tag of $100. While some may not view it as an accessory I've been on film crews where this little recorder was waiting in the wings in case the **Sound Devices 702** or **633** went down. If you're looking for a cheap capture solution for small projects, I would suggest it as well.

2. Rode VideoMic GO: $90

While it doesn't capture the kind of audio that the **Rode NTG line of shotgun mics** will, the **Rode VideoMic GO** captures quality sound for its price tag. I've used this same mic several times over the years in order to capture scratch-track audio, which is extremely helpful when you get into post-production.

3. Audio Technica Condensor Mic: $99

In the event that you didn't capture all of your audio while in the field, you'll need to capture some ADR. For that you'll need a quality condenser mic. The **Audio Technica** is a great little mic, but you also might want to check out the Blue Snowball, MXL V67G, Behringer C-3 or the AKG P120, all of which are under $100.

4. Rode smartLav: $66

This is an interesting **lav microphone.** Say you're working on a documentary or industrial video when your wireless lapel mic goes on the fritz. You need this audio and this shot and you only have a limited amount of time. Well, grab your smart phone and connect the **Rode smartLav** to it and open the app. Just like that, you have a backup for under $100.

5. Nady DSM-1X Digital Meter: $75

I never really thought about needing to measure the sound level of a space. However, I've had several **sound recordists** tell me they've used them when **filming in an industrial space** where there are large spikes of sound. They would walk with the meter toward the source of the sound while watching the dB level, easily discovering how close they could get to the sound without harming the recording equipment.

6. Comprehensive Audio Adapter Kit: $90

It never fails, you're out in the field and you need some sort of adapter, but that was one of those minute details that you forgot. Well if you've ever found yourself dealing with this before just know that you aren't alone, it has happened to me before as well. But, in order to prepare for the next time this will happen here is a great little audio adapter kit.

7. Leatherman Sidekick Multi-Tool: $42

This is easily the greatest tool I've ever seen on set. A good friend of mine and fellow filmmaker brought one of these on set and it was a simply a godsend. While it's not necessarily a piece of "audio" equipment, it will come in handy at some point. For example, when I was on a documentary crew, the sound recordist had a heck of a time pressing the small battery lock release on the **Sound Devices 702 field recorder.** Enter the Leatherman Sidekick. Problem solved.

8. ProTapes Gaff Tape: $20

Next to the multi-tool, the best tool for audio — and really any part of film production — is **gaff tape**. It's amazingly handy. I was recently working on a documentary film and we needed to attach the boom mic to a C-Stand. When we discovered we didn't have all the parts necessary to pull this off, we whipped out the **gaff tape** and strapped the boom pole to the arm of the C-Stand. It worked perfectly. You can also use **gaff tape** when you need your subject to **tape a lapel mic to the inside of their shirt or jacket** so you can get crystal-clear audio.

9. Vulta Hurricane Flashlight: $37

As soon as you say that you won't need a **flashlight**, you'll need one. When working on set everything is lit in a specific way. So the light is directed toward the subject or characters. This will sometimes leave you in a shady or dark spot where it can be cumbersome to find little things like lapel clips or adapters. **So make things easier on yourself and keep a small flashlight handy.**

10. Sennheiser HD 280 Pro Headphones: $75

Last, but definitely not least we need **headphones.** These same headphones were recommended to me by a film composer I work with, and I've used them for over two years now. When you put these on you'll notice right away that you hear a nice flat sound, and as you should know, when you're capturing sound you want to make sure that this sound is flat. **This allows you to hear everything as it is without any manipulation.**

September 1st
10 Crucial Pieces of Audio Gear Under $500

Filmmaking is an expensive career. Keep your budget in check with these crucial pieces of audio gear under $500.

It's easy for us filmmakers to become so absorbed in the visual side of production that we lose sight of the audio. In reality, **capturing great audio is just as important as capturing great visuals**. A great story isn't just crafted in imagery. It also needs a voice and supporting sound to help flesh it out. So, after conferring with my composer and sound engineer, I've compiled a **list of ten crucial pieces of audio gear that will help you capture your film's voice and sound without breaking the bank.**

1. Zoom H6

Before you can capture audio with a microphone, you need something for that mic to connect to. You can go with a shotgun mic that attaches to your camera, but that's really best for capturing scratch track audio. For your final audio, **you want to use a field recorder** much like the ol' reliable Sound Devices 702 recorder. However, if you don't feel like shelling out 2k for a field recorder, you should consider the **Zoom H6.**

Price: $399

2. Directional Mic

Now that you have your recorder, **let's get a mic to capture that audio.** For my films, our sound engineer runs a directional mic for the majority of the film and for foley work, as it offers the most flexibility when on set. See this article from Film School Online for a breakdown regarding placing mics and booming. While he uses a Rode NTG-8, which can take a chunk out of your budget, he suggests that you can capture quality audio using the Rode NTG4 or NTG-2.

Price: $269 (NTG-2)

Price: $369 (NTG4)

3. Lavalier Mic

So you have your boom mic, which gets you spacial and foley audio, but now you want something that gets you crisper dialogue audio, especially for interview settings. **For this you'll need a lavalier or lapel microphone.** There are a lot of options, but as Chad Johnson explains in the video below, the Sanken COS11D is used by most film and television professionals.

Price: $379

4. Wireless System

If you're conducting a sit down interview, then you really don't need to worry about a wireless system. However, if you want to mic characters on set and you don't want to see any wires, **then a wireless system is the way to go.** There are several types of wireless systems out there; the Sony UWP-D11 and Azden 105 Series are two that I've seen several times on set. However, for my sound designer, the Sennheiser G3 is the tool of choice. While it is just *slightly* north of $500, it does come bundled with the Sennheiser ME2 lavalier microphone. In the video below, Dave Dugdale runs through the wireless systems I've mentioned, with the addition of the Shure FP.

Price: $574

5. Rode Blimp 2

So now you have your mics, but you've noticed that your directional mic is completely exposed and is getting hammered by wind noise. Not to worry — a solution to cut out all of that noise is easily available **by getting a windscreen like the Rode Blimp 2.** The Blimp is the industry standard windscreen. It perfectly suspends your directional mic inside its sturdy casing. It has a quick adjustable grip and an XLR input connector at its bottom. The price tag is a little higher than you'd expect, but it's well worth the investment.

Price: $299

6. Rode Boompole

Boompoles are an absolute must for your directional mic. **There are several options for boompoles**, such as the K-Tek KEG-100 or Gitzo 3560. But the Rode Boompole is cost effective and solidly built. Check out the following Ric Viers video where he uses a Rode Boompole and gives you a few tips and tricks.

Price: $149

7. XLR Cables

Okay, so now you have your field recorder, your mics, your wind screen, and your boompole. You're set to record — but how are you connecting your mics and wireless systems to your recorder? **You'll need the cheapest tool of this entire list... XLR cables.** Be sure to get an assortment of lengths from 5 feet to 15 or 20 feet, because you never know when you may need them. Extend the life of your XLR cables by remembering to roll them correctly. How does one correctly roll an XLR cable? Randy Coppinger explains below.

Price: See Sweetwater Cable Finder for Options

8. Headphones

We're just about ready to check our audio levels, **so we need a pair of headphones to help us hear the levels.** For this, you'll want a closed-back type of headphone that gives you a flat sound, which allows you to hear the sound close to naturally. There are a ton of options when looking at headphones. Really, it comes down to personal preference. The most widely used prosumer headphones are the Sennheiser HD 280 Pro.

Price: $99

9. Storage

Now you need to add storage to your field recorder so you can save that audio for later processing. **Audio files will never rival the size of video files**, but you'll still want a decently sized SD card to slot into your field recorder. For that, let's look at Monster Digital 64g microSDXC. See the TbonesTech video on SD Card hacks just below.

Price: $99

10. Logic Pro

You have all of your equipment in the field and you've captured great audio. Now what do you do with it? You send it along with your video files to whatever NLE system you prefer. But for final mixing, most professionals, **especially sound designers**, like to use an audio mixing software such as Audacity or Audition. While Pro Tools is still the industry standard for Hollywood, its $899 price tag puts it out of reach for many. Apple Logic has been making strides toward the professional arena, and as my composer told me recently, "its lower cost and ability to do what Pro Tools does makes it a no brainer." First Institute has a great video where they compare and contrast Pro Tools and Logic Pro X just below.

Price: $199

September 2nd

ADR: Automated Dialogue Replacement Tips and Tricks

Recording, editing and mixing ADR is an essential part to becoming a successful filmmaker. From pre-production ADR to post, we've got you covered.

ADR (Automated Dialogue Replacement) is a method of superimposing dialogue that has been recorded in a controlled, acoustically treated space. Location dialogue oftentimes becomes problematic when the ambient noise of the environment is too high, the equipment malfunctions, or when the talent is just not projecting over what should be background noise.

Almost every modern Hollywood film has anywhere from **30% to 70% ADR dialogue**, so it's an integral part overall of any film's success. If executed properly, **ADR can even salvage entire scenes**.

A Word About ADR Looping

Before we begin, there are a few key elements to ADR that you must strategically plan to set up the recording session correctly. By **looping,** play back of a repeating loop from the film is fed to the recording talent while simultaneously recording the new dialogue. There are two types of looping: **visual looping and audio looping.** With visual looping, the actor will listen to the location take several times to get a feel for the delivery before attempting to track the dialogue. When recording however, the talent will not hear the previous location take but will watch the scene to match lip sync. In their headphones/monitors they will hear the line they're delivering real-time. Visual looping requires a split video feed if the ADR is not recorded in the control room.

Audio looping will typically produce the most desirable results; however it is usually much more time extensive. The session is performed the same way as visual looping, excluding the video monitor and without muting the original dialogue track. Many ADR engineers even use a hybrid of these techniques.

Always break up the looped lines into smaller sections to maintain consistency and sync. For better sync when beginning the line, try recording three beeps exactly one second apart each, with the final one being one second before the first word starts. This provides an audio cue; essentially a metronome, to start the talent in the correct rhythm of the ADR line.

Treating Your ADR Recording Space

In post-production, you have much more control over your audio then you do when recording on location. **The overall goal is to obtain a clean ADR recording so later you can put the dialogue in the appropriate acoustical space with EQ and reverb.** If you are not in an acoustically treated environment, follow these tips and tricks below to treat a given space:

- **Use thick blankets to dampen hard surfaces if early reflections occur** (on the floor under talent, use C-stands to construct walls)
- **Place talent so that the largest area in the room is facing them** (again, minimizing reflections)
- **Hang a small blanket, towel or felt over talent's music stand**
- **Eliminate all ambient noise** (air conditioner, fridge, fans, etc.)
- **Overall, deaden the sound as much as possible to yield best results**

ADR Equipment

When recording ADR, **it is important that you use the same microphone used on location to capture the dialogue.** The goal of ADR is to convincingly match the dialogue in frequency response and tonal characteristics to the location audio with ideal mic placement and acoustics. All microphones have different frequency responses and polar patterns yielding different tonal characteristics, so match accordingly.

Digital audio workstations such as *Avid Pro Tools, Ableton Live, Logic Pro, Adobe Audition, Nuendo* and *Cubase* will satisfy all of your recording and looping needs. It's important to utilize audio production software as the recording and looping capabilities of video editing software is typically inferior.

- **Microphone**
- **Preamp / Interface**
- **Digital Audio Workstation (DAW)**
- **Headphones**
- **Video Monitor**

ADR Microphone Placement & Delivery

Depending on what mic you are using, it is important to maintain some distance between the microphone and the talent to create a sense of realism to what you see. If you are using a shotgun microphone, try a distance from **10 inches to 2 or 3 feet**, depending on how wide the camera angle is in relation to the talent's distance from the camera. For shotguns, it's best to place the microphone **just off axis and pointed downwards, slightly to the left or right** of the talent. Shorter shotguns should be closer. Don't forget a pop filter if necessary!

How the actor delivers the line is a very crucial process affecting the delivery and tone of the ADR. **If the talent is replicating the same body language and mood as is used in the scene, it will aid a great deal to the quality of the lines and ease your workload in post-production.**

Post-Production, Ambient Tone & Reverb

Now that you have obtained a clean ADR recording, you can begin adding the appropriate acoustical space to your tracks. Before you begin, it's important that all of the ADR dialogue is in sync. There are a few tools and tricks to utilize bringing out the best sync: *VocALign Pro* is a powerful plugin that processes your ADR into near-perfect sync. By using the waveforms from the original location audio, *VocALign Pro* performs a series of time stretches and contractions to sync the ADR. Another option is to edit the ADR manually, but this can be very time intensive.

Next, add your ambient tone, or "room tone" that was recorded on location. This will fill the spaces between the dialogue and insures what you're seeing coincides with what you're hearing. Finally, add EQ and reverb, tastefully putting each phrase in it's appropriate acoustical space. Many engineers use **convolution reverbs** (a reverb plugin simulating a real acoustical space).

September 3rd
Affordable Software Every Filmmaker Should Have

One of the last things to usually make its way into our toolbox is software. Let's look at affordable software options for your video production arsenal.

Every filmmaker and video producer needs software. Whether you're in pre-production, principal, or post there is some sort of software that you'll need to process your daily tasks. The downside is that this software isn't always cheap. Fortunately, there are **affordable software options** out there for whatever specific production task you need complete.

Day-to-Day Operations

No matter if you're an indie filmmaker, run your own video production company, or you're a motion designer, you'll have **day-to-day operations** that take time to process. Make these processes easier with these simple to use applications.

QuickBooks

If you're **processing payments from clients** for the work you are doing, then keep all of your accounting information streamlined in one app through **QuickBooks**. It's a fairly inexpensive asset and at the end of the year you can send all documentation to your CPA for processing.
COST: $7.99 A Month

Square

If you need an endpoint solution for sending out invoices to clients, then **Square** could be a good application for you. Setting up an account is free and comes with a credit card reader. It also integrates with **QuickBooks**.
COST: 2.7% Charge on Each Transaction

Appointy

Scheduling is probably one of the hardest aspects of our business, as we're always on the go. While **Square** also offers scheduling services, they aren't exactly cheap. There is another app called **Appointy** that does exactly what **Square** scheduling does, but it offers that service for free.
COST: Free to $60 a Month

Skype

Communication is key in our business and there are several solutions, but **Skype** is one of the best out there. This application allows you to message, to video chat, and to share your desktop with collaborators. If you have an **Office 365** or **Microsoft Account,** you can gain access to **Skype**.

COST: Free For Individuals, $2.00 A Month For Business'

Google Docs

While Office 365 is a great option, it also costs the average user just over $8 a month in dues. So, for those out there that want an even cheaper document editing solution, **Google Docs** has you covered. As long as you have a Google account, Docs is free. There are paid solutions for business owners in the form of Google Apps, but those are not necessary for **Google Docs**.

COST: Free with Google Account

Celtx

If you write your own scripts for narrative films, commercials, or even industrial videos, then **Celtx** can help you. Basic access is free, but if you want extended options and access, you'll need to pay a monthly fee of either $8.25 or $16.58 a month. While **Celtx** isn't as robust as **Adobe Story,** its free pricing for Basic Access is better than the $9.99 a month fee for Story. However, if you are a Creative Cloud subscriber then you get Story for free.

COST: Free for Basic Access

Non-Linear Editing

Now that you have your day-to-day operational software, let's take a look at post-production software that is affordable and necessary for you to complete your work. We'll start with non-linear editing software options. We will list all major options.

Adobe Premiere Pro

Adobe Premiere Pro is a favorite among independent filmmakers and video professionals. Its ability to integrate seamlessly into other Adobe software is a huge bonus. There are two options for **Premiere Pro:** one is the monthly subscription for the single app. The other is a monthly "Complete" subscription to Creative Cloud, which **Premiere Pro** is apart of.
COST: (APP) $19.99 a/mo. or (Creative Cloud) $49.99 a/mo.

Final Cut Pro X

While the price point may not sound that affordable, **Final Cut Pro X** is actually one of the cheapest professional non-linear editing systems out there. While initially panned when it first released, Apple has done a solid job of releasing updates to move the software closer to what the former industry standard **Final Cut Pro 7** was.
COST: $299.99

Avid Media Composer

Avid Media Composer is the industry standard for video editing. While for many years its price point was just out of reach for most video professionals, that has changed recently. There are now two ways to purchase and gain access to **Media Composer.** One is through a monthly subscription, while the other is through a one-time fee for the current version release. However, while the monthly subscription is being hailed as affordable, it's still pretty steep for professionals just starting out.
COST: $49.99 a/mo. or $1,299.99

Lightworks

Lightworks is an Academy and Emmy award-winning software most notably used by Martin Scorsese's longtime editor, Thelma Schoonmaker. Its robust system has made it a favorite of many big name editors. Purchasing options come in three forms: monthly, yearly, and outright. Some may want to explore the outright license, as its price point is just a little more than **Final Cut Pro X**.

COST: $24.99 a/mo., $174.99 a/yr. or $437.99 outright license

DaVinci Resolve Lite

While not originally a editing software, **Resolve** is the new kid on the block. Blackmagic Design offers a lite version of the **DaVinci Resolve** for free, but the paid version unlocks all of the tools. However, the paid version is one of the more expensive options listed.

COST: Free Lite Version or $995.00 Full Version

Motion Design

You have your editing software, but now you need to create some smooth graphics for your project. For that you'll need a good motion graphics editor. While we are aware of several other effect software options out there like Apple Motion and The Foundry's Nuke Studio, for independent filmmakers and new video professionals there are really only two options that make the most sense.

Adobe After Effects

For many motion graphic and special effects professionals, **After Effects** is THE software to use. With an amazing wealth of available plugins from Video Copilot, Red Giant, and The Foundry, **After Effects** is like the swiss army knife of motion graphic software.

COST: (APP) $19.99 a/mo. or (Creative Cloud) $49.99 a/mo.

Fusion 7

Blackmagic Design jumped into the motion graphic arena when they purchased **eyeon Fusion**. And just like they do for **Resolve**, Blackmagic is offering users an industry standard software free. Keep in mind, though, that this is the free version.
COST: Free Lite Version or $995.00 Full Version

Audio Software

One of the last things filmmakers or video professionals usually think about is **audio editing**. Luckily there are some great options out there for us to utilize. We'll give you our top four software options.

Audacity

It doesn't get much better than free, and that is exactly what **Audacity** is: free. Developed by volunteers and distributed under the General Public License, **Audacity** is a surprisingly easy to use and beefy audio recording and editing software.
COST: Free

Avid Pro Tools 12

For the longest time, **Pro Tools** has been the industry standard for audio editing. And for the longest time, it was one of the more expensive softwares to own. But, just as Avid has begun to offer a subscription model for **Media Composer**, they are doing the same for **Pro Tools**, which gives you access to a professional grade software at an affordable price.
COST: $24.92 a/mo.

Apple Logic Pro X

Logic Pro wan't built specifically for filmmakers or video professionals, but it can work some magic for you if you do indeed add it to your toolbox. Originally built for music producers,

Logic Pro X is much more in-line with the music world… but its easy-to-use interface, simple timeline editing, and integration of video allow it to be a fairly robust audio-editing software for film. Its price point isn't overwhelming either.
COST: $199.99

Adobe Audition

Finally, you guessed it… there is Adobe. Just like with **Premiere Pro CC** or **After Effects CC**, a single subscription to **Audition** can be purchased for $19 a month. **Or you can purchase the Complete Suite and get Premiere, After Effects, Photoshop, Illustrator, and Audition plus many more apps** for $49 a month.
COST: (APP) $19.99 a/mo. or (Creative Cloud) $49.99 a/mo.

Our Personal Thoughts

While I spent my early career working with **Final Cut Pro 7**, **After Effects** and **Pro Tools,** my preferences have changed. Now I use **Avid Media Composer, After Effects** and **Logic.**

I do have **Creative Cloud**, and I think it is a great value, and more and more I'm being sold on **Premiere Pro CC.** Again, this is my personal advice, but for young filmmakers and rookie video professionals, I would highly suggest paying for the **Creative Cloud Complete subscription.** It offers you the most flexibility. You can pre-visualize your project, edit it, and even market it *all* within the software lineup of Creative Cloud.

September 4th
Audio Checklist for Video Editors

Implement these audio tips for success and raise the quality of your video editing projects!

Nothing screams "amateur!" like bad audio. Even if your project has stunning visual images, your project will suffer if proper attention isn't paid to creating a quality, complimentary audio track. We've put together the following tips for the video editor looking to improve the sound mix of their projects!

Only use high-res audio in your projects

MP3s may be useful for web applications, but in video **WAVs or AIFFs are better choices**. These file types are less compressed and will sound cleaner and crisper. MP3s can also prove to be finicky in some video editing applications, like Final Cut Pro. An additional step you can take to avoid complications in post is ensuring that **all the audio elements in your project have the same sample rate** – the standard for digital video is 48 kHz. Check out our previous post on the best audio formats for video editing for additional information.

Let music drive the video

Your goal is to use music to enhance the feeling of your video, not work against it. Pull a handful of songs that you think will work for a particular scene or project. Then, **VERY roughly lay out the video track and audition each of these songs underneath it** to see how they work together. Once you've decided on an audio track, *then* use that **music as a guide for editing the video** (in most cases cutting to the tempo and beats).

Keep your audio tracks organized

Assign different audio tracks in your project to different audio types. For instance, keep all dialogue on tracks 1-4, all music on tracks 5-8 and all sound effects on tracks 9-10. Think to yourself, "if another editor had to sit down at this project would they be able to quickly identify each audio clip?" It's best practice to keep the project organized as you go, but it's **ESSENTIAL to clean it up before archiving**. Keeping an organized timeline will likely save you time and a bit of sanity.

Use sound effects to enhance action

Sound effects are often one of the last things to get added to a mix, so it likely falls off when you're up against a deadline. Instead, **think of sound effects early in the post process**. When you're reviewing footage take notes of instances where sound effects may add value to a scene. If you're working with a sound designer, discuss opportunities for incorporating sound effects in the mix. **The right sound effects can help set the tone and add pacing to your project.**

Don't skimp on the room tone

Connect with the on-location audio person before the shoot to ensure they're **recording room tone every time the scene or environment changes**. Anytime the on-camera sound drops off (this can often happen between cuts) make sure you're using room tone to cover this audio dead space. This will keep the mix sounding most consistent and be less jarring to the listener.

Test your mix

On what device, will your project be seen? With the wide variety of digital video devices, it's important to **listen to your mix just as the intended viewer would**. Get a strong baseline mix in your audio or video editing application, and then refine it to fit the final delivery format. For instance, you may want to consider adding extra bass to an audio track that will primarily be heard through treble heavy low-grade computer speakers. Keep the **final** output in mind when doing your **final** mix.

Utilize meters when setting levels

Your ears will fool you. It's impossible to keep a consistent mix when adjusting from your own hearing alone. If you're making adjustments by ear, you'll likely find that the overall mix will get louder and louder through the timeline. As you become accustomed to the audio level you'll unknowingly raise the audio little by little, so that the end of the project sounds significantly louder than the start. Avoid this editing mistake by utilizing **the audio meters within your video editing application**. A standard in digital video is to keep most audio around -12 db with audio spikes not exceed 0db (12 db of headroom). If you're outputting for web it's likely you'll want to run the mix a bit hotter to account for computer speakers (around -6db). Everyone's hearing is different so use the audio meters to get a consistent result.

September 5th

Audio Editing Tip: Matching ADR and Location Audio in Post

Mixing and matching ADR with location audio can be very challenging, but these audio editing tips will help you get much better results every time.

Nobody enjoys having to record **ADR**. It's a fairly grueling process that usually occurs at the tail end of a production when you just want to wrap things up and get your project out the door. What's even more frustrating than having to record it in the first place though, is attempting to match the sound quality with your source/location audio.

Imagine a scenario where you're editing a project that was shot entirely on a busy city street. Most of the location audio sounds solid, but there are a few takes that just aren't working. Maybe the noise from the street bled through too much on a critical line or there was a technical issue with the mic, ultimately leaving you with the reality that you need to record **ADR** for a portion of the scene.

Once you go back into the studio with your talent and rerecord their dialogue to match with picture, the work has really only begun. It goes without saying that **clean, studio recorded audio tracks are going to sound very different from on location recordings**, so ultimately you'll need to take some measures to get the audio to match up.

In a best case scenario, you'll send your edited timeline to a dedicated ProTools artist who will help finesse the audio until it's perfect. But in some instances, you may very well be left with the task of tweaking the audio yourself, and if that's the case you should always adhere to these **audio editing tips**:

Remember Why You Recorded Room Tone

Assuming you've done your job properly on set, you should have room tone recorded for each location you shot at. Room tone of course, is simply a track recording of ambience in your location which can be used during the audio editing process.

One of the most critical steps in matching **ADR** with location audio involves the addition of room tone, which can be an art unto itself. Always ensure that you are not only adding in room tone, but mixing it down so the levels are equal to the ambient levels on the rest of your dialogue tracks. Also be sure to add crossfades carefully at the top and tail of your clips to ease in and out of the room tone clips.

Just with this single step alone, your audio track will start to feel far smoother, as there will no longer be an absence of natural background noise when playing through the **ADR** segments.

Know How to EQ

Much like how cameras all have their own distinct looks to them, microphones all have their own characteristics and sounds. It's highly unlikely that the mic that's being used to record your **ADR** is a perfect match for the mic that you were using on set, so you will notice some differences in audio quality right off the bat.

For instance, you may find that your location audio has more high end (treble), while your **ADR** recording is more bass heavy. This can easily be adjusted and compensated for with a little bit of EQ work, which can go a very long way in helping the different recordings to blend together.

Start by getting your basic levels where they need to be so that all of your tracks match at least from a gain standpoint. Then adjust your highs, mids, and lows on both the source audio and the **ADR** recordings to try to find a good happy middle ground. Once you've found the right balance, the majority of the heavy lifting is done. If you'd like a deeper look at EQ basics, check out the post *Basic Guide to Understanding EQ* over at B&H. It isn't a software-specific approach to EQ, rather it's a general look at the science behind the process.

Reverb Matters

One of the other critical elements to take into account when dealing with **ADR** material is the lack of reverb. Assuming you've recorded in a professional soundproofed studio, your source **ADR** tracks will have little to no reverb at all. In contrast, depending on where you shot your original footage — it is very likely to have at least some degree of reverb.

Imagine you shot a scene in a cathedral with a huge amount of reverb in it, and then attempted to place in some **ADR** tracks to replace a few lines. Obviously, the sound quality would be extremely different even if room tone had been added and a proper EQ was completed. Ultimately the difference would probably be a direct result of reverb (or lack thereof).

Always be sure to not only apply reverb in your editing system, but also take the time to fine tune it so that it matches with your location audio as closely as possible. Reverb can literally come in all shapes and sizes, so you need to ensure you are taking enough time to not only select the right effect, but also fine-tune the settings if you want to get the most realistic and flawless results.

September 6th
Audio Resources for Filmmakers

These online resources will help filmmakers get the best results when working with audio!

Sound production is a big part of filmmaking/video production that is often overlooked. Whether you are making films, documentaries, corporate communications or wedding videos, the following resources will help you **better understand audio** and get better results!

1. FilmSound.org

FilmSound has a helpful FAQ on **Audio Post Production**, as well as articles from 3 time Oscar winning video and sound editor Walter Murch (Apocalypse Now, English Patient, Cold Mountain). The site is geared toward **sound editing and design in feature film production** and features excellent resources for those looking to get started in the business.

2. Tips for Making Your Film Sound Great

These tips from the pros at Skywalker Sound were taken from a recent Sundance Film Festival panel on **successful sound design**. Discover some of the most common sound design mistakes filmmakers make, and how to avoid them. As a bonus they share their top picks for sound design from film history.

3. Videomaker "Audio How To"

Although Videomaker is perhaps best known for their coverage of production and post, they offer a ton of info on **sound design for filmmakers** as well. Covering everything from quick tips to reviews of the latest audio gear, be sure to check out their frequently updated audio "How To" section.

4. Recording Awesome Location Sound

These tips from LAvideoFilmmaker.com **will help you record better location sound** for your project. Specifics covered include how to choose the best mic, optimal microphone placement, recording ambient sound and basic tips for working with audio in post. While you're on the site be sure to subscribe to their FREE email newsletter on filmmaking tips.

5. Audio for Film

If you're new to **filmmaking or sound design**, these basics from MicroFilmmaker are a great primer. In this post, you'll learn the 3 components of a solid soundtrack (dialog, sound effects and music), as well as some useful info on creating a successful sound mix.

6. Audio Tips for Video Editors

All too often, audio work is cast aside in post-production in favor of spending more time on achieving impressive visuals. This is a crucial mistake. In this post, you'll pick up a few tips for **optimizing your audio workflow** *during* your video edit. Picking the right audio monitors (speakers), basic sound mixing and essential audio effects are all covered.

7. Location Sound/Audio Post Forum

DVX User is best known as an active camera and filmmaking community, but they also have a forum for **Location Sound/Post Audio**. Start with the "Audio 101" thread which covers common audio filmmaking questions. If you have a specific audio question be sure to post it in the forum!

8. Sound Series by Clinton Harn

Filmmaker and audio pro Clinton Harn teamed up with Zacuto for a info-filled blog series on audio *for* video. Topics covered include picking the right mic (and the differences between mics), capturing sound in cars and creating a working budget for **sound recording and design**.

9. Mike Russell Adobe Audition Tutorials

Mike Russell's free Adobe Audition tutorials teach you practical skills (noise reduction, sweetening audio). Anyone using a **Adobe based post production workflow** can seriously benefit from his often-updated YouTube channel. Also, be sure to check out his 5 free presets (email) to use in Audition. As an example, check out his video below on recording **high quality voiceovers** in Adobe Audition:

10. NoFilmSchool – Audio with a Crew of 1

NoFilmSchool is a wealth of information for filmmakers and video pros. In a recent post, they tackled the task of **recording audio** as a one-person crew. Lots of good info here about recording audio with DSLRs to external recorders and mic placement.

September 7th
Audio Tips and Tricks: Removing Echo and Reverb

Use these audio tips (and a couple of plugins) to easily remove reverb and echo from dialogue.

Recording sound dialogue can prove challenging on set. Sometimes we find ourselves **sacrificing ideal audio conditions for a beautiful shot**. Whatever the case, we've all come across dialogue audio recorded with too much **natural reverb present** within the room.

If budget and time allows, **ADR** is the higher-quality option to replace your cavernous dialogue recording. Though as filmmakers often know, the **best option isn't always the most realistic in completing your project.**

In any case, there are a few great **plugins** (compatible with Adobe Audition, Premiere Pro, and most audio/video editing software) that can actually "de-verb" your dialogue audio.

Don't want to buy them? All of these plugins have trial-versions you can try out for free. Let's take a look below:

- **Acon Digital DeVerberate** ($99.90)

- **SPL De-Verb** ($59.00)
- **iZotope RX4** ($1,200)

Here's a video tutorial from Curtis Judd of Learn Light and Sound that covers the removal of echo and reverb from dialogue audio using two of the above plugins: **Acon Digital DeVerberate** and **SPL De-Verb**. After the video, we'll look at the steps Judd took in his process.

Acon Digital DeVerberate Step-by-Step Tutorial

1. Open the plugin and select **reduce room reverb** from the preset menu. **Listen** to the dialogue audio with and without the plugin engaged.

2. Next, adjust the **reverb time** (the time it takes for the original source sound to reflect off of the walls and come back to the microphone) in the **source reverb settings** box. As a general rule of thumb, larger rooms require a greater amount of reverb time (in seconds). Enable the **difference monitoring** box. This allows you to hear the amount of reverb the plugin will be filtering from your dialogue audio. Adjust the **reverb time** parameter gradually while playing back the audio. Adjust until you **begin to hear only the reverb from the dialogue**.

3. Uncheck **difference monitoring** to hear what effect the plugin has on the dialogue. Next, adjust the **reverb level (dB)** parameter (the amount of reverb to reduce/add) balancing between **reverb removal and avoiding artifacts**.

4. Although your dialogue audio should be sounding pretty good at this point, there may be some artifacts in the audio from the reverb reduction. Next, we will use the **spectral smoothing** parameter to reduce these artifacts. Use this parameter carefully as **higher values may bring back some reverb**.

SPL De-Verb Step-by-Step Tutorial

1. Upon opening, you will find this plugin has a very simple interface with only two parameters: **reverb reduction**, and **output gain**. Select the preset titled **Less Room – more direct** from the preset selection menu.

2. Adjust the **reverb reduction** parameter until you cancel out most of the reflections, resulting in **dry and direct dialogue**. As you turn the parameter **counter-clockwise** you will hear more reverb reduction.

September 8th
Audio Tips for DSLR Filmmakers

Treating audio as an afterthought is a huge mistake. Up your sound game with these audio tips for DSLR filmmakers!

Although many filmmakers know just how critical **great audio** is with regards to the success of a film project, it's still one of the most overlooked aspects of the filmmaking process. This is unfortunate, as poor sound quality can hinder all of the other elements that we work so tirelessly on. In the end, nothing else matters **if the sound quality is poor.**

Whether it be **distracting background noises** that have been picked up (such as wind or cars passing by), or **poorly recorded dialogue**, these issues greatly affect the overall viewing experience and absolutely must be dealt with in order to achieve any sort of success with a film project.

So for those of you **DSLR filmmakers** out there that are looking to **up your game with regards to audio**, here are a few key tips to get you started.

Don't rely on your DSLR

First and foremost, you need to remember that just because the picture quality on your DSLR may be great doesn't necessarily mean the sound quality is great too. The fact of the matter is, **DSLRs are not meant designed to capture professional quality audio** – no matter how many manual controls or functions they may have. The internal limitations of your DSLR can never be compensated for by using better external devices (such as a high quality shotgun mic) as **the camera's limitations will always be the bottleneck** as far as sound quality goes.

Just because your DSLR has manual control over levels or a headphone jack doesn't mean that it's going to record great audio. It simply means that it's somewhat competent at recording audio in a pinch or can be used to record reference audio. For professional sound quality, **always use an external device** (whether it be as simple as a Zoom H6, or a more complex mixer/recorder) in order to achieve professional level sound.

Scout Locations

Do your field research! This is by far **the cheapest method for achieving great sound** available to you as a filmmaker. It costs you absolutely nothing to devote a few days during pre-production to go to your various locations and do some audio tests. You might feel that this isn't necessary, but when you get to set and realize that you are shooting in the middle of a flight path, **you're going to wish you scouted that location properly.**

The scout itself can be very simple. Just go to your location at approximately the same time of day that you are going to shoot and **start looking for red flags.** If you're shooting on a rooftop, make sure the wind isn't out of control. If you're in a field, be aware of the background noise created by crickets, birds, and other wildlife. If possible, **bring your sound recordist with you** and actually do tests with your equipment to see what noises you're picking up – if any.

Like I said, doing this **costs you nothing but a bit of time upfront,** and it could potentially save you a ton of time and headaches both on set and in the ProTools suite.

Always Record Room Tone

For those that aren't familiar with the term, "room tone" is essentially the ambient sound of a room. **Room tone is always recorded on professional sets** so that the audio editor has scene-specific background noise to work with if he or she needs to patch over any sound issues in their ProTools session. Location audio professionals will typically **record room tone for every single location** they are covering in order to pick up the **general hum and subtle noises** that are present in every room. For example, if you were to record room tone in a 'silent' kitchen, you would inevitably pick up the sound of the refrigerator buzzing, maybe a door creaking in the background, a slight hum from the lights on in the room, etc.

Room tone is usually **recorded at the end of every scene for 30-60 seconds** while the entire cast and crew stands silently, or clears the room. Why is this important to your sound quality as whole? As I touched on above, in post-production, you typically **use room tone to help blend together multiple takes of audio** so that there is a consistent bed of sound that seamlessly melds together all of the dialogue and ADR tracks.

You can also use room tone to **match ambient sounds when you shoot multiple takes of the same scene** and there are differences in the background noise. For example, if in one take the air conditioner goes on and in another it turns off, you will want to use room tone (of the air conditioner on) to keep the sound of it present in the entire scene. Here's a video from thesubstream that covers the ins and outs of recording room tone.

Final Thoughts

For top-tier production value when making a film, **it's vital that you pay just as close attention to your film's audio needs as you do its visual needs.** If you can be one of the few micro-budget filmmakers that actually prioritizes sound, you will certainly reap the benefits of going the extra mile.

Pristine sound adds a whole other dimension to your film and ups the production value in ways that the camera never will be able to. Understanding your cameras capabilities, doing sound tests in each of your locations, and recording room tone for every scene are three of the simplest things you can do to vastly improve your film's sound quality.

September 9th

Fundamentals of the Boom Operator and Location Mic Techniques

The boom operator employs the technique of suspending a microphone above a subject allowing for versatility and movement of the talent and operator while retaining excellent audio quality.

The #1 rule to recording professional dialogue on location is getting the **microphone as close to the talent's mouth as possible** while maintaining good frequency response. To get optical microphone placement, one needs to **block the set** before shooting begins. With the help of the cinematographer and director, the boom operator should know exactly what camera and actor movements are taking place. The process of blocking the set eliminates the boom entering the camera frame, boom pole shadows, and uncoordinated movements.

Boom Operator Equipment

The boom pole allows you to place the microphone above any given subject while staying out of the camera frame. Usually made out of a lightweight carbon fiber or aluminum, there are varying lengths of boom poles. **Professional boom poles will extend to a maximum of 12 to 20 feet.**

The shock mount consisting of elastic bands or dense rubber attaches the microphone at the end of the boom pole. This reduces low-frequency rumble from the boom operator's hands and fingers, sudden movements in position, or the XLR cable against the outside of the pole.

The microphone, obviously the most important aspect in location shooting. Depending on where you're shooting (indoors or outdoors), there are usually two types of hyper-cardioid microphones used by professional boom operators: **Shotgun mics and short hyper-cardioid mics.**

Shotgun mics are commonly used outdoors where there is a considerable amount of ambient background noise. The long slits in the barrel help reject mid and high frequencies, though not all low frequencies are rejected (use a low-cut filter). One drawback to longer shotguns is that they are so directional in their narrow pickup pattern, natural qualities of a source such as the human voice are lost due to the lack of exterior background reflections from the source. **They are the ideal microphone for noisy, outdoor situations.** *Right image is a typical shotgun frequency pickup pattern.*

Small diaphragm hyper-cardioid microphones are less dramatic in their rear and side frequency attenuations and rejections, delivering a natural quality from a sound source. The drawback being the lack of rejection; considerable background noise is audible. A short shotgun wouldn't be ideal in an environment with loud traffic, winds, crowds, etc. **When indoors and in quieter environments, they are the ideal choice.**

Booming from Overhead

Suspend the microphone above and slightly before the talent, either placed in the center of multiple actors or angled slightly towards whoever is delivering dialogue. **Because the microphone is closer to the head, booming from overhead is an industry favored technique.** Vocal presence is important to a clean recording. **When booming from overhead, the mix between all the actors delivering dialogue sounds more natural, meaning less mixing in post-production.**

Booming from Below

Place the microphone slightly ahead and below the talent, angling the mic directly at the source of the sound. This technique can be ideal for small spaces or limited workspace. **Booming from below is not as ideal as booming from overhead because of added bass frequencies coming from the chest cavity.** If the actor is wearing noisy jewelry or is making noise with their hands, perspective may also be skewed from the sound effect appearing louder. That said, **booming from below can be effective in certain situations.**

Windscreens

The big furry balls and zeppelins you see are all wind screens of some type: microphone covers that attenuate wind noise. This synthetic acoustic fur, typically referred to as a "dead cat" has traditionally been used to reject wind noise. Rycote has developed a new windscreen technology using the new 3D-Tex material, which improves wind attenuation. Let's take a look at three of the most popular microphone wind screens currently on the market:

1. Rycote Super-Softie

This new slip-on windscreen incorporates the new 3D-Tex material which they claim is better then traditional fur. The "ice-cream cone" shape and design maximizes dead space surrounding the microphone, making it an aerodynamic solution with no parallel sides. With sizes from 12 cm – 18 cm, the Rycote Super-Softie retails at $135.

2. Rycote Baby Ball

This mini ball zeppelin for small diaphragm condenser microphones, provides ample dead space around the capsule. A classic design, this type of mini ball zeppelin has been used in studio sets around the world. Also at a reasonable $135, this is a trusted investment.

3. RØDE Blimp

The new RØDE Blimp is now one of the lightest modular windshield and suspension systems on the market. At $299, this zeppelin-style windshield fits any RØDE or third party shotgun microphone. The fur windscreen included, this should be in the arsenal of every boom operator.

September 10th
Get Great Location Audio When Working as a One-Man Band

There's no substitute for having a sound recordist on your crew, but there may be times where you need to multi-task and record audio yourself. These tips will show you how to do it right.

We all know that audio is just as important (if not more important) than video when it comes to **the audience experience.** Audio is much less forgiving than video, which is why a great looking film with poor audio will never be received as well as a mediocre looking film with great audio. It all comes down to how our senses react to the content we perceive.

Even so, many of us make the mistake of neglecting audio – especially on really small shoots. Personally, speaking, even though most of my shoots have full crews (including an audio team), I also have many shoots were **I'm working as a one man band.** In the latter scenario, I'm typically shooting, directing and rolling audio all at once, which can be a real challenge. Through a lot of trial and error (and many big mistakes along the way), I've managed to develop some techniques that work really well for me when shooting under these conditions. Like many of you reading this, I am not a **professional sound recordist**, but that doesn't mean I can't employ the right techniques to capture professional quality audio.

Here are three fundamentals that you should always follow when **recording audio without a boom op.**

1. Use a Lav and Boom

Even though you might not always have the luxury of working with a dedicated **location audio recordist** on set, you can still emulate their workflow to ensure you're getting the best results. Most sound recordists prefer to have two mics covering their talent: **a boom and a lav.** The boom mic is usually preferable as it typically generates the cleanest sound and doesn't run the risk of getting muffled or hit the way a wireless lav mic will.

At the same time, **a lav is critical to use simultaneously.** Some shooting conditions won't allow you to get the boom as close to your talent as you would like, or there may be more than one character speaking at once, and the boom is unable to cover both effectively. The bottom line is that **using two mics gives you a safety net.** If there's an issue with one, the other is a great backup.

Typically on set, I'll have my boom mic set up on a stand and the lav mic hidden under the clothing of my talent. Both are running into my **Zoom H6 recorder**, and in post I'll choose between the two tracks depending on the specifics of the scene in question.

2. Always Go Manual

Whether you're recording audio straight to your camera or using **a dedicated recorder** (such as a Zoom or Tascam) you're going to want to set your levels manually. This is one of the most common mistakes that inexperienced filmmakers make on set, which results in really awful sounding amateur audio.

When your levels are set automatically, the quality of your recordings is diminished substantially. Automated systems are constantly boosting and reducing their levels in an attempt to catch up with the variances in levels being recorded — but no system works perfectly, and there are always issues. One example is the **hissing sound that'll occur in between lines of dialogue.**

When nothing is being spoken in the scene you're shooting, the automated levels will boost up really high to compensate, and you'll be left with a lot of white noise. And even though you may be able to correct this in post to some degree, it'll never sound the same. When your talent starts speaking (and breaks the silence) the levels will drop very quickly and you end up with a **strange audio artifact** that just doesn't sound professional.

The solution to all this, of course, is to set your levels manually. Simply run a few lines with your talent before you start recording and **make sure that the levels aren't peaking.** Now you'll have a consistent result throughout your entire take, and can rest assured that you won't generate any of those strange artifacts associated with auto-levels.

3. Record A Backup Track

When you're working as a one man band, you don't have the luxury of **monitoring your audio** as closely as you would if were your sole task. In many cases you're going to be spread pretty thin while checking your focus, directing your talent, and handling all sorts of other things on set, which means you're prone to error on every front. Audio is no exception.

One of the most common issues that you'll run into when working this way (as it relates to audio), is improperly set levels. We've already gone over why it's so important to record your audio manually, but the downside to manual audio is that your recordings are **prone to peaking.** For example, your actors may have run their lines and sounded great during your test (and level setting), but then in the scene they get much louder or one of them screams. Now all of a sudden your levels are peaking like crazy, and you might not even notice since you're so bogged down handling other aspects of the shoot.

The solution to this potential problem is to **always record a backup track.** Many audio recording devices will allow you to record a safety track (usually -20db lower than your regular track), so that in situations like this, you can pull clean audio from your backup track to patch over any moments that peak. You also might have the option (depending on your setup) to split your audio and record to two different devices – let's say your camera, and an external recorder – each set to different levels. The method that you use isn't the important part, what really matters is **creating a safety net for yourself to fall back on** in case of any technical issues.

September 11th
How to Clean up Audio in Premiere Pro in 30 Seconds

Need to get good audio fast? Just follow these quick steps in Premiere Pro and Audition.

A video is only as strong as the audio supporting it. But if you're in a pinch, you may not have the time to perfectly finesse your audio. Let's take a look at how to quickly fix your audio in **Premiere Pro** — with a little help from Adobe Audition.

1. Send to Audition

No matter your individual circumstances, if you have unneeded background noise in your audio, the best tool to clean it up is the *Noise Print* feature in Adobe Audition.

Luckily for you, if you're editing with **Premiere Pro**, you should have Audition already installed on your computer. To send an audio clip to Audition, simply right click on the track and select *Edit Clip in Adobe Audition.*

2. Capture Noise Print

The first thing you need to do before you apply the *Noise Print* effect is capture your background noise without the vocal parts. You can do this by selecting a voiceless area in your track with the

Time Selection Tool. Play your track to make sure you've selected only background noise and no voice.

Now it's time to capture the background noise. To do so, simply navigate to *Effects>Noise Reduction>Capture Noise Print* or hit *Shift+P*. Your background noise is now saved into Audition.

3. Apply Noise Print

After you've captured the *Noise Print*, it's time to take the noise print out of your original audio clip. First you will need to deselect your noise print area. To do this, click anywhere in your timeline with the *Time Selection Tool* selected. Now navigate to *Effects>Noise Reduction>Noise Reduction*. A window will pop up that looks like this:

You'll see two important effects:

- **Noise Reduction** — the amount of noise that will be reduced.
- **Reduce By** — the number of decibels that the noise will be reduced.

The best way to ensure that your audio will sound the best is to adjust each parameter by hand. But if you're in a hurry, just set *Noise Reduction to 50%* and *Reduce By to 15db*. After you've set your noise print levels select *Apply*.

4. Send to Premiere

Now it's time to go back to Premiere, but first you will need to save your audio out of Audition. Simply hit *Command+S* and your audio will be automatically saved and replaced in your **Premiere Pro** timeline.

5. Vocal Enhancer

Now that you've taken out most of your background noise, it's time to enhance the vocals. Grab the *Vocal Enhancer* effect in your effects panel and drag it onto your audio clip. You will need to adjust the vocal enhancer for your subject.

Navigate to the *Effects Control panel* and select the dropdown arrow under *Vocal Enhancer* until you see the custom setup option. Click the *Edit* button. You will see a box that pops up. *Select Male or Female,* depending on your subject.

6. Set All Peaks

Now that your audio is sounding great, it's time to level it for your individual production. To do this, simply *right click on the audio* and select *Audio Gain*. Select *Normalize All Peaks* and *set the level to -6db*. You should now have decent audio that's perfect for corporate videos, quick commercials, or news packages.

September 12th

How to Pick the Best Video Production Mic

Sound is vitally important to any film or video production. Here are some things to consider before picking out your video production mics.

Capturing quality audio is incredibly important to your film or video. But in order to capture that sound, you need to have **quality production mics** to go with your recording device. Picking the right **production mic** for the job isn't always easy though. There are a lot of questions you need to ask yourself before you make that purchase. Let's go through some of those questions and see if we can help you find the right **production mic** for your needs.

1. What Will the Mic Be Used For?

The most important question you need to ask yourself is: **what am I using this mic for?** Different productions and scenes call for different mics, so it's really important to know what the situation is before you purchase your mic. Let's look at the three major options for mics and what part of the production they best fit into.

Shotgun Mics

Shotgun mics are good for several things on a production set. They get their name from the way they record sound. You point the mic at what you want to capture and it not only gets this sound, but it grabs surrounding sound. You can use shotgun mics to capture the dialogue of a scene or the sound details of a scene. They are also used quite often for capturing foley sounds and ambient room tone. While shotgun mics are extremely good in spaces, they tend to pick up more sound than you need for dialogue. With that in mind, your best bet is to utilize a shotgun mic in conjunction with a lav.

- The Rode NTG3
- Sennheiser MKH416
- Audio-Technica AT8035

Lav Mics

A lavalier mic (or lapel mic) is the gold-standard mic for capturing dialogue. These mics capture incredible audio when conducting an interview for television, documentary film, or industrial video. Lavs come in a wired version and a wireless version, with both versions being small enough to hide beneath the collar of a shirt or on the underside of a jacket. You'll want to get these mics as close to the center of the chest as possible. Lavs are light enough that a little gaffer tape will be all you need to stick the mic under your subject's shirt. Just remember to be courteous and professional when applying a lav mic.

- Sennheiser ME 2
- Shure WL185
- Sony ECM44BC

Video Mics

Video mics are a type of shotgun mic, but these particular mics aren't really for capturing the final audio for a production. They connect straight to the camera in order to capture scratch-track audio that will allow your editor to easily sync the video and high-end sound together in post.

- Rode Video Mic

- Sennheiser MKE 400
- Shure VP83F

Once you know what your production needs are, you can begin searching for mics — but there are just a few more questions to ask before you make your purchase. Before we get to those questions, let's check out this video from Film Riot where Ryan Connolly gives us some advice on mics for production.

2. What's the Size of Your Production and Budget?

Answering this question will go a long way in determining what you need and what you can afford. No matter if you're working with a large budget or an indie budget, there are options for you to get quality **production mics** to capture your audio. Just be wary of breaking the bank as Film Shortage recently pointed out.

If your camera costs a couple hundred then it's not really worth buying a microphone that sets you back a couple of grand, as the quality of the two won't match up.

The key here is to be really sure that you set a budget for yourself and stick to it. Audio equipment can get expensive without you realizing it, so make sure the **production mic** you're selecting will do the job you need it to do. Again, let's check out this video from Ryan Connolly and Film Riot as he runs through specific **production mics**.

3. Be Mindful of Pickup Pattern

Pickup pattern is how well a microphone hears different sounds from different directions. Depending on what you're recording, you'll want to look at the pickup pattern before making a determination on what **production mic** to purchase. Knowing the directional response of your mic will help you tremendously when going into production. Let's go over those pickup patterns and help you learn what mics are what.

Omnidirectional

Omni mics are beasts. They capture audio in a circular pattern, which means they are pulling sound from all directions. Because these mics are pretty much a catch-all mic, they're often used as the built-in microphone for most cameras. You can also use a standalone omni mic when you need to cast a wide audio net. Its ability to capture a wide range of audio has made it a favorite to documentary filmmakers who want to capture wide audio during observational moments. There are also some lavalier mics that are omnidirectional as well.

Bidirectional

Bidirectional mics are great mics to use when needing to capture ADR (automated dialogue replacement). The directional pattern for these mics comes from the left and right side, while the range from top and bottom is minimal. Other than ADR for film and animation, these type of mics are used quite often in music recordings.

Unidirectional

When you think unidirectional mics, you can think shotgun mics. As discussed above, you point the mic at what you want to capture and it not only gets this sound, but it grabs surrounding sound. These mics are often used for capturing production audio on set and for recording foley and ambient sound as well.

Cardioid/Hypercardioid

Cardioid mics make up the majority of the handheld mics that we use. They capture sound in a odd pattern, which is usually described as being heart-shaped. These types of mics are great for capturing vocals and come in many different shapes and sizes, from the standard mics for singers to lapel mics used for interview dialogue. For an in-depth look at each one of these pickup patterns, let's check out this great overview from Videomaker.

4. There Is No Such Thing as a One Mic Shoot

Well, okay. *Technically* there is. But this is something I learned early in my career: no matter if you're a big-budget filmmaker or an independent videographer, you'll want to capture dual audio. This could be as easy as running a video mic in conjunction with a shotgun mic. As we mentioned above, this will allow you to capture scratch-track audio and pro audio for final editing.

Just remember that you want to capture the best audio you can. Great audio will go a long way toward masking a lot of mistakes. As Scary Cow points out in an article on recording amazing audio for low-budget productions:

Horrible picture can be passed off as "style" when accompanied by perfect audio, but poorly recorded and mixed audio will make a great picture seem amateurish and poorly-executed.

So again, be sure to use all options available at your disposal. Redundancy is a good thing when talking about production audio. don't just slap a lav on the talent. Also use a shotgun mic on a boom pole to get an extra layer. If your camera doesn't capture scratch-track audio, connect a mic to it. Three solutions for one sequence. It sounds like overkill, but when the time comes to edit the film, the editor has a lot of flexibility. This is a good thing.

5. What Mic Accessories Do You Need?

Just getting a **video production mic** alone will get you rolling, but you're going to need a few accessories to achieve optimal quality. Here are a few items that will help in the long run.

Shotgun Mic Accessories

Shotgun mics alone aren't going to get you the quality audio you want. One of the first things that you'll want to grab is a quality boom pole. Then you'll want to protect your mic, so look at getting either a Rode Blimp or a standard windscreen. The Blimps usually come with a pistol grip and shockmount. If they don't, you'll want those as well. K-Tek also makes a fantastic collapsable boom pole that's more flexible than the standard pole.

- Boom Pole
- Rode Blimp
- Dead Cat Windscreen

- Pistol Grip
- Shockmount

Lavalier Mic Accessories

Lavalier mics don't have as many accessories as shotgun mics, but there are a few things that are absolutely necessary to have before you record. At some point you're likely going to need to go from a mini 3.5mm adapter to an XLR male adapter. Your lavalier mic will more than likely come with its own windscreens and clips, but trust me… at some point these are going to just get up and walk away. Invest in extras. Lastly, you'll want some trusty gaffer tape. This comes in handy when your wanting to mic up your talent with a lav mic.

- Mini to XLR Cable Adapter
- Windscreens
- Alligator Clips
- Gaffer Tape

September 13th
How to Set Audio Levels for Video

Bad sound can easily ruin good footage. Use these tips when it comes time to set audio levels for video and film projects.

As a filmmaker and videographer, you probably spend a lot of time trying to get the most beautiful shot possible on set. Then when you sit down to edit the video, more time is spent color correcting and grading. Then it's time to move on to exporting, where you pick the perfect codec that will **output good colors** while minimizing compression.

However, when it comes to audio there's usually not much more effort put into it than simply, "sounds good".

Audio is probably the most **overlooked and under-appreciated aspect** of the filmmaking process. Audiences can forgive subpar cinematography, but subpar audio will make even the most loyal audiences disengaged. There seems to be a lot of misinformation out there about the correct way to level audio in videos, so let's take a look at how to correctly **set audio levels for video** in the modern industry.

Correct Audio Levels

There's a lot of debate online about **the right way to level audio**, but there's one thing that everyone can agree on: **you should never go above 0db**. Even though your NLE may allow you to raise your audio levels all the way up to 6db, it's advised by virtually everyone that you should keep your audio below 0db. This is because your audio will begin to clip after 0db, resulting in horrible distortion.

Think about it as a ceiling. As soon as your audio peaks and hits the ceiling, **it will begin to get distorted.** This is why explosions in hollywood movies sound awesome and explosions in bad YouTube videos sound like muffled junk. Most major NLEs and audio editing software will have **red indicators** pop up anytime your audio goes above 0. If you're getting this warning, then your audio is too loud. For safety, **no peaks should be above -6db.**

Most video editors agree that the overall audio level of your audio mix (all of your audio combined) should normalized **between -10db to -20db**. I personally level my videos around -12db with occasional peaks to -8db. The trick here is to stay away from 0db as best you can. Experts differ on the exact numbers — because there are no exact numbers. Editing audio is a lot like editing video. At the end of the day, **your ears should be your guides if you've adhered to the technical rules.**

Some people say that if you are creating a video for the web, then you should get closer to 0db… but it all depends on the video you are producing. If you're creating a film, you might want to have more range between your average mix level and your peaks. If you're doing a simple web commercial, it might make more sense to have less range and a higher overall average level. You'll figure out what works for you over time.

Recommended Levels

Here's a few of my recommended level suggestions.

- **Overall Mix Level:** -10db to -14db
- **Dialogue:** -12db to -15db
- **Music:** -18db to -22db
- **Sound Effects:** -10db to -20db with occasional spikes up to -8db.

These recommendations are a little on the quiet side when compared to some industry experts, but I find it much better for an audience to turn up the volume than run the risk of peaking or distortion.

Before you finalize your film or video, take off your fancy studio headphones and **go play your video on the platform in which your audience will be watching it.** For example, if you're working on a TV commercial, try watching your video on a TV to see how it sounds. It's not uncommon for music producers to listen to their tracks in a car before they sign off on distribution. The same should be true for you. Whether it's on a laptop, iPhone, or TV, listen to your video on the medium in which your audience will be watching and you'll quickly find audio quirks.

It should also be noted that film distributors and TV broadcasters often have their own standards for audio levels, so you should absolutely consult with them before setting your audio levels. In NTSC countries, for example, peak audio levels must not exceed -10db with occasional -8db spikes, whereas PAL countries must not exceed -9db.

Do I Need to Use Bars and Tone?

You've probably seen **color bars** on a local TV station or at the beginning of an old tape recording. **Bars and tone** are used to calibrate a system to optimally playback your video or film. Bars are for color, so we'll cover those in another article. Tone, however, exclusively deals with audio and **it's really simple to understand.** Tone is just a reference engineers use to correctly output your video at the appropriate level. And it sounds like one long beep.

Some people say that tone should be set to the average loudness of your video, but this is only an opinion. In fact, there is no set-in-stone standard for the loudness at which tone should be set it all depends on the broadcasters preferences. For example FCPX's tone default is -12db and Premiere Pro's is -20db. The trick is to simply **keep your tone decibels between -6db and -24db.** Truthfully, in most circumstances, you probably won't even need to put bars and tone at the start of your video.

Good Audio is More Than Levels

While levels do play a big part when it comes to creating professional audio, there's a lot more that needs to be considered and adjusted to get the best audio possible. Effects like compressors, limiters, noise reducers, and (most importantly) EQ will all help contribute to a well balanced and professional sounding video.

September 14th
How to Turn a Closet into a DIY Sound Booth

Do you need high-quality voice-over on a limited budget? No problem. Here's how you can turn your closet into a DIY sound booth.

There will likely come a time when audio needs to be performed beyond what was captured on set or location. This additional audio comes in many forms: **a soundtrack, sound effects, voice-over, narration, and even ADR.** Usually the soundtrack and sound effects are purchased for your project or created by sound specialists. But when it comes to voice-over and ADR, most filmmakers or video producers are on their own.

While you can rent time in a studio space to record audio in a sound booth, the cost to use such spaces can be detrimental to a budget. In order to soften the financial blow, many filmmakers and video producers capture the voice-over and ADR on their own. The problem, however, is still the need for a space to record this audio. Luckily, most of us have closet space available.

Let's see what's needed to turn a closet into your very own **DIY sound booth.**

1. The Space

The very first thing you need is space. You can use a hall closet, linen closet, or pantry for this space. **A closet beneath stairs is a great place to start as well.** No need for anything huge, just enough space to fit one person comfortably.

2. Make Spatial Adjustments

Once the space has been decided upon and cleared of all clutter, you'll likely need to make some adjustments. **You may have to remove shelving or racks in order to maximize the space.** You definitely want your surfaces to be flat for the next step: sound proofing.

Also, don't forget to add a light if there isn't one already in the closet. **Lighting is essential.** Power could be a necessity for you as well, depending on what you'll use the space for beyond just capturing vocal tracks. So, be aware of where your outlets are. If there are no outlets in your closet, which is probably the case, then you'll want to contact a licensed electrician to aid you with this part of the adjustment.

3. Soundproof the Space

Now that you've picked your space, made some spatial adjustments, and smoothed out the wall surface, it's time to move onto the soundproofing part of the project.

One soundproofing solution is **a blanket**. These can be either a sound blanket or a packing blanket that you can purchase at many hardware stores. Another solution would be to **purchase egg crate foam**. You can easily find this at most department stores for a very minimal price. Finally, there are **acoustic panels** and professional sound foam. Both of these options will be a bit more pricey, unless you build your own panels.

Once you purchase any of these solutions, you'll want to either use tacks, nails, or adhesive to apply them to the walls, ceiling, and the door of the closet. If your closet space has hardwood flooring, purchase a small rug or section of carpet to place on the floor. For vocals, you'll want to cover as much surface area as possible. For more *"acoustic"* needs, leave some surface area visible.

4. Gather Your Equipment

Now that your space has been soundproofed, make sure you have the right equipment. For the inside of your closet, you'll need a mic, mic stand, pop shield, XLR cable, music stand, stool, and headphones. Once you have these pieces of equipment in place, you need to make sure that they can reach the mixer or interface, so cable extensions may be a necessity.

Remember to listen to your equipment in the space before you finalize anything. Sometimes you may find that only covering 70% of the closet in foam will work perfectly for you. So run tests and record some vocals and listen to the playback. If you're happy with the sound, then you're good to begin recording professionally.

5. No Closet, No Problem

What if you desperately need a sound booth but just don't have any available closet space at all? Well, fear not... a sound booth doesn't have to be a closet specifically. All you need is four walls (one with a door) and a ceiling.

There are pre-built sound booths available out there that work perfectly. However, if you're the type of person that likes to build and customize, then by all means get started.

If you just don't have the time or resources to build a large scale sound booth, then a possible solution is purchasing or making a small portable sound booth. These can usually get the job done if you're just needing some quick vocal work. They can be built or bought pre-built for a fairly inexpensive price.

September 15th
On-Location Audio – 3 Tricks Every Filmmaker & Sound Person Should Know

Reducing background buzz and hum when recording location sound can be a challenge! Follow these 3 simple tips to get cleaner location sound on your next shoot.

Want to drive yourself crazy? Try removing **audio buzz or hum** during video editing. Isolating **bad audio frequencies** without distorting dialogue, or intentional on-camera sound, can be a frustrating challenge.

It's always best to get the cleanest **on-location sound**. You'll save yourself time in post-production and will likely have a better sounding product then if you were to attempt a post-production fix.

3 common sources for **on-location background buzz and hum** are:

- Heating, Ventilation and Air Conditioning Systems
- Lighting
- Refrigerators

The following **on-location sound tips** will address each of these problem sources and how to minimize their effect on your audio.

Play Weatherman

A/C units may be the #1 culprit for picking up **bad background audio**. They rumble, hum and can really muddy up an audio track. To top it off, they're erratic…turning on and off at random intervals (leading to irksome **shot inconsistencies**). The only way to insure that you don't get

A/C hum is to kill the system while you're shooting. BUT, nobody likes burning up under hot production lighting...

TRICK: As soon as you arrive on set (figure, you're going to arrive about an hour or more early to setup lighting, shots, etc.) radically adjust the heater or A/C unit. Let the unit overcompensate. If it's hot out, turn the air conditioner on blast. Freeze the room. In cold weather do the opposite. Then, when you're ready to start rolling, turn off the unit. This trick will buy some time where the talent and crew aren't miserably uncomfortable on set.

Blankets & A Step Stool

So what about the times when you can't control the A/C unit? Big office buildings are notorious for this...

TRICK: You can soften the **A/C unit hum** by covering up vents with blankets. Professional sound blankets are ideal, but if you're on a budget or in a pinch, even your standard blanket or comforter could be a satisfactory replacement. The step stool allows you to access high or hard to reach vents.

If you have **buzzy ballasts** from location lighting, obviously the first line of attack is to turn them off. Lighting that stays on all the time (such as emergency lighting) may require you to physically remove the bulb while shooting. The step stool also aids with this.

Freeze the Keys

Refrigerators can't be easily moved out of a location, so it's best just to **turn the power off** while rolling on-set. With the door shut, a refrigerator can stay cool for a while...but you don't want to forget to turn it back on!

TRICK: Remember to power it back on before leaving the set by **placing your keys in the refrigerator when you unplug it** (tip from MacProVideo.com). There's no quicker way to get banned from a location than to let a refrigerator full of food spoil!

For on-location audio success, follow these tips for **reducing background buzz and hum noise** before the cameras ever start rolling!

September 16th
Scoring Your Film Project for Success

If you're interested in understanding more about the dark art of film score composition check out these great resources to help you make better films.

Understanding what a film composer does, **how best to work with your film score and how to create well mixed film soundtracks** (bringing together both the sound design and the score) is crucial to creating the other 60% of your film – the sound. In this roundup of interviews and tutorials you'll learn tips and insight from industry leading **sound designers** and **film composers**.

If you're looking for high quality film and video music, without the cost of creating a unique film score, **be sure to explore our exclusive** Library of Handpicked Tracks at CR Production Music.com.

Film Composing Masterclasses

In this excellent 10 minute highlight video from composer Gabriel Yared's British Film Institute (BFI) Masterclass you will **learn a ton about crafting a score** and how to approach a scoring project in the first place:

"Who is the director who wouldn't dream of having an ally, someone who takes his hand and say 'Come let's try things. You have this idea, OK, let's put it there – it works. OK lets try something else, let's be bold! Let's go somewhere else…" – Gabriel Yared

This hour and a half panel discussion from the National Film and Television School (NFTS) is a long one, but worthwhile for anyone serious about audio. Annabelle Pangborn (head of editing for the NFTS) delves into the many opportunities to **use soundtracks, both musical and otherwise, to add impact to narrative drama.** Additionally she chairs a panel discussion 'focusing on some of the different approaches to composing film music and the crossover with sound design.'

Interviews with Film Composers

Film composer **Michael Giacchino shares six lessons on film score composing** in this excellent Vulture article, featuring tracks from some of his films including *Up*, *Super 8*, *Star Trek* and *The Incredibles*. It is interesting to read how each film's score was an evolutionary process of creativity that is all really about tapping into the heart of the film.

"It was a tough thing to get to, because in the beginning, I was trying to appease what I thought Star Trek music should be," he says. "Everything I was writing sounded spacey — what you would expect from a film like that." After hitting wall after wall, writer Damon Lindelof eventually provided him with sage advice: "Why don't you forget we're making aStar Trek movie and write a score to a film that's about two guys who meet and become the best of friends?"

"[Lost taught me] how to be quick, be fast, don't overthink things, go with your gut, and get it done as efficiently and properly as [I] can," he says. Giacchino didn't discuss musical ideas with J.J. Abrams or anyone on the show — there wasn't time."

Film Music Mag has an in-depth interview with composer Matthew Margeson, co-composer on *Kick-Ass 2*. Matthew has also worked on a whole raft of huge hollywood features, network TV shows and computer games in his career to date. Matthew's interview provides a valuable view into the world of film scoring, especially as **working as part of a team and the journey you might take to work your way up to being a fully credit film composer.**

There is an old saying that whatever you're currently working on is the demo piece for your next gig. It's true. Also, a big part of this is the collaboration between filmmaker and composer. I mean, if you look at all of the contemporary greats, Elfman, Williams, Horner, anyone really....

there tends to be very solid director / composer team. Sometimes a composer's work schedule for the foreseeable future can really be contingent on what his work partners are up to.

September 17th
3 Quick Ways to Be a Better Film Director

Film directing is much more than being 'in-charge'. Utilize the 3 tips below to be more effective on-set.

The success of a film often hinges on the **effectiveness of the director**. Are you doing all you can to be the best for your crew and talent? In this post, we take a **look at two quick and easy techniques** that will help you **become a better director.**

1. Hire the Best

It's said that an organization is only as strong as it's weakest link and the same is true for a film. If you've had experiences similar to mine than you know how catastrophic it can be when a crew member with a negative attitude is on set. Not only does it take away from the overall morale of the crew, it will show in the finished product. This is why it is extremely important to **hire good crew members** that will be able to do their job with a good attitude.

Follow the motto, *"hire slow, fire fast."*

Put in the time up front to ensure an individual is right for your team before offering them a position on your project. Have you already worked on a film with them in the past? What do other individuals who've worked with them have to say about their work ethic, skills and attitude?

Hiring good crew members will also free up a lot of precious time for you to **focus on your creative vision**. It's really easy to get bogged down with worrying about all of the technical nuances associated with a film and completely forget about the actual content that will be shot. If you hire a reliable crew however, it is much easier to **hand off responsibilities** that would have normally taken up a lot of your time on set.

The **relationship** between you, the director, and the actor is highly important to the success of the film. In most cases a film production will span over the course of a few months. So just as with crew members, it is important to cast **an actor that you can build a great working relationship with**. Actors that come with big egos are **hard to work** with and tend to bring down morale.

2. Be Hospitable

If you are an indie-filmmaker you are probably not going to be able to pay your crew very much money (if any at all), so it is extra important to make sure everyone is **as comfortable as possible** on your set.

One of the easiest ways to keep everyone happy and comfortable on-set is to provide the crew and actors with **food and drinks**. Don't get the cheap stuff either! Would you be happy with a Twinkie and a bottle of water? If you are shooting over the course of a few of days don't think that pizza and sandwiches won't get old. **Hospitality goes a long way** on a 14 hour shoot.

3. Communicate Openly with Talent

It's highly recommended that you, the director, **take an acting class** to understand the processes that actors go through to prepare for a role. Film directors usually come from a technical background so it is hard to know the lingo and approach that actors respond best to. Even if it's just one class, a course in acting will help you better relate to your actors.

During pre-production (and while on-set) **ask your actors questions** about their roles. Through asking questions you will be able to identify any inconsistencies in the actor's perception of the role and the creative vision you have for it. Without this dialogue you will waste a lot of time on-set correcting inconsistent visions towards a role. **These conversations should happen before you arrive.**

Remember the Golden Rule

In conclusion, a good rule of thumb when directing is the golden rule, "**Treat others the way you would want to be treated**". With good hiring and an empathetic mindset you will more likely gain the respect of your cast and crew.

If you are interested in learning more about being a great director we have prepared a **recommend reading list**:

Film Directing Shot by Shot: Visualizing from Concept to Screen
by Steven D. Katz

Directing Actors: Creating Memorable Performances for Film & Television
by Judith Weston

Getting Better as a Director: Learning How to Talk to Actors
by NoFilmSchool

September 18th
5 DIY Tips for Product Demo Videos

If you're in the world of video production, you'll likely shoot a few product videos at some point. Here are a few DIY tips and tricks for getting them right.

Shooting a **product demonstration video** is a must for a company of any size. You can easily make a good-looking **product demo** — you just need to be aware of some of their pitfalls and keep a few DIY tools handy.

1. Camera

Admittedly, this first tip isn't very DIY. But it's important to find a camera that works well in most **lighting** and gives you **flexibility over its settings** (manual control over the shutter, aperture, etc.). **HDMI out with live monitoring** is a must if you're working by yourself. Without it, you're going to have a hard time judging exposure, focus, and framing while you or your hands are in the shot.

Remember, **HDMI out does not always mean live monitoring**, so do your homework. Also, unless you want to take long breaks to recharge your battery, make sure the camera can record while charging. You might want **multiple batteries** ready to go as well.

2. Tripod

Have you ever tried to do an overhead shot with a normal tripod? Overhead shots can be a **complete nightmare** without the proper equipment. If you don't want to splurge on a tripod arm attachment, you can **rig up a monopod on a boom stand with gaff tape**. It helps if the monopod has a ball head to get the angle just right.

Of course, this technique also depends on the weight of your camera. You can always get a few **sandbags** to stabilize the stand or find some other counter weight for the boom. This is a simple **DIY solution**.

3. Lighting

Continuous **LED lighting** that can change between tungsten and daylight AND has variable power is ideal, but can get expensive quickly. There are plenty of kits out there — but if you're running low on funds, there is an easy **DIY fix**.

Head over to your local hardware store and gather a variety of bulbs in different wattages and different color temperatures (incandescent to daylight) to make sure you have **enough power and the right type of light** for each shoot. You'll also need to purchase at least **two to four inexpensive clamp lights** (size is up to you) and it never hurts to have extra clamps on hand.

I also highly recommend using a soft box. Making your own is pretty simple and cheap.

Just make sure to test your lighting while you're in the shot. There's nothing worse than meticulously lighting your shot, then realizing you are **casting a shadow**.

4. Reflectors

Reflectors are not that expensive, but if you need flexibility in size, there is an easy solution. **White foam core** reflects and diffuses well, can be cut to size, and can be clamped onto just about anything. Need silver or gold? I've seen some people use foil paper, but that gets wrinkled easily. **Just buy up some plain silver and plain gold wrapping paper and tape it onto the cut-out foam board.** Easy enough!

5. Tabletops or Desktops

It's important to use a tabletop with a color that generally contrasts your product. Black on black is rough. We don't all have the luxury of having different desktops or tabletops. In a pinch, you can buy an appropriate size poster board (black or white) that contrasts in color to your product (assuming you're doing tight shots). You could also get a few pieces of plywood and stain them to get the look that you want.

Every DIY solution will have some quirks. Once you figure them out, you can make great **product videos** on a budget easily!

September 19th
3 Affordable Ways to Capture Great Dolly Shots

You don't have to spend a lot of money to capture eye-catching dolly shots. Here are a few pro options that won't bust your budget.

When storyboarding your next film or video project, you may decide that one particular scene would benefit greatly from a **dolly shot.** Of course, you may not have the budget to purchase a dolly platform and track.

Luckily, there are a variety of solutions out there to cheaply capture a great dolly shot.

1. Camera Sliders

Camera sliders are perfect for capturing short **dolly shots.** I've personally used the Glidecam VistaTrack slider on two film productions and it captured exactly what was needed. While it wasn't the most affordable of all the options below, it was cost effective when compared to purchasing an actual **dolly system**, which can easily run $1500-$2000.

- Glidecam VistaTrack - $599
- Manfrotto Camera Slider - $499
- Varavon Slidecam - $385
- Benro MoveOver4 – $199

2. Table Dolly

If you need to capture a short **dolly shot** and you're using a DSLR, then look into **a small table top dolly**. These lightweight solutions are great in a pinch and many can support quite a bit of weight, which can help if you're using one of the smaller cinema cameras by Blackmagic Design or RED. By using this solution, you can capture effective **dolly shots** on multiple small surfaces. And because of its ease of use, you can capture multiple angles in a matter of minutes, as there's no real set up time between shots.

- Cinetics CineSkates Pro - $150
- Pico Flex Dolly - $110
- iKan Table Dolly - $90
- Digital Juice Orbit – $66

3. Tripod Dolly

If you can't afford a slider and you don't have a smooth surface to utilize a table top dolly, then the **tripod dolly shot** is going to be your best option. This simple-to-use tripod add-on will need a solid smooth surface to really get you the results you're looking for. However, if that's not possible, there are fairly inexpensive track options for this type of dolly.

- Sachtler – $540
- Manfrotto - $319
- Libec DL-5B – $260
- Davis & Sanford - $139

September 20th

How Low-Key Lighting Can Instantly Make Your Film Dramatic

Make your scene moody and atmospheric with low-key lighting.

Want to quickly add dramatic tones to your scene? Try turning off a light. In the following post we'll look at **low-key lighting** and its cinematic potential.

What is Low-Key Lighting?

Low-key lighting is a lighting effect that uses a hard light source to enhance shadows in your scene. Unlike high-key lighting (in which shadows are minimized), **low-key lighting** is all about shadows and contrast.

A low-key image is one that contains predominantly dark tones and colours. Like high-key images, they convey atmosphere and mood. But where a high-key image feels airy and light, a low-key is usually dramatic and full of mystery.

Low-key lighting is typically used when the director wants to either isolate a subject or convey drama. Just because a scene is shot with **low-key lighting** doesn't necessarily mean it must be scary, but, if you want your audience to be uneasy, **low-key lighting** is a great place to start. **low-key lighting** helps to minimize distractions in your frame, so it really helps to guide your audiences eyes where you want them to be.

How to Shoot Low Key Lighting

A typical **low-key lighting setup** consists of one large light, plus reflectors and diffusers as needed. It can be easy to overcomplicate your film set with too many lights. **Low-key lighting** is simple and effective. If you're having lighting trouble on set, try simply turning off a light. A **low-key lighting setup** might be the way to go.

Low-Key Camera Considerations

Low-key is all about shadows, so, just like with any dark shoot, you'll need to take all of the normal **low-light** precautions.

1. Invest in Good Lights

It can be easy to spend your entire equipment budget on camera gear. Don't make this mistake. A small investment in lights will go a long way. For most **low-key lighting** situations you'll want to use a large soft source like a softbox.

2. Use a Fast Lens

Low-key lighting tends to be shot in darker locations, so you'll want to make sure you have a fast lens nearby. Because of the whole camera noise problem, this tends to be a better decision than simply getting a camera that's good in **low-light.**

3. Monitor Your Levels

When shooting low-key lighting, you'll end up with some really funny looking histograms. This is normal, but be mindful of your pixel information. Even if your blacks are black, you want to **make sure your subject isn't underexposed or overexposed.** You can always edit the color in post, but you can't adjust pixel information if your subject has absolute black or white points.

4. Use Negative Fills

A negative fill is essentially a dark cloth or board used to absorb light. This is important for **low-key lighting** as you want to control any incidental light that hits your subject.

5. Shoot in RAW

Shooting a low-key scene is only the beginning. After your footage is captured, you'll want to manipulate color levels while editing. For this reason, it's best advised to shoot in RAW instead of a compressed format.

Conclusion

Low-key lighting isn't something that has set-in-stone rules. Instead, low-key is really more of a theoretical concept used to convey a lighting style between film crew members.

September 21st
How to Create a Soft Hazy Look Without a Fog Machine

Fog machines and hazers continue to be some of the most widely used tricks of the trade on film sets of all shapes and sizes, but they certainly aren't the only way to give your footage a soft hazy look.

One of the greatest challenges in digital cinematography today is offsetting the extreme sharpness that most modern digital sensors capture. For years, DPs have **used hazers to create immersive and dream-like atmospheres**, and in today's digital landscape this technique is more useful than ever. A small, almost unnoticeable amount of fog or haze can go a very long way in "taking the edge off" of your overly sharp digital footage. But in some cases, it just isn't practical or possible to use a proper hazer, and other solutions should be considered.

There are countless reasons why you might not be able to use a hazer —lack of budget, location regulations, power issues, etc. Thankfully though, there are many **alternatives to traditional hazers** that can ultimately serve the same purpose.

It's worth noting that not all of the suggestions below are going to give you the same look that a real hazer would give you, but they are capable of solving one of the same problems: **overly sharp footage**. So next time you need to shoot something and are unable to pull together a proper haze system, consider these alternatives.

1. Diffusion in a Can

Products like Fantasy FX canned fog are excellent alternatives to hazers, especially when you don't have access to a power supply. For instance, you may want to **add a bit of haze to a shot inside a small cabin** to create some atmosphere, but don't have access to a generator or power at your location. Diffusion in a can allows you to spray the room with a high-quality haze that can last for up to two hours. As you might imagine, this option isn't going to be as powerful as a haze machine, but for small spaces and highly controlled environments, it's an excellent solution.

2. Stockings on the Lens

This is the oldest trick in the book, but still one that's employed on sets of all kinds — from student films to Hollywood features. The idea is simple: **Stretch a stocking across your lens** to soften the image dramatically, creating a hazy glow within your images.

As I mentioned above, techniques such as this one won't emulate the look of a hazer, but will instead provide an alternate aesthetic if you want to soften your image. One of the nice things about **using a stocking on your lens** is that you can ensure consistent results, without a whole lot of effort. In his article *Diffusion for the Digital Age – Using Stockings,* Shane Hurlbut discusses exactly how to achieve the effect. This video shows what you can expect the results to look like:

3. Camera Filters

If you don't like the idea of using a stocking on your lens or are going for a more subtle look, there are many **lens filters** you can consider that will help to **soften your image** beautifully. In particular, Pro-Mist filters are some of my favorite to use, as they **add just enough softness to the image** to mitigate the harsh digital footage. This video shows a comparison between Pro-Mist and Black Frost filters, both of which can help you achieve similar results:

4. Do It in Post

I don't typically recommend adding diffusion in post — but sometimes there's no choice. The bottom line: nothing you can do in the editing room will effectively **replicate the look of capturing a softer image in camera**, whether you're using a hazer, filter, or any other technique. That said, there will certainly be times when you may have no other option but to soften your image in the editing room, and it's still a solid backup option if you're ever in a pinch.

Many software platforms (like Red Giant's Magic Bullet Looks) have diffusion effects built right in, and with some fine tuning, strong results can be had. Alternatively, for the more seasoned editor/colorist, using DaVinci Resolve or other professional color grading systems can give you more control over your final result. For instance, in Resolve you might choose to pull a luma key on your highlights and add a faint amount of blur to them. This technique will give you a lot of control over **how much diffusion/softness you'll add to your image**, and will serve to help you achieve fairly realistic results.

September 22nd
How to Create Artistic Fashion Films

Whether you're shooting the runway or a stylized documentary, here are a few great examples and tips for creating engaging fashion film projects.

Fashion films are a cinematographer's dream – moody, stylized and often experimental. Unlike commercials, which are forthright in their messaging and typically utilize an "appeal to the masses" approach, **fashion films** aim for a softer sell and typically target a niche audience. The proliferation of web video has led to an increase in this 'genre.' Brands have taken notice, using this platform as way to forge deeper connections with their audience.

Whether it's through product placement in narrative form, documentary-style personal profiles or simply through a video lookbook, the following projects represent some of the best **fashion films**. Then, read on for considerations on gear, music and talent when shooting your own fashion film project.

Fashion Films: Story & Style

Your story will differ depending on your audience, product, and client, but the goal is all the same... inspire people to buy the product. Obviously this looks much different than simply creating a commercial. In fact, most **fashion films** don't mention the products at all. Instead, good **fashion films** often highlight the products in a subtle way. What story do you want to tell?

Different Fashion Film Genres

Although '**fashion film**' is a bit of a nebulous term, we can break it down into a few potential subgenres…

1. Product Placement Films

Unlike traditional commercials where the product takes center stage, the following videos don't push the sell.

For example, this film created by Jessy Moussallem for Vanina is a great example of an inspiring **fashion film**. Part music video, part choreography video…you wouldn't overtly know they were pushing a product at all. Some incredible cinematography work went into creating this stunning **fashion film**.

The following video created by Öctagon was designed to inspire people who like skateboarding to buy their products. It's an unconventional approach for a skate video – highly stylized, black and white color grade, visual effects. It's futurusitic, a bit dystopian and edgy…and it works.

In this skateboarding video created for New Balance, we see a few skateboarding celebrities using the products. The video is a little more "corporate" than the other videos in this genre, but it's a good practical example of that sweet spot where a commercial meets a film.

2. A-Day-in-the-Life Film

"Day-in-the-life" documentaries are arguably the most popular style of **fashion film** out there right now and for a good reason.the "lifestyle" approach connects with audiences. These documentary-like films showcase a subject doing various things which the potential audience would find interesting, but unlike 'Cool People Doing Cool Stuff,' day-in-the-life films focus on the beauty in the mundane.

In this film created by Free People, we follow a girl as she travels throughout a mountain landscape. Notice how the style of the film complements the clothes she wears. This is a topic we'll discuss in more detail below.

The day-in-the-life style has become so synonymous with **fashion films** that it's become a parody in itself. In this mockumentary, Viva Vena flips the script and makes fun of the day-in-the-life films that they frequently create. While you'll probably want to take a serious approach to your film, it's definitely a funny watch.

3. Narrative Films

One popular way to create an artistic **fashion film** is to use a narrative approach. A narrative **fashion film** typically focuses on thematic mashups where the filmmaker will try to combine different styles and themes to complement the clothing or products.

This film created for Bibi Lou showcases two themes that were clearly an objective for the filmmakers: class and fun. The cinematography, location, and clothes highlight the high-class nature of the clothing, while the content, music, and VO make it more fun. You'll notice that the narrative isn't quite as traditional as a 'normal' short film.

This film created for Ted Baker is more traditional in its approach to storytelling, but you'll notice that the clothing seems to 'pop' a lot more than in a traditional film. This is because when making a f**ashion film**, there's a focus on making the products look good. This also translates into making meaningful set design choices and spending extra time on color in post.

This film created for Love Stories is exactly what the name brand implies. The film is simply a narrator talking about his love for a girl, with lighthearted cinematography to make the entire film feel more empathetic. It's interesting to see that, instead of focusing on spectacular cinematography, the filmmakers focused more on creating a fun story.

4. Music-Driven Films

A music-driven **fashion film** will highlight the clothing by cutting incredible cinematography together with a good music track that evokes the right tone for the clothing being presented. If you're looking for the right music for **fashion films**, I highly recommend checking out our library here at CR Production Music.com

This film created for JT by Jessica Trosman is one part music-driven video, one part experimental film. The film definitely complements the artistic nature of the clothing Jessica is trying to sell.

Another great example of a **fashion film** is this music video called *Snooze* created for Forty Five Ten, Tootsies, and Haggar. The film is essentially indistinguishable from a traditional music video. This style can be a fun way to showcase your client's brand in a non-traditional way.

5. Experimental Fashion Film

If you want your **fashion film** to stand out, experimental is the way to go. However, the biggest challenge when creating an experimental film is to create an engaging film that doesn't isolate the audience. You don't want someone to be so weirded out by your unconventional storytelling that they don't look at the clothing! It's a fine line... but when done correctly, an **experimental fashion film** can be quite effective.

This film created for Upton Belts uses contrast to emphasize the bold nature of the belts being sold. The film is successful by being visually stunning and approachable for mass audiences.

This film created for Ioana Ciolacu is a little more experimental in it's approach to storytelling, but if you investigate the brand, it actually falls right in line with their clothing style.

6. Fashion Documentary

A behind-the-scenes or documentary approach can give viewers a behind-the-scenes look, while humanizing a brand.

This documentary simply showcases Naked and Famous Denim's process and values through interviews and b-roll footage. As far as craft goes, the film looks fairly easy to create, yet the content makes it just as good as the other videos in this post.

This film created for Helen Rödel is a simple VO with b-roll footage of the creation process. But the thing that really makes this film stand out is the cinematography. The shots are up close, intimate, and raw... just like the clothing brand.

7. Lookbooks

In fashion, a lookbook is simply a booklet that showcases clothing or products that will be released in a given fashion season. Some companies are choosing to create **lookbook films** as well. These can look very different depending on the brand/intent.

This lookbook created for Urban Outfitters is simply a series of models on a white backdrop wearing the clothes with a very unique motion graphics effect applied to them. The result is a cool overview of the clothing styles and an entertaining video.

This is another example of a lookbook created for Ezekiel. The film pairs footage of a small European village with the clothing to supplement the tone that Ezekiel was going for.

Finding Music for Fashion Films

Behind every great **fashion film** is a great music track. Music has the power to radically change the way your audience perceives your film… and subsequently the clothing. When picking the right track, you want to focus more on how the track will complement the clothing. This all depends on the type of clothing you will be selling. For example, if you are creating an ultra-sleek modern **fashion film**, you might want to choose an edgy electronic track. Whereas if you are creating a lifestyle video for a sweater brand, you might want to choose something a little more folksy.

When it comes to selecting the right music for a **fashion film**, you have two options: pay an artist to create a custom track or license a royalty free track. Paying an artist can generate some amazing results, but it can also be crazy expensive. Not to mention the process of creating a custom track can take a lot of time and effort.

So your best option is to license a track from a royalty free music site. Here on CR Production Music.com we have thousands of custom tracks designed to be embedded seamlessly into your **fashion films**. Our artists handmake tracks with character and emotion.

Color Considerations for Fashion

If you want to take your footage to the next level, then color needs to be a cornerstone part of your post-production workflow. This is especially true if you're creating a **fashion film**. Color, or more specifically color palettes, can make the clothing 'pop.' While the example below is a bit extreme, it does highlight how important it is to think about all of the colors in your scene.

You'll notice in the video that the colors seem to be more vibrant than most videos you watch, but that's simply not the case. Instead, the colors are emphasized because they contrast well with the other elements in the scene. You won't just see someone wearing a bright shirt… you'll see the shirt as it stands in contrast with the mountains and snow.

The entire frame was colored to make the clothing colors stand out the most. It's basic color theory. When you intentionally draw out colors in your video through set design and post-processing, you can make your footage look very professional and inspiring.

One color resource that I like to use is Coolors.co. On their site you can lock in certain color values and see what colors go well with them. When fashion designers are designing clothes, they use color palettes… so why should you abandon color palettes when you edit the footage? Spend a little extra time planning out your footage color and you'll be amazed by the result.

Gear Considerations

When making a **fashion film**, tone is king. Before you select your camera, you need to figure out the overall tone of your scene. Will it be modern, hipster, authentic, etc.? After you've chose a style and tone, then you should select your camera. Most **fashion films** want to showcase how beautiful the clothing is, so you probably want to get a camera with a high dynamic range. Also, for color purposes, recording in RAW is a must.

If your budget is slim, you could go with a Canon DSLR like the **Mark III** with a magic lantern hack or a **Blackmagic Cinema or Pocket Camera**. If your budget is middle-of-the-road, you could use something like a **RED SCARLET or a Blackmagic URSA**. If you're going high end, you will always get good results with a **RED EPIC or an ARRI ALEXA**. Be sure to bring enough cards as well. RAW footage ills up cards incredibly quickly.

While the camera is certainly important, don't forget about lenses. If you're wanting to get really up-close shots, you'll want to make sure you rent or buy a macro lens. And while we're on the subject, you should probably use prime lenses only when shooting a **fashion film**, as they will generate a shallow depth of field and a crisper image.

Where to Find Models for Fashion Films

If you don't already know a good model, then there are a few online resources out there to help you find the right model for your gig. The most popular site to find models online is Model Mayhem, but the models are almost all amateur. They'll require quite a bit of direction once they get on set. Model Mayhem is cheap though — sometimes free, actually — so if you're working on a low-budget fashion film, it's probably the best way to go.

Another option would be to call a **modeling agency in your area**. They will likely be able to find you an experienced model, but you'll pay for it. If you're working on a medium to high-budget shoot, this is the way to go.

September 23rd
How to Direct Scenes Containing Minimal Dialogue

Master one of a film director's most important skills: Directing scenes that contain minimal dialogue.

It may sound like a cliche, but the old adage of **"Show, Don't Tell"** is as relevant today as ever. As filmmakers, most of us understand the notion that film is a visual medium and therefore the best stories are often told by **tapping into powerful visuals**. However, many filmmakers fail to actually put this ideology into practice and **their films run the risk of lacking depth**.

There are countless incredible films that have an abundance of dialogue, and the style or genre that you like to work in may call for more heavy dialogue scenes. Regardless, knowing **how to direct scenes with minimal dialogue** will inevitably improve your results not only in the more textural moments in your film, but also in the verbal moments too. When visual cues, metaphors, and powerful imagery couple together – **the end product can really shine.** For example, here are a few notable (**and wildly dissimilar**) light-on-dialogue scenes from classic films:

From Terrence Malick's Days of Heaven

From Big Night, directed by Campbell Scott and Stanley Tucci

From Stanley Kubrick's 2001: A Space Odyssey

So whether you are someone that likes to **direct content with less dialogue**, or simply want to improve your understanding of the visual storytelling as a whole, read on. These tips will help you get great results when transitioning into this type of storytelling.

1. Imagine your scenes as dialogue.

A huge challenge for many filmmakers is conceptualizing and writing material without a lot of dialogue. **More often than not, the dialogue-free scenes in films end up being nothing more than transitional moments** with very little inherent value unto themselves, with the exception of helping to glue together other pieces in the film. The mistake that many filmmakers are prone to making is not conceptualizing their dialogue-free scene in the same way they would a verbally driven scene.

What I often recommend to filmmakers is that they imagine there is dialogue in a scene that doesn't have any. I will ask – **What do you want to tell the audience?** How does this move the story forward? What new character info do we get from this? The same kinds of questions you would consider when writing a dialogue scene… Once these questions have been answered, **coming up with concepts for visuals that can illustrate them** becomes much easier. You're no longer just thinking about arbitrary images, but rather meaningful information in a visual format.

2. Don't overdo coverage.

In film, a lot of the time **less is more.** This notion applies very obviously to shooting films without a lot of dialogue, yet this is one area where many filmmakers go very wrong. Inexperienced directors will often feel like they need to build up a certain moment, and overcompensate for the fact that it has no dialogue by over-covering the scene. They will get a **dozen angles that they don't really need** and actually prevent the viewer from focusing on some of the important visual cues in the scene.

3. Find symbolism.

Every shot that you show in your film needs to be important and relevant to your story or characters or both. While it may be relatively simple and straightforward to **direct a dialogue-free scene** that's simply progressing the story, it's more difficult to execute well on the character level. In order to really tap into something emotionally powerful, **your visuals need to have symbolic and metaphorical meanings** that ideally are subtle enough to hit the viewer on a subtextual level. It's amazing how powerful subtext is to the average viewer, and many dialogue-free scenes that make use of symbolic or metaphorical imagery are able to convey far more to the audience than any amount of dialogue would be able to. Always look for ways to add meaning to your scenes through the use of objects, colors, wardrobe, props, or any other vehicle that may allow you to do so.

4. Break up important moments.

Another big trap that filmmakers tend to fall into is trying to cram **too much information into a single non-verbal moment.** So for example, the filmmaker might want to convey a detail about one of their characters (let's say that the character is a recovering alcoholic that relapses). That same filmmaker might decide to create one long visual scene that somehow shows the character being tempted by alcohol and then giving in... But placing too much information in one scene like this can feel very cheesy and soap-opera like in many ways. The better option is to **break up the moment** and tell it in two or three pieces.

By planting seeds for the audience and leaving bread crumbs, so to speak, your viewers will be led to their own conclusions about your story and characters — **and that will give your film a deeper meaning to them.** In the example above, if you were to show a few moments leading up to the character starting to drink again (let's say, having wine spilled on them, watching their boss drink in front of them, etc.), you are able to nudge the audience to the conclusion you want them to draw **without being too forceful.**

5. Show more character

When in doubt, always focus on your character development when **working with non-verbal material.** The most interesting and dynamic character information can be portrayed best in scenes without dialogue, so always take advantage of this fact. Ask yourself what you can show your audience in this dialogue-free scene, moment, or film that you wouldn't otherwise be able to in a scene with other characters. Maybe you choose to show your main character alone, and give insight into who they are behind closed doors... Whatever choice you make will work as long as it is centered around **conveying character detail in an interesting and visually motivated way.**

September 24th
How to Properly Calibrate Light Meters

Avoid a faulty reading by verifying the accuracy of your light meter with this quick tip.

I live in a rural area and get calls for jobs that never leave me enough time to get my **meters calibrated professionally.** I've devised a system that works for me in a pinch and I wanted to share it with all of you.

First, you'll need a still camera with a **histogram display** feature. A histogram is a digital version of the zone system. The middle of a histogram is the same as **zone 5**, or "middle" gray. An 18% gray card is "middle" gray in value.

The idea is to expose that middle gray card to **render a middle gray spike** in the middle of the histogram. If accomplished, then you have achieved a **perfect exposure** — a feat necessary for calibrating your meter accurately.

I'm illuminating the card with the available light coming through a skylight. Know that the reading will be more consistent if you light the card with instruments, however, since many of you don't have lights, I'll go without as well.

Fill the frame with the gray card and **set up your still camera to reflect a basic cinema situation**. With my shutter speed at 1/50th of a second with ISO 800, I've matched the native speed of the ARRI ALEXA. The only remaining variable is the f-stop which will be set to put the exposure spike in the middle of the histogram. In this test case that f-stop ends up being a 2.8.

Then quickly take your test **spot meter reading** before there is any deviation in the available light, clouds, wisps, etc. If your meter is well calibrated, it should render a reading very close to a **2.8** or in my case **exactly a 2.8**. I don't worry too much about a tenth or two over or under. If you are calibrating an **incident meter** use a flat disk, hold the meter in front of the gray card and pointed at the camera. Your exposure should be at a **2.8** or very close to it.

I know that many of you don't use a meter, but they can be very useful in verifying the speed of the chip in the camera you might be shooting with. To ascertain this issue, **shoot a gray card at the exact exposure your calibrated meter displays at the native ISO** of the camera. Send the footage to a post house and ask if that gray exposure is where it should be on their scopes. If it is, then the native speed is truthful. If it isn't, then adjust your meter to reflect that over or under metric.

I recommend that **everyone should at least own a spot meter**, because you never know when you might have to shoot a film on *film*. You can't light from a monitor on film; a meter reading must be taken and it has to be pretty close to perfect — or else. So go on ebay and purchase one. My bet is that you'll find a reason to use it every day even on your next digital shoot!

September 25th
Mastering The Film Slate

In this post we explore how to make sense of a film slate. This universal icon of filmmaking – 100 years strong – is still a vital tool in the filmmaking process.

The humble film slate (or clapper board) has withstood the test of time in **filmmaking** and today still plays a vital role in keeping track of every set up, take and most importantly, syncing separate sound to picture.

If you're a **camera assistant** you need to know what should be written on it. If you're an assistant **video editor** or an editor, you need to understand how to make sense of what is written on it. Otherwise using the clapper board becomes a waste of everyone's time.

Top Tips for Slate Happiness

1. **Get everyone's names spelt correctly**. This is the most important thing to get right on day one, especially seeing as both the names on it are usually your bosses.
2. **Write in capitals** so its easy to see.
3. **Speak up** when you're reading out the slate info as you might be quite far from the mic.
4. Give the clapper board a decent whack so that the **click is solid** and also heard.
5. **Add a corrective note** if you some how fall behind or are shooting 'pick-ups'. The slate is useless if it provides inaccurate info.

A Slate Masterclass in 3 Parts

The excellent filmmaking website The Black and Blue has a three part masterclass on 'Deciphering the Slate' which is a brilliant and exhaustive primer on how to write up a film/videoslate, as well as how to make the most of the info once you've got it. Each part is chock full of useful links to other posts and resources so its well worth taking the time to explore the posts in full.

Part 1 of Deciphering the Slate describes each section of the film slate and what to write in it. It also provides details of what to write in several different common filmmaking scenarios.

Part 2 of Deciphering the Slate walks through some of the more detailed intricacies of a film slate including what to do for shots without sound, vfx plates, reshoots, pickups and more.

Part 3 of Deciphering the Slate provides 12 examples of completed slates in which camera assistant Evan Luzi provides some insightful analysis of what's going in each one.

September 26th
Streamlining the Director/DP Relationship

Working with a new director or DP can be a tricky process that takes some time to develop. Here are some filmmaking tips to help streamline that process, and to make sure your production is getting the most out of that relationship.

With advancements in technology and professional production equipment constantly becoming more affordable, it seems that timelines (and usually budgets) for projects become smaller and smaller every year. This means that you have to work more efficiently — and as a solid team — to finish with a project that everyone can be proud of.

One of the best ways to do this is to make sure that the **director** and the **director of photography** have a clear and singular vision for the execution of the project. Here are some suggestions for ways to make sure the two are in sync.

Start with a Lookbook

An image can be a hard thing to explain with words. One easy way to make sure that the visual style of a project is decided on and agreed upon is to **begin the process with a lookbook**. A lookbook is a collection of images that define the look and tone of the image that you're going for.

It can be any number of things... paintings, photographs, stills from another film, anything that is a representation of what you want to do visually. It helps to take notes on each image, so that you can reference what it is about that image specifically that will support your story/look.

I prefer to **use a cloud-based file storage service for creating lookbooks** (Dropbox, Google Drive, etc). This way, while on set or scouting a location, you can always pull up the lookbook and effectively communicate a visual idea on the spot. Evan E. Richards runs a blog with a comprehensive selection of screengrabs of various films that's a great resource for **building a lookbook.**

Learn Their Process Early On

Everyone does things differently. Some **directors** will want to have a lot of involvement in how the image is created, down to the placement of the camera and focal length of the lens. Other **directors** aren't interested in those details, and will fully look to the **DP** to deliver the look that they're going for, with little to no direction otherwise.

This needs to be discussed ahead of time. That bit of information will completely **define the nature of the DP's job** on that project, and it can be different every time. It's important for everyone to know their role on set, and for all expectations to be made perfectly clear before the production begins. Some of these topics are touched on in this Hollywood Reporter roundtable of **Oscar-nominated directors discussing their craft.**

Get Everyone Involved

It's not acceptable to bring the DP in right before the shoot. The **DP** should be able to walk the locations well ahead of time, taking photos, looking for power (if needed), and getting an overall game plan on load-in and the plan of attack. This will make it easier for them to create lighting diagrams for each of the setups as well, which is a huge timesaver (and will also allow them to put together the gear list for the shoot). A great app for creating lighting diagrams is Shot Designer.

It's important to work together in creation of a shot list (check out the awesome Shot Lister app) and game plan for each shoot day based on the location scout. This should be done before anyone starts to put together a schedule, and (in most cases) before booking the talent.

It is **the director of photography's job** to know what time will work best for each location (sun through windows, sun positions for best backlight, etc). If they never get to see the locations, there's no way that they can do their job. This is one of the most overlooked issues in low-budget productions.

Keep an Open Line of Communication

There's always time to talk. No matter how short on time you are, it will almost always *save* you time if you stop to pull your **DP** or **director** aside and have a quick chat about what's going on and (hopefully) figure out what isn't working. Sometimes you just have to get away from the rest of the crew and actors to really get some real thinking done.

When things are moving and decisions are constantly being made, it's really easy to get in the swing of things and lose track of what's actually going on. Always be asking yourself: *Are we executing the plan? Am I supporting my colleagues process? Are we achieving the look that we laid out in the lookbook?* And most importantly: *Are we making something we're all going to be proud of?*

If there is ever any doubt, pull your **director** or **DP** aside and figure out how you can fix it — and do it sooner than later.

Know Your Role in the Relationship

In the end a film can look lousy but work because of a great performance but not the other way around. That's something always worth remembering. – Roger Deakins

One thing a **DP** should always remember is the pecking order on set. **The director is always in control.** While filmmaking is a very collaborative process, it's important that the **DP** keep the ultimate vision of the **director** and execution of the project at the front of their mind at all times. If you don't watch out for it, ego can set in and arguments can begin because the **DP** wants or takes too much control.

However, that works both ways. If the **director** isn't assuming the lead role in the execution of the project in a way that cannot be questioned, someone else is going to have to step up to make sure the project is completed. There is an art to doing this in a way that gets the best work out of people, while also getting the best out of the project.

When working quickly, and under stressful guidelines, these things can be a weak point in the hyper-sensitive ecosystem that film sets usually become. It's important to be aware of everything, and everyone's feelings, especially when it comes to the way that the **director** and the **DP** work together.

September 27th

The Art Department: Design, Construction, Decor, and Props

The Art Department is often the largest film crew. Hundreds of employees make up several divisions, including Art, Sets, Construction, and Property. Let's take a closer look.

The art department is responsible for visual aspects of filmmaking. This includes everything **on a set**, as well as the **set itself**. The department is supervised by the **Production Designer**.

Throughout filming, sets must evolve. Either they are adjusted, or new sets are constantly built. Many members of the **art department** are on standby, in case any changes must be made. The positions are incredibly creative and require immense amount of skill and attention to detail. Here is a breakdown of the art department and the duties of each member.

Production Designer

The term **production designer** was created by William Cameron Menzies. At the time, Menzies (featured below) was working as the **art director** on the set of *Gone with the Wind*. He coined the term due to the film's massive scope.

The **production designer** is responsible for the entire visual appearance of the film. To achieve the overall look, they will coordinate with the art department, costume department, makeup department, and more.

They not only work closely with the **director** to bring his vision to life, they also work with the **producer** to **calculate the needed budget**. The cost will depend on the type of film, whether the art department has to achieve a modern style set, a fantasy castle, or a sci-fi space ship.

Depending on the production, a **production designer** may even be hired well before a **director**. They will look at scripts to estimate the cost needed to bring the story to life. Once a **director** is in place, they will collaborate on how to best shoot the film. **They will either decide to build sets, use visual effects, or shoot on location.**

Once decided, the **production designer** will deliver sketches and outlines to the **art director**, who in turn delivers their work to the **construction department**. The final sets built by the **construction department** will then help **set decorators** and **prop buyers** determine their needs for the film.

The Art Department

The overall **art department** includes a sub-department also called the **art department**. This department includes the preliminary designers who will plan the overall look of the film.

Art Director

The art director reports directly to the **production designer**. They oversee the artists and designers who help create the overall look of the film. It is their job to supervise the planning and practical design of sets and set pieces. On large-budget projects, there may be multiple art directors. If so, the main position will be the **Supervising Art Director** of **Senior Art Director**. On smaller projects, the job of the **production designer** and **art director** are typically combined.

The **art director** will analyze a script to make note of all necessary **props** and special **set pieces** that may require an extended time to design, build, or acquire. They will also oversee the creation of all necessary plans that will be given to the **construction department**.

They are also responsible for the **maintenance of sets**, making sure any rebuilds or changes are made on schedule. The will manage the creation, dressing, and striking of all sets and locations.

Assistant Art Director (First Assistant, Second, Third)

The **assistant art directors** are responsible for carrying out the **art director's** plans, including measuring locations and other necessary information the **production designer** needs. They are also responsible for researching and making props, assisting with model making, and surveying sites. On larger productions, **assistant art directors** will manage the smaller locations or sets.

Standby Art Director

This is an **art director** that monitors the art department during filming. If there isn't a **standby art director**, the responsibilities fall to the **props master** and **on-set dresser**.

They will watch the video playback monitor to make sure all set pieces appear as needed. They will coordinate with **standby painters** and **standby carpenters** if any last-minute changes are needed on set during filming.

Draughtsman (Set Designer)

Draughtsmen are responsible for the technical drawings of sets. Their drawings, computer models, and physical models will include all measurements and materials needed for construction. On many sets, a **draughtsman** in usually the **first assistant art director**.

Concept Artist (Illustrator)

A **concept artist** works on a specific set piece. This includes the design of creatures and monsters to the look of a space ship.

Graphic Artist

This position creates physical graphic elements for a set. A **graphic artist** will create newspapers, posters, fliers, contracts, logos, signs, etc.

Storyboard Artist

These artists will turn a screenplay into a set of detailed illustrations. **Storyboard artists** will create storyboards, which the production team uses to plan out every shot. These visualizations are often created well before shooting begins.

The **storyboard** will show the entire film from the point of view of the camera. It will show camera angles, a character's actions and position, as well as all other major elements needed for a shot. They will also list any necessary movements on screen, like a character jumping or an object falling.

Model Maker

When a **draughtsman** requires a specific model, it is the **model maker's** job to draw and then construct the miniatures. They can use a range of materials to create the models, including clay, wood, metal, plaster, and plastic.

Art Department Coordinator

With the large amount of employees in this department, the **art department coordinator** is responsible for monitoring daily operations. They will work among the various departments to verify that all sets and props are ready on time. The will also manage the departments budget, and schedule the sets construction, dress, and strike.

The art department coordinator will also create location notes. These detail everything from details of construction, needed set dressing, and props. They will use these notes to gain licenses and permission for location shoots, as well as verifying health a safety protocols are met.

Sets

Set Decorator (Stylists)

The **set decorator** is responsible for decorating a film set. This includes furniture, drapes, fixtures, paintings, and overall decor. They are also responsible for **dressing props**, which includes everything from cars and animals to dishes and household items.

Set decorators also work with product placement and acquiring approval to use copyrighted items. Prior to a shoot, they will photograph all items and assign them to each set. On set, they will manage the **swing gang** and place everything in the appropriate place. After the shoot, they will make sure the set is broken down and that everything is returned to the responsible rent house.

Leadsman

The **leadsman** or **lead man** is in charge of the **set dressers**. They direct the crew that places all the furniture, drapes, and dressing props on set.

Set Dresser (Swing Gang)

Set dressers (also called the **swing gang**) place and remove all dressing props. They are responsible for practically everything on the set: furniture, rugs, drapes, lamps, decor, doorknobs, etc.

Swing gang is most often used referring to the **on-set dressers**, those making any last minute changes prior to cameras rolling. Any parts of the set that are not permanent are referred to as the **swing set**. These are items that can be move around on set or easily removed if they don't work for the overall look of the shot.

Buyer

The **buyer** is the one responsible for purchasing or renting set dressing. They work with stores or rent houses to schedule deliveries and purchase any necessary dressing props.

Greensmen

A **greensman** is a **set dresser** that is specialized in landscape and plants – *greens*. This includes real and artificial plant life.

Construction Department

The construction department is responsible for building the actual structures that make up the set. Framing walls, doors, or constructing entire buildings.

Construction Coordinator (Construction Manager)

The **construction coordinator** oversees the entire **construction department**. They order all construction materials, schedule workers, and supervise the actual building of the sets.

Head Carpenter

The foreman of the carpenters and laborers.

Carpenters

Carpenters are the expert wood workers on set. The build, install, and remove wooden structures. The not only construct the actual physical set, they also make any wooden props and furniture.

Key Scenic

This artist is responsible for surface treatments. The **key scenic** can paint wood to give it an aged or distressed look. They also make props look more realistic, like painting foam to look like a rock or brick. They can also paint a window to look like stained glass.

Painter

A **painter** is responsible for the final appearance of a set. The are responsible for all surface preparation, priming, painting, and finishing. The can also apply special finishes, like marbling or graining to sets.

Plasterer

These artists apply plaster to walls, ceilings, and floors. They also create moulds for interior and exterior walls, or use fiberglass to create intricate panels – like a spaceship.

Sculptor

Sculptors typically create large set pieces like busts, statues, or elaborate miniatures. They use an array of materials, such as foam, clay, metal, and wood.

Property Department

The property department, or **Props**, is responsible for all practical movie props. These are not including in the set dressing or costume department, but rather used by an actor in a scene. This includes food, firearms, swords, or specific items like a proton pack or custom vehicle.

Props Master

As the chief of the **property department**, the **props master** is in charge of finding or making practical props. If the film is a period piece, they are responsible for making sure that the props are accurate to that era.

Prop Maker

The artist or technician that creates custom props. This can includes creating any type of casings, or wiring electronics to make a functioning prop.

Weapons Master (Armorer)

This prop manager is in charge of all firearms, swords, or other weapons. They are also trained and licensed to use the weapons, and will often collaborate with the stunt manager and actor to maintain set safety.

September 28th
The Basic Fundamentals of Lighting a Green Screen

Learning how to evenly light your green screen backdrop will give you better results when it comes time to edit your video.

Lighting a **green screen** is fairly simple from a technical perspective, yet many DPs who don't have much experience with chroma key work are prone to making some unfortunate mistakes on set. Unlike traditional film lighting, which is all about finding contrast and mood by balancing light and shadows, lighting a **green screen** is all about evenness and consistency.

For the purpose of this post, I'll describe a **basic green screen lighting setup** that involves only two background lights. While two lights might be all you need for many scenarios (such as an interview setup), keep in mind that the basic principles outlined here can be applied to wider and larger **green screen** setups too — you just may need to add more light.

The most crucial thing to remember when lighting your **green screen**: any area of the backdrop that appears in the frame must be **lit perfectly even** and **exposed correctly**. If your backdrop is lit properly on one side but underexposed on the other, your compositor or editor will have a very tough time pulling a clean key. The same applies to a backdrop that's either over or underexposed. Any attempt to pull a key from a backdrop that isn't actually reading as green on camera will inevitably be a failure.

Lighting Green Screen Backdrops

The key is the same for achieving soft light in any other shooting scenario — use big, soft light sources. If you point a hard light source (such as tungsten light with no diffusion) at your **green screen**, you're going to run into trouble. The light will have a hot spot and there will be a gradient surrounding it, ultimately giving you an uneven light to work with.

Conversely, if you were to point a tungsten light (let's say a 2K source) at the **green screen**, but use a large 8 x 8 frame with a silk to diffuse the light, you'll be in great shape. Personally, I prefer to use double diffusion when shooting on a **green screen**. My ideal setup typically involves a bright light source that's first diffused by a standard 4 x 4 silk on a C-stand, and another 8 x 8 frame in front of that silk for an additional layer of diffusion. This ensures that the light is as even and soft as possible.

Placing Green Screen Lights

Assuming your needs are relatively simple, you can use a minimum of two lights to illuminate your backdrop. Using the setup described above, I recommend placing one light (with diffusion) on either side of the **green screen**, a few feet back on a 45 degree angle.

Right off the bat your results should be pretty close, and you can fine tune/adjust the angle of each light to make sure they're not overlapping too much in the center. In other words, you don't want to have a hotspot in the middle of your frame if both lights are spilling into each other. Be sure to adjust your lights and use flags when necessary, so your lighting is as even as possible.

It should also go without saying that you'll want to **use the exact same lights on either side of the green screen** for the sake of consistency. If you're using two different lights, you could run into exposure issues (or even worse, color temperature issues) which could once again cause headaches in post. With regards to the rest of your lighting setup, these will be creative decisions and are ultimately up to you.

If you want a more dramatic look on your talent, **you can light them from the side.** Alternatively, you might use two more flood lights on the talent's face to create an even flat light. No matter what creative look you're aiming for, the **green screen** will always need to be lit the exact same way.

On bigger productions, you may need to use overhead lighting, additional sources, or more diffusion, but the basic principles outlined here will apply no matter what.

September 29th
The Right Gear for Your First Production Assistant Job

Having the right gear for your first production assistant gig will not only benefit your reputation on set, but also guarantee work in the future.

No matter where your media-related career begins, at some point filling the role of **production assistant** is almost inevitable. The good news is that these jobs eventually lead to more gigs where you'll have ample opportunities to demonstrate your knowledge and skills.

Being adequately prepared for your first role as **production assistant** and having the necessary gear is vital to satisfying the production's goals and your own future career opportunities. Here are some suggested items to consider purchasing beforehand.

Gaffer Tape: $18

Gaffer tape is truly an indispensable tool. No matter the type of production you're working on, gaffer tape will be needed. With all the cords and markers that go into big shoots, tape is a necessity that isn't always readily available in the moment. Having the means to help the key grip or your fellow **production assistant** on the spot is beneficial for you and everyone working.

Tool Pouch: $16

A standard small **tool pouch** that can be worn on your belt is not only cheap, but tells others on set that you're prepared for the job. What goes in the pouch? I recommend keeping a flashlight, vice grips, and a small pocket knife. You can even buy an **all-purpose tool and tool pouch** on Amazon for less than $20.

Dress for the Weather: $30-$100

Always keep a rain jacket on standby. Being outside for twelve hours a day, six days a week, you're bound to run into foul weather at some point. The rain will pass, and production will pick back up — and you can't beat being dry for the rest of the shoot.

Hiking/Waterproof Shoes: $50-$100

Not only is the landscape unpredictable, but as a **production assistant** you'll need to be able to go anywhere, at any point. All-purpose hiking boots simply are perfect when it's time to trudge through mud. And you *will* be trudging through mud.

Work Gloves: $20

Due to the unpredictability and vague nature of being a **production assistant**, you never really know what you'll be asked to do on set. Having a pair of **all-purpose work gloves** can help you maintain a solid grip and protect your hands when heavy lifting is required.

Ear Piece: $13

Most productions will provide the necessary communication tools like walkies and earpieces. However, if certain equipment fails to work, having a backup (or an extra set for a fellow PA in need) will only help the production — and your reputation.

Sun Protection: $25

Having personally experienced being on set in mid-July in the middle of Louisiana for fifteen hours straight, I can assure you — the sun is your enemy. On top of making sure you're covered in sunscreen, a hat is strongly recommended to keep the rays at bay.

Bonus: Helpful Hint

Never sit down. **Directors and producers are always watching.** Demonstrating why they hired you can only benefit you in the long run.

Being a **production assistant** is a great way to start on your path to success in the film industry. Hopefully some of these options will help you down the line on an intense shoot. The hours are rough, the pay is little, but being on set and contributing in any way possible is **worth the pain**.

September 30th
Tips for Keeping a Long Dialogue Scene Visually Interesting

No matter how great your writing might be, heavy dialogue scenes can begin to feel boring. Here's how to keep things interesting on those longer takes.

Previously, we talked about directing scenes with minimal dialogue, and this article is essentially focused on the exact opposite challenge – **heavy dialogue scenes.** While shooting a one or two-page scene with lots of **dialogue** might be fairly straightforward, things get much more complicated when you get into lengthier page counts.

For instance, when you're shooting a conversation between two people sitting at the dinner table… If you were to cover it in the traditional sense (a wide and two close-ups) you'd **run out of steam after a minute or two in the editing room pretty quickly**, and things will likely start to get pretty boring. However, if you can follow at least one of the tips on this list, you'll be in much better shape.

Move the Camera

A **roaming camera** (whether handheld or on a steadicam) will always hold the viewers attention better than a static shot. Just as it's important that you choose the right type of camera movement for your scene, it's also important to choose the right movement for your audience. With long dialogue scenes, always look for ways that you can move that camera, whether it's panning back and forth between your actors, circling your talent, etc. to **keep your audience visually stimulated.**

Move Your Actors

If you're hellbent on no camera movement at all, either because it doesn't work with the mood you're setting or it's technically impossible, then consider **moving your actors** instead. Say for instance you're shooting the dinner scene as described above, and it's six pages long. Why not have one of the actors get up at the two-age mark and walk to the kitchen to get something? Whether the other character follows or not, you now have a new background and new angles on both characters and have subsequently **added more dimension to the scene.**

Cross the Line

Those of you that went to film school have had it drilled in your heads to never 'cross the line' (which is of course the **imaginary axis** the camera sits on), but rules are made to be broken.

Assuming you don't want to use a roaming camera and want your actors to stay static, crossing the line is a great way to completely change the perception of a scene by simply **capturing reverse coverage.** If there's a beat in your scene where the tone or pace changes, consider using a **cutaway shot** to bring you across the line and then shoot the remainder of the scene from the other side. If nothing else, it will keep things interesting and **let the viewer subtly know a change has occurred.**

And there really is no better way to understand the craft of shooting a heavy dialogue scene than by watching great films by some of the **masters of dialogue.** Filmmakers like Quentin Tarantino and Richard Linklater are notorious for their use of dialogue, and both employ a variety of techniques to keep the viewer stimulated.

October 1st
Traits of a Good Film Crew

Picking the right film crew isn't hard if you know what to look for. In this post, we share a few tips to aid in the success of your film project.

Sometimes the most difficult part of making a film is finding the right people to make it with you. There is a reason why professional filmmakers get paid so much money to do their job, **they are worth it.** However, even if your budget is nonexistent there are a few qualities to look for in a crew member that will help you **sort out the good apples from the bad.**

A good crew member...

- Helps solve problems on set.
- Improves morale on set by complementing **instead of complaining.**
- Is concerned with making the film as great as possible even if it means shooting late.
- Is more concerned with making a film than getting lunch, eating snacks, taking breaks.
- Is able to admit when he/she has made a mistake.
- Will offer help to other crew members once their work is complete.
- Is concerned with the success of the entire team rather than getting praise for themselves.

A bad crew member...

- Complains outwardly about long working days and early mornings.
- **Shows up late** to call times and blames it on traffic and phone alarms.
- Criticizes the decisions made by the director or producer in front of other crew members.
- Brings down the moral on the entire set.
- Only does things when he/she is told to do them.
- Misses pre-production meetings.
- **Wants to receive praise for everything** they do.

Based on that criteria do you think you are a good crew member or a bad crew member? **Are you a good crew leader?**

How to Assemble an Awesome Crew

Now you may be asking, "Where do I find these good crew members?" Well, the answer to that question is not as simple as going to FindaFreeCrew.com and selecting people...you're going to have to put in some leg-work.

Finding a good crew always begins with good networking. As any good filmmaker will tell you, one of the most powerful tools you can have is networking skills. This means as a filmmaker you should be spending time with other filmmakers. Once you have a network asking for help isn't as difficult.

Build Excitement

It is very important to hire people who are **excited** about your project. A crew that isn't excited about a project will be very difficult to motivate and subsequently will not create a good finished product.

You can build excitement through interacting and tagging crew members on social media, inviting crew members to brainstorming sessions and highlighting crew members on the film's website. On the same note, crew members who are **eager to gain work experience** will probably be more reliable than those who are simply trying to make money.

If your budget is low it might also be helpful to ask crew members with access to **good equipment** to be a part of your shoot. This might save you precious money that would have been spent somewhere else. This is definitely where your developed relationship will have to come into play. There's nothing worse than having an audio person volunteer to help bring equipment then not show up. Not only would you be out a crew member you would also **not be able to shoot your film**.

Set Expectations

The line between a good crew member and a bad crew member can sometimes be blurred under poor leadership. It is your duty as a director/producer to **communicate exactly what you expect** from your crew every step of the way.

Expect good work but **be patient with crew members** if they don't have a lot of experience. Never boss people around especially when they are helping you for free. Nothing screams amateur than a director who is impatient and rude to his crew.

Give a schedule to everyone on set so they will know what to expect. In my own experience I've found that a **checklist** with each step of the production process increases the morale and buy-in of every crew member.

Be sure to maintain relationships with your crew after a project has been shot and make everyone feel involved during every phase of production. This will give your crew a greater sense of ownership and will keep them motivated to help you on **future projects**.

October 2nd

What All Producers Need to Understand About Working with Directors

For a film to truly succeed, its lead producer must understand how to effectively collaborate with the film's auteur. Unfortunately, no two directors are exactly alike.

The **producer/director relationship** can arguably make or break a great film. A talented **director** needs a dedicated **producer** to help bring their vision to life, and that **producer** needs to be working with a **director** that they truly believe in. But really, having a complimentary working relationship is just the tip of the iceberg. There are so many complexities involved with the creation of any film. For a great **producer** to achieve the best possible final product, they absolutely need to adhere to these guidelines:

1. Understand Your Role as a Support System

Unfortunately, it's quite common for **producers** to neglect one of their most crucial tasks – to ultimately support the **director** to the point where they're performing at the top of their game. A great **lead producer** is far more than just someone who pulls together the crew and keeps the schedule running on time. A truly great **producer** will always be able to get the best creative work possible out of their **directors** by being honest with them, supporting their decisions, and pushing them (even when the going gets tough) to finish each stage of the film to the best of their abilities.

As a **producer**, I'd argue that your role is partly that of a psychologist: you need to understand what your **director** needs in order to maximize their potential, which will ultimately benefit the entire production by leaps and bounds.

2. Don't Try to Direct

Some of the worst collaborations I've ever had with **producers** were with individuals that didn't know their roles. The most effective **producers** understand that they're there to bring someone else's vision to life, and not to interfere with that vision. That's not to say that a **producer** shouldn't have a vision of their own, but rather that their vision needs to be focused in a different place.

The vision of the **producer** should be big picture oriented. Above and beyond production and post, they need to be able to see the path to success with the film – including distribution, marketing, and countless other elements. When too much emphasis is placed on trying to do the **director's job** for them, ultimately everyone loses.

3. Picking the Right Director Is Paramount

To use a music analogy, finding the right **director** to collaborate with is just like finding the right bandmate. You need to work with someone who you respect, can tolerate for months on end, and who you trust immensely. It isn't enough to just work with a **director** because they have some clout and you think they can open some doors for you with regards to talent, financing, or otherwise.

Fostering a positive collaboration between yourself and your **director** starts with finding the right person to work with. Someone whose style you understand and respect. Someone whose personality gels well with yours. And someone who's willing to work through the rough patches with you. If you don't choose your **director** wisely, you won't be able to see eye to eye on most things, and the film will very likely falter as a result.

October 3rd
What Are Focus Charts and Why Do You Need One?

Ever used a focus chart? Learn more about this important filmmaking tool and discover how it can help your next production.

The very first thing you need to do before you ever roll on a single camera is obtain **critical focus**. By making absolutely sure you have **critical focus**, you're ensuring that your final product is of professional quality. Most cameras have a magnify feature option that allows you to crop in closely to a subject and set your focus.

Basic Filmmaker has a great four-part series on how to get the **critical focus** you need. Here's the first part.

There are several tools you can use while on location or on set that will help you **capture critical focus**. One such tool is a **focus chart**.

What Is a Focus Chart?

Basically, a **focus chart** acts like a target. It gives you multiple areas to zoom in on in order to get the focus you need. You will usually see a **focus chart** utilized in a controlled studio environment, but it isn't always necessary. **Focus charts** are typically used when working with shallower depths of field. It's common to see **focus charts** used on a product or low-light shoot.

Focus charts can also be used for calibrating lenses and testing your camera's autofocus. Using a **focus chart**, you can quickly determine if your lens or your camera is causing chromatic distortions.

Where Can You Get Your Hands on One?

When you first do a search for **focus charts**, you'll find that they aren't cheap. The less-expensive ones are around $100, while some can get as high as $1500 or more. If you're on a budget, you can download Distant Blue's Focus Chart App. It's free and essentially turns your smart phone or tablet into a **focus chart**.

If you would rather have a printed version of the **focus chart**, but don't have the money to purchase one, then you can make one in Illustrator.

October 4th
Why a Script Supervisor is Essential to Your Film's Success

Ever spent countless hours filming only to discover crucial continuity mistakes, rendering your film a mess? Preserving your film's continuity is key to maintaining the script's credibility.

You're on set. The entire crew is hard at work on the last scene before you wrap. The lighting is perfect, your camera operator has an amazing shot, excellent audio, and the actors are all delivering. You complete the scene in a timely fashion thanks to your crew's excellence. After wrapping your film, post-production immediately begins. **In editing, you discover that your film cannot be cut.**

Despite your crew's professionalism and excellence, your film lacks consistency: there are tons of continuity errors. Who was maintaining this continuity (or lack of it)? The script supervisor (called the continuity supervisor in the UK) has the extremely important task of maintaining your film's continuity from shot to shot. They are essentially the editor's representatives on set.

When every shot, action, and motion is consistent in your film, then you have achieved good continuity. The shooting schedule for a film may continue over a period of a few days, months, or even years. This places an even greater emphasis on maintaining proper consistency between shots.

Responsibilities of a Script Supervisor

It is the job of the Script Supervisor to make a log of every action that is shot:

- What was the camera shot (close up, medium, wide, etc)?
- Were there any technical problems with lighting, camera or audio equipment?
- Is the take a Print (P), No Good (NG) or BUST?
- Did your director want you to notate any particular take as the one to stand out?
- Were there any complaints or special notes from either your DoP (Director of Photography) or director?

The majority of feature and short films are shot with only one camera. Of course, the director or DoP may prefer more coverage for a scene. This would entail moving the same camera to various angles and changing focal points and camera lenses for the same scene. Obviously, this can take some time. Maintaining continuity despite this movement can become extremely difficult, but is aided by the help of the script supervisor's notes. Always plan the extra time to shoot additional takes.

If the continuity was broken in any way, enough time should be allotted to correct this. **It is the script supervisor's responsibility to ensure that the film will cut.**

The Continuity Report

The script supervisor's notes are outlined in a continuity report that is created throughout the shooting process. This report should contain the following information:

- **Daily log of the shoot**
- **Particular action that is occurring in the shot**
- **Camera configurations**
- **Audio and picture quality**
- **Crew list**

To further avoid continuity errors, an assistant to the **script supervisor** is usually a necessity. Two sets of eyes are definitely better than one when it comes to catching subtle errors on set. To maximize the impact of the assistant, it is important that they have a different vantage point than the **script supervisor**.

Some mistakes can easily be fixed on set, however if overlooked an expensive reshoot may be your only option. To help avoid that, the assistant can take pictures of each actor's exact movements, wardrobe, makeup, hair and props. This will help immensely if you're forced to split a scene up by a few hours, days, or even months.

Let's Wrap

You owe it to yourself, the crew and the actors to be on top of your film's continuity. Hiring a trusted **script supervisor** will ensure that your film will be cut without having to compromise your edit. Don't overlook this seldom-discussed, but entirely necessary, on set position!

October 5th
Yesterday's Cinematography Tool Reinvented for Tomorrow

Alpha Wheels redesigns a classic filmmaking tool for the future of film gear. Gain absolute precision and control over camera movement on gimbal stabilizers with these futuristic hand wheels.

Hand wheels are one of the oldest tools cinematographers have utilized on set. They offer control over **cranes**, **dollies**, and a variety of **camera mounts**. The team at 1A Tools wanted to bring that same level of precision control to stabilizers like the MoVI and Ronin.

Now, these aren't the first **hand wheels** designed for gimbals — others, like the PLC Veracity Control Wheels, have been available since 2014. However, the Alpha Wheels feature a sleek and stunning design, and its open API offers endless possibilities. What also sets Alpha Wheels apart is the ability to use the wheels in Cine Designer, offering total control in previsualization.

We've built the software to practice camera moves in a very realistic 3D environment. – Cinematography Database

Here's a look at the Alpha Wheels in action.

The Alpha Wheels system comes in two variations, lightweight aluminum or heavy-duty brass. The aluminum allows for easy transportation and remains incredibly responsive. The much more durable brass will fall in line with similar hand wheels already used on major sets. They are three times the weight of the aluminum wheels.

I spoke with 1A Tools co-owner Boyd Hobbs about the new Alpha Wheels.

As working DPs, when we conceived of the Alpha Wheels, we didn't stop at gimbals and remote heads. We thought of all the platforms we want to use wheels for, and we imagined a set of wheels with an open, flexible design that we could use on every job, no matter the type or budget.

For filmmakers with a MoVI, the **Alpha Wheels are directly compatible with the MoVI** controller. A single cable delivers both data and power. This setup allows operators access to multiple MoVI/MIMIC/joystick/Alpha Wheels combos. There are also updates coming to those with the DJI Ronin.

We are actively **working on improving the Ronin integration**. It can work right now through any off-the-shelf Futaba controller for those that really want it. We want to finalize our recommended workflow. This workflow will be published before we ship.

As previously mentioned, a standout feature is the ability to use the Alpha Wheels in pre-production. The system uses an API to integrate with Cine Designer. It isn't just the Cine Designer angle that's most exciting, but the public release of the API. **The open API will allow endless possibilities.**

We walked through Cinegear this year with a prototype asking vendors what they thought and it was honestly incredible. The potential uses are endless. Everything from post VFX work, dynamic lighting grids, moving truss, new types of remote heads. The wheels are a great interface for cameras because they give you responsive, real-time, tactile control. And now that so much of the industry is gaining levels of remote control or motorization, there is a need for responsive, real-time, tactile control in so many corners of the industry.

We would be thrilled to see it used outside the film industry. For many people once they see it in use and hear that it has an open API, that's when lightning strikes and they can imagine a use in their own field. That's why we are opening it up. Our creativity made the wheels. Now it's open for anyone else's creativity to apply them.

Communication protocols will include: Serial via USB, Serial via Lemo, CAN BUS, Raw Encoder Data, and stepper motor compatible Step and Direction signal. 1A Tools will publish an open API on their website for each protocol as they become available.

Technical Specs:

Supported Outputs via Interfaces

- Freefly MoVI M15 via Spektrum DX7S/MOVI Controller
- Freefly MoVI M10 via Spektrum DX7S/MOVI Controller
- Freefly MoVI M5 via Spektrum DX7S/MOVI Controller
- Cine Designer via Micro USB
- DJI Ronin (Coming Soon)

Weight

- 6 lbs w/ aluminum wheels
- 9.5 lbs w/ aluminum wheels and base
- 16 lbs w/ brass wheels and base

Open API Outputs (Subject to Change)

- Serial via USB
- Serial via IO Port
- CAN Bus via EXT Port
- Step and Direction Pulses via EXT Port
- Raw Encoder Data via EXT Port
- Analog via IO Port

Power Inputs

- 7-30V Unregulated via 2-Pin Lemo (Arri Polarity)
- 5V Regulated via IO Port
- 5V Regulated via Micro USB

October 6th

Your Crash Course in Assistant Directing

From shooting schedules to protocol on set, assistant directing is a lot more than meets the eye. Here's a step-by-step guide to help you become a qualified 1st AD.

The **assistant director,** not to be confused with an assistant *to* the director, is one of the most integral parts of any functioning production.

Side note: The **first assistant director** is often referred to as the **1st AD** or **AD** for short. On top of all responsibilities below, the **AD** is also in charge of a department of **other assistant directors** (2nd AD, 2nd 2nd AD, 3rd AD) and **production runners.**

The **AD** coordinates all production activity and serves as the liaison from the crew to the creative line on set. It sounds simple when you put it that way — but it's actually one of the most involved positions in both pre-production and production. Becoming qualified for the job takes lots of patience, practice, and brain power. And multitasking will become your middle name.

Step 1: Break Down the Script

Once the **script** is deemed **locked** by the writer and director, you will begin breaking it down. Make sure it is the latest version because this process is not one you'll want to do over. Read the script once for story, then grab your favorite pack of highlighters.

You will re-read the script over and over to make note of every aspect that will require attention. This is usually done by dividing it up into the following categories to keep things organized for your department heads: **characters**, **animals**, **locations**, **atmosphere**, **vehicles**, **props**, **wardrobe**, **hair** and **makeup**, **special effects**, **stunts**, and **sound effects**. Use a different colored highlighter for each category when you are reading through, and make sure to **create a key** for other's reading your script breakdown.

After highlighting and taking notes, you will **break the pages down into eighths**. A script is broken into **eighths** to help accurately **time the script** and decide **how much can be filmed each day**. You will start at the top of each page and **break the script into eight even rows** (approximately one inch each).

If the scene exceeds eight rows it becomes one page and whatever the remaining eighths are. **One page** translates to **one minute** of screen time. If a scene is **3 and 4/8ths** of a page, it should translate to approximately **3:30 of screen time** and so forth. You will use this information to create a **shooting schedule** later on.

Once you are finished marking up your script, you can create script breakdown sheets — **one sheet per scene** that summarizes all elements necessary from each department to bring that scene to life.

Step 2: Create the Shooting Schedules

You must first decide **how many days** your project will take to film, then you can decide in **what order** you will shoot.

When deciding how many days it will take to film, you must establish how many pages you will be shooting per day. Time to pull out the **script breakdowns!** You will analyze each scene separately to figure out how many days are needed to shoot each scene. For most scripts, it is safe to say you can **shoot three to four pages in a twelve-hour day** at a reasonable pace, and sometimes up to six or seven pages a day when your crew is an efficient, well-oiled machine. However, be sure to consider extra time when you have animals, children, large crowds, special effects, stunts or location restrictions in your script.

Once you've decided how many pages you will shoot each day, you will arrive at a total number of shoot days. Make lists of all of your **actors,** all of your **locations,** and all of your **setups** in each location. The setups will be determined by looking at your **director of photography's shot list** and communicating with the **camera** and **lighting teams.** Now it's time to schedule your shoot!

You want to "shoot-out" actors, locations, and set-ups. If the first and last scene of your film take place at the same location with the same people, it would not make sense to split them up. You would **group those scenes together** in the schedule to save time and money. This is what is referred to as "shooting-out." Use your **pages-per-scene** and **pages-per-day total numbers** as the outline for your schedule and fill it in aiming to **shoot-out your actors, locations, and set-ups.**

Step 3: Put Together the 'Day Out of Days'

The 'Day Out of Days' or the **DOOD** is a spreadsheet that's used to tally the number of days each of your cast members will be working.

It is arranged as an easy-to-read chart with columns for each day and rows for each cast member. The letters in the grid represent days on set. An "**S**" is used for the actor's start day, "**W**" for a work day, "**R**" for a rehearsal day, "**T**" for a travel day, "**H**" for a holding day, and "**F**" for the finishing day.

The **DOOD** makes it easy for each actor to see when they will be called to set, and for the producer to see how many days each actor will need to be paid for.

Step 4: Become the Timekeeper on Set

As the **AD,** you are in charge of running the set efficiently, knowing what is going on with each department at all times, and maintaining a **positive attitude** throughout. Here's how you're going to do it:

- Start out by **introducing yourself** to every crew member on set. This is important because you must be accessible to the crew, but they need to know **who's boss.**
- Be confident in your abilities, your schedule, and your knowledge of the script. You did **plan out the whole shoot** after all.
- Allow time for **blocking** and **rehearsal,** but not too much time.
- When it's time to roll, be loud with your calls and don't forget to **use your walkie.** Standard calls: lock up the set, call for quiet, ask everyone to settle, then roll camera, roll sound, and you're ready for action.
- If you are ever running behind, **communicate, communicate, communicate.** Talk to each department for solutions, and always talk to your director about what is going on.

The **AD** keeps each shoot day running smoothly and on schedule to make sure that the production meets its goals. He or she is in constant communication with the **director,** letting them know how much time they have left for each shot. When the schedule gets tight, the **AD** also decides with the **director** whether it is time to move on to the next shot, or if they can afford to reallot time from another shot to keep going.

October 7th
5 Editors that Broke the Hollywood Studio System

As the Hollywood studio system began to crumble, these editors turned a new generation of young filmmakers into household names.

In the late 1960s, the United States of America found itself in a transitional stage. The younger generation had attached themselves to art, music, and film. Young filmmakers were unlike any directors before them. They had grown up with movies and the meticulously studied them. By the 1970s, these young directors were breaking box office records.

Names like Scorsese, Spielberg, and Lucas became legendary after this period. Behind those directors were some incredible editors who were also breaking traditional molds. Following the footsteps of the pioneering women in film editing, **these women would cut some of the most praised work in American cinema.** They were the editors of New Hollywood.

Anne V. Coates

Anne Voase Coates had dreamed of working in film. Her uncle, J. Arthur Rank, was a founding member of Pinewood Film Studios. His company, the Rank Organization, also controlled Denham Film Studios and the Odeon Cinemas chain. Rank was a devout Methodist, who produced many religious films.
Anne had expressed her desires to work in film, but her uncle had reservations. He attempted to break her spirits by having her cut many of the religious films he was producing. His hope what that she would lose interest in the industry and return to her work as a nurse. However, **Anne found the work invigorating.** She fixed film prints of religious short films and sent them on various British church tours.
There were some wonderful women editors who helped inspire me to go into editing in England. In a way, I've never looked at myself as a woman in the business. I've just looked at myself as an editor. I mean, I'm sure I've been turned down because I'm a woman, but then other times I've been used because they wanted a woman editor. – Film Sound

Her passion landed her a job as an **assistant film editor at Pinewood Studios.** The first film she worked on was *The Red Shoes* for director Michael Powell in 1948. She worked under editor Reggie Mills, who despite not talking much, taught Anne a tremendous amount of discipline when it came to editing a film. Mills would go on to win the **Academy Award for**

Best Film Editing for *The Red Shoes*. By 1952, Coates would receive **her first credit as an editor** for *The Pickwick Papers*.

In 1962, Anne V. Coates would work with director David Lean to **masterfully edit the epic film *Lawrence of Arabia***. The film was an astronomical success, and the editing techniques used by Coates are still studied and used today.

I suppose the most challenging film I cut was "Lawrence," because we had such a huge amount of film – I believe it was 31 miles! – which gave me an abundance of choices. – Turner Classic Movies

The most famous edit in the film is the *literal* match cut. The film cuts from the image of a match to the sun over the Arabian desert.

In this documentary look at the making of the film, Anne V. Coates discusses editing *Lawrence of Arabia*. She explains the difficulty of editing the film in London, while the sound crew worked in Shepperton Studios.

Coates worked seven days a week for four months to complete *Lawrence of Arabia* on time. Her worked paid off, as **Anne won the Academy Award for Best Film Editing**. *Lawrence of Arabia* was nominated for ten Oscars, winning seven.

Two years later, **Anne was nominated for her second Academy Award** for her work on *Becket*.

There are nonlinear small things in my editing sometimes that you might not even have noticed. I started jump-cutting from one place to another quite a lot. When I was editing Becket, the producer, Hal Wallis, said, "You can't do that. You can't cut from this shot to that shot without a dissolve as they are 50 miles apart." I said, "Guess what? I've done it and it works perfectly." And it's still in the film. – Editors Guild

She received her **third Oscar nomination** for the 1981 film *The Elephant Man*. The film was a challenge, as producer Mel Brooks didn't want the audience to see the Elephant Man's face until later in the film.

By the 1990s, the changes in the film industry meant that **Anne would have to learn an entirely new editing process.**

When Frank Marshall and Kathleen Kennedy offered me Congo, they said, "Well, you have to do it digitally because the special effects system couldn't do it otherwise." ***So, they had me taught on Lightworks****. . . It's just another tool, really. Once I got that in my mind, I progressed* *faster. And then, when I did Out of Sight, Steven Soderbergh had a sound man who could link up with an Avid [Media Composer] but not with a Lightworks.* **I moved then from Lightworks to Avid, and I've stayed on an Avid ever since.** *– Editors Guild*

Anne V. Coates is still working in the industry, recently surpassing the length of Margaret Booth's storied career. She just completed the 2015 blockbuster film *Fifty Shades of Grey*. To date she has been nominated for five Oscars, winning one. She has also a member of the Order of the British Empire.

Thelma Schoonmaker

While studying at Columbia University, Thelma Schoonmaker answered a *New York Times* ad for an **assistant film editor**. She would cut successful European films to fit US broadcast time standards. In that job, she learned the art of negative cutting.
Schoonmaker then signed up for a six-week filmmaking course at New York University (NYU). **It was there she met a young Martin Scorsese.** Scorsese was struggling to finish his short film, *What's a Nice Girl Like You Doing in a Place Like This?* A professor asked Schoonmaker to help Scorsese finish the film, and thus started the legendary Hollywood duo. She would edit Scorsese's first feature film, 1967's *I Call First* – renamed *Who's That Knocking at My Door*.
In 1970, Thelma Schoonmaker edited *Woodstock*, the documentary on the famous American music festival. The film showcased the performers through a series of superimpositions and freeze frames. The film earned Schoonmaker her **first Oscar Nomination for Best Film Editing**, a nomination rarely awarded to documentary films. (In 1996, *Woodstock* was selected for preservation in the United States National Film Registry by the Library of Congress.)

Even though Schoonmaker earned an Academy Award nomination for her editing, **she was unable to join the Motion Picture Editors Guild**. To acquire union membership, Schoonmaker would have to first work as an apprentice and an assistant. She refused to do so, and was thus forced to work on a series of small films and documentaries for the next decade.

In 1980, Scorsese called upon Schoonmaker to edit his film *Raging Bull*. Initially she had to decline, due to the fact that she was not a member of the Editors Guild. Apparently, her work and friendships over the years played in her favor, as the union was influenced to offer her membership. **Schoonmaker finally joined the Motion Picture Editors Guild** and got to work on *Raging Bull*.

In this presentation at EditFest NY 2010, Schoonmaker talks about her experiences editing the improvisation between Joe Pesci and Robert De Niro.

10 years after her original Academy Award nomination, Schoonmaker was once **again nominated for Best Film Editing**, this time taking home the Oscar for *Raging Bull*. **Schoonmaker went on to edit every single Scorsese film since.**

Not only did Scorsese help Schoonmaker achieve success as a film editor, **he also introduced Schoonmaker to her husband, director Michael Powell.** Powell was the director of the previously mentioned film, *The Red Shoes*. Powell was also a great influence on Scorsese, who had studied Powell's films.

After Michael Powell's death in 1990, Scorsese and Schoonmaker would go on to preserve his memory by restoring his films. In this fantastic video, the three can be seen together in the editing bay.

In 1991, **Thelma Schoonmaker received her third Oscar nomination** for her work on Scorsese's *Goodfellas*. Here's a look at Scorsese and Schoonmaker working on the sound mix. Though *Goodfellas* was nominated for six Oscars, only Joe Pesci won an award.

In 1995, Schoonmaker oversaw the Scorsese documentary *A Personal Journey with Martin Scorsese Through American Movies*, which was a part of the British Film Institute's celebration of the first 100 years of film.

Schoonmaker garnered her **fourth Academy Award nomination** for *Gangs of New York*. Two years later she **won the Academy Award for Best Film Editing** for *The Aviator*, and two years after that **she won another Academy Award for Best Film Editing** for *The Departed*. Her most recent Oscar nomination was for the film *Hugo*.

Thelma Schoonmaker's seven Academy Award nominations for Best Film Editing is the second most nominations in Oscar history. She trails Michael Kahn by one nomination. Schoonmaker is currently tied with legendary editor Barbara McLean.

Dede Allen

Dorothea Carothers "Dede" Allen began her career at Columbia Pictures in the 1940s. She first started as a production runner, eventually working her way up to sound librarian and eventually assistant film editor in the special effects department.

One of her **first projects as an editor** was the 1959 film *Odds Against Tomorrow*, which was directed by Wise. Wise **served as Allen's mentor**, often encouraging her to experiment with her editing. Wise was an editor turned director; he edited the legendary masterpiece *Citizen Kane*. In 1961, Dede Allen edited the hit film *The Hustler* starring Paul Newman. (The film's sequel, *The Color of Money*, was directed by Martin Scorsese and edited by Thelma Schoonmaker.) Dede Allen later collaborated with Paul Newman on *Rachel, Rachel*, *Slap Shot*, and *Harry & Son*.

As the Hollywood studio system crumbled, film editors took on a much more significant role than ever before. Traditionally, editors were studio employees that did not need attribution for their work on any particular film. This all changed in 1967, when **Dede Allen became the first film editor to ever receive a solo opening credit on a film.** The film just happened to be her most renowned and praised work – *Bonnie and Clyde*.

Dede Allen's work **broke from standard Hollywood editing techniques**. She implemented the use of jump cuts, or would open a scene with a close-up. It would be the finale of *Bonnie and Clyde* that would become her most famed use of quick paced editing. In less than a minute, Allen cuts over 50 times during the ambush scene.

In the 1970s, Allen would often collaborate with director Sidney Lumet, editing his films *Serpico*, *Dog Day Afternoon*, and *The Wiz*. Dede Allen earned her **first Academy Award nomination for Best Film Editing** for *Dog Day Afternoon*.

Warren Beatty, who had talked to Dede Allen about journalist John Reed during the production of *Bonnie and Clyde*, brought Allen on to edit the 1981 film *Reds*. It took two and a half years for her to finish the film, longer than any other film she had worked on. The John Reed story earned 12 Academy Award nominations, including **a second Oscar nomination for Best Film Editing** for Allen.

In 1985, Allen edited the John Hughes classic *The Breakfast Club*. She also edited *The Addams Family* in 1991. In 1992, Dede Allen accepted the role of **head of post-production at Warner Bros.** She would return to editing in 2000 with the film *Wonder Boys,* which garnered her **third and final Oscar nomination.** Dede Allen died in 2010 at the age of 86.

For an in-depth look at her career, take a look at one of her final interviews before her death.

Verna Fields — "Mother Cutter"

Verna Fields began her film career as a sound editor in the late 1950s and early 1960s, working on films like *El Cid*. By the mid-1960s, she was teaching film editing at the University of Southern California (USC). She would also edit occasional projects, like *The Legend of the Boy and the Eagle* and *Targets*.

In 1968, Fields made her directorial debut with the documentary *Journey to the Pacific*. **Verna Fields hired two editors to help her with the documentary, George Lucas and Marcia Griffin.** George and Marcia married in 1969.

Impressed with her work as a sound editor on his film *Targets*, director Peter Bogdanovich asked Fields to edit his films *What's Up, Doc?* and *Paper Moon*. At the same time, George Lucas had Verna Fields and Marcia Lucas edit his film *American Graffiti*.

Both *Paper Moons* and *American Graffiti* were nominated for the 1974 Academy Awards. *Paper Moons* received four nominations. *American Graffiti* earned five nominations, including **Best Film Editing for Verna Fields and Marcia Lucas.**

That same year, Fields began editing the *Sugarland Express*, the **directorial feature film debut of Steven Spielberg.** For her skill and attention to detail, **Fields became endearingly known as 'Mother Cutter.'**

Even though she was surrounded by up-and-coming talent, Verna Fields edited her last feature film in 1975. She worked on Spielberg's next film – *Jaws*. Verna Fields would absolutely go out at the top of her abilities, as *Jaws* is an absolute master class in editing. Here is an intense breakdown of one of the films scenes.

Verna Fields **won the Academy Award for Best Film Editing for** *Jaws*, beating out Dede Allen's *Dog Day Afternoon*.

Following the success of *Jaws*, **Verna Fields became the Vice-President for Feature Production at Universal Studios.** She remained in that position until her death in 1982.

Marcia Lucas

As previously mentioned, Marcia Griffin married George Lucas in 1969. She worked as an assistant editor on *THX 1138* and *The Candidate*. Marcia Lucas would then collaborate with Verna Fields on *American Graffiti*, earning **her first Oscar nomination.**

While Martin Scorsese was without Thelma Schoonmaker in the 1970s, Marcia Lucas edited *Alice Doesn't Live Here Anymore* and **served as Scorsese's supervising editor** for *Taxi Driver* and *New York, New York*.

In 1977, the world was introduced to *Star Wars*. Directed by George Lucas, **the film was edited by Marcia.** Not only did Marcia serve as the films editor, she helped rewrite the piece. In an interview with Rolling Stone, George Lucas said,

I was rewriting, I was struggling with that plot problem when my wife suggested that I kill off Ben, which she thought was a pretty outrageous idea, and I said, 'Well, that is an interesting idea, and I had been thinking about it.' Her first idea was to have Threepio get shot, and I said impossible because I wanted to start and end the film with the robots, I wanted the film to really be about the robots and have the theme be the framework for the rest of the movie. But then the more I thought about Ben getting killed the more I liked the idea.

Marcia was also crucial to the film's climactic Death Star finale. To build the tension the original sequence lacked, Marcia had to re-order the shots from the beginning. She told George: *If the audience doesn't cheer when Han Solo comes in at the last second in the Millennium Falcon to help Luke when he's being chased by Darth Vader, the picture doesn't work.*

Her intuition proved right, as *Star Wars* was not only a blockbuster hit, but also a hit with the critics. Marcia Lucas **won the Academy Award for Best Film Editing** for her work on *Star Wars*.

Marcia would go on to edit *Star Wars: Episode V – The Empire Strikes Back* and *Star Wars: Episode VI – Return of the Jedi*. Those would be the final films she would ever work on. Following a divorce from George Lucas, Marcia has withdrawn from the public view and kept to herself since.

October 8th
5 Simple Steps for Creating Epic Vlogs

Unsure of where to start your journey into the highest reaches of the vlogosphere? This quick guide will help you along the path toward vlogging success.

Vlogs — routinely produced, bite-sized, personality-driven videos featuring day-to-day activities and lifestyle content — are one of the hottest **videography trends** of the last few years. The biggest **vloggers** aren't just big. They're *huge*. Good Mythical Morning alone has collected almost **11,000,000 subscribers** and garnered over 2,5oo,ooo,ooo views since 2008. People are making money as professional YouTubers — and you can too with these easy steps and equipment suggestions.

1. Choose the Right Camera

Versatility is one of the most important qualities to consider when picking **the right camera for everyday shooting**. You need to be able to get up and go without worrying about the capabilities and/or limitations of your camera. **Vloggers** have quite a few camera options at their disposal:

- Canon PowerShot G7 X – $649
- Canon EOS Rebel T5i -$649
- Sony Cyber-shot DSC-RX100 IV – $948
- Canon EOS 70D – $999
- Sony Alpha a7S II – $2,998
- Sony Alpha A7R II – $3,198

Of course, remember that your camera is only a means to get your story to the people. Successful **vloggers** know that **telling an interesting story** is *everything*. Find an angle. A unique focus. Filtering the world through a **one-of-a-kind perspective** is the best way to compel people to watch.

2. Maintain a Steady Shot

Given the hectic, unpredictable nature of **filming a vlog**, it's tough to know what the shots will be or where your day might end up. Maintaining a **professional, visually appealing aesthetic** is a top priority when trying to gain subscribers and followers. Spare your audience a case of motion sickness and stabilize your camera.

Gorillapods, like the one seen above, are stellar for **quick tripod setups**. They're also perfect for maintaining a steady shot at a comfortable distance from your face. Manfrotto's PIXI Mini Table Top Tripod (seen below, via B&H) is an excellent accessory for point-and-shoot cameras. Plus, with the KLYP+ attachment, you can even use the PIXI Mini to **stabilize an iPhone**.

Keep in mind, you don't necessarily have to think small. Sometimes you just can't beat a **standard tripod** when capturing a time-lapse or still shot. Solid models start at less than $100 — just find one that fits your needs and budget.

3. Pay Attention to Audio

Vlogs are not meant to be cinematic masterpieces. They're fast-paced, brief, and directed at viewers who aren't expecting world-class quality. Nonetheless, bad audio can **ruin your final product** and chase away your audience. If you want keep your subscriber's eyes glued to the screen, make sure their ears are satisfied. One of the best audio recording options on the market is the Rode VideoMic Pro, which will set you back about $200.

Again, you simply can't beat consistent, clear audio. Unless your **vlogs** require boom mics and intricate staging, Rode's the way to go.

4. Don't Neglect Lighting

Lighting for a **vlog** is a bit tricky. You're usually on the go, or you don't have time to stop and properly light yourself or your subject. Obtaining a well-lit shot takes practice, but knowing how to **position your body and camera in relation to the sun** or nearest light source is crucial. Small LED panels (like the Z96 above) are moderately affordable, coming in between $100–$200, and they can be attached to the top of your camera.

5. Perfect the Edit

All the footage you capture throughout the day/week/month is worthless if it doesn't end up **pieced together** in an entertaining way. **Video editing** can be tedious, but it's vital to the success of your project — so be prepared to spend some serious quality time with your NLE. Some YouTubers (Casey Neistat, for instance) prefer **Final Cut Pro X**. Others, like Ben Brown, edit in **Premiere Pro**. Just go with the one you're most comfortable with because you're going to be working with it constantly. The scheduled, routine nature of **vlogging** demands it. Getting into the flow of shooting and editing a video per day/week/month takes discipline, but it is possible. Below, previously mentioned travel vlogger **Ben Brown** demonstrates how he edits his **daily vlogs**.

Get Inspired: Six Successful Vlogs

Vlogging can be liberating, emotionally and creatively. Frankly, there are no rules for content, structure, length, you name it. **Vlogs must simply be engaging.** They must compel people to **subscribe** and return for every new episode.
For some **vlogging inspiration**, check out these successful channels. Notice each creator's approach and the atmosphere they cultivate. Remember, it's their one-of-a-kind view of life that keeps people coming back again and again.

Sam and Niko (from Corridor Digital)

Casey Neistat

Mr Ben Brown

Raya Was Here

Ethan and Hila

Vagabrothers

October 9th

Cutting Commercials: Editing 15, 30, and 60-Second Spots

Learn how to decide the right length you need for a commercial spot, and find out how to work with loops and short tracks to recut the same spot three times.

The **best length for a commercial** or ad is an often-debated topic. For a typical ad, most national broadcasting stations allow either a 15-second, 30-second, or 60-second slot. Choosing the right length is going to be difficult, as every product and company differs. **Some companies go ahead and produce all three commercial lengths**, using each ad in different markets. They may use a 60-second spot for national television, 30-seconds for local television, and a 15-second spot for web ads.

Shorter commercials have been increasing in popularity. Advertisers can spend less on 15-second time slot versus a 30-second slot. This allows them to run the ad more often and for longer periods of time. According the *New York Times*, that's why the 15-second spot was first created in the late 1980s.

By the mid-2000s, 15-second spots accounted for over 36% of all commercial time sold by the major broadcast networks. It's not just a cheaper time slot too, as it's also cheaper to make a shorter commercial. With the increasing presence of internet ads, advertisers are finding that the brand performance of a 15-second spot is equal to a 30-second spot. It's also more shareable, as 15-second social videos are shared 37% more than 30-second or 60-second ads.

With the increasing popularity of 15-second ads, why do you still need to cut 30-second and 60-second spots? Well, larger companies may prefer the storytelling aspect of a longer ad. Also, the decision for the final run time may not even be decided until well after editing has commenced. **This is a struggle for many video editors**, and it's the reason why **CR Production Music.com offers so many different lengths for each of our tracks**. Let's look at some tips and tricks for editing commercials of different lengths.

The Best Type of Ads for 15, 30, and 60-Second Spots

You know how the hardest part of editing is trimming everything down into a great video? Well, now after you finish the video — you will have to do it TWO MORE TIMES. It can be enough to drive you crazy. **The shorter the final length, the tougher the edit.** Ease your pain by knowing what the company is looking for in their commercial.

60-Seconds

Is the point of the commercial spot to tell a story? Then you will most likely need to use a full 60-seconds. This allows the most time to tell a brand story and leave viewers with a longer message. The downside is that this may be too long for most viewers. In fact, it's been noted that an audience begins to lose attention around the 45-second mark. 60-second videos are also great at **introducing a whole new ad campaign to viewers**, which can result in shorter versions of the same ad, as well as different spots in the future.

When Geico and the Martin Agency launched a new ad campaign deemed the "unskippable" promos, they first introduced a 60-second version to show the concept to audiences. This version carries the gag from the 13-second mark when the dog first starts eating food up until the end.

30-Seconds

Commercial spots that focus on humorous campaigns benefit the most from 30-second spots. Viewers also have 75-80% the recall of a 30-second spot compared to a 60-second spot. With the right joke or amount of humor, the 30-second spot can also be more memorable than a 15-second ad. However, some believe that the 30-second ad is dying.

To further the example of recutting the same ad three times, **here is the 30-second version of the same Geico ad**. Note that the dog starts eating at the 10-second mark, shaving off three seconds from the previous ad. The ad ends before the dog gets on the table to eat the other plates.

15-Seconds

If the company is looking for the biggest return on a limited budget, **a 15-second spot may be the best answer**. These ads also tend to be more focused on sharing product information and using easy-to-explain messages. They can also be aired more frequently — and as mentioned previously, they are more likely to go viral on social media. The downside is that not all brand stories can be told in 15-seconds, and it can be difficult to convey larger messages. That said, shorter ads have a better chance of being repurposed for use on television, online, mobile, and in-store displays.

In the 15-second version of the Geico ad, the dog starts eating at the 12-second mark, and only eats from the father's plate. It's 1/4 of the length of the original 60-second ad, yet the joke still works in every version.

*Pro Tip: Keep in mind that broadcasters and stations have varying definitions of length. For example, some broadcasters request that a 30-second commercial is actually 30-seconds on the dot – not one frame more or less. Other stations may require that the ad be 29.5-seconds. Be sure to verify what is needed.

How to Trim a 60-Second Spot into a 30-Second Spot

If you are working with a talented and experienced director, you will hopefully find that every shot was perfectly timed to a stopwatch. Commercials rely on an actor's performance set to a specific time per shot. If you don't have this luxury, the edit is probably going to be a tough one. Without a perfectly timed shoot, you will find yourself fighting the script in post.

If the 60-second spot was already scripted and timed out, but the 30-second wasn't — you will need to trim wherever you can. Hopefully you can start by getting rid of a second or two from each clip. Delete any unnecessary establishing shots. Was there a four-second shot of a house and then a two-second shot of the front door? **Well, now it's just a two-second shot of the house.** You can easily establish a space quickly and move on, the viewers will be able to keep up.

Another trick is to **start with your audio.** If you are editing an existing song, get it down to 30-second and make sure to keep a quality sounding song throughout the piece. Another option is to use a shorter version of the song — like the ones provided by CR Production Music.com. Throw in a 30-second version of the same track, and then trim clips to the music.

How to Trim a 30-Second Spot into a 15-Second Spot

Going from 60-seconds to 30-seconds is hard enough, but trimming down to 15-seconds can be brutal. You will struggle with making sure you keep all the right clips, and you have to accept that you may need to delete some of the best footage to make the edit work.

If the original ad had a voice-over narration, **be prepared to heavily edit the audio — or ditch it entirely.** Like the previous note, throw in the shorter version of the same track, and then trim clips to the music.

After you finalize your edit, **be prepared to compress the 15-second file for a multitude of different formats.** Not only do stations want uncompressed high-resolution files (if not still tapes or disks at some places), you will also need to compress for web streaming on sites like YouTube as well as social media. Be sure to check each social media sites guidelines for optimum media.

October 10th

Documentary Film Editors Talk About Their Process

Some of Hollywood's top documentary editors got together at Sight, Sound and Story 2015 to discuss their process. Here are some highlights from their chat.

Documentary film editors Andy Grieve (Going Clear: Scientology and the Prison of Belief, The Armstrong Lie), Zac Stuart-Pontier (The Jinx, Catfish), and Pax Wassermann (Cartel Land, Knuckleball!) sat with Garret Savage (My Perestroika, Ready, Set, Bag!) in conversation as part of Sight, Sound and Story's annual New York City event, presented by Manhattan Edit Workshop on June 13th. Here's some of what they talked about.

Garrett: *What kind of thoughts or advice can you give on how to start a film and how not to start a film?*

Andy: *I think about it as compartmentalizing information. The worst situation is like when you're on the subway listening to music and your headphones are tied in a knot. You don't want to end up like that. Start small. Don't think, "This is the first scene, this is the first clip, this is how I start or end the film," just watch the footage and make small things and gradually connect* things together. I never tie knots I don't think I can untie. A lot of times I don't even do much cutting, I just kind of watch and add locators, or cut selects before I really start to assemble scenes. For me a mistake would be cutting a bunch of stuff that becomes useless. It's getting ahead of the process.

Garrett: You don't like creating a ton of select sequences, you like creating fewer rather than more?

Andy: That's evolved with technology because you can have longer sequences. I just don't like to have tons of bins open which can be messy. You can find the process that works for you. I know editors that write out tons of note cards and put them all over the wall. Everyone has their own sort of process, but in a bigger sense it's about not being overwhelmed and finding a way to keep things separate, and then once you're ready, start putting it all together.

Pax: I have a discussion with the director about why they wanted to make the film and what moments they really want to pop in the film. A lot of times those moments aren't reflected in the footage. Sometimes you do have to cut a scene to get the director's confidence in order to have the room to play. With the younger directors that's even more necessary because they're more nervous and anxious.

But first do a very quick overview of watching everything, making a lot of notes, holding on the first impressions. I make all kinds of stickies with all sorts of musings and ideas. It gets kind of ridiculous, but I try to hold onto those thoughts because by the time you get the first rough cut those first impressions are gone and you can't get those back.

Then you make a basic overview reviewing stuff, some of it watching very intently, definitely not going crazy with selects. Selects become a burden at a certain point. You can become beholden to the selects when what you really need to do is just look at the footage. Keep it all open for as long as possible, especially selects for an interview.

Zac: You don't know what's important yet.

Pax: Right. I don't really watch the interviews that much in the beginning. Some directors do a ton of interviews. It depends. You can get beholden to the bites then. If you really obsess over the sound bites, you don't really have a great film, you have a great interview.

Then, find a scene that epitomizes the spirit of the movie. Usually it's a scene that's in the middle of the movie. I would say the biggest mistake is to cut the beginning of the movie and obsessing over it. It'll never be the beginning you end up with. If you do that, you're not discovering the film enough.

Zac: I always think it's interesting that there's such a different mindset for when you're starting a film versus finishing one. I always think when I'm finishing a film that I'll be so much faster on the next one, but starting a film is this constant relearning. It's always sluggish. The more times I go through that, I get more confident of the different stages I have to go through. That first stage is so overwhelming and you have to get through that process. You have to learn the footage and it needs to get into your head. The goal is to be a sponge, absorbing it all. I like to put simple things together. They're not even scenes yet, but I organize things into subjects and then turn those into scenes.

Andy: After I cut selects for an interview, you don't even use half of them. Then I go back to the transcript and use stuff you had no idea was going to be useful. I don't know why that always happens. Maybe because the more sound-bitey stuff jumps out at first but then it doesn't feel as real. Then you wind up finding stuff that's much less transparent but fits the message of the story much better.

Garrett: What percentage of the job is the diplomatic, therapeutic part?

Pax: When there's a team of editors it's much more about verbalizing the entire idea. Sometimes that's the same as working with a director that's sitting next to you the whole time. They want to know what you're doing, and where you're going, so part of the diplomatic thing is getting really good at pitching your ideas. Editing is probably more craft than art, and while there's certainly a lot of art in it you have to be able to have inspiration, and it has to be free-flowing, and verbalizing it is very hard.

Andy: People are much more impatient now. I find it hard to actually sit and actively edit with someone. To have someone watch while I'm cutting, I feel tension and frustration from that person that it's not happening fast enough. I find it better to try not to do that as much as possible. People don't know which part of the process you're in. They see you put a shot up and they say, "oh no, not that shot," but you don't want them to comment because you're not there yet. The actual act of editing is less collaborative now.

Zac: *I think with features it's easier. You're more picking takes, as opposed to a documentary, you're trying to invent this thing out of nothing. So it's hard when someone says they don't like something, but you want them to consider the whole thing. It's such a long process and you want to keep it focused. You can really get bogged down in little things. It's hard to tell a director that you're not changing a shot right at that moment when you're dealing with the structure of the narrative, when all you're trying to find out is if this scene can go before this scene. I can fix the individual shot.*

One of the amazing things about documentaries is they continue to grow as you work on them. It's this organic thing even though the footage doesn't change. It's constantly staying new when it's working.

October 11th
Gutter Editing and the Uninflected Shot

Here's how to use the juxtaposition of uninflected shots and the gutter between them to make a compelling edit that keeps your viewers actively engaged in the storytelling process.

What is 'The Uninflected Shot'?

In his famous 1988 book, *On Directing Film*, David Mamet points to the **uninflected shot** as the crucial building block of cinematic storytelling. An uninflected shot is the opposite of a tableau shot, and **contains a minimum of visual information**. A shot of a hand, a spoon, a key, and a face can all be classified as uninflected.

When an uninflected image is paired with another uninflected image, the association elicits meaning in the mind of the viewer. Mamet considers this type of editing to be **more effective** than turning to a Steadicam shot or single take that merely follows characters and waits for something interesting to happen. Using the juxtaposition of uninflected shots is editing 101, but is so inextricably linked to the medium of film and video that it often gets taken for granted, and remembered only for its flashiest moments.

2001: A Space Odyssey via MGM

This famous graphic match in Stanley Kubrick's *2001: A Space Odyssey* is a juxtaposition of **uninflected shots**. But the bone isn't simply a bone. It's just become an important tool, something we wouldn't know without the shots and ideas that preceded it.

Intellectual Montage

Any shot of a single thing can qualify as uninflected. However, the problem with **uninflected shots** is that they easily slip into inflection, which is to say that they carry more meaning than the most simplified and stripped down classification.

This leads us to Sergei Eisenstein's concept of intellectual montage, which works when **the latent meaning in a shot is awakened** through the collision with another shot. This shot collision is a conversation between images that gives rise to new meaning in the mind of the viewer.

Intellectual montage can get pretty intense, especially when text gets thrown into the mix, as evidenced in the overwhelming assassin training video in the *Parallax View* (1974):

The Kuleshov Effect

Lev Kuleshov, Eisenstein's teacher for a short period of time, was another early Russian filmmaker, theorist, and a crucial experimenter with the idea of uninflected shots. He conducted a well-known experiment known as the Kuleshov effect wherein he paired **three sets of static, uninflected images**. Each set included the face of a man, Ivan Mosjoukine, with a separate uninflected shot.

The first pairing suggests hunger. The second suggests sadness. The third suggests lust. The decoding process and resulting association of the images is left to the viewer, who actively fills in "the gutter," or space between the images, with meaning.

Comic Books

Scott McCloud explores this idea of "the gutter" in his book, *Understanding Comics*. While the book is primarily about comic and graphic art, there are many filmmaking correlations. McCloud discusses the use of "the gutter" as a way to actively involve the reader, and in the case of movies, the viewer.

While the image of one man swinging an axe at another man is not the most uninflected image, it does function through an important omission. The juxtaposition with a second image containing a skyline and shriek compels an association on the part of the reader, who **completes the act of killing** merely suggested by the two images. The famous shower sequence from *Psycho* (1960) works by way of a similar principle.

Using the gutter is about leaving out information and entrusting your audience to fill in the gap. It's about visual restraint and building narratives through simplicity. After all, **the narrative power of any material is only as good as its ability to elicit involvement** on the part of your viewer.

Conclusion

Brevity and precision in shot selection and juxtaposition is like iceberg storytelling. Hemingway's six-word story (even if it may be an urban legend) is an example of the literary power of the uninflected shot: "For Sale. Baby Shoes. Never Worn." It's deceptively simple and yet **suggests something quite powerful** by forcing the reader to fill in the gutter. As you plan out your next film or video, consider your own use of the uninflected shot. As you **write your shot list and make your storyboards**, consider if your shots can be simplified to elicit greater audience involvement through the power of intellectual montage. Can you be making better use of "the gutter" between shots to actively involve your audience? With single takes and "oners" on the rise, it's easy to forget the effectiveness, and effectiveness, of a good old-fashioned cut. It doesn't take a lot of time. It does take some planning, imagination, and a little bit of trust in your viewers.

October 12th

How to Achieve Perfect Slow-Motion Results in Post

Overcranking in camera will give you the option to achieve beautiful slow-motion work in post. But if you don't follow the right formula in the editing room, your results will be less than ideal.

The 180-degree shutter rule states that your **shutter speed needs to be double that of your frame rate.** So if you're shooting at 24p, you'll want your shutter speed to be set to 1/48. If your shutter speed is any higher or any lower, you'll get unwanted results — either a sharp "fast-frame effect" or a slow-motion blur.

If you've been shooting for a while, then this may be second nature to you. But in the editing room, things can often get confusing for filmmakers…

Let's assume you've **captured a 48fps clip at a 1/96 shutter speed.** In post, if you were to slow that clip down to 50%, you'd end up with a perfect slow-motion effect since it would effectively play back at 24fps with a 1/48 shutter. But if you didn't slow that clip down at all, and just dropped it into a 24fps timeline, you'd essentially be working with a 24p equivalent shot that has a 1/96 shutter speed instead of 1/48. This would give your footage that fast-frame look I described earlier and clearly wouldn't adhere to the 180-degree shutter rule.

The point of all this, is that it's very important to **know the exact percentage you need to slow your footage down in post** in order to maintain that 180-degree shutter. The 48fps example is an easy one, since it's exactly double that of 24fps.

Here are some **common over cranked frame rates** with the respective percentages they should be slowed down to in post (in a 24p project/timeline):

- 30fps = 80%
- 48fps = 50%
- 60fps = 40%
- 80fps = 30%
- 96fps = 25%
- 100fps = 24%
- 120fps = 20%
- 150fps = 16%
- 180fps = 13%
- 240fps = 10%

If you're working with a frame rate that's not on this list, you can simply use this formula to calculate your target percentage:

24 / Amount of FPS = Slow Motion Percentage.

And of course if you're shooting in a different frame rate (such as 25fps PAL or 30fps NTSC), then simply use your project frame rate in place of "24" in the formula.

October 13th
How to Correct Underexposed Footage

You've underexposed your shot and now it's too dark to tell what's going on. Don't panic. Instead, use these techniques to correct underexposed footage.

We've covered how to salvage overexposed shots, but what about the opposite? Everyone at one point has offloaded their footage to find that, disappointingly, **a shot was underexposed**. Depending on the severity of the shot, you might still be able to salvage details from the **midtones** and **shadows**. Here's the underexposed shot we'll be working with.

Upon initially trying to **correct underexposed footage,** one might increase the exposure or ISO settings to add more 'light' to the clip in order bring back detail. However, this isn't going to work in your favor.

Here's Adobe's definition of the exposure effect: *The Exposure effect simulates the result of modifying the exposure setting (in f-stops) of the camera that captured the image.*

Increasing the exposure affects every aspect of your image, and ultimately you don't want that, as it's going to bring out the dirty noise. Here is a look at the result of **increasing the exposure** of the overall image. It leaves the **shadows** and **lower midtones** very murky.

How To Correct Underexposed Footage

Take the following steps to **bring your subjects out of the darkness** and keep your shadows clean.

Small disclaimer: Of course, if your shot is completely shrouded in darkness, you're not going to claim back much of that detail without completely ruining the image. If your blacks are already at (or below) 0, then you'll likely find that shadows will start to form into clunky areas of noise. If your shot is **a few stops underexposed**, this tip will bring life back into an underexposed image. This method **delivers detailed shadows** while **maintaining the midtones** that we boosted.

Step 1: Adjust Midtones and Highlights

First, you need to make a few simple adjustments with the **midtones** (Gamma) and **highlights** (Gain). These need to be **increased**. No matter what software you're using, from the basics of the **built-in 3-way color corrector in After Effects** to **DaVinci Resolve's dashboard**, you're going to be able to adjust these properties specifically.

You'll need to have the **waveform scope** active so you can see where your whites and blacks are sitting. By adjusting those settings, I've been able to bring the image back to a reasonable exposure for the scene. As this specific scene was dimly lit to start with (it's in a restaurant at night), it's important to **respect the location's lighting** when bringing the exposure back into the shot. Our waveform says that we have good midtones, the blacks are black, and we have a few highlights peaking naturally.

Step 2: Adjust Shadows

Our **shadows are a little milky** despite the waveform saying we are sitting near 0 black. Not to mention they are also noisy. To fix this, you want to take the curves (again, all editing platforms should have a curves control) and **pull the lower the midtones down**. Our shadows are now starting to look black. Although it looks as if we've lost detail in the man's shirt, when the clip is playing you can still see the detail.

However, we now have this **blue cast** within the shadows. This is another by-product of bringing detail out of the shadows. To remove this, you can either **push red into the shadows on the Lift control**, or (preferably) you can **use the blue curve to remove those lower blue midtones/shadows**.

Step 3: Reduce Noise

Finally, clean the image with a **noise reduction application.** Your image should now look a lot better than it did before. **Boosting the midtones** will be a better use than just increasing the exposure or brightness — by doing that you will bring a lot of noise out of that darkness. Finally, it should be noted that **underexposed images** will more than likely be absent in saturation. You may also need gently to **boost the saturation of the underexposed image.**
Here's a handy recap:

- Increase midtones and highlights while lowering the shadows.
- Apply curve to pull down the lower midtones.
- Apply correction curve to remove unwanted color casts.
- Boost saturation (if needed).
- Apply noise filter.

October 14th
How to Edit Comedy Scenes for Maximum Laughs

Learning how to edit comedy takes a very specific and unique set of skills. It's arguably one of the hardest genres to cut. These tips will help you maximize your laughs every time.

No matter what genre they're working in, an editor's job is undoubtable a difficult one. That said, **editing comedy** comes with its own set of principles and challenges that can often make it that much harder to tackle. Unlike many other genres that have a lot of leeway in terms of pacing and timing, **comedic edits** need to be extremely tight and specific in order to land well with an audience.
For those of you out there **cutting comedy**, whether it's in a commercial or feature-film format — these tips on **how to edit comedy scenes** are for you!

1. Go Multicam Whenever Possible

Comedy scenes are often shot with a two or three camera setup in order to catch spontaneous moments and have proper coverage on improvised dialogue. If you're fortunate enough to be given source footage for more than one camera on the scene you're editing — always take advantage of that.

In other words, don't simply edit your scene as you would have if it were shot with a single camera... you won't be taking advantage of the material you're given. Great comedic actors will most often have near-perfect comedic timing. When working in a multi-cam session, you'll be able to maintain the beats in the scene much more organically and effectively.

2. Know When the Beats Aren't Landing

Whether you're cutting a multicam project or not, there will be times when the comedic timing of a scene simply doesn't work. Perhaps it takes too long to get to a punchline, or there isn't a long enough awkward pause after a joke has been dropped.

As a **comedy editor**, it's your job above all else to be the authority on what's working and what's not. When things just aren't landing, you need to know when to cut or when to pad the scene. It's amazing how just a few extra frames added or trimmed can be the difference between a joke landing or not, so always stay sharp with regards to timing.

3. Test Your Footage

There are pros and cons to testing (or running a focus group) on any type of film. More often than not, it's incredibly helpful for comedies. As we've already touched on, **comedy is all about timing** – there's no better way to know if your timing is working than by watching others respond to the material.

After weeks or months in the editing room, certain jokes will feel funny to you just because you know they're coming, and others will have lost their novelty entirely, which may tempt you to cut them unnecessarily. Before you go too crazy in the editing room, be sure to test the film — even if it's just for a group of friends to gauge their reaction. Seeing when and where people laugh, which jokes go over their heads, and which moments people respond to most will be very telling.

October 15th

How to Give Your Video a Vintage Look

From lenses to post-production tweaks, there are lots of ways to give your footage a vintage look. Capture some old-school vibes with these video tips.

Hipster trends come and go, but it seems **vintage color grading** is here to stay — and rightfully so. **Vintage color grading** can be a fun way to give your projects a unique vibe. So, if you're looking for a new approach to stylizing your footage (or you're simply interested in how to create a vintage look), follow the quick steps below.

Vintage Lenses

One of the best things you can do to **give your project a vintage look** is shoot on a vintage lens. Unlike modern lenses, vintage lenses tend to distort colors around the edge of the frame, a phenomenon called chromatic aberration. Typically you'll find lots of chromatic aberration in older or cheaper lenses. This isn't ideal for modern video projects, but it's perfect for creating a vintage look. You can usually pick up a vintage lens on eBay for around $50 and buy an adapter to fit whatever mount your camera uses.

Keep It (Slightly) Soft

One of the key differences between modern video and vintage video is the sharpness of the final image. Typically, on vintage film, images degrade over time. This leads to an overall soft video or images. To simulate this on your camera, you can **turn down the sharpness in your camera menu settings** or simply **add a slight blur** to your final video. If you're using a program like Adobe After Effects to stylize your footage, **simply add a 3 to 4-point fast blur.**

Film Overlays

You've probably noticed how grainy vintage footage is. In order to simulate this on your own, you need to **download a free grain pack** online. Fortunately, there are quite a few out there. After you've downloaded your free grain pack, it's time to overlay it onto your footage. For most circumstances, you'll probably want to use a **soft light overlay blending mode.** I personally recommend turning down the opacity on an overlay blending mode until your grain looks perfect.

Decrease Contrast

Now it's time to start color grading. In order to make your footage look vintage, you'll want to **turn down the contrast just a little**. Vintage footage doesn't hold black or white levels as well as modern video. In most video editing applications, you can simply **add a contrast effect** and dial it down by about 20%.

Bring up the Black Levels

Modern Hollywood films typically have very dark black points in their video. This has become synonymous with theatrical color grading, and it's a very popular approach in the indie filmmaking community — but it's not a very good approach to **creating a vintage look**. The best thing you can do when working on a vintage color grade is bring up your black levels just a little bit. You want your blacks to map to a dark gray instead of deep black. You can get this look by using either the **curves effect** or the **levels effect**. It really just depends on your favorite color grading tools.

Bring Down the White Levels

You'll also want to **bring down the white levels** in your video. I recommend mapping the bright whites down to a light gray. Just like when working with the black levels mentioned in the step above, you can use either the **curves effect** or the **levels effect** to achieve this look.

Warm up the Highlights

Now it's time to adjust the overall color of your project. In order to do this, I recommend using the **curves effect**. In the curves effect, **navigate to the blue curve** and bring down the highlights, but keep the shadows about the same. This will warm up the highlights in your image and give your footage just a slight sepia look. You don't want to take this too far — you can quickly begin to make your film look a little too western. Just remember, warming up your highlights just a touch can go a long way.

Turn Down Saturation

One thing that's easy to see in **vintage video** is the lack of bright colors. This is simply due to the fact that vintage film degrades with time. All you need to do to simulate this look is simply **turn down the saturation** of your final video. You can easily do this in most video editing applications by adding a saturation effect. You don't want to go too crazy — a saturation decrease of 20 to 30% should be perfect.

Light Leaks

If you want to take your **vintage video** a step further, one of my favorite things to do is **add a light leak**. If you're not familiar, a light leak is essentially a pre-rendered video asset that simulates light spillage on old film.

October 16th

How To Increase Your Editing Speed Dramatically

As editors, we are always looking for the best way to tell a story. In most cases, the best possible version is only found after many passes of editing. Luckily, there are many things you can do to increase your editing speed significantly and get to the finish line faster.

Editing, like any other part of the creative process can be both highly enjoyable and immensely frustrating. When things are going well, it's an extremely rewarding experience that allows us to finally see our projects come to life. On the other hand, it's possible to get into slumps when editing (especially early on in the process) that can prevent us from finishing on time, and even worse – ending up with a subpar cut of the film.

I've always been a big believer that with any creative process (editing included) the best way to get to the finish line is by having a mold to work from. **I've never edited a project and simply locked off the first cut that I did, and I really don't think that anyone should.**

You always want to challenge yourself to get better results and to tell your story in the most efficient and effective way possible. Many times, this means that you will need to go through many different iterations of your edit – which is completely fine. In fact, it's encouraged.

You might have a general idea of what your film is going to look like, but truthfully you will never really know until you can watch a finished version. For this reason, I suggest getting a first rough cut of your project completed as **quickly as possible**. After all, if the edit is going to change so drastically throughout the process anyways, you are better off getting the first pass done sooner than later (even if it's flawed), so you at least have something to work from. Not to mention, you don't want to spend too much time finessing edits and smoothing over cuts on a first pass of anything, since you are likely to lose just about all of that hard work.

Here are my tips for getting through your edit faster, so you can start to focus on the revisions more effectively.

Organize like crazy.

Organization may not exactly be the sexiest part of the editing process, but if you do your legwork up front and actually set up your project file properly, you will be able to work way faster once you're actually in the thick of things.

Organization includes everything from creating proxy files (so that you can edit quickly, even from a laptop), to logging and labeling all of your footage properly. The last thing that you want to do is get halfway through an edit while on a roll, and then have to stop for **20 minutes** to go and look for a clip. Organize your footage like crazy and you'll thank yourself later.

Don't worry about audio edits.

Your audio is going to sound pretty bad during the rough cut of your film. Obviously if your sound recordist did their job properly, the actual audio itself will be high quality. But in the context of your edit, it **may not sound great at all**. Certain takes will be louder than others, there will be gaps where no room tone is placed, sound effects will be missing, and loads of other issues will arise.

It will be tempting to just go ahead and start finessing your audio so that it sounds far more clean (especially if you have to show your producers a cut), but I would advise against wasting time doing this. No matter what, it's going to get re-done, and let's face it – you're probably not that proficient with post-audio. So leave it to the pros, and do what you do best – edit! Even if it means having to listen through some crappy audio during the rough cut/assembly stages.

Avoid going through every take.

Depending on how you (or your director) shot the project, you may have a ridiculous amount of coverage to go through. If this is the case, I would advise against going through all of it initially, as you simply don't need to. Some editors like to go through every take first and do '**selects**' where they will place their favorite clips in a timeline, but in many cases that's a waste of time, considering you aren't going to use 90% of that material.

Instead, go through the edit intuitively and ask yourself '**what comes next?**' every step of the way. By doing this, the edit will feel far more organic as you are making choices based on your intuition, and it will move much more quickly as well.

Learn your keyboard shortcuts.

If you haven't already started editing with **keyboard shortcuts**, then drop what you're doing and learn how to edit that way now. On a really small project (like a 30 second commercial) this may not be as much of a factor, but when dealing with a substantial short or feature film you can save a lot of time by not juggling the mouse and keyboard so much.

You wouldn't believe how much time you actually spend physically moving between mouse and keyboard when editing, not to mention the fact that keyboard shortcuts are in themselves much faster than 'drag and drop' mouse editing.

Use placeholders.

Sometimes you're on a roll editing a scene or sequence, but then you hit a wall. Something's just not working creatively. Maybe you can't find the right temp track to use, or there isn't a good enough transitional shot to bring you into the next act. Whatever the issue may be, if you start to get stuck on **something trivial** – just move on.

You don't want to waste an hour of your precious time trying to finesse an edit or work on a scene that just isn't gelling. Instead, don't be afraid to just drop in a placeholder (which could simply be a title card, explaining the scene that will go there), and move on. After getting through a few more scenes and **maintaining your momentum**, it will be a lot easier to go back to that placeholder and figure out what you want to do there, since you'll be looking at it with fresh eyes.

October 17th

How to Organically Incorporate Close-Ups Into Your Edit

Close-ups and extreme close-ups have the power to be intimate, terrifying, and hilarious. Placing these shots naturally in your work is tricky — but not impossible.

Close-ups have been around since the beginning of film. They're used in everything you watch and are an essential part of filmmaking. Whether you're **shooting commercials**, **music videos**, **corporate video** or actual **movies**, close-ups are a necessity and need to be utilized in the proper way at the appropriate time.

Building Tension

Sergio Leone was a master of the close-up. Not only would he use super-wide lenses for extreme close-ups of eyes, hands, guns, and mouths, but he would edit his scenes in a way that built tension like nobody's business. Instead of using actual camera and body movement to convey the tense nature of a scene, Leone would cut from **medium shot** to **close-up** to **extreme close-up** while moving back and forth between characters. The result was intense to say the least. In doing this, the audience moves with you from one desired gaze to the next. This quick, direct cutting gives the viewer no time to think — just feel.

An extreme close-up of the eye is a classic method for **showing character reactions and emotions**. A dilating, widening, or shutting eye conveys a sense of suddenness and tension that is hard to replicate with other body movements. Roman Holiday released this wonderful video compilation of extreme eye close-ups to show you the possibilities and appeal of using these shots.

Transitional

Close-ups can be an excellent way of **transitioning** to the next scene. Because of the screen-filling, eye-encompassing nature of close-ups, the object in frame is usually the ONLY object in frame. Nothing else matters. When moving from scene to scene, cutting away to an object or person that might also be in the next scene is an excellent way of transitioning by means of distraction.

This method of transition is put to perfect use by Edgar Wright. Wright has discussed in the past why he likes close-ups and how close-ups can be implemented in an intelligent way. Every Frame A Painting also produced an enlightening video on why Edgar Wright's editing and camera work is some of the best out there. Worth the watch!

Using Macro

Regardless of the genre or style of video you're producing, **macro lens** close-ups can be seamlessly woven into the plot — or they can be exceptionally jarring. When a character is looking at something, cut to that extremely close-up shot of the "something." On the opposite end of the spectrum, wake your audience up with a jolting close-up.
The above image is from Jonathan Glazer's *Under the Skin*, set against the **white backdrop**, the central alien character discovers an ant crawling on her finger. The **staggeringly close shot** of the ant makes it seem monstrous as it moves around on her massive finger. This shot immediately disappears and returns to wide, leaving the viewer suspended and wondering what they just saw. The cut makes the shot of the ant that much more **appalling** and **disturbing**.
Taking a more light-hearted approach to a macro shot of ants, director Peyton Reed, used macro lenses to get actual shots of ants and the environments for *Ant-Man*. This creative use of **macro photography** is an excellent example of how **close-ups** can produce a stunning experience for the audience.

October 18th

How to Organize a Feature Film Edit Like a Pro

Organize your feature film edit like the editor of Mission Impossible: Rogue Nation, Eddie Hamilton.

Editor Eddie Hamilton has worked his way up the Hollywood blockbuster editing ladder to what has to be the top spot — **cutting a summer tent pole franchise hit, *Mission Impossible: Rogue Nation*.**
I recently put together a little **round up of some of Eddie's best interviews** on the topic of editing director Christopher McQuarrie and producer/star Tom Cruise's latest adventure over on my own blog, but I thought it would be a great idea to **draw out some of the fine-grain detail of how Eddie organizes his edit** in this post.

Eddie shared some of his workflow tips in this fantastic interview with PVC writer Steve Hullfish, which provides some of the detail in this post, as well as other interviews with Eddie that I've read or heard over the years. Eddie's essential philosophy is that **everything should be so clearly labelled and logically laid out** that any other editor could sit down in his chair and quickly find anything they needed.
The image above is a screenshot of Eddie's Avid Media Composer timeline for the first reel of *Mission Impossible: Rogue Nation*.

Organizing a Feature Film Edit

Organization of your edit begins at the project level with your Bin structure. In the interview with Steve Hullfish, Eddie walks through his preferred structure which I've visualized for you in the above image.
So what's going on? Well, films were traditionally broken down into reels which were about 11 minutes each, due to the practicalities of handling 1000 feet of 35mm film. This is the way in which Eddie breaks the film down into manageable chunks. It also helps everyone keep tabs on which reels have been signed off or need more work. These are stored in the Cutting Copy bin.

The cutting copy archive allows Eddie to **keep track of every version of the film** that's ever been screened or delivered to someone, organized by date. The scenes are grouped and **all of their slates labeled and organized in bins**, which will sort in the correct alphabetical order. It should be noted that Eddie cuts in **Avid Media Composer**, which allows multiple editors to work on the same project with the same media and open and lock specific bins while they're using them and then update for every editor globally. The image I've made above was created in **Adobe Premiere Pro**.

Labelling a Feature Film Timeline

In this screenshot from the image at the top of this timeline **you can see how Eddie labels his Media Composer timeline** to keep track of what is on each track. The important thing to do when using a naming system like this, is to be diligent with the placement of each element of your sound mix so that everything stays where it should. Something like Roles would achieve the same result in FCPX without having to be careful about where things are physically.

The mono dialogue tracks allow Eddie to work with the sound recordists original recordings for that microphone and **he prefers to add in the audio keyframes to dip each line of dialogue he uses** to create the best sounding version of the film he can in his edit suite. This is instead of using the supplied 'Editor's Mix' from the location sound recordist, which are intended for dailies.

One of the most obvious things you get from looking at a picture of Eddie's timeline is the copious amounts of **color coding** he does. In the video presentation below, Eddie mentions that **he color codes odd-numbered scenes in green and even-numbered scenes in blue** so that *"when you're pacing out the movie you can see how long the scenes are relative to each other."*

Another timeline tip that Eddie shared was his process for choosing takes. Eddie's assistant editors create a huge **selects timeline** of every single line of dialogue and they lay them out in chronological order. Also each camera angle, or presumably multi-camera angle, is then organized by track with all wide shots on V1, all Over the Shoulders on V2, all medium shots on v3 and so on. This allows Eddie to very quickly watch through all takes of a line and pick his favorite. **It also makes it very efficient to allow the director to see alternatives** if they wish to swap something out.

Editing with a Gaming Mouse

In this excellent NAB 2012 presentation, Eddie shares some **valuable technical tips on how we approached co-editing *X-Men First Class*** with Director Christopher Nolan's go-to editor, Lee Smith.

One of the tips he shares is his use of the Razer Naga Ergonomic Gaming Mouse to speed up his workflow. **I've pulled out his programmable mouse mapping** from the video so you can make it your own. He skips past a couple of numbers so I've inserted my own suggestions. If you're interested in this kind of thing, check out this post on editing keyboards, controllers, mice and more.

October 19th

How to Properly Backup Your Footage on Set Without a DIT

If you can't afford to have a Digital Imaging Technician on your crew, use these tips to help ensure your footage is safely backed up every time.

We recently discussed the ever-changing role of the Digital Imaging Technician. As technology evolves, the importance of having a **dedicated DIT** on set is becoming more and more crucial. After all, if you're spending countless hours prepping for a project, and potentially thousands of dollars shooting that same project, **you need to ensure that your media is protected as safely as possible.** Further, a great **DIT** needs to be aware of the quirks associated with different cameras, media types, formats, and other variables that will change from shoot to shoot. Again, though, not every production can afford **a dedicated DIT** and often times an AC or even a director will end up backing up their own footage. **If this sounds like you, be sure to follow these three steps:**

1. Always Use At least Two Hard Drives

Hard drives are extremely finicky and even the best of them will act up when you least expect it. I've had the unfortunate experience of having a drive die on me in the middle of the project and learned the hard way that **you always need a second backup.** Personally, I now make three backups of all of my footage and keep them on three separate drives just to be safe. It may sound like overkill, but when one of your drives fails and you've lost months' worth of work – **you'll wish you'd just spent an extra $100 for another backup.**

2. Never Backup from the Backup

One of the biggest mistakes that non-DITs will make when backing up footage is duplicating their backup drive instead of creating a new backup from the memory card. It's very possible that when you transfer footage to a hard drive from your memory card that there could be an issue or a corrupted file in that backup. As you might imagine, if you were to then take that backup and save it to another drive, the corrupted file would transfer over and both backups would be flawed. Instead, always make sure to **back up to one hard drive first, and then use the original memory card to create an additional backup.**

3. Always Have Extra Memory Cards on Set

If you think you only need two cards for the project you're shooting, **then bring four.** Having too few memory cards on set can cause all sorts of issues when it comes to backing up your footage. For instance, if your cards aren't transferring as fast as you'd like, you may have no choice but to **wipe a memory card** before it's been backed up a second time, leaving you with only one original backup. Or alternatively, you may have one of your two backup drives die on set. Having a second set of memory cards allows you to leave your files on them if one of your drives fail **and ultimately the cards can serve temporarily as your second backup.**

October 20th
The Art of the Freeze Frame

Learn how to use the simple effect of the freeze frame to hold your image on screen and in the minds of your viewer.

What Is a Freeze Frame?

A **freeze frame** halts the perceived movement in your image, effectively converting it to a **still shot** reminiscent of a photograph. **Freeze frames** are self-reflexive, so they call attention to the **filmmaking process** and to the **filmmaker**, but they are invaluable in **adding emphasis**, covering up for **lack of footage**, or creating a **note of ambiguity**.

In the days of shooting with film, the selected shot was optically reprinted to achieve the effect. With digital technologies, freezing your image has become as easy as tapping a few keys — so the real question becomes **how and when** should you use the **freeze frame?**

Ways to Use It

Freeze frames can be used at the beginning and throughout your movie. It's all a matter of setting the stylistic tone of your work. For example, you may want to give your title card a little extra punch as Soderbergh did in his 1998 film, *Out of Sight*.

Soderbergh continues his playful use of the **freeze frame** during the opening act of *Out of Sight* as a transitional device and as a way to introduce a new character (another great place to use **freeze frames** early in a film, especially if you are running voice over on your soundtrack). In his film, *Election*, Alexander Payne uses **freeze frames** during his character introductions for a comedic effect.

Martin Scorsese uses the **freeze frame** to great effect in films like *Goodfellas*, *The Departed*, and *The Aviator*, as you can see in this video compilation of Scorsese's editing techniques. Justin Morrow includes **freeze frames** as one of Martin Scorsese's influential editing techniques in this article.

Freeze Frame as an Ending

It seems that the most common —and memorable — use of the **freeze frame** is at the end of films. Employed in this manner, the **freeze frame** can be a way to avoid showing **gruesome details of a character's demise** and instead leave your viewers with a note of **romance** and **ambiguity**. Though many of these endings are the stuff of legend, **this is your official spoiler alert.**

Instead of seeing the titular characters from *Thelma and Louise* (via MGM), plummet to the bottom of the Grand Canyon, we are left with their car hanging in mid-air, seemingly defying gravity as the two characters hang above a chasm representative of their situation both as **outlaws** and as **rebellious women** in a male-dominated world.

Another famous use of the **freeze frame** as a substitute for a bloody finale can be found in *Butch Cassidy and the Sundance Kid* (via 20th Century Fox). When the two main characters are trapped and outgunned, **they confront their fate head on.**

The **freeze frame** can present an opportunity to halt — and highlight — the atrocity of violence, as seen in the final frame of *Gallipoli* (1981). The splotch of blood on the main character's chest echoes a shot early in the film when the same character races through the red ribbon of a finish line.

One of the most famous **freeze frame** endings occurs in François Truffaut's French New Wave classic, *The 400 Blows*. Although the final **freeze frame** does not suggest a violent death for the main character, Antoine Doinel, the image creates uncertainty, ambiguity, and concern for the life of Antoine.

It's not uncommon to use a **freeze frame** of the main character as a backdrop for conveying story information that happens after the plot of the film. *Animal House* (1978) uses this technique to a comic end, but the approach can have a more serious tone, as evidenced by the final **freeze frame** in *Bloodsport* (1988).

While we're considering Jean-Claude Van Damme's involvement in the **freeze frame** ending, let's not forget this classic pose from *Street Fighter* (1994).

The **freeze frame** isn't immune to parody, as made evident in the ending of *Police Squad!* (via Paramount and ABC).

The **freeze frame** ending gives a moment of **pause** and **consideration** for your audience. Everything that preceded the final, frozen instant can take on additional dramatic weight and helps in the transformation of a seemingly ordinary film ending into a **mythic one**.

October 21st
The Editing Genius of Michael Kahn

Michael Kahn is one of the most successful film editors in the business. Here's an in-depth look at his legendary career.

The most interesting thing about legendary editor Michael Kahn isn't that he started by editing *Hogan's Heroes*, or that he became Steven Spielberg's go-to editor. No, the most interesting thing about Kahn is that he never really wanted to be an editor in the first place. He began his journey working in a New York mailroom and slowly moved up the ladder to become an apprentice. He advanced to assistant editor and finally head editor of the classic television series *Hogan's Heroes*. From there his career shot off like a rocket. Let's take a detailed look at his classic career, one that made Edgar Wright say:

We were shown a montage of Michael Kahn's credits. It was possibly the most epic, daunting and yet inspiring body of work I've seen at any awards show, technical or otherwise.

The Apprentice

Kahn began his career producing commercials for a New York ad agency, but soon found himself working in post-production after being offered a job at Desilu. The production company was owned and operated by the legendary television duo Desi Arnaz and Lucille Ball, but Kahn found himself being essentially the "male secretary" for editorial supervisor Dann Cahn. He became Cahn's apprentice and was soon urged by John Woodcock to join the union.
By joining Woodcock, the young Kahn would begin working on his very first television show, *The Adventures of Jim Bowie*. Kahn would say, "It was a wonderful time to be in the editing business because we had fourteen or sixteen shows on the air. Some were comedies and some were dramas." Kahn would learn valuable lessons at this stage of his career, lessons such as discovering how to manipulate the film to do what he wanted it to.

Cutting for Television

By the 1960s, Kahn moved up from an apprentice to assistant editor and began working toward the '8 Year Rule.' This was an old rule that editors followed that dictated they had to work professionally as an assistant editor for eight years before they could edit a film or television show as the main editor.

A friend of mine, Jerry London, got a chance to work on Hogan's Heroes; he did the pilot. He said, 'If you come with me as my assistant, after the fifth or sixth show I'll make you the editor. Jerry London was true to his word. Michael spent the next six years of his career editing over 130 episodes of the classic comedy series.
Video from Manhattan Edit Workshop
From the success of *Hogan's Heroes,* Kahn was able to garner attention which led to his move from television editing to film editing. His first film was a drama called *Rage,* directed by Oscar-winner George C. Scott. Kahn would utilize the techniques he learned as an apprentice (such as the use of slower cuts) to impress Scott so much that he requested to work with Kahn again on his next film *The Savage is Loose.* This extended collaboration would garner Kahn editing jobs on films like *The Devil's Rain, The Ultimate Warrior* and *The Return of a Man Called Horse.* Directors started saying 'hey, that's an interesting idea, I didn't think of that.' And that sort of encouraged me on, then I tried other things – I kept trying things. And directors seemed to appreciate it – Michael Kahn, Editors Guild

Close Encounters with Greatness

By 1977, Michael Kahn was already having great success in the film industry when a young director named Steven Spielberg, fresh off the success of *Jaws,* came looking for an editor to cut together his sci-fi epic *Close Encounters of the Third Kind.* Kahn once remarked that cutting his teeth in the fast-paced environment of television set him up perfectly to work with Spielberg, who works quickly and captures a wide range of coverage.
Video from Manhattan Edit Workshop

The result of this collaboration would be multiple Oscar nominations for the film and Kahn's very first nomination for film editing — an award that he would lose to Paul Hirsch, Marcia Lucas and Richard Chew for *Star Wars*.

Kahn quickly picked up more work during Spielberg's down time, editing *Eyes of Laura Mars* for Irvin Kershner and *Ice Castles* for Donald Wrye. After these two films, Kahn would see a string of hit films come to him from Steven Spielberg, as well various other directors like Robert Zemeckis, Richard Donner, Frank Marshall, and Tobe Hooper.

In 1981, Kahn would score big with his editing work on Steven Spielberg's legendary film *Raiders of the Lost Ark*. He would follow this win with Oscar nominations for *Fatal Attraction* and *Empire of the Sun*.

Part of the Oscar Elite

After editing some of the most revered films of the 1980s, like *Poltergeist*, *Indiana Jones and the Temple of Doom*, *The Goonies* and *Indiana Jones and the Last Crusade*, Kahn would have an amazing run over the next ten years. Starting with 1991's *Hook*, directed by Steven Spielberg, Kahn would edit *Jurassic Park*, *Twister*, *The Lost World: Jurassic Park*, and *The Haunting*.

Video from Manhattan Edit Workshop

Kahn edited two films during this era that would give him legendary status within the editing community: 1993's *Schindler's List* and 1998's *Saving Private Ryan*. Because of his ability to effectively craft a story and master the techniques of editing, Kahn would be awarded two more Oscars for both films. In the video below, Kahn talks about the process of editing the opening scene from *Saving Private Ryan*.

Video from Manhattan Edit Workshop

From 2000 to 2010, Kahn wouldn't slow down at all, editing *Catch Me if You Can*, *Peter Pan*, *War of the Worlds*, *The Adventures of Tintin*, *War Horse*, *Munich* and *Lincoln*. He earned Oscar nominations for the latter two films.

Since 2011, Kahn has stopped editing films for filmmakers other than Spielberg, who calls Kahn his big brother. In an article from Flickering Myth, Kahn had this to say about working with some directors:

Some directors don't like you to edit until they are ready to run it with you; then what you have to say is minimal because he tells you what he wants and you sit there and type out the visuals. But that's not editing... I want to make a contribution to the film.

So far in his career, Michael has been nominated for eight Oscars, the most of any editor. His three wins tie him with other legendary editors like Thelma Schoonmaker, Daniel Mandell, and Ralph Dawson.

The Editing Style of a Master Craftsman

Michael Kahn recently completed editing *Bridge of Spies*. He's also slated to edit *BFG* and *Indiana Jones 5*. But his long list of credits isn't what makes Michael Kahn so great. It's his attention to the creative process of editing. It's his incredible ability to know when and why you need a cut or a transition and how to blend the scenes together that made him a legend.

Kahn also purposefully never goes to the set to watch the production. He's often said that he wants the film to come to him fresh without any preconceived ideas. He told Cinema Editor Magazine that he doesn't edit the way he does because he went to school. He says it was the years working as an apprentice and assistant editor that taught him how to be a real editor.

It's not about knowledge; it's all about feeling or intuition. Good editors or musicians or directors—what makes them special is that they feel things... Your feeling is what you're getting paid for. It's your ability to cinematically touch things.

Get a deeper look into this master editor's career straight from the source in this great one-on-one interview with DP/30.

October 22nd
The Hidden Stories Behind Weird Post-Production Terms

Ever wonder where some of those strange post-production terms came from? Here are some origin stories you might not know.

The industry is full of strange and confusing terms that make sense only to those who use them every day. Have you ever wondered where all these strange terms came from? Let's take a behind-the-scenes look at those weird **post-production** terms.

Keyframes

In modern animation applications, a keyframe designates a value at a certain point in time. These modern-day applications can interpret the data between keyframes so you don't have to. This is called tweening, and it's a recent advance in technology.

In the golden days of animation, every frame had to drawn by hand — but it wasn't the job of lead animators to draw every frame. Instead, more experienced animators would draw only the 'key' frames in a scene and more inexperienced animators called Inbetweeners would create the drawings between the key frames. For more information regarding early animation techniques, I highly recommend checking out *The Illusion of Life* by Frank Thomas and Ollie Johnston.

Masks

In post-production, masking is the process of designating a portion of the frame to not be affected by a given effect. In Photoshop you might use a mask to only blur out a background and not your subject. In After Effects, a mask can be used to help with compositing 3D elements. But the history of masks goes back much further than Photoshop. In fact, the term is derived from physical masks which literally block portions of your face.
Masking has long been used in fine arts as a way to shield portions of a canvas from being affected. In fact, masking tape derived because it was used to *mask* out certain objects that weren't meant to be painted. Today masking has evolved to become an essential part of a digital artists workflow and it all started with physical art.

Feathering

In modern software, feathering is essentially the smoothing out of edges. But why is it called feathering?

It actually plays homage to a classic painting technique in which artists would use feathers to smooth out a transition between two colors. Feathering was also used by early photo editors as a way to smooth out ink. Even in modern home painting, some people use feather dusters as a way to smooth out paint color transitions. Feathering continues to be an essential process for editors and motion graphic designers alike.

Matte/Matte Painting

In film and photography, a matte is reference footage used to composite a foreground onto a background. While the history of mattes in film is quite dense, the term *matte* first originated from the early set extension process known as matte painting. These early matte paintings were scenes painted on glass using, you guessed it, matte paint.

Over the years, mattes would evolve to become modern-day color keying, but digital matte painting continues to be a process used in contemporary films. For more info on the history of matte painting, check out this fantastic video created by John Hess of Filmmaker I.Q.

Rotoscoping

The original patent for a rotoscope, invented by Max Fleischer

Rotoscoping is essentially cutting an object or subject out of a scene one frame at a time by hand. While the process is easier for modern filmmakers, it's still very tedious.

In the early days of film, an artist would use a rotoscope to project a frame onto glass. The artist would then go in and trace the subject by hand. While the process was traditionally used for cartoons, it has transitioned over time to be used mainly for VFX work.

October 23rd
Tips for Editing Travel Videos While Abroad

Away from your editing bay? Here are a few handy tips for editing travel videos on the go.

While editing from a work station is always ideal, sometimes we simply aren't afforded that luxury — especially when traveling. So what are we to do as editors when all we can do is edit with a laptop? Let's take a look at five ways to **create stunning travel videos** when you're away from your workstation.

1. Archive Footage Well

The first step when **editing travel videos** (or any video for that matter) is to **log the footage well**. Depending on your file structures and footage, your folders may take on different names. I've found the best thing to do is organize by **Trip>Location>Event**. Use descriptive words to name each clip, as you never know when you might want to access this footage later.
If you archive your footage right the first time, you'll be able to better locate individual clips. I suggest using an **external SSD** in a protective case to log your footage when traveling. Not only will the read/write speeds be faster than an external HDD, but you'll also have the added benefit of a more rugged hard drive.

2. Define a Narrative and Tone

While you may not have the luxury of a script when **editing a travel film**, your video should nonetheless tell a story in some way. Even if the story is very basic, it's much better to use basic storytelling techniques in your video. For example, it probably makes more sense to **start out with establishing shots** to give your viewers context rather than throwing all of your b-roll together.

Beautiful Overview

The choice to use high frame rates also helps the audience notice more subtle details that might have normally gone unnoticed. When editing a **highlight video** like this, it's good to think about continuity. You don't want to simply slap your footage together. Instead, give your audience a context and ask yourself if any shots take away from the overall tone of your video.

Follow My Footsteps

Another way you could make a travel video is to do a sort of **"day in the life"** concept where you put yourself or your fellow travelers in the film. This example from Junior Braun is a great example of this style. Notice how the audience is going on a journey with Junior, from the car ride to the sights he visits.

This video by Juan Rayos, in which we follow a few long boarders down a mountain, is another good example of this style of execution.

When editing this style of film, it's important to **create a setting through introductory shots**.

Stunning Timelapse

If you're a lone traveler, then a **timelapse video** may be for you. Timelapse videos are an editor's best friend, as they are normally shot in RAW and give you a lot of flexibility in post. This video from Martin Heck is a great example of what can be shot with simply a camera and tripod.

Here's another great example of a **travel timelapse video**. It's important to note that if you want to get good **timelapse shots of stars**, you will probably have to get pretty far out of town. If you can't, I recommend using the new dehazer tool in Photoshop to clean up light pollution.

If you end up editing a timelapse film, **spend a lot of time working with color**. A little extra time spent tweaking your footage will pay dividends when you share your final video with the world.

Concept Videos

If you want to make your entire vacation/trip more video focused, you could always shoot a more conceptual video. This video created by Rick Mereki is an interesting take on travel. Each shot had to be carefully planned, but the finished video ended up looking fantastic.

Another interesting concept by Rick is this mashup of different food plates from around the world.

3. Use Grading Presets

When traveling, you likely won't have much time to sit down and **color grade** each individual shot, so you'll probably want to use some **color grading presets.** This will allow you to simply add a blanket grade to your entire video that matches the overall tone of your travel footage. There are a lot of really good color grading resources out there. The most popular is Magic Bullet Looks. It'll set you back **$399,** but it's the way to go if you want to add professional color grading presets to your footage. Additionally, you could always use some **free color grading presets** (or even make some yourself) that emulate color grades from your favorite videos. However, if have time to color grade each clip by hand, you absolutely should. This will require you to **shoot in a RAW or low-compression format**, but it'll be worth it if you have time to make an awesome video.

4. Music Tells Your Audience How to Feel

When it comes to travel footage, music is your best friend. Music has the power to radically **change the way your film is perceived by your audience.** Before you sit down to pick the right music, ask yourself what tone you want the video to have.
One rookie mistake is to choose music that's too upbeat for the tone of your video. Try to pick music that reminds you of the feelings you felt when at that location. Here at CR Production Music.com, we have custom, curated tracks from every genre that are **specifically designed to work seamlessly with your film.**

5. Keep Graphics Simple

There's a time and place for complex titles. A travel video is not one of them. Travel videos should draw your audience into a location while minimizing distractions. So you will probably want to keep to cross dissolves on solid white text.

October 24th
Video Editing Quick Tip: Matching Shot Colors

Matching shot colors between two clips is easier than ever with these simple tips for Premiere Pro and Final Cut Pro users.

Keeping your shots well-lit and **consistently colored** throughout your project can be one of the most challenging aspects of **video production.** Whether you're shooting with different cameras, shooting at different times of day, or receiving footage from many different shooters, **maintaining a consistent visual aesthetic** can be difficult — but not if you know how to properly ensure your shots are colored the way you want them to be. Let's look at the best way to make it happen.

Matching Shot Colors in Final Cut Pro

Final Cut Pro offers the easiest way to **match color,** thanks to the accurately titled **Match Color** tool. The method is fast, efficient, and can cut time from your workflow. Larry Jordan recorded an excellent tutorial showcasing the simple process and the steps needed to **maximize quality** and **efficiency.** He uses vastly different clips to attain totally different looks for his footage.

First, select the clip you want to change. Under the **Enhancements** menu, select **Match Color.**

Next, scrub through a different clip that you want to match the color from. Then hit **Apply Match.** Voila!

Matching Shot Colors in Premiere Pro

Matching color in Premiere Pro isn't as simple as it is in Final Cut Pro, but it's still relatively easy nonetheless. Instead of offering a one-click route, the best option is to physically tweak the colors.

Jordy Vandeput from Cinecom gives us a condensed walk-through on which steps to take in order to **match clips** correctly. He begins by stating the obvious: Consider every single **object**, **person**, and **background** in the shot in order for the transition to look natural. The three most important settings to address — in order — are **color temperature**, **exposure** and **saturation**.

Though this may seem tedious, it does allow you to work in greater detail with your images.

October 25th

Wisdom for Editors from Leading Post-Production Professionals

In this post, post-production pros lend their editing advice gained from years of personal experience.

Great direction for those starting out in the industry or for industry vets looking to improve their craft.
I often get asked advice from those starting out or looking to break into the industry…

What should I study in school?
How can I become more employable?
What makes an editor successful?
After years of passing on my own anecdotal recommendations, I recently reached out to some of the industry's leading editors and post-production educators to hear their response when presented with the question "What advice do you have for new or aspiring editors." Although the responses came from industry leaders spread out across the world, through analogous experiences, much of the wisdom and suggestions were strikingly similar.

HARD WORK & CLIENT RELATIONSHIPS

Often it seems aspiring editors become micro-focused on the "tech" that goes into this work. It should not be overlooked that editing is a collaborative human-based effort. Whether between editor and production crew or editor and a client, a big aspect of the post-production process involves working with others to execute a creative vision. Knowing the tech is essential, but equally important is the ability to work in a collaborative environment. Much of the input that we received from pro editors echoed this sentiment, focusing on the importance of finding success in collaboration.

@kyl33t ALWAYS be direct and honest. no mind games, no building resentment. Just communicate, collaborate, and compromise. There is a fine line between willingness/strong work ethic and being taken advantage of.

@originalsmiley Learn patience.

@Philiphodgetts If you don't understand: ask! Don't assume anything – confirm you've understood correctly.

@ericosterberg Be someone people can sit in a room with for 10 or 15 hours at a time and you'll get many freelance calls.

@conigs Be friendly. Talk to the producers/directors/clients in your room. Make them want to work with you.

@rhedpixel If you have a bad feeling, say something.

@Dr0id Give.

@ThePageBoy Learn to find new tactful ways of explaining why an idea is "stupid".

ORGANIZATION

On this blog, we've often said "organization is the key to efficient editing" and much of what we heard from industry pros backed this up. With digital production we're seeing larger amounts of video shot and culled together for projects. This increase in data means an even greater need for smart organization practices. Spending the time on the front end to organize media and generate metadata means greater time savings during the cutting process.

@davemehrman Stay organized. Knowing where files are saves time and headaches. Keep your files organized. When you know where things are, you can focus on the story.

@little_lucylu Take time to name things correctly. Untitled sequences will be the bain of your life otherwise.

@ukjoncollins Good organisation is 90% of editing.

@philiphodgetts Do great log notes and know your basic tech (or go look it up).

@ronsussman It's all about attention to details. Organization is key. Look for the unexpected moments.

@comebackshane Take the time to review your footage, and get organized. Editing is faster when you know what you have, and where it is.

STORYTELLING & GOOD EDITING PRACTICES

Good storytelling comes from experience and creative thinking, but it also comes from self-awareness. Some of the best editors are those that can take a step back from their position in the process and instead look at the video as the intended viewer would. Editors tend to develop a relationship with the footage as they work it, becoming attached to shots or sequences. Instead, strip away any context you may have developed for the footage during the production/post process. Examine it strictly for its storytelling potential. Does it make the scene stronger or weaker?

Along with tips for good storytelling some of the feedback we got was how to improve the actual editing process. Check out some of these tips and good editing practices...

@mjeppsen "Learn to kill your babies." The shot/scene/style you love may not best serve the story.

@macgarp Make a decision and own it.

@camkingvidguy Timing, pacing, story. Study storytelling. Software doesn't matter if you can tell what makes a great story.

@dvbgregory Have passion for your edits and see your edits as your shooting.

@ronsussman It may indeed be the best take but that doesn't mean it will work in context. This is why I don't pull selects.

@matthewcelia Editing is really only about the in and the out points and the order you put it in. Everything else is extra.

@Cineblur The power of a cut. Don't overuse the dissolve. It gets old and boring.

@andymees The best transition is a simple cut ... dissolves are for editors that can't cut.

@britmic Cut on an action, no matter how small

@**little_lucylu** Don't call it final until the bill has been paid. Version numbers are your friend!

@**Chris8Video** Learn keyboard shortcuts and stop fumbling w/ the mouse.

@**EditorBron** I put all footage from a bin on a timeline. I don't only log it. Scrolling through lets you quickly pick out which shots will work.

@**twilsbach** Producer/network notes. Address the underlying concern, not just the specific fix. Also, learn your keyboard shortcuts.

@**DRGlenngreenRX** Don't be afraid to save separate versions w/progressively bolder choices & extreme reshuffling of timeline

TOOLS & GEAR

Being adept with a wide variety of hardware and software tools makes you more employable and will likely lead to the creation of a stronger product. Much of the advice that we heard from industry pros supported the view that although it's not the software that equals success, having a wide knowledge base of different tools can lead to greater success as an editor.

@**IEBAcom** Don't learn how to use only one tool.

@**1987velle** Use what's right for YOU. Not because ever one else uses it. Take reviews of gear/software with a pinch of salt. Test out yourself.

@**lafcpug** Don't listen to the pundits about what tool is best. Seek your own truth. And learn all the tools.

@**michaschmidt** It's not the app you are using that counts. It's the editor and the ideas that matters.

@**rhedpixel** 90% of technical problems are cable problems.

@**oflanada** Be YOUR best with YOUR gear. When you reach your full potential with gear you have, you'll have the opportunity to get better gear and start the process over.

@**ParadiddlePix** Non-linear software is a tool for you to finely craft a story. Every project is a story. Every edit decision must have motivation.

SELF IMPROVEMENT

Finally, we heard from many pros that stressed the importance of continuing education and self-improvement. This is an industry that is continually evolving with new technologies, new challenges and new modes of business. Staying informed of new advances will lead to greater opportunities and success.

- **@MulhernMedia** Practice! Look around for inspiration. Try new things and show off your talent to as many people as possible.
- **@oflanada** Keep learning. Eat, breath, and live the craft. Soak up everything you can from pros and others willing to help.
- **@DylanReeve** Try to understand underlying principles to your software and process.
- **@editblog** You're never done learning...either the craft or the technical side. You can learn from anyone, even those under the editor.
- **@LB_Cuts** Take every job you get. Especially the ones you think are too tough for you. You'll learn quickly & realize how much you can achieve.
- **@ale_zorio** Be strong and never give up.

October 26th

3 Ways to Stabilize Motion in After Effects

There are multiple ways to smooth out and stabilize motion in After Effects. Here are the three most important techniques to know.

On top of being a pretty fantastic compositing and motion graphics software, **After Effects** is a great tool for smoothing out video footage. While it's always better to keep your footage as smooth as possible when on set, if you sit down to edit your footage and realize it's too shaky, it's not the end of the world. In fact, there are multiple things you can do. Here are three tools for **stabilizing footage in After Effects.**

1. Warp Stabilizer

- **Pro:** Easy to use. Professional results.

- **Con:** Can sometimes lead to warping.

The **warp stabilizer** is going to be your best bet when you need to **stabilize motion in After Effects.** As a drag-and-drop effect, the **warp stabilizer** is incredibly easy to use. In a nutshell, the **warp stabilizer** works by analyzing your entire frame and creating mini track points on objects in your scene.

The warp stabilizer effect uses background rendering. This allows you to work on other things while the effect is processing.

The **warp stabilizer** is particularly cool because it allows users to **adjust the stabilization intensity.** If you want your objects to be locked down, simply turn the smoothness down to 0. If you want there to be a little more movement, turn it up to 100 or anything in between.

The **warp stabilizer** also uses background rendering to process its effect. This allows you **work with other effects** while the warp stabilizer is analyzing the footage.

Users can also deselect any mini track points that may be attached to objects that are moving too much in the frame. For example, if you wanted to **stabilize footage** of a shopping mall, you wouldn't want the **warp stabilizer** to stabilize the footage based on the shoppers walking around. This would lead to incredibly shaky footage. A better alternative would be to deselect any points that are connected to people and leave the points that are connected to static objects.

The following tutorial from Evan Abrams shows us how to **use the warp stabilizer to stabilize footage in After Effects.** Notice how the warp stabilizer works better when your footage is shot at a higher shutter speed.

2. Stabilize Motion Feature

- **Pro:** Locks shots down.
- **Con:** Can lead to awkward warping. Must be adjusted by hand. Can create gaps on the edges of a frame.

Before the **warp stabilizer** was introduced into **After Effects,** users had to use the **stabilize motion feature** to smooth out their footage. This legacy tool can still be found in **After**

Effects today. That's not to say that the **stabilize motion feature** can't be used in a modern workflow. If you want your shot to be 100% stable, the **stabilize motion feature** is the way to go.

However, be prepared to adjust everything by hand when working with the **stabilize motion feature**. You might have to track your footage multiple times if your track points begin to wander while tracking.

3. ReelSteady

- **Pro:** Smoothest stabilization possible. Easy to use. Masking capabilities.
- **Con:** Price.

One new plugin to hit the stabilization market is ReelSteady for After Effects. **ReelSteady** works a lot like the **warp stabilizer** tool in **After Effects** — but the stabilization found in **ReelSteady** is much better. Just take a look at the following demo video created by **ReelSteady**. You'll notice that the **warp stabilizer** creates wobbly edges in the video, but **ReelSteady** makes the entire frame incredibly smooth.

ReelSteady also has quite a few added features that make it fantastic for doing next-level tracks. For example, users can create masks to block out certain areas of your frame. This is great for deselecting a subject that moves prominently around your frame.

The only negative with **ReelSteady** is the price ($399). Unlike the other options on this list, **ReelSteady** isn't included in **After Effects**. But if you want to have the smoothest footage possible, **ReelSteady** is the way to go.

October 27th

5 Alternatives to Popular Video Editing and Motion Design Plugins

Want the look of professional editing plugins without the cost? These alternatives may do the trick.

The professional plug-in community has really expanded in the last few years, with amazingly powerful effects being created by small and independent software companies. The capabilities of these plugins is largely impressive, but unfortunately, the price is often out of reach for those that are learning or simply need the plugin for one project.

We scoured the 'net for some **free alternatives to popular video editing plugins**. They don't have quite the feature set of their paid counterparts, but they'll get you buy when you're in a pinch.

1. Alternative to Magic Bullet Looks: Download Free Presets

When it comes to applying color grades in your video editing app, you can't go wrong with the Magic Bullet Suite. Using MB you can apply almost 200 preset looks to your footage in After Effects, Premiere Pro, and more. The presets are fantastic and provide unique looks, fast. The Magic Bullet Suite can be purchased for $399 from RedGiant's website.

That said, there are a number of free color grading presets on the 'net that can look **just as good** as the Magic Bullet Suite. Sites with **free color grading presets** include PremierePro.net, Studio 1, or Fenchel-Janisch. Even if you don't love the end result you can tweak the presets in your favorite editing software, then save the changes as your very own preset.

All of these preset options (including Magic Bullet) are only quick solutions. If you really want to get amazing color on your films you should try color grading from scratch.

2. Alternative to Optical Flares: Create Your Own Lens Flares

Video Copilot's Optical Flares is arguably the best lens flare plug-in for After Effects and Nuke. With Optical Flares users can create custom lens flares while controlling parameters like intensity, color, and shape. Optical Flares also comes with dozens of **high-end presets** that allow users to quickly add professional lens flares into their compositions. It retails for $125 on Video Copilot's website.

Using a combination of shape layers, blending modes, and expressions you can make your very own lens flares without Optical Flares. The following video tutorial by YouTuber **Ch-Ch-Check It** shows us how it's done. The techniques outlined in this video tutorial can also be applied to simulate other light based effects like **light leaks** or colored lens distortions:

3. Alternative to Trapcode Particular: Research the Effect

Another great tool from Red Giant Software, Trapcode Particular is the industry standard particle generator for **After Effects and Nuke**. Trapcode Particular gives users added functionality beyond that of built-in particle generators. It can be purchased for $399 from Red Giant's website.

While Trapcode Particular can certainly save you a lot of time, it isn't always necessary to get your desired look. Do a quick Google search to see if your effect can be accomplished using built-in effects and particle generators in After Effects (like Particle World). More often than not, you will be able to get a **similar effect** without needing to buy Particular – it'll just take more time to create it.

For example, on the Trapcode Particular homepage Red Giant states that Particular can be used to simulate realistic smoke. The tutorial below (created by Vox Lab) shows us how to create smoke using only native After Effects plugins and effects.

4. Alternative to Element 3D: An Opportunity to Learn 'Real' 3D

When Element 3D hit the market two years ago it was a game-changer for After Effects users. In short, Element 3D allows users to easily import and manipulate **3D objects** in After Effects. Gone were the days of layering 2D objects in 3D space to simulate depth. Other features, like the ability to add textures and keyframe movement, make Element 3D a powerful tool that every serious AE designer should own. Element 3D can be purchased for $199 from Video Copilot. However, using other professional design programs – like Maya, Cinema 4D, or Blender – you can create anything that you could create with Element 3D…and more. If you don't own Maya or Cinema 4D, try Blender. It's completely free and updated regularly. While the learning curve is steep with these programs it is **certainly worth it**. With the Cinema 4D 'integration' into After Effects, it's more important than ever to be comfortable in that application. Additionally, it makes you a catch for potential clients and employers.

5. Alternative to Twitch: Create Your Own Glitch Effect

Twitch is an After Effects plugin that was designed to add glitch effects to your video. Using Twitch, editors can adjust various glitch operators like blur, light, and scale. Twitch can be purchased from Video Copilot's website for $45.

Every single glitch effect found in Twitch can be created with a little time and effort in After Effects. Using the wiggle expression, combined with various effects and free video assets, you can quickly create professional glitch effects **without third party plugins**.

October 28th

14 Tips for Faster Rendering in After Effects

Speed up your rendering times in After Effects with these quick tips.

Rendering is an annoying (but unavoidable) aspect of the motion graphics process. However, there are a few steps you can take to make your **After Effects renders** as fast as possible.

1. Use the Right Graphics Card

After Effects is an incredibly intense program for your graphics card (no surprise, right?) And while there may be hundreds of graphics cards available for your computer, only a few are recommended by Adobe to run After Effects. Adobe specifically recommends certain GeForce, Quadro, and Tesla cards. You can find the full list on the system requirements page on Adobe's website. If you're using a sub-par card, you'll likely see an instant render speed increase when you switch.

2. Upgrade Your RAM

If you work day in and day out in After Effects then upgrading your RAM is the way to go. Adobe recommends at least 4GB of RAM to run After Effects, but you'll benefit from much more than that. It's not uncommon for professional AE users to have **32GB of RAM or more**.

3. Use a Solid-State Drive

A solid state drive is a quick way to increase not only rendering speed in After Effects, but also the overall speed of your computer in general. If you purchased your internal or external hard drive for less than $100 it's time for an upgrade. With a **solid state drive** After Effects will be able to load assets, reference the cache, and load effects much faster.... all leading to reduced render times.

4. Use Two Hard Drives

When you render your footage to the same hard-drive your project is saved on, you are forcing that hard-drive to perform two operations simultaneously: read and write. While this doesn't lead to render times that are twice as slow, it does lead to reduced render times. Instead, try using one hard drive to run the program with assets and another hard drive to render the finished video.

5. Turn On Multiprocessing

After Effects has the hand ability to render out multiple frames at the same time using multiple processing cores. By default, multiprocessing isn't turned on in After Effects, you have to do it by hand. To do so navigate to After Effects>Preferences>Memory & Multiprocessing. A screen that looks like this will pop up:

Simply click the check box next to '**Render Multiple Frames Simultaneously**' and adjust the settings to your liking.

6. Reduce Pre-Comps

Pre-comps are a funny business inside of After Effects. When it comes to creating an organized and convenient workflow in After Effects, pre-comps are a extremely efficient. However, pre-comps aren't always best when it comes to creating fast render times. This is because pre-comps require pixel information to pass through **multiple compositions** before rendering to your hard drive.

7. Clean up your Compositions

Just because you can't see a layer inside your composition doesn't mean it isn't being rendered by your CPU. So before you send your composition to the render queue make sure you **delete/trim any unused layers** inside your composition.

8. Trim Layers Off-Screen

Files that are actually out of the video frame will still take a toll on the rendering time, especially if you are using 3D cameras. If your goal is to optimize render times you need to use the trim feature (option + [or]) to trim your layers up to the exact frame that they will be used in your composition.

9. Turn off Ray-Traced 3D

Ray-Traced 3D layers was one of the coolest features introduced into After Effects in CS6 – finally a way to create 3D models directly in After Effects! This excitement was short-lived though, as Ray tracing takes way to long to be practical for everyday use. Make sure your composition is set to Classic 3D instead of Ray-Traced 3D before you render. If you don't you will see your render time increase by at least double.

10. Close Other Programs

It can be easy to forget, especially when using the Adobe Dynamic Link, but before you render a composition in After Effects you need close out all the unused programs running on your computer. This will free up space for your CPU to run After Effects.

11. Choose the Right Codec

Less compressed codecs like MOV take longer to render in After Effects than smaller codecs like H.264 or ProRes. It's important to ask yourself what your video will be used for once it's done. Will it be on TV or simply embedded on the web? If it's going online, chances are it's going to be **incredibly compressed** anyways. So maybe you don't need to export your video as lossless?

12. Turn Off Motion Blur, Depth of Field, & 3D if Unnecessary

When it comes down to increasing your render speed in After Effects you need to ask yourself, "will this feature be used in my video?" Often you can toggle unused features off to make your render times much faster. For example, if you don't need your layers to have **motion blur** you can toggle the motion graphics button to off. If you have a 3D camera do you really need to have depth of field or are you trying to get a 2D flat look? If your layers are set to 3D is it for a good reason? Could you simulate 3D by scaling down your objects and moving them in 2D space?

13. Be Selective with Effects

Not all effects are created equal. Some take more time than others to render. To speed up render times you need to become very selective about the effects you use. Most effects have been optimized to render across multiple threads on your CPU, but there are a few that will only allow After Effects to use one thread at a time. If an effect only uses one thread it will take much more time to render. These effects are:

- **Auto Color**
- **Auto Contrast**
- **Auto Levels**
- **Cartoon**
- **Lens Blur**
- **Particle Playground**
- **Shadow/Highlight**

This list of effects was created by Edward Korcheg from Template Monster.

14. Newest Version of AE

While each update to After Effects may not seem revolutionary, Adobe is constantly trying to make After Effects faster and more optimized for users. It is important to install the latest version of After Effects available to you. Sure, back in the day it was a large financial commitment to purchase each Creative Suite update as they would be released, but now that the Creative Cloud is prevalent you should always have the **latest update**.

Bonus: Use Media Encoder to Export Compositions

One of the biggest problems with using the render queue in After Effects is the fact that you can't do anything else while rendering. However, this is a **"hack"** that you can use to render AE compositions and still work on another project, using Adobe Media Encoder. Simply import your AE project into Media Encoder and you will be able to select which composition you wish to export. Because this doesn't go directly through After Effects you will be able to work on other projects during this process.

October 29th
After Effects, Quick Tip: Depixelating Vector Files

Are your vector files pixelated in After Effects? Enable 'Continuously Raster'.

Adobe Illustrator is vector based, meaning you can adjust the scale of Illustrator files without a loss in quality (it uses a system of equations to calculate the shapes of your object rather than pixels).

However, if you've ever tried importing illustrator files into After Affects you may have realized that they remain pixelated when you scale them up in your composition. The enable/disable feature called "Continuously Raster" is unknown by many AE noobs, but is needed to get your vector files to scale smoothly in AE.

1. Import an .ai, .eps, or .pdf file
After Effects accepts all four of these vector formats.

2. Move the vector file to your composition.
Simply drag and drop.

3. Select 'Continuously Rasterize'.

It's the box that looks like a sun. If you can't see it select the "Toggle Switches / Modes" button at the bottom of your comp layer. It should pop up now.

If you follow these steps your vector files will be smooth when scaled up rather than pixelated. This technique also works with pre-comps, so if you happen to have something like text inside of a pre-comp but need to scale it up you can hit the "**continuously rasterize**" button and you will now be able to scale it up without it being pixelated.

October 30th

After Effects Quick Tip: How to Change the Render Sound

Customize the render alert in Adobe After Effects with this simple hack.

If you've used After Effects for any extended period of time than you know there is no sound more satisfying than the **render sound**. Each time the high-pitch ring sounds off you know your render has completed, leaving you with an exported video and a smile. But what if you could change that render sound to whatever sound you want?
In the Quick Tip tutorial, we will show you how to change the default After Effects render alert to any other sound. This tutorial will only cover changing the sound on a Mac but if you use a PC you can find out how to change by navigating to the Creative Cow forums.

1. Find the After Effects CC 2014 (or CC) App Icon

You can find the app under Applications>Adobe After Effects CC 2014>Adobe After Effects CC 2014.

2. Select "Show Package Contents"

Right click on the app icon and select show package contents.

3. Locate the "sounds" folder

This folder can be found by clicking Contents > Resources > Sounds.

4. Replace rnd_okay with WAV file

Each sound located in the sounds menu is an alert for an After Effects function. If you are looking to change the render sound simply replace the **rnd_okay** file with a similarly named WAV file. The new sound must be a WAV file and it must be called **rnd_okay** in order to work.

There you go! Now you can change the render alert in After Effects and make it all your own.

October 31st

After Effects Quick Tip: Linking Layers to Checkboxes

Learn how to turn a layer on and off in After Effects using the Checkbox Control.

if you work in a team environment or want to create a template for multiple projects, the Checkbox Control is a handy tool you can add to your AE projects. Unfortunately, many people don't use Checkbox Controls because they can't be created without writing an expression, but don't be intimidated! Once you have a Checkbox Control in place you can quickly turn layers on and off in any comp in your project. The controller is a simple way to turn on/off layers without having to track them down in your compositions.

1. Create a new adjustment layer.

The adjustment layer will simply be a place for the checkboxes to live. It doesn't really matter what the adjustment layer is called, but you might want to call it something like "Controller" if you are planning on using this technique in a template.

2. Add the effect "Checkbox Control" to the Adjustment Layer.

Simply grab the "Checkbox Control" effect from the Effects panel. It can be found under **Expression Controls> Checkbox Control.**

3. Open the opacity of the layer you want to check on and off.

Find the layer that you want to turn on/off with a controller. Select the layer and hit the "t" button on your keyboard. This will call up the Opacity options.

4. Add the expression:

if("PICKWHIP TO CHECKBOX" *==0) 0 else 100;*

Right click on the stopwatch next to the Opacity parameter. You will open up the expression box. Simply type in: **if(**
After you type in **if(** you need to grab the pick whip (the swirly logo to the left of the expression box) and drag it to the "Checkbox Control" effect in your adjustment layer. After Effects will drop in some code that looks like this: this Comp.layer("Controller Layer"). effect("Checkbox Control")("Checkbox").
You will then type in: **==0) 0 else 100;**

The expression basically says if the Checkbox Control is equal to 0 (turned off) than the opacity layer will be 0. The "else" parameter says that if the Checkbox Control is equal to anything other than 0, it will return a value of 100. So for the checkbox control it will either be 0 if unselected and 1 if selected. So 0 value for opacity if unselected or a 100 value for opacity if selected.

5. Your layer should now turn on and off depending on whether the checkbox is selected.

Your checkbox control should work perfectly now. One thing to note is that the checkbox control *will* work across multiple compositions. This is especially helpful if you are wanting to nest compositions.

November 1st
After Effects Tip: Simultaneously View Multiple Compositions

Speed up your workflow in After Effects by simultaneously viewing two different compositions.

Nesting is a great way to stay organized in After Effects, but it can be frustrating jumping back and forth between comps and nested comps.

1. Logically name your compositions.

When working with multiple compositions it is really important to stay organized. Give your compositions a more logical name than simply "Comp 1" or "Pre-Comp".

2. Create a new comp viewer.

Click "New Comp Viewer" in the drop-down menu in the top of the composition viewer. A new composition panel will now pop up.

3. Select the composition you wish to view.

From the composition drop down menu you can now select the composition you wish to see.

4. Lock the comp screen.

Lock the compositions by clicking the lock icon near the menu bar.

5. Changes in the pre-comp will be reflected in the master comp.

Because After Effects doesn't organize comps by folders, viewing multiple compositions at the same time is a great way to **perfect your designs without having to jump back and forth between compositions**. This same technique can be applied to other panels in After Effects, like the effects panel and the layer panel.

November 2nd
Cinema 4D: The Iris – VFX/Mograph Experiment

Maximize basic geometry from Cinema 4D with plug-ins from After Effects.

Whoa! We love this animation created in Cinema 4D and After Effects by motion design pro Aharon Rabinowitz. In the follow up tutorial, Aharon provides a load of insight into how simple geometry can be used, in conjunction with some really cool plugins, to create an interesting and detailed 3D animation.

VFX Breakdown

In C4D Aharon creates a simple polygon object and then uses the C4D plug-in called *Greebler*. This plug-in allows for the addition of multiple artifacts in varying shapes and sizes on top of your geometry. Once the desired settings are in place through the *Greebler* plug-in Aharon exports the project out as a OBJ Sequence. He uses an add-on from *AEScripts* called the *Plexus OBJ Exporter* to export out an OBJ Sequence.

Once the sequence has been exported he moves into After Effects. In AE he utilizes a number of plug-ins and add-ons such as Video Copilot's Element 3D, of which Version 2 is releasing this November. One of the issues that Aharon has with importing his sequence into *Element 3D* is the carry over of the UV Mapping. Since he exports it out as a sequence rather than an object, the texture mappings setting are different in *Element 3D*, which restrict mapping.

After applying a standard material preset in *Element 3D* Aharon adds lighting, fog, ambient occlusion and depth of field through standard AE effects. Then he uses a combination of Red Giant plug-ins such as *Knoll Light Factory EZ*, *Magic Bullet Looks*, *Mojo* and *Trapcode Shine*. This is a great example of using a multi app, multi plugin workflow to impressive effect.

November 3rd
Creating 3D Flip Down Text in After Effects

Combine multiple text animators in After Effects to create overshoot for a great-looking organic animation!

Text animators in After Effects are awesome. They allow you to have great, **complex text animations** while being able to make easy modifications to the text's content. Here's how to make one of my favorite quick animations: **3D flip down text** with some **overshoot**.

First, type out your text in a new layer. This animation works best with **multiple lines** of text.

Next, you'll want to twirl down the text settings, click on the "**Animate**" arrow, and select "Enable Per-character 3d". This lets After Effect's text animators see each letter as a separate 3D object for animation purposes.

Now we get down to the actual animation. Click the animate arrow again, and select "Rotation" to add a text animator with a rotation property.

We're going to be adjusting the **X Rotation**, but if you try to change the rotation now, you'll notice that the anchor point is mid-letter. That's not particularly helpful for our animation, where we want the text to flip down from above. You could adjust the anchor point using another text animator, but there's actually an easier way…

Above the text animator, you'll see "More Options". Twirl that down and you'll see the two values that will let us change where the rotation is anchored to: **Anchor Point Grouping** and **Grouping Alignment**. We'll change Anchor Point grouping to "line" so that the anchor point is the same for each line, and we'll move the Grouping alignment so that the mark (shown below – you may want to click the image to enlarge) is just above the line of text. This is where the text will flip down from.

Now that our anchor point is set correctly, we'll change the X Rotation so that the text rotates away from the camera by about 90°.

We also want the text to fade in so you don't see it before it flips down, so we'll click on the "Add" arrow under the text animator and select "Opacity", then set that to 0%.

Now that our properties are set, we'll do a little work on the timing of the animation. Twirl down the "**Range Selector**", and "Advanced" inside that. We'll set the animation to be based on "Lines" instead of "Characters", change the Shape to "Ramp Up", and set both **Ease High** and **Ease Low** to 100%.

Now that all of our options are set, all we need to do is keyframe the Offset from –100% to 100% and you'll see something like the below.

So what's missing with the above? It feels a little flat, and some **overshoot** would do it some good. Overshoot is when the animation **goes past it's end point**, then **settles back** to where it should end. To do this with text animators, we'll a second text animator for rotation. Go back to to the "Animate" arrow and select "rotation". This will add a brand new text animator with rotation properties.

What we want to do is set the rotation to indicate how much overshoot we want to see. I chose –30°.

We need to change the Range Selector for this text animator to "Lines" like the first one, but we're going to set the Shape to "**Round**", which will make it go from the start value to the value indicated below, then back.

We'll add two keyframe to change the second text animator's offset from –100% to 100%, just like the first animator, and there you go!

The second animator give it a nice little overshoot, which adds a bit of **organic motion** to the movement. It's fun to experiment with **multiple text animators**, instead of trying to cram everything into one. Text animators are incredibly powerful, and one of my favorite After Effects features. Hopefully you'll find new ways to use them in your work!

November 4th
Exporting Tip: Creating Multi-Aspect Compositions in After Effects

While After Effects may be an extremely powerful VFX and motion graphics tool, it can be just as useful for workflow tasks — including creating multiple deliverables of the same project.

It's extremely common today for clients to request **multiple deliverables** of the same project, often requiring different aspect ratios and formats. For instance, television broadcasters in some markets may still request a 4:3 center cropped version of your 16:9 television project. By the same token, other broadcasters may be fine with a 16:9 version of your project — but your master file may exist in a wider (2.39:1) aspect, which means that you'll need to deliver several variations of your final project.

Personally, speaking, it's quite common for the projects I work on today to require at least **three or four different deliverables**. There's typically one high-quality ProRes master, an h264 web master, and a reframed 16:9 broadcast deliverable at the very least.

In order to streamline the process when delivering three or more files to my clients, I'll often use pre-created compositions in **Adobe After Effects** to save time. Specifically, my compositions/deliverables have been set up using the following two steps:

Step 1: Create Master Composition

Create a master After Effects composition (in full 4K resolution) that will house the high-quality master file of the project.

Step 2: Create Secondary Compositions

Create secondary After Effects compositions with various aspect ratios and resolutions that all contain a scaled version of the master composition in the timeline.

I have a project template that's been set up in this way, so whenever I need to create deliverables, I can simply drop my master file into the master composition (step one), and it'll automatically populate in the secondary compositions (step two).

That way, since my project template was already set up before hand, all I need to do is drop the master file into the right comp, and the rest of the work is automated for me. **The only final step involves adding each comp to the render queue and sending the files off to the client.** Every project is different and not all of my projects require the exact same deliverables, which is the case with most filmmakers. That said, I try to include as many possible variations of frame sizes and aspect ratios as possible in my template (4:3, 16:9. 720p, 1080p, etc.) and then I'll only add the comps that I need to the render queue for any given project.

This is just one of countless ways that **Adobe After Effects** can be used to enhance and streamline your workflow — and it works like a charm every time.

November 5th
How to Create Heat Waves in After Effects

Learn how to create displaced heat waves in After Effects with this easy-to-learn technique.

Heat waves are surprisingly easy to create in **After Effects**. With a few effects and a single adjustment layer, you can create realistic heat displacements with minimal effort. Let's take a look at how to **create a heat displacement effect in After Effects**. Let's begin:

Step 1: Create New Solid

Create a new white solid in **After Effects.** Simply go to **Layer>New>Solid** or hit **command+Y.** Make the layer white and name the layer "Wave Matte." Click OK.

Step 2: Mask the Solid

Make a mask around the area in which you want the wave effect to be. Feather out the edges to about **250 pixels.**

Step 3: Add Turbulent Displace

Add the **turbulent displace effect** to the **Wave Matte** layer. For my example I set the amount to 245 and the size to 100.

Step 4: Set Keyframes

We don't want our waves to be stationary. So in order to make the waves move, you should **set keyframes to both the offset and the evolution parameters.** Set a keyframe that will move the offset upwards over time and set a keyframe moving the evolution forward. There are no hard and fast rules about what the layers should be set to. Simply mess around with the movement until your waves seem realistic.

Step 5: Create Adjustment Layer

Create a new adjustment layer by going to **Layer>New>Adjustment Layer** or simply hitting **Option+Command+Y.**

Step 6: Set Luma Mask

Move the adjustment layer below the **Wave Matte** layer and change the **Track Matte** to **Luma Matte.** The **Wave Matte** layer should be invisible now.

Step 7: Add Effects to Adjustment Layer

Add a **turbulent displace effect** to the Adjustment Layer. Turn the amount and size down to 30. Set a keyframe for the evolution so that it makes one **full rotation every five seconds**.
Add the **Fast Blur effect** to the Adjustment Layer. Don't turn it up too far. Set the blurriness around **4** and check the **Repeat Edge Pixels** box.

November 6th
Increase Your After Effects Work Speed by 30% With Macro Keys

Give your hands a break and speed up your After Effects workflow! Let your hardware do the work for you with programmable keys!

As my knowledge of **After Effects** grew, I found myself looking more into the program's hotkeys for more repetitive tasks, in hopes of spending less time navigating menus. This certainly sped up my workflow to an extent, but with some hotkeys being combinations of three and even four characters, I still had to take the time to pause, recall, and set up my hands in awkward position to press said combination.

I found that **using hardware with programmable keys** created a big jump in my productivity. Programmable keys allowed me to, say, scale a layer to match the composition width without having to think about it. Once I memorized that key location, what was previously a conscious, distracting action, became second nature.

It may sound trivial, but when applied to everything from layer transform actions to typing expressions, it can speed things up to a surprising degree. If this guaranteed boost in **After Effects** efficiency appeals to you, there are several affordable options you can choose from.

1. Macro Keypads

Price: $100 – $500
The XK-24 USB Keypad via X-keys

For most digital artists, **dedicated macro keypads are the ideal device.** While they aren't necessarily the cheapest, they specifically cater towards video editors and the likes. These are especially great if you simply want more buttons in addition to your current peripherals. With many button counts to choose from, and various layout options, you can most likely find something that will fit perfectly in your current work station. **They even feature different backlighting color options!**

The XK-4 Stick via X-keys

Moreover, pads such as X-Keys include **customizable key labels**, so that you can simply identify your keys by their individual icons. While you can technically do this with a DIY setup or a keyboard with built-in macro keys, these labels are designed to allow you to re-use them easily in the future, rather than having to peel a sticker each time.

2. Keyboards with Macro Keys

Price: $30 – $200

The Apex 300 Keyboard via SteelSeries

If you would rather your **programmable keys** be integrated into your keyboard to prevent some clutter, or also simply happen to be in the market for a new keyboard, you may want to look into purchasing one that has **programmable keys** built in. Unlike dedicated macro keypads, most keyboards of this design are geared more towards PC gamers, so they'll force you to memorize the position or number dedication of your individual keys. However, if you have decent muscle memory, you may find that it's worth the slight inconvenience.

The G710 Plus Mechanical Gaming Keyboard via Logitech

Gaming keyboards are usually fairly flashy, but there are a few conservative, professional-looking options available as well. There are even a few options with mechanical keys, if you prefer them to the more common membrane keys. One of the cooler aspects of gaming keyboards is their ability to **program macros on the fly** without opening their software. For instance, if you find that a certain project will repeatedly use a specific expression, you can press a "macro record" button and it will automatically assign your following keystrokes to the chosen key.

3. MMO Mouses

Price: $30 – $100

The G600 MMO Gaming Mouse via Logitech

In a similar vein to the keyboards we just discussed, gaming has provided some great mouses that are surprisingly handy for programs like **After Effects**. MMO gamers typically require many easily accessible macro buttons for split-second actions. While the **After Effects** workflow isn't this intense, one can certainly benefit from being able to access so many functions without having to relocate your hands. This is my personal favorite of these options, and it has eliminated most lag I deal with from minor tasks.

The Razer Naga MMO Gaming Mouse via Razer

I find this to be by far the most efficient way to deal with complex keystrokes and recurring expressions, simply based on the physical convenience of the buttons. Additionally, gaming mouses generally feature more precise movement, with the ability to toggle sensitivity levels on the fly. If you don't necessarily need upwards of twenty programmable buttons, there are many more streamlined options with just a few additional buttons for you to map.

4. DIY Macro Keypad

Price: $10 – $30

USB Numeric Keypad via Amazon

If you're interested in any of these options, but lack the budget to invest in one, worry not! With simple open-source program called HIDMacros, you can transform an every day number keypad into your own dedicated programmable macro keypad!

You may already have one laying around, but if not, you usually can find them for around $10 new. If you have an extra full-sized keyboard laying around, you can use it with HID Macros as well. Add some home made sticker labels if you'd like, and you're good to go!

While there are a number of ways to improve the speed of your work flow within **After Effects**, doing so with the purchase of new hardware is a satisfying shortcut amongst more tedious, knowledge-based progression. **Ideally, the use of macros will benefit you as much as it helped me.**

November 7th

Pro Tip: How to Create After Effects Assets in Adobe Illustrator

Designing your own motion graphic assets makes your animation unique. Here's how to easily create After Effects assets in Adobe Illustrator.

We'll start by creating everything in **Adobe Illustrator** and then moving it all into **After Effects**. The beauty of creating in **Illustrator** is that the elements are vector based, so we can scale them as needed once we bring them into **After Effects**. The most important thing to keep in mind here is that **we will be working in layers**. It's very easy to go straight to creating once you open **Illustrator** — and that will put everything on a single layer.

Drawing the Asset in Illustrator

The reason we are creating different elements on separate layers is because each layer, when imported into **After Effects**, will become its own layer in the composition and can be animated individually. If all of the elements were made on one layer in **Illustrator**, they will all merge together in **After Effects**, essentially being no different than a still image.

First, **create a new document** (File -> New). You'll want to set the resolution to the same size that your **After Effects** comp will be. For this example, I'll go with **1920×1080**. Be sure your color mode is set to **RGB**.

Now we can begin creating. I will be creating a set of animation icons and want my final animation to take place on a bubble, so I'll **create that first in the bottom (currently the only) layer**. Notice that I've named the layer — whatever you name the layer in **Illustrator** is what the layer will be named in **After Effects**.

It's very important to keep things organized as you create; you don't want to get forced into a distracting game of *Where's Waldo* with your layers.

I've created a new layer for the person icon I drew at the bottom (aptly named "GuyAtBottom"). This will allow me to animate the "Bubble-BG" and "GuyAtBottom" layers independently when I bring this into **After Effects**.

For the next icon, I have a chat bubble with four circles in it. I want the chat bubble itself to animate on the screen. Then, after the chat bubble is completely on the screen, I want the little circles inside it to animate on one at a time. In this situation, **I need to put the bubble and each circle within it on their own layers.**
We've only got two little icons and a simple circle background, **but we're already at seven layers**. This is why it's important to **label as you go** and not come back to do that afterwards. Not labeling your layers properly is why we can't have nice things.

For the third icon, I have four buildings that I want to animate individually as if they're growing out of the ground. But while I was creating them, I got too excited and **forgot to put them on their own layers.**
Easily fixable — just **create a new layer for each building** so you can separate them. Then select the second building only (the first building will stay on our current layer).
Now, hit **cmd-x (Mac)** or **ctrl-x (PC)** to cut the building. Select the new layer you created for the second building. With that layer selected, hit **cmd-shift-v (Mac)** or **ctrl-shift-v (PC)**. This does what's called a 'paste in place,' which pastes whatever you've cut or copied in the exact same place that you cut or copied it from. However, since we had the new layer selected, the building was pasted onto the new layer instead. Now we can separate the other buildings as well.

I've now separated the towers. I also went ahead and created a few extra icons that I want to animate in **After Effects** using the same technique. Time to bring this into **After Effects**. To save your project, simply hit **cmd+S on a Mac** or **ctrl+S on a PC**.

Importing the Asset Into After Effects

Once you have **After Effects** and your project open, go to **File -> Import -> Files**. When the dialog box pops up, select your **Illustrator project file**. At the bottom of the dialog box, be sure you tell it to import as "**Composition – Retain Layer Sizes**." This tells **After Effects** that you want to work with your layers and to keep the bounding box at the edges of the layer and not at the edges of the entire comp. If you imported it as footage, it would merge all of your layers together.

Now that the **Illustrator project** is successfully imported into **After Effects**, you can see that a comp has been created for us. When you open that comp, you can see that all of your layers are there from **Illustrator**. Also, the individual layers can be found in the project tab and used elsewhere within your animation.

Pro Tip: If you're working in **After Effects** and notice that the shape of one of your icons (or whatever you're making) is off, you can go back into **Illustrator**, fix the shape, and **save the project like normal**. When you alt-tab back to **After Effects**, the change will take effect without messing up your animation. Just be sure that you don't *MOVE* the asset in illustrator; this could throw your animation off.

Since I made each asset on its own layer, I can change the color of each. added a slight drop shadow to the circle, and animated each layer as I saw fit.

Next time you have a motion graphic you need to get done quickly, **use this technique to see exactly what it's going to look like on the final frame.** You can show the client a near-final looking still frame without losing valuable animating time.

If they decide to change one of the icons (or whatever you're making), you can replace the content in that layer in **Illustrator** and all of the animation keyframes and attributes you've applied to the layer in **After Effects** will still be there, but with the new icon!

November 8th

Proper Green Screen Tips and Techniques

Get the green screen tips and techniques you need to properly shoot a composited sequence for your next project.

Working with a green screen presents a series of unique challenges, both in production and in post. Sometimes we jump right into green screening without really taking the steps to capture a proper sequence. The end result: Your audience knows that they're seeing something shot on a green screen instead of a well-composited scene.

Traditional artists take time and planning to produce a work of art. Directors take the time and effort to **develop a scene before shooting it**. Green screen capturing requires that same attention to detail. So to help you out, we'll share a few important **green screen tips and techniques**.

Pre-Visualize Your Scene

When it comes to **shooting on a green screen**, planning ahead is vital. Concept art and storyboards are a great way to visualize the scene before the cameras even start rolling.

Know What's Real and Not Real

When shooting on a green screen, it is also vitally important to have a good grasp on what is real and what isn't. As many may know, not everything in the environment needs to be created by a computer. Sometimes you need real props working in concert with your character and the CGI. In many cases these assets need to interact with one another in the space, and this is why it is incredibly important to know what needs to be real *and* not real.

The Importance of Lighting

Whether you're going for a natural look, or for low or high key, the environment and the characters need to be lit in order to convey the scene clearly to the audience. This process is just as important when lighting for your green screen. Not only do you need to light your character in order to match the lighting of the environment they will populate, but you need to light the physical green screen itself. By doing this you make the time you spend chroma keying out your subject much easier.

Framing and Camera Movement

It is very important to NOT have flat imagery in your green screen work. Flat imagery is obtained by placing the camera directly in front of the subject with the subject standing still in the scene. The only real instance where the use of this framing works is during an interview process. You can avoid flat imagery with several solutions, but the two most important are **framing and movement.**

By **framing properly** you can have the character enter and exit the frame. You can give the character something to do in the sequence and decrease the dreaded flat imagery. You can also add **camera movement** in the scene along with the movement of your character. By adding these two together you create an environment that the audience **feels the character can physically explore and exist in.**

Brandon Clark has posted a short test video that shows him utilizing a moving camera with a character and tracking points within the green screen space.

Processing your Green Screen Sequence

With your green screen sequence now shot, you need to key out your characters and props from the green screen itself. The best way to go about this process is to either use **Adobe Premiere, After Effects** or **Nuke 9** along with a set of plug-ins. By using any of these pieces of software, along with the plug-ins and the previously discussed techniques, you can get your scene keyed out and ready for post-processing in no time.

November 9th

Quick Tip: Allocating RAM in After Effects

Is your computer optimized for After Effects? In this post, we share a simple tip to rev up your processing speeds in AE.

If your rendering time is taking longer than expected, a change in **RAM allocation** may be all you need to speed up After Effects.

I confess, when I starting using After Effects a few years back I was befuddled at the long rendering times. My computer was new and had plenty of RAM, but rendering was taking *forever*. Then, I learned this quick tip that has dramatically altered the performance of the app. Hopefully it'll do the same for you!

Adobe gives you the option to change how much of your computer's RAM is being used by After Effects (and the other applications in the Creative Suite). Depending on the RAM you have installed in your system, you will want to experiment with your allocation settings. **After Effects is 64 bit**, which allows you to take full advantage of your available RAM (*from Adobe*):

- You can render much larger compositions—both for preview and for final output—with larger frame sizes and larger source files.
- RAM previews can be much longer.
- You can work with higher color bit depths without encountering memory limitations.
- After Effects can cache more items, which reduce the frequency with which frames and components of frames are re-rendered.

Modifying your AE RAM allocation settings is simple. Here's how it's done:

1. Open up After Effects

2. Go into your AE Preferences

Click on After Effects > Preferences > Memory & Multiprocessing.

3. Change 'RAM for Other Applications'

4. Click 'Ok'

And you're done! You should see an increase in your rendering speeds in After Effects. If your computer is still going slow you might need either a new graphics card or maybe even a better processor. *If you want more info about how to optimize your machine for After Effects check out the system requirements or memory and storage pages on Adobe's site.*

November 10th

Quick Tip: Exporting with Alpha Channels in After Effects

Learn how to export video with an alpha channel in this After Effects quick tip.

Alpha layers are an incredibly efficient way to composite footage during the video editing process. The alternative is importing your composition into After Effects which can take way too much time. Follow these simple steps for exporting graphics or elements with a transparent background (alpha channel) in After Effects.

1. Make sure your background is transparent.

You can easily tell if your background is transparent by clicking the checker-box button in the composition panel.

2. Add your composition to the render queue.

Simply navigate to Composition > Add to Render Queue or hit Control+Command+M

3. Click the output module: "Lossless"

It is in the render queue on the bottom left.

4. Set the video output to RGB + Alpha.

Navigate to video output in the box the pops up and scroll down to RGB + Alpha. Your video will now include 4 different channels when it exports. Click Ok.

5. Render

Just hit the render button…and your done!

Now your footage has a transparent background layer, so you can place it above other footage in your video editing timeline. In this method of exporting your video you get **variable** alpha layers which means they can have varying degrees of opacity, but some export methods only feature **binary** alpha layers which are either off or on, no in-between.

November 11th

Simulating Depth Using Vanishing Points in After Effects

Turn your 2D images into 3D worlds with the astonishing Vanishing Point feature in After Effects.

Vanishing Point is one of those really cool effects in **After Effects** that will always be impressive no matter how many times you use it. In a nutshell, Vanishing Point simulates a 3D environment by creating a simulated 3D projection. While it doesn't work in every situation, if you have a room with good four-corner perspective, you can create some amazing results. And convert it to this using Vanishing Point in **After Effects**:
Let's take a look at this awesome feature inside of **After Effects** and discuss a few ways to make your Vanishing Point videos even better.

Step 1: Create a Vanishing Point Grid in Photoshop

In order to create a Vanishing Point in Photoshop and **After Effects**, you need to use a combination of both Photoshop and **After Effects**. First things first, you need to open your photo in Photoshop then navigate to **Filter>Vanishing Point** or simply hit **Option+Command+V**. You will see a window pop up. In the window, select the **Create Planes** tool **(C)**. Make a small rectangle around the back wall of your Vanishing Point image. Make the box as straight as possible.
After you set the edges of your base plane, you can drag the edges of the frame to create the Vanishing Point effect by holding down command. You will probably have to adjust the edges if they aren't 100% flush with the edges of the walls. You can do this by holding down command and adjusting one edge and corner at a time. If for any reason your plane turns red, you may need to stretch the edges of your frame further in z-space.

Step 2: Export for After Effects

After you've created all four edges in your frame, it's time to export your video to **After Effects**. Before you hit that 'OK' button, navigate to the menu button in the upper left of the Vanishing

Point window and then hit **Export for After Effects**. You will need to designate a place to save the .vpe file on your computer.

Step 3: Import Vanishing Point File

Open up **After Effects**. With an **After Effects** project open, navigate to **File>Import>Vanishing Point**. Now select the Vanishing Point file on your computer and hit 'OK.' You should now see a folder with five images pop up in your project panel along with a new composition.

Step 4: Adjust the Composition

Click inside the new composition and you will see a composition made up of five images, a parent, and a camera. By default, the width of the composition will be the same as the width of the image file in Photoshop. You will likely want to change the width of the composition to a standard 1080p composition, but you can simply select one of the presets in composition settings.

Depending on your scene, you may need to adjust the rotation of your parent. If you need to move in or out of the scene, I recommend using the zoom feature versus physically moving the camera in 3D space.

Tips for Creating Better Vanishing Points

Depth of Field

If you want to make your new 3D Vanishing Point look even more real, you should try adding a simple depth of field to your scene. A depth of field can simulate a real-life environment and really help sell your composition.

To do this, navigate to the camera options in your timeline turn the depth of field on. You can then adjust the depth of field by messing with the aperture and blur level.

Lights

One of the cool things about working with a Vanishing Point: the layers created in photoshop will actually work in 3D space. So like any other 3D composition in **After Effects**, you can adjust your layers to accept 3D lights. This can create some really cool results if you are wanting to integrate 3D motion graphics into your scene.

3D Models and Text

There are a lot of reasons why you may want to put text or objects into your 3D scene. No matter what the reason, it's easy to do. Simply turn 2D layers to 3D and place them in your scene. You can also use 3D effects like Trapcode Particular and Element 3D in your Vanishing Point 'room.'

November 12th
Use the Puppet Tool in After Effects to Add Life to Animation

Add subtle animation and bring your designs to life with the Puppet tool in After Effects. Here's everything you need to know.

When working with image assets (especially vector designs), subtle application of the **Puppet tool in After Effects** can add life to your animation.
In this example, I'm animating a background design of a bird and other design elements scaling up.

The bird feel pretty lifeless, so I'm going to use the **Puppet tool** (the pushpin icon in the menu bar, as seen below) to give it some subtle movement. The **Puppet tool** lets you add "pins" in the image, then move and warp the image based on where you move the pins.
Each time you click on the image with the **Puppet tool**, you add a "pin" which acts as a kind of soft joint. I'm going to start by adding my initial joints, as well as adding a few joints that I won't be keyframing, to keep certain parts of the image from moving. I'm going to place pins on the tips, middle joint, and beginning of its wings, the tips and beginning of his tail, and the middle of the head and the neck.
By default, as soon as you add a pin, it puts an initial keyframe for that pin wherever your playhead is.

From here, I'm going to move back a few frames and **do my deforming**. I want it to look like the bird is spreading his wings and tail as it scales up, so I'm going to deform it by bringing the tips of its wings down a little and the mid-point of its wings down and a little towards the center of its body.

I'll take the three bottom points on the tail and move them all in a bit towards the top tail joint. Then I'll take the head pin and drag it up just a little, so that it looks like the bird is lowering its head as it spreads its wings into a flying position.

Previewing this, it does look like its wings are stretching out, so now I'm going to move those keyframes to line up with the scale I already have on the layer.

You'll notice it looks a little… funny. This is because the **Puppet tool** movement isn't eased at all. I'm going to select all of the deform keyframes and right click, setting them to "Easy Ease." After that, I'll jump into the Curve Editor and drag the influence on the end keyframes to about 50%.

This gives us a nice, eased movement.

Subtle application of the **Puppet tool** can make a big difference to still designs by adding a hint of life-like movement that simple transforms simply can't. There are all sorts of places this can be applied, **just remember to do small movements** – they'll translate well without looking *too* fake.

November 13th
Using Neat Video: Exceptional Noise Reduction for Video

Is grainy footage ruining your project? Neat Video packs a powerful punch for reducing grain and noise in footage. In this post we'll show you how to get the most out of it in your projects.

Digital noise is an inevitable, undesirable facet of working with video. Unlike film grain, we find digital noise ugly and wish to eliminate or limit it. Luckily, noise reduction tools exist to combat grainy footage. While native software noise reducers suffice for many projects, sometimes additional firepower is required for egregiously dirty shots.

Enter Neat Video, a professional noise reduction plugin. At its price point (free or up to $199 – depending on the version), it's become an industry standard. However, its interface is anything but intuitive. Let's wrap our heads around it.

How Neat Video Works

Neat Video profiles a portion of the image to evaluate the noise in the overall frame. It is optimal that this portion should contain as few characteristics as possible. Good profiles might contain a piece of pure blue sky or a shadow region that lacks detail. Neat then reports a *Quality* level on this profile as a percentage. The higher the percentage, the more effective the reduction.

Once it's gathered a profile for our shot, the *Noise Filter Settings* tab activates. The intra-frame controls are tweaked inside the plugin and temporal reduction is controlled outside the plugin.

Treating a Clip

Low light in a concert hall, a pretty classic candidate for potential noise. The noise is in this one for sure: We'll be working with an extremely noisy RED clip shot in a low-light concert hall. My chosen software is Davinci Resolve, but Neat works in a host of applications like After Effects, Premiere, Final Cut Pro, and others.

To use Neat Video in Resolve, add a new serial node and open up the FX panel. Drag the *Reduce Noise* plugin onto the new node. We'll worry about the parameters here later. Click the *Options* button. Click the FX icon all the way on the right interface, above the timeline. *Some parameters will come up but click* Options *for now.*

Neat Video works really well with minimal user input. Clicking *Auto Profile* lets Neat evaluate the image for the best possible profile. You can also set this yourself, but it's difficult to beat *Auto Profile*.

Neat Video found a profile at nearly 80 percent quality for my shot, whereas mine were somewhere around 50 or even 30 percent. Best to let it do its thing.

To evaluate the reduction, do one of three things:

- Toggle the *Preview* button to see the original and filtered results.
- Hold your mouse button down to see the original shot, and release your mouse to see the filtered results.
- Click and drag to draw a square around an area. The inside shows the filtered result. The outside shows the original image.

Draw a square around any area to see the filtered and original versions next to each other. Depending on the shot's noise level, you may not be seeing dramatic results. You can zoom into the image to get a finer detail of everything that's going on.

You can zoom in quite a bit to see what the noise reduction is doing. There are also a number of views showing just the luminance channel or each separate color channel that you can use for further analysis.

This view shows the three separate color channels. Check out how noisy the blue channel is compared to the others. You're slacking, blue channel! Neat Video works pretty well as is, but depending on how much time you have in session, there may be some time to tweak to find what looks good. You can adjust your *Noise Levels* and *Reduction Amounts* inside the *Noise Filter Settings*. Note that the *Luminance Reduction* is set lower than for *Chrominance* because our eyes are more sensitive to luminance than chrominance. Proceed with subtlety! Don't go too far and risk blurring the footage.

Once you've got the profile where you want it, click *Apply*. You may not get real-time playback, but that's what the *Render Cache* is for. Select the *Playback* menu, and scroll to the bottom to *Render Cache* and select *Smart*. Resolve knows what your graphics card can handle in real-time and which nodes it needs to render.

Neat Video Parameters

The most useful parameter is the *Radius* button. It allows Neat Video to analyze the noise profile forward and backward by the number of frames you specify. The maximum Neat can evaluate is five frames before and after your current frame, which will be especially processor-intensive. You may see dramatic results by just kicking the *Radius* up to three. Just know, the default setting of one evaluates three frames: the current one, and one frame before and after it. *Threshold* controls how aggressive you want the temporal filtering to be. The *Adaptive* option can be used when the shot veers greatly in composition, causing the noise profile to change over time. As you may have guessed, *Interlaced* is for dealing with interlaced footage. Chances are you won't need this if you're dealing with modern cameras that shoot progressively.

The noise reduced shot looks much more palatable, especially when it's moving.

Our scopes readout before the noise reduction. Note how the lower register appears to be smeared. That's the noise. Our much-improved scopes, yielding pretty dramatic results.

Neat Video is an awesome noise reduction plugin that works with many professional pieces of software. It's highly processor-intensive and will balloon your render times even if you have a decent graphics card, so make sure to factor in that time when working with demanding clients. In Resolve, using Neat Video in conjunction with the *Render Cache* is the preferred workflow. Placing the reduction node near the beginning of your node tree ensures it will stay rendered as you add additional corrections. When wielded with subtlety, noise reduction is a great tool and can dramatically improve image quality.

November 14th

3 Tips for Picking the Right Font for Your Business

So you've picked a stellar name for your company, crafted a catchy tagline, and chosen the perfect colors for your brand. But you're not quite done. Don't forget about an oft-overlooked component of visual communication: fonts.

Just as colors elicit an emotional response, so too do fonts. For better or for worse, they evoke certain associations, feelings, and moods. Some fonts — Comic Sans, Papyrus, Curlz MT — are universally reviled, while fonts like HTF Didot and Akzidenz Grotesk are hailed for their elegance, beauty, and craft.

Fonts communicate more than just words. Your choice of typography instantly says a lot about you and your business, and it influences how people perceive your messaging. The right font will drive your message home, and the wrong font will distract your audience and detract from your credibility.

Read on for three essential tips to help you choose the right font for your brand.

1. Decide Which Characteristics You Want Your Brand to Convey

First, consider these questions: What are the most salient qualities of your brand? What's your brand personality — is it serious and trustworthy, or jovial and fun? What do you stand for, and what do you want to communicate to your users?

Also think about your target market. What are their interests and aspirations? How do they communicate? This knowledge will help shape your brand identity.

2. Make Sure Your Font Style Aligns with Your Brand's Character

The next step, to pick a font that matches the mood and feel of your brand, is key. Every font has a distinct personality and character, so you need to be thoughtful when you select one. Some fonts are elegant and refined, some are whimsical and playful, and some are traditional and formal.

Generally, fonts can be broken down into several broad categories:

Serif

Serif fonts have little "feet" and carry a traditional, classic feeling. They are considered to convey authority, reliability, confidence, and respectability. Some corporations that use serif fonts in their logos include HSBC Bank, CBS television network, and Tiffany & Co. Font examples include Baskerville, Garamond, Caslon, and Palatino.

A subset of this group is **slab serif** fonts, which have thick, blocky serifs. They're often used in headlines, and their geometric serifs give them an air of confidence and strength. Font examples include Rockwell, Archer, Egyptian Slate, and Memphis.

Sans Serif

Sans serif fonts lack the "feet" and generally have a clean, simple, modern, and sensible feel to them. Companies such as Facebook, Hulu, and YouTube all use sans serif fonts in their logos.

Some typography experts recommend using sans serif fonts for the web because they're easier to read on screens, but as our screen resolutions continue to improve, many say that serif fonts work just as well on the web. Font examples include Helvetica, Avenir, Arial, and Futura.

Script

Cursive fonts (which includes most handwritten fonts) generally embody femininity, elegance, creativity, and friendliness. Corporate logos using script fonts include Cartier, Instagram, and Coca-Cola. Use these sparingly; they're not ideal for body copy because they have low legibility in paragraph form.

Novelty

Novelty fonts are bold, quirky, fun, and eye-catching. They are designed to be loud and flashy, which creates visual interest and makes them great for headlines, but also makes them difficult to use. It's a good idea to use them sparingly — one novelty font is enough — and pair them with a more minimalist font for the body text.

You can explore hundreds of free fonts at Font Squirrel and Google Fonts, and then decide which one best matches the tone of your messaging and represents the spirit of your brand.

3. Make Sure Your Fonts Are Readable

Readability is a major priority when you're designing. You could have a brilliant message, but it's all for naught if it's not legible. Designer Jessica Hische has a "Il1 rule": if you're working with a sans-serif font, try typing a capital I, a lowercase l, and a number 1 next to each other, and see if you can tell the difference between them. If you can't, then you might encounter some trouble. (Verdana, the font used in the example to the right, passes the test.)

Good typography is crucial to building a strong brand identity and creating a favorable first impression. But with so many fonts out there, it can feel overwhelming to pick the right one. Feel free to experiment with different ones and refine as you go. As long as you match the font with the mood and purpose of your messaging, and it embodies your brand identity, you'll deliver a strong message to your readers

November 15th
5 Easy In-Camera Effects

Why process those camera effects in post when you can do them directly in-camera? Check out these 5-easy in-camera effects.

Not all visual effects are done in post-production. In fact, some really awesome (and easy to achieve) effects can be done directly in-camera. Here are the in-camera effects that explains how a few of the most eye-opening in-camera effects are done.

1. Forced Perspective

Forced perspective is a technique that uses spacing and distance to make **objects appear larger or smaller** in relation to other objects.

2. Lower Shutter Speed

Using a lower shutter speed is generally done for two reasons. The first: because the location is dark and you need to let in more light. The second is to **create motion blur to make the action seem more fluid**.

3. Faster Shutter Speed

A faster shutter speed is utilized extensively by professional sport filmmakers. Because of the high shutter speed, you can essentially "freeze" a moment. When using this in conjunction with camera movement, **the action seemingly becomes more violent.** This technique works great in combat sequences.

4. Lens Whacking

Lens whacking is done by **detaching the lens from the mount and then holding it close enough to allow the sensor to still gain an image.** The result is very surreal and ethereal.

5. Lens Flare

Lens flare is the natural effect of **non-image forming light entering the lens and hitting the sensor**, creating the characteristic streak of light.

November 16th
5 Online Resources for Getting Started in Visual Effects and Motion Graphics

Looking to start a visual effects career or develop new motion graphics skills? These online VFX education resources are cost effective and convenient!

Whether you just finished high school or are mid career, not everyone has the time or money to attend school full-time. In this post, we explore affordable online options to **learn visual effects, CG and motion graphics**.
Check out each site, watch the preview videos and read the FAQs to find the **online VFX education resource** that best fits your needs and interests.

1. FXPHD

FXPHD mimics a traditional format of universities, giving you a 10-week schedule of training. You can join anytime during the 10 weeks and the classes are taught by industry professionals.

	Standard three course membership costs $359, includes required 4th class, Background Fundamentals.
How it Works:	You download the classes; it is not a subscription service. You have 2 weeks to sample the available classes (first 2 classes) before committing to 3 classes.

Features:	Access to a variety of software via VPN during the 10 weeks. Access to the class forums, where you can ask questions and interact with fellow students. You can also download hi-res footage that you can use for practice. Some of the intro classes offer certification exams. There are Challenges (background fundamentals) where you submit work for feedback.
Focus:	Broad. Though they offer a lot of VFX and motion graphics classes, as well as classes in cinematography, editing, color grading, and audio. They have 9 class tags, where you can search classes by subject.

2. Digital Tutors

How it Works:	Subscription service (Monthly Plan $45, 6 Months $225, Yearly $399) You have access to files to use for the classes and on your reel.
Features:	1300+ courses with 24 Learning Paths that guide you to what classes to watch. Classes are broken into levels and offer quizzes and tests. A good starting place for beginners is CG 101, a collection of fundamentals for 2D & 3D. There are also tips on creating a demo reel and portfolio. They offer new classes each month (see listing below).
Focus:	Broad. Subjects include 2D, 3D, CAD, Game Development and Video VFX. Also covers traditional skills (drawing, illustration, color theory), as well as a variety of software.

3. CMIVFX

How it Works:	Annual Subscription $299.99 (includes training materials) or you can buy a video stream of any individual class.
Features:	New classes weekly. Instructors (mentors) are well known industry artists.
Focus:	Specific. Hi-End VFX for movies and media (software include Nuke, Houdini, Maya).

4. Simply Maya

How it Works:	Video Credits allow you do download only the parts of a tutorial that you'd like to watch. You can also opt for a Lifetime Membership $395 or purchase a video tutorial from the Simply Maya Shop (individual downloads)
Features:	Tutorials cover a range of Maya related topics including rigging, lighting, modeling, shading and rendering. There's also an active Community Forum and Maya resources (models, rigs, shaders, materials, scripts).
Focus:	Specific. Courses are limited to Maya software based training.

5. VFX Learning U

VFX Learning U is an Indiegogo project (funding Dec. 2013) of VFX Learning.

How it Works:	A suite of VFX training tutorials from VFXLearning.com Choose the FX Technical Director package for $300 or purchase case studies individually (1 for $50 or 4 for $150).

Features:	70 hours of training on Maya and RealFlow. The Technical Director package which covers how to create Hollywood style VFX. Each training video comes with project files.
Focus:	Specific to feature film style visual effects.

Other Paid VFX Education Options

If you're looking for a more traditional online VFX school, check out these options (all over $500) which offer a structured set of visual effects classes.

- **Escape Studios**
- **Animation Mentor**
- **Gnomon School of VFX**

November 17th
8 City Logos with Bold and Beautiful Design

Designing a city logo is a lot like branding a company, except there are infinitely more historical, cultural, societal, and political implications to consider. Every city in the world has a distinct identity that gives it a soul and a sense of purpose, and it is the daunting job of designers to capture this identity with a single image.

We found eight of the world's most compelling city logos that accomplish this, and dug into the stories behind the designs.

Amsterdam, Netherlands

The municipal logo for the capital of the Netherlands is as minimalistic — and direct — as it gets. It adopts the city flag's red color as well as its St. Andrew crosses (also a shorthand for the city's infamous Red Light District), and affixes the city's name to it. The original 2003 design had "Gemeente Amsterdam" (City of Amsterdam) on one line, but an upgrade by design studio Dedato B.V. in 2014 added a line break to nest "Amsterdam" below "Gemeente" and provided a cleaner look to the current version of the logo. A logo that, for all its simplicity, is effective in its modern look. The stacked Xs are somewhat evocative of the canal houses that line the city's waterways — tall, neat, and ordered, just the way the Dutch like them.

Cape Town, South Africa

Cape Town's logo, designed jointly by agencies Yellowwood and King James in 2014, came with a mission to visually represent the city's forward-looking frame of mind ("Making Progress Possible. Together" is the city's motto). That led the agencies to look to the horizon, literally, and find inspiration in the city's most famous landmark: Table Mountain. The mountain's silhouette became the foundation of the new logo, linked and repeated to form a circle. The additional concentric circles were created to convey a city both "layered and harmonious," and the vibrant colors capture the energy of the city's culture.

Kostroma, Russia

When the city known as "the soul of Russia" hired designer Natalia Chobanu in 2013 to create a new logo, she set out to merge the city's traditions with a modern design. The logo — like the culture — is built on tradition. According to Chobanu, the shape of the logo is directly drawn from cultural artifacts like a kokoshnik (a traditional Russian headdress for women), the halo of a Holy Mother icon, and even part of an old map of the city. Those inspirations were then abstracted into the geometrical figures found in the finished product, which make it look both unexpectedly (and intentionally) modern and vibrant for an old Russian city.

Melbourne, Australia

In 2009, the Australian city assigned design firm Landor the task of rebranding their city's image for the first time since the 1990s. Landor had a few goals, like advertising the city's sophistication to the world, and creating a logo that would remain modern for years to come. While dreaming up possible logos, they explained, "the diversity of Melbourne became a sacred concept." They captured this beautifully in two ways: The diverse shading of colors in the logo (see more variations here), as well as the linked and overlapping polygons that make up the symbolic "M." Together, it all creates a fun and modern vibe that would convince anyone to visit Melbourne.

Montreal, Canada

When the French-Canadian city's logo was designed and unveiled by Georges Huel & Associates in 1981, it featured a beautiful rosette accompanied by the text "Ville de Montréal." A minor update in 2005 aside ("Ville de" was dropped, and "Montréal" was shifted to the left of the flower-like image), the logo has remained unchanged. Not just because it became so beloved by the city's people, but because the number of intended meanings layered into the rosette is a dizzying feat of symbolism. A few examples: It's an adaptation of part of the city's coat of arms; each quarter of the rosette is both a V and a M, to represent the initials of "Ville de Montréal"; the heart-shaped petals represent love for the city; the four petals evoke the ethnic groups that founded the city (French, English, Scottish, and Irish). It's a remarkable accomplishment to stack so much meaning into one simple design, without sacrificing aesthetic.

Prague, Czech Republic

Created in 2002 by design firm Studio Najbrt, the main objective of the new logo was to provide "a symbolic hand extended to all visitors coming to Prague and a reminder of the city's history as a center of different cultures and nationalities." That's why, in addition to channeling the city flag's color scheme, the logo features several variations on the city's name. Each one is "Prague" in a different language, and meant to reflect the Czech Republic capital's diversity. The eye-drawing white line that separates the "Pra" root from its suffixes is also a wonderful symbolic touch, conveying the idea that the city has a core foundation, but one mean to be built upon — whether by residents or tourists.

São Paulo, Brazil

In anticipation of both the 2014 Brazil World Cup and the 2016 Rio de Janeiro Olympics, designer Rômulo Castilho was given the task of creating a logo that would "promote São Paulo as a unique destination full of opportunities, services, and culture." That uniqueness is immediately captured in the logo's vibrant colors, which readily evoke Brazilian festivities like Carnival. The firework-like shapes emanating outwards from the city's name cleverly creates the impression of a city bursting with life, services, culture and — above all else — fun.

Tokyo, Japan

Created by ad agency Hakuhodo, and revealed in October 2015 in anticipation of the 2020 Toyko Olympics, the city's new logo is very simple. However, the simple design has big conceptual ambitions. The designers created it to encourage those looking to fill in the inferred blank space before the ampersand with themselves. In that way, the logo becomes a vehicle for engagement, true to the massive metropolis of Tokyo and the endless opportunities (traditional, modern, and downright weird) it offers. The logo effectively says to tourists, and even to residents, "Make this city yours."

November 18th
10 Examples of Horrible Hollywood Special Effects

Check out ten moments from big budget blockbusters that made it virtually impossible for viewers to suspend their disbelief.

Between Christopher Nolan's scientifically accurate black hole in *Interstellar* to the full-sized Millennium Falcon in JJ Abrams's upcoming *Star Wars: The Force Awakens*, it's a good time to be alive for fans of both **CGI and practical effects**. Of course, for every jaw-dropping moment of movie magic, there are at least ten instances of unintentional FX hilarity. For example:

1. *The Mummy Returns*

The Rock is practically a special effect unto himself. He's charming. He's massive. Entire franchises (*G.I. Joe*, the *Fast/Furious* films) have been revitalized by his undeniable charisma and screen presence. So it makes sense that the filmmakers of *The Mummy Returns* would give him the day off during the shoot of the movie's climax. Speaking of *G.I. Joe*...

2. *G.I. Joe: The Rise of Cobra*

As an old school *G.I. Joe* comics fan, I had high hopes for this movie. I mean, they cast Joseph Gordon-Levitt as Cobra Commander and Christopher Eccleston as Destro. What could possible go wrong? Turns out, as witnessed in Destro's transformation scene...a lot. VFX powerhouse MPC did many of the effects.

3. *X-Men Origins: Wolverine*

Every time Hugh Jackman spikes his hair and lights a cigar, a yacht spontaneously appears in the backyard of a Fox executive. So you'd think they wouldn't skimp on Wolverine's defining Adamantium attribute. And the GIF above would prove that you're incorrect.
YouTuber ILoveRyanReynolds (who from their content, most certainly loves Ryan Reynolds) offers up a 4 part behind the scenes look into production of *Wolverine*:

4. *King Kong*

Peter Jackson's Weta Workshop is a legendary special effects house. You know you're going to be seeing something amazing when their logo appears in the credits of a film. I think the most amazing thing about this dinosaur demolition derby is that it didn't end up on the editing room floor. Peter Jackson actually completed a production diary of the film, chronicling the filmmaking process. It's avaliable from Amazon, as well as a web version here.
Of course, Weta is also responsible for such special effects masterpieces as the *Lord of the Rings* trilogy and the 2014 *Godzilla* remake, so we can cut them some slack.

5. *The Twilight Saga: Breaking Dawn – Part 2*

For a film series that's chocked full of questionable special effects this one may take the cake. Just look at the baby. Look at the baby!

6. *Hulk*

I get that the over-the-top proportions and palette of the Hulk make him hard to portray as a realistic character, but somehow the Marvel Cinematic Universe pulls it off. Unfortunately, the same can't be said about Ang Lee's rubber skinned take on the big green icon.

7. Star Wars: A New Hope (Special Edition)

Oh, hey. It's Jabba the...what? I am not doing George Lucas a favor by following up this CGI abomination with a video that features the amazing Practical Effects Jabba.

8. Star Wars: Return of the Jedi (Special Edition)

I refuse to believe that Boba Fett would go to this super-lame party. Here's the original version. As a kid, it truly felt like this his was the kind of strange cosmic disco that would be playing at an intergalactic gangster's palace. This scene has 99 problems, but Practical Effects Jabba ain't one.

9. Harry Potter and the Sorcerer's Stone

The filmmakers could've had Harry, Hermione, and Ron fighting Shrek and it still wouldn't looked as cartoonish as some of the scenes in this movie.

10. Jaws 3

Is this the greatest moment in cinematic history?! Originally produced in 3D, *Jaws 3* was directed by Joe Alves, the man responsible for creating the famously hard-to-work-with mechanical sharks used in Steven Spielberg's original *Jaws*.
The documentary *The Shark is Still Working* is a fascinating and entertaining look at some of the difficulties that occurred on the set of Jaws. It's definitely worth a watch.
Now that we've wallowed in VFX failure, you can go do good work!!

November 19th

10 Motion Graphics and Visual Effects Resources for Editors

In today's world, video editors are often expected to have Motion Graphics/VFX Skills. The following resources are beneficial for extending your graphics skill set.

The days of 'just being an editor' are over. Most editors are now required to wear multiple hats and juggle various **video editing, motion design, encoding and color grading** applications on a daily basis. On most freelance jobs I am often using Adobe Photoshop and After Effects for graphics tasks, Maxon Cinema 4D for 3D work, along with Premiere Pro, Final Cut Pro and Avid Media Composer for video editing.

With the recent free addition of **Cinema 4D Lite into After Effects Creative Cloud**, more video editors will now be integrating 3D into their work. In this post, we've rounded up 10 resources will help you strengthen your After Effects and Cinema 4D skills – **free After Effects templates**, **motion graphics plugins** and loads of free training and tutorials!

Mograph is a collection of forums for **working in motion graphics**.
The site covers the art and business of the industry along with forums on resources, jobs, and tutorials. There's also a reels and portfolio page where the best motion designers share their work – great for inspiration. Mograph is a good place to network to and learn more about the industry.

Vfxer

Vfxer is a **Cinema 4D & After Effects** resource run by a husband and wife team (Simon & Claire). Besides useful AE and Cinema 4D tutorials, they have sections on visual effects news, inspiration and free stuff (weekly mailing list).
Be sure to check out their collection of 10 free pre-fractured 3D models that can be used in Element 3D or Cinema 4D.

Greyscale Gorilla

Greyscale Gorilla is the brainchild of VFX guru Nick Campbell. Over the last few years Greyscale Gorilla has become a leading **motion design and visual effects** force online, with frequently updated tutorials, news and their own 3D and visual effects products.

aescripts + aeplugins

aescripts + aeplugins offers quality scripts and plugins for a variety of video editing and motion design applications (After Effects, Cinema 4D, NLEs). These are particularly helpful when you are looking to extend what you can do in an app. For instance, need to animate characters mouths in **After Effects** without losing your sanity? No problem, there is Auto Lip-Sync ($39.99)

The scripts are affordable, with some even being 'name your own price'.

ToolFarm/AE Freemart

Motion Graphics artist Michele Yamazaki runs/writes for both of these sites. **AE Freemart** covers cool resources for **After Effects,** including free After Effects templates and plugins. Toolfarm sells plugins but has evolved into a resource for editors/artists. They cover the latest motion design and visual effects news, as well as having a blog and **free After Effects tutorials**.

Lesterbanks

Lester Banks round ups the best of After Effects & 3D tutorials from the web. Most of these are intermediate to advanced and are aimed at the working editor/artist. This is a 'must bookmark' site for anyone that works in motion graphics and video editing on a daily basis.

Imagineer Mocha Tutorials

When tracking motion in your video footage, you can generally get better tracks quicker using Mocha AE (bundled with After Effects), rather than simply tracking inside of **After Effects.** It is a powerful app but can be a bit overwhelming at first for some editors. Check out these **free tutorials for getting started with Mocha AE,** as well as more advanced tutorials for their flagship app Mocha Pro (used for the face replacement in the popular TV show *Grimm*).

School of Motion

New to Motion Graphics/VFX? Joey Korenman is a Creative Director who shares his knowledge of creating motion graphics on his website, School of Motion. The tutorials and articles cover most all the software tools of the trade (Photoshop, After Effects, Cinema 4D, & Nuke.) School of Motion is a good resource for those starting to learn After Effects & Cinema 4D.

Motion Graphics Exchange

Motion Graphics Exchange is a motion design resource with **free After Effects templates**, tips, presets, expressions, and scripts.

You can search the site by category or topic – a helpful time saver. Say your looking for a wiggle script. Simply type in 'wiggle' and you'll get a list of wiggle expressions and tips.

Helloluxx

Tim Clapman is an expert on Cinema 4D and teaches classes at FXPHD. He offers advanced tutorials on Cinema 4D for those taking their skills to the next level. His work is high end and really inventive, so a bit of C4D experience is probably suggested before jumping into these terrific tutorials!

Motionworks

Motionworks combines **free After Effects and Cinema 4D tutorials**, with industry news and showcase of great examples of motion design projects. Aside from free training on the site, be sure to check out the in-depth paid training and tutorials for AE and C4D.

November 20th
10 VFX Moments That Changed the Industry Forever

The history of filmmaking is marked by amazing moments of game-changing movie magic. Check out these jaw-dropping VFX innovations that radically changed the industry.

The debate over practical versus digital has been raging for a long time. Some argue that the look and feel of practical sets make things seem tangible and tactile. Others love digital **movie sets** because they free the filmmaker to insert things they otherwise couldn't.
No matter which side of the fence you plant your flag, both types of effects have been responsible for some iconic moments that changed the industry. Let's take a look at a few game-changing **VFX** sequences.

1. In the Beginning, There Was Kong

Before Douglas Trumball wowed us with the Jupiter sequence in *2001: A Space Odyssey* and before ILM broke our brains with *Star Wars* and *Jurassic Park*, there was a man named Marcel Delgado. A master of stop-motion animation, Delgado revolutionized the industry with 1933's *King Kong*, creating special effects unlike any that had previously been seen. You could equate this moment to the first time audiences saw *Toy Story* decades later. It was, as they say, a a big deal.

Inn 1949, Delgado would team up with a young sculptor named Ray Harryhausen to perfect stop-motion techniques in a film called *Mighty Joe Young*.

2. Harryhausen and the Argonauts

After his fateful collaboration with Marcel Delgado, Ray Harryahusen would go on to develop many stop-motion animation sequences for film. But none of them had the impact that a certain 1963 film had. Just five years before*2001: A Space Odyssey*, Harryhausen created magical animation sequences for the fantasy film *Jason and the Argonauts*. Regarded by Harryhausen as his greatest work, *Jason and the Argonauts* stunned audiences across the country with one of the most famous **VFX** scenes of all time as Jason and his Argonauts battled a host of skeleton warriors.

The effects of this film would ignite the imaginations of many young up-and-coming visual effects artists like Stan Winston, Henry Selick, and Richard Taylor. Harryhausen would also be awarded the Academy Lifetime Achievement Award for his work and influence on the film industry. During the ceremony actor Tom Hanks said:

Some people say Casablanca or Citizen Kane... I say Jason and the Argonauts is the greatest film ever made.

3. Douglas Trumbull's Space Odyssey

Five years after *Jason and the Argonauts* was released, a sci-fi film would take things one step further. Using miniatures and massive sound stages, director Stanley Kubrick would gather a team to handcraft the future before our very eyes. Even though this was an amazing feat, the real game-changing **VFX** moment came during the "Star Gate" section at the end of the film. For this, a young special effects artist named Douglas Trumbull used a technique called slit-scan photography. He would also charge water with various inks, paints, and chemicals to create portions of space.

These techniques had never been done before. When the film hit screens, it completely revolutionized the film industry — and inspired a young filmmaker named George Lucas to finally tackle a massive project he had been trying to develop for some time.

4. A New Hope With Industrial Light & Magic

In 1975, George Lucas began developing his latest film, The Adventures of Luke Starkiller. In order to fulfill the visual effects needs for production, Lucas reached out to **VFX** artist Douglas Trumbull. However, Trumbull declined the opportunity, as he had already committed himself to creating the **VFX** for a Steven Spielberg film called *Close Encounters of the Third Kind*. To help Lucas out, Trumbull suggested his assistant, John Dykstra. From this moment on, Lucas and Dykstra would form a visual effects company known as Industrial Light & Magic. Their first project? *Star Wars*.

For *Star Wars*, Dykstra gathered a collection of amazing talent that included **VFX** artists like Ken Ralston, Richard Edlund, Dennis Muren, Joe Johnston, Phil Tippett, and Steve Gawley. This team developed a motion-controlled camera and used it against black backdrops in order to film highly detailed spacecraft models. The moving camera would pan around the models and give them a sense of motion that would then be superimposed.

This could quite possibly be the biggest moment in all of film history, as *Star Wars* would go on to completely flip the industry on its head and inspire an entire generation of filmmakers and **VFX** artists.

5. Mr. Lasseter and the Stained Glass Man

In 1985, a young artist named John Lasseter (who worked with Industrial Light & Magic's *Graphics Group*, later to be known as Pixar) developed the first fully functional computer-animated character for the big screen. This character was the "Stained Glass Man" from *Young Sherlock Holmes*. At the time of its creation, it truly was a remarkable feat. No one had seen a fully rendered character like that before. From this moment on, the world of **VFX** changed forever — but it didn't just happen over night.

It would take some time before the industry would trust the use of fully rendered animated characters. But this moment, though small and not always known by most people, was indeed a massive moment in film history. Of course, John Lasseter would go on to create and direct *Toy Story*, but the work he left behind at Industrial Light & Magic would inspire longtime VFX supervisor Dennis Muren to convince filmmaker Steven Spielberg to take a chance with 3D rendered characters for his next project.

6. Rubber and Digital Dinos in the Same Frame

In order to prove that his team could pull off such a feat, Dennis Muren and his team at ILM collaborated with Stan Winston's creature shop to bring 1993's *Jurassic Park* to life on the big screen. This is where things really turned for the world of CG and visual effects. Now the industry had concrete evidence that the **VFX** industry could indeed create computer-animated imagery that looked real. ILM took a gamble, believing that if you give the audience enough tangible assets, you can extend that environment with optical illusions that they will accept. This is where we get into the theory of "the perfect blend," which *Jurassic Park* nailed: mixing digital dinosaurs with the practical dinosaurs created by Stan Winston and his creature shop. This is the launching point for the type of **VFX** seen in many modern films.

7. Bullets Fly Reeeeeeeally Slow in the Matrix

Six years after *Jurassic Park,* the game changed once again as Neo twisted and leaned and ducked to avoid Agent Smith's bullets on an urban rooftop. It wasn't the choreography and gunplay that shocked people… It was the way the sequence was filmed, in 180 degrees of motion.

VFX supervisor John Gaeta developed the process known as "bullet time" by using a large array of still photography cameras. These cameras would then flash and take pictures in quick succession. These still photographs would then be placed into an NLE system where they would be edited together to create a sweeping moment of slow-motion action.

8. The Lords of MoCap

Just a short few years after *The Matrix*, director Peter Jackson and **VFX** supervisor Richard Taylor collaborated to bring the world of Middle Earth to the big screen when they developed *The Lord of the Rings* trilogy. While there were plenty of old-school SFX techniques on display, there was one process that made this one of the very best moments in **VFX** history: the introduction of Gollum and the process of Motion Capture or Performance Capture. Richard Taylor and his crew at Weta Digital had actor Andy Serkis wear a specialized suit that allowed them to capture the motion and facial expressions for the character. Once this performance was completed, the data was sent to artists who crafted the 3D version of Gollum. It wouldn't take too long for this process to catch on in the industry — and soon a film would be created almost exclusively through this process.

9. In the 3D Mindscape of James Cameron

Director James Cameron has always been one to really push the limits of his film production. So it was no surprise when he released *Avatar*. While there were plenty of flesh-and-blood characters in the film, the majority of what is seen was accomplished through Performance Capture. Weta Digital expanded on what they learned with *The Lord of the Rings* to capture more facial emotions from the characters, including eye movement. The film also ushered in a new wave of 3D theater experiences, which exploded after the film's release.

10. Breaking Reality With the Virtual

The world of entertainment is on the cusp of something pretty amazing. The idea of **immersive cinema** has been around for many decades. In fact, **VFX** legend Douglas Trumbull has been working on ways to make this a reality for many years. But the next game-changing technological leap might very well be **virtual reality**.

With VR headsets and related camera tech waiting just around the corner, it wont be long before we begin to see the fruits of this new technology. In fact, you can already see some of it through the Industrial Light & Magic xLAB. This facility works toward the creation and development of immersive entertainment built around the *Star Wars* franchise.

November 21st

Cinematography Tip: Creating the Illusion of Speed

Creating the illusion of speed can be surprisingly difficult, regardless of whether or not your subject is actually moving quickly. Here are some common techniques you can apply to your filmmaking to turbocharge on-screen action.

Making action appear faster than it is, or even simply as fast as it is actually occurring, is a bit more complex than one might think. **Visible speed depends on a variety of factors, ranging from camera settings to framing.** In most cases, you can't shoot a real car chase at breakneck speeds, so let's take a look into some of the Hollywood trickery involved in high-speed action.

Motion Blur

We'll start with the basics. **Motion blur is one of the most important things to consider when exaggerating motion.** It is generally the result of an object moving very fast or slow in comparison to the camera. **The larger the difference in speed between an object and the camera filming it, the more motion blur that object will create.**
In most cases, **motion blur is best applied to background objects, rather than the subject of the shot.** For instance, motion blur is great for tracking shots in which the camera is traveling a similar speed to the subject. However, you would want minimal motion blur when your subject is quickly flying by the camera.
The viewer's focus should never be on a blurry object or person, so be sure to limit its use to unimportant, passing objects, unless there is a specific exception in which you want to draw attention to the blur.

Technically speaking, **high motion blur is achieved with a low shutter speed,** and vice versa. For example, if shooting at 24 fps, a shutter speed of 1/50 would produce a lot of motion blur, whereas a shutter speed of 1/2000 would virtually eliminate it. **Be sure to always set your shutter speed to at least twice your framerate (For 24fps, set to 1/48 or higher. For 60fps, set to 1/120 or higher),** as anything lower will result in choppy, unnatural-looking footage.

The iconic speeder bike chase of *Star Wars Episode VI: The Return of the Jedi* is a classic example of effective application of motion blur. Interestingly enough, **this sequence was shot by walking through the forest and shooting one frame at a time**, then superimposing the speeder bikes over the resulting footage. **Because photos aren't restricted by a frame rate, they can use very low shutter speeds to increase motion blur beyond the limitations of reality**, which was great for depicting the blisteringly high speeds of the futuristic speeder bikes.

Framing

The way a moving object is framed can drastically affect how fast it appears. **When shooting a moving object, especially from the side, tighter shots such as a medium shot or close up will emphasize speed. This is because usually objects appear faster when close, and slower when far away.** This optical illusion is the reason that passing airplanes tend to appear very slow despite moving very quickly. **The smaller the subject is in the frame, the smaller the distance it will appear to travel.** When the subject takes up the majority of the frame, less of the background will be visible at once, resulting in the illusion of covering more distance. **Narrower lenses are best suited for these types of shots.** The opening motorcycle sequence of *Skyfall* demonstrates this idea perfectly.

Conversely, **when shooting a moving object from behind or in front, a wide-angle lens would be more appropriate.** Narrow lenses tend to compress visual depth, while wider lenses expand it. What this means: if you were to film the same object approaching the camera directly, with both a 250mm telephoto lens, and a 14mm wide-angle lens, the object would grow in perceived size much more quickly and drastically with the wide angle. This accentuation of distance on the Z-axis is **great for fly-bys, close-ups of the moving subject,** and again, any shots of the front or rear of the moving subject.

For this, let's look at another modern motorcycle chase shot quite differently from the James Bond sequence, from another action film centered on espionage. This year's *Mission Impossible: Rogue Nation* featured one of the best motorcycle chases in cinematic history, if not the best. As you can see, the shots that illustrate the most speed utilize wide angle lenses and are shot behind or in front of the subject.

Setpieces and Camera Placement

Another way to highlight speed is by placing and moving the camera correctly. As mentioned before, objects appear to pass more quickly when close to the camera, and in turn generate more motion blur. Because of this, **it's often best to include objects that pass very close to the camera or subject.** Having things such as cars passing both behind and in front of your subject can add familiar points of reference for the viewer to interpret the rough speed of said subject. Note that **high-speed sequences in films avoid bland environments** with few nearby objects, as such locations make it hard to tell how fast anything is traveling. Even this scene from *Star Trek: Into Darkness* is sure to include debris for reference, as in reality, outer space is mostly empty and very difficult to accurately judge speed in. Lacking setpieces can be compensated for to an extent, by giving the camera more movement instead.

If shooting a subject traveling on land, **placing the camera lower to the ground will further indicate motion**. This is why many car chases are largely shot at bumper level, such as this awesome introductory chase scene from *Mad Max 2: The Road Warrior*.

Camera Movement

Camera movement is arguably the most crucial factor in establishing the frantic tone of a high-speed situation. While **shaky cam** has recently become an overused staple of modern Hollywood action films, employed to mask poor choreography, its effectiveness should not be underestimated, as it **adds a sense of urgency and chaos.**

Additionally, **camera movements** such as pans, tilts, dollies, and trucks **that follow the direction of the subject will emphasize velocity**. The camera being unable to keep up with the subject and seeming to fall behind is another nice touch to further diversify your scene's visuals. The 1998 thriller *Ronin* demonstrates some great camera movement, as does the aforementioned *Mission Impossible: Rogue Nation*.

Fly-by shots like these are perfect for visualizing urgency and pedestrian perspective, especially when cut to very briefly (quicker cuts infer less time for characters to see the action).

On the contrary, **moving the camera *toward* an approaching object or *away* from a retreating object can increase perceived speed**, as demonstrated in this shot from *Harry Potter and the Deathly Hallows: Part 1*.

Keep in mind that these techniques are best used in moderation; abusing any of them can break the audience's immersion, as seen in this absurd, unconvincing scene from *The Fast and the Furious*. It applies the majority of the previously discussed tricks to such a drastic degree, that they draw attention to themselves and result in a cheap-looking, over-stylized mess — though the cheesy visual effects don't help its case.

Using cinematography to manipulate the audience into seeing something that isn't quite real is critical to maintaining suspension of disbelief — and the illusion of speed is no exception. Audiences are constantly improving their ability to recognize falsity, so simply fast-forwarding your footage won't cut it. Hopefully, with these tips, you can bring your high-octane ideas to life.

November 22nd
Combining Practical Lighting With VFX

A deceptively simple technique that mixes practical lighting with VFX is proving to be one of the most visually impressive methods of creating atmosphere in recent memory.

Using **LEDs** for more than just a **light source** is a trend taking off in filmmaking. By using them as **markers, subject lighting,** and **interactive practical effects,** filmmakers are slowly but surely making new use of one of the most dynamic tools available for filmmakers.
One recent production to make use of this **visual effects technique** was 2016's *Ghostbusters* reboot/remake/sequel/what have you. Regardless of your thoughts on the film, the method used to shoot their **character VFX interactions** was genius.
For a room full of extras, interacting with an **imaginary dragon-demon-ghost** is difficult for many reasons. On top of the lighting issue, having the crowd sync up with one another while following something that isn't there can be extremely difficult to pull off. By using an **LED-**

covered drone, the crowd and central characters have a **reference point to use for their reactions**, and the light given off by the LED is beneficial as a reference for the **VFX team**.

How cool is that? Whether your shoot calls for glowing monsters or not, **using a drone as a marker** for your actors is pretty genius.

Lighting Your Subjects

As seen in the *Ghostbusters* breakdown above, Paul Feig **draped his extras in LED lights** to give them a ghostly blue aura. For projects needing **spiritual** or **supernatural** elements, this idea is cost effective and brilliant. Of course, as seen below, this wasn't the first time a production made use of LEDs in this way.

For the *Watchmen* character of Dr. Manhattan, Billy Crudup wore an entire **LED suit** to bathe his nearby costars in real blue light. Again, just like with *Ghostbusters*, this technique gives **the VFX team a great reference point** for the character's height. The following **behind-the-scenes look** reveals the detail and intricate work that went into creating Dr. Manhattan. It's well worth the watch, even if it is from six years ago.

LED lights can also be used as physical objects that actors maneuver and manipulate themselves. One major film from last year put LED VFX to work in the most obvious and genius way.

Using Objects

2015's low-budget indie darling *Star Wars: The Force Awakens* made use of this **LED technique** with its **lightsabers**. As seen in the stunning VFX breakdown video released a few weeks back, all of the film's lightsabers are actual glowing swords held by the actors.
This year we were also treated to a masterful fan flick featuring the infamous *Phantom Menace* villain **Darth Maul**. Working with a relatively small budget, the German production made use of **LED lightsabers** as well. Even if your film has nothing to do with Star Wars, using these **LED props** can be beneficial when working in the **sci-fi genre**. The **behind-the-scenes video** is excellent for anybody dreaming of one day adding their own contribution to the *Star Wars* universe.

Sure, these means of production are more likely to be used for big-budget studio pictures. Nonetheless, this way of thinking is basic filmmaking prowess at its finest. The filmmakers found a fast, practical way of shooting what they needed in a manner that's not out of grasp for low-budget projects. **LEDs** can be used a wide number of ways and they should never be overlooked as a good VFX marker, light source, and interactive prop.

November 23rd
How Long Does It Really Take to Create a Logo?

When General Mills decided to launch its first new cereal brand in 15 years, the company knew it was facing a major challenge. "There are very few new brands coming to cereal," explains Alan Cunningham, senior marketing manager of cereal innovation with General Mills. "We really needed to break through with something different."

Designing an engaging brand identity, therefore, was paramount. General Mills needed to create a logo so enticing that it could convince consumers to try something entirely new. The product concept — cereal shaped like tiny pieces of toast — came first, then the name (Tiny Toast, of course). That's when the design work began.

"It was a long process of trying to figure out what was right," recalls Kyle Jensen, vice-president and design director with Minneapolis-based creative studio Ultra Creative, the firm that designed the graphics associated with the Tiny Toast brand. All told, it took Ultra Creative and General Mills a year and a half from initial product idea to final design. The product hit the shelves in June, and the Tiny Toast brand was born.

Navigating a New Design

More often than not, logos look deceptively simple. How long could it possibly take to create that Nike Swoosh or Apple apple? But as General Mills can attest, it can take months and even years to design a symbol that truly embodies a brand's character and speaks to consumers.

There's a lot of pressure on brands to get it right. Companies like Netflix, Airbnb, MasterCard, and Instagram have all updated their iconic logos, and the results aren't always well-received at first. Airbnb's new symbol, for example, was meant to embody the brand's ability to deliver a sense of belonging to global travelers, but the company came under fire when the public pointed out it looked like everything from a guitar pick to parts of the human anatomy. Instagram's simplified logo, unveiled earlier this year, was polarizing, too.

Over time, consumers come to connect with brands through their logos. A change can be jarring — and yet, a new logo is often a must. The new Netflix icon is part of a growing trend toward designing for smaller screens as brands try to keep pace with consumers' evolving device preferences. Wired magazine called the Netflix "N" "the latest in a spate of redesigns by tech companies looking to update their visual brand for the mobile age."

So what's a brand to do? To ease the transition to its refreshed logo, MasterCard made a point of retaining its "50-year-old familiarity" and well-established visual language, while simultaneously creating a more digital mark. Instagram, meanwhile, created a social video that shows its customers how the new logo was derived from the well-loved original.

The Making of a Mark

"The logo is the most identifying element of the brand and what creates instant recognition," explains Rovena Aga, creative director with a luxury resort in Manila, Philippines. "It is the soul of a brand and your first introduction to it."

And like a first impression, brands better make sure it counts.

For Aga, the logo design process starts with the client briefing. During this discovery phase, the designer familiarizes herself with the company, its values, mission, vision, and employees. "We learn about how they perceive themselves, and how they would like to be perceived," she said. Next comes the market and competitive research phase, which leads to brainstorming. Aga always sketches on paper first — "writing down key words and just letting the thoughts flow" —

allowing her to experiment with graphical elements like colors and shapes. She never dismisses these early ideas, as they help her stay on track.

Eventually, she takes the process digital using software like Adobe Illustrator, chooses a font by trying out multiple variations, and identifies the three best options in the pack. These she presents to the client, and the fine-tuning begins.

Different Strokes for Different Designers

In some ways, to create a logo is like creating a work of art: it might take hours, days, or years to achieve the desired outcome. "It varies wildly," said Mike McGowan, a designer with the the University of Michigan's Office of University Development and a longtime freelancer. "I'm currently working on a fairly simple identity project that's gone on for well over six months."

There are times, however, when the answer is immediate — an "aha!" moment that reveals everything. As McGowan points out, it can take a 20-minute cab ride to create a logo: Famed graphic designer Milton Glaser thought up the I ♥ NY logo in the back of taxi on the way to a meeting about New York State's marketing campaign. On the other end of the spectrum, it took several creative teams and about 200 designs to come up with the logo for FedEx that's still being used today.

Like Aga, McGowan has learned there's no better way to start than by putting a pencil to paper. "I like to use really cheap printer paper. It has a good tooth, and because it's so thin I can use it like tracing paper," he said. McGowan considers everything in these early days, from whether the company name can be abbreviated, to whether the acronym can become a word (like NASA), a monogram (like Chanel's logo), or presents a graphic solution (like FedEx).

Eventually, he too goes digital. "After digesting (the client's) feedback, I almost always make a nice and tight vector drawing of the logo, trying to make it as close to finished as possible," he said.

But different designers have different preferences, and unlike Aga, McGowan doesn't invest much time in those initial, "fast and messy" drawings. "If you do," he said, "they become precious and it's hard to let that idea go, even if there are better ones."

The Proof is in the Preference

In the case of Ultra Creative and General Mills, letting go of those early designs was crucial, particularly after market research and testing. The length of the Tiny Toast logo design process wasn't just due to ongoing experimentation, but also the fact that the packaging and brand identity conceptualization were conducted simultaneously.

"Many times, you design a logo and try to shoehorn it into the brand design, but (Tiny Toast) was all done together," Jensen said. General Mills' R&D team didn't just investigate the product's market potential early on, but also after the logo was starting to take shape. "Focus groups are fantastic for getting answers to a handful of questions," said Cunningham, "but when evaluating the first moment of truth, you have to go in-store."

To assess whether its preferred logo options could effectively convince consumers to try Tiny Toast, General Mills planted mock-up boxes on actual grocery stores shelves. Some customers were taken to the product and asked for their initial impression. Others were left to discover it on their own.

"Some of the early designs we really liked failed in-store," Cunningham said. "They didn't have enough energy to pop, or were a little too flat." That's when the company made some "huge pivots," including abandoning the idea of incorporating characters, which Cunningham notes "were fun, but aged the cereal down."

Before landing on the right logo for Tiny Toast, which Jensen said was built around the shape of the toast top to emphasize the alliteration in the product's name, Ultra Creative and General Mills went through 10–15 different logo designs.

Cunningham reports that after its launch, Tiny Toast managed to generate 700 million impressions of earned media. It's hard to imagine that the carefully crafted Tiny Toast logo didn't play a part in its success.

Why Redesigns Aren't Faster

Market research was also a big part for of the logo development process for computer software company WhiteSource. After introducing a new product six months ago, the company went from catering exclusively to executive-level decision makers to software developers as well.

The original logo represented the startup well, but WhiteSource didn't think it would resonate with developers; they needed to create a logo that spoke to both audiences. "The problem was that we are still selling to management C-level and VP level. Developers aren't the ones buying the product, just the ones using it," said Maya Rotenberg, director of marketing with WhiteSource.

Working with a graphic designer, the company came up with two ideas: An animated gopher that was in line with the branding approach other companies take for their developer tools, and a hard hat that represented WhiteSource's commitment to protecting the site-build process.

WhiteSource interviewed nine of its customers about each concept, and also held an informal roundtable discussion on Reddit. "We were told the gopher gave the sense of a developer tool, and that the second option looked like a hipster with a beard," Rotenberg said. Interestingly, the company had already been referring to the icon as the "hard hat hipster" internally. Once it saw that the logo appealed to its customers and that they appreciated its unique character, their logo choice was clear.

Even though WhiteSource was redesigning a logo rather than starting from scratch, it took two graphic designers seven weeks to finalize the color scheme, graphic language, and various iterations. The company wanted to be sure its logo served its evolving business needs.

It was a similar story with online international freight marketplace Freightos. It, too, needed to redesign its logo to appeal to a new audience after expanding its product.

"We started by asking who we were, and what we wanted our logo to reflect," said Guy Laor, the director of UX (user experience) and design at Freightos. "It's not actually so easy, because when you conduct research within the company you hear about 30 different opinions."

Laor says it took several months to align everyone at the company, which facilitates global shipping, around the simple idea that it shouldn't be hard to move things from place to place. That led to the adoption of a series of squares representing the goods inside a shipping container.

After many conversations about color palette and font, and tweaking the logo to work online, in print, and on different screen sizes, Freightos and its designer were satisfied. All told, the process took two months.

The final Freightos logo captures the idea of moving shipping containers from place to place. (Freightos)

How long does it take to create a logo? The answer is simply that it depends on the brand and its designers, and how much market research they need to conduct. The concept may come quickly. It may take months. When a logo does come together, most companies will tell you it just feels right.

And when it does, the odds are good your customers will agree.

November 24th
Life After 'Life After Pi': The VFX Industry One Year Later

Has anything changed in the year since *Life After Pi* exposed the business model issues facing VFX houses like Rhythm and Hues?
Released in February of 2014, the documentary *Life After Pi* chronicled the demise of major VFX studio Rhythm and Hues due to the **non-sustainable practices existing between VFX houses and movie studios**. Did the issues exposed in *Life after Pi* lead to positive change in the VFX industry? Let's take a look at what we learned in the doc and what lies ahead. For your reference, here's *Life After Pi*, directed by visual effects art director Scott Leberecht.

1. Billing and Predicting are Never an Exact Science

Every time a bid is created for a client you have to look into a crystal ball. Several years ago Debra Kaufman wrote in an article on Creative Cow:

VFX facilities have operated for years without standardized contracts and viable bidding practices. They have been and continue to be vulnerable to changes in technology and studio policy.

As *Life After Pi* asserted, many VFX studios use a process known as a 'fixed bid'. This means each bid is constructed based on the production company *(*Universal, Disney, WB, etc.*)* giving the VFX studio a rough 'blue print' of the film. So, essentially the production company is saying, "here is what we want to do, and we know changes are inevitable, so you'll need to account for those changes and include them in the bid."

There is a lot of estimation and guesswork that goes into trying forecast the future for a bid like this. Right off the bat we should see that using a bidding system such as the current fixed system is **not a solution for large scale VFX projects.**

2. The Problem with Cost

Next up is the cost of creating visual effects. At present, VFX are more than likely going to be one of the most or*the* **most expensive item on a budget sheet.** Unfortunately that cost wont go down, because in order to house the people, hardware, and software needed for VFX work, it will cost large sums of money. Mike Seymour, co-founder offxguide, said in a recent article:

The early days of the studio system looked much like all the big VFX companies which are folding on a daily basis. They would build huge sound stages, buy expensive equipment, hire employees (actors, directors, tech) and keep them on staff year round to produce movies. The problem was, when they **weren't producing movies, they were wasting money.**

This dead money can happen two ways for the VFX studio. One **is not having work**. When you're in between projects or bidding on a new project, there is a lot of dead money out there with no revenue coming in. A way to fix this is to have the VFX studio maintain a much smaller staff that consists strictly of managers and directors. You then contract work out and create a bidding process for contractors to come in and work on specific projects while reducing your overhead cost considerably.

Another way VFX studios have dead money is the **overages on current projects**. As expressed in *Life After Pi,* VFX studios have to complete several revisions which takes them beyond the time and material budget in the fixed bid. So the tab for all of this extra time spent on revisions is being picked up by the VFX Studio. So, the real question is **why are VFX studios having to process so many revisions in the first place**?

3. Lack of Visionary Leadership

As a filmmaker and visual effects artist, I agree with *Life After Pi*'s assertion about a lack of visionary leadership. More times than not, I hear VFX supervisors talk about the lack of face time with the director. It's hard to complete anything on time when there really isn't any one-on-one time with the director. The smart move for directors would be to **bring the core VFX team in during pre-production and keep a running dialogue going throughout production**. By treating the VFX team as an invested collaborator, **you reduce revisions by a large margin**. Kristy Barkan made a great observation in her SIGGRAPH article when she quoted the film saying:

Studios would not permit a director to shoot for a week or two on set, and then say — 'Eh, tear down this set and build a new set.'

A great example of this type of collaborative process is the relationship between Peter Jackson and Richard Taylor of Weta Workshop. Jackson has always been good about getting Richard and his team involved early in the process. This is an approach that George Lucas had with ILM and the *Star Wars* franchise.

4. Who Exactly Have We Lost?

As of 2015, each one of the fifty highest grossing films have used some form of visual effects. Nineteen of the top fifty earned **more than one billion dollars**. Surprisingly, several of the studios that worked on many of these projects are no more. In fact, betwen 2003 to 2013, twenty-one VFX studios either **declared bankruptcy, restructured, or closed their doors for good.** This list includes Rhythm and Hues, Digital Domain, and Modus.

In the 1970s and 80s, hot on the heels of successful VFX-heavy films like *2001: A Space Odyssey* and *Star Wars*, there were four VFX powerhouses: Apogee, Boss Films, ILM, and Dream Quest Images. Today, only ILM still exists. At present, VFX companies are relocating due to increased tax incentives outside of Hollywood. Because of this, artists are having to uproot their families and move to new cities regularly.

Bryant Frazer stated in an article for StudioDaily that the current landscape is, "leaving many U.S. VFX artists out of work, in transit to new Canadian offices, or leaving the industry entirely."

5. How to Stop the Bleeding

Many industry insiders have different opinions on how to curtail the financial issues facing VFX Studios. Many have called for Unions or a Trade Organization to help level the playing field, but each one of these come with their own set of obstacles – and in the case of the Trade Organization, fold because of lack of funding.

The first right step might be **adopting a time and materials model** over the problematic fixed bid method, as suggested by Mike Seymour in his article on FXGuide. The time and material model is often used in other professional industries like construction, architecture, and design. The model is easily explained: **a buyer pays a contractor based on work performed.** All time and material spent constructing said work is covered by the buyer.

Magnopus is one such VFX studio that is utilizing this type of business model. Heading up this venture are Rodrigo Teixeira and Alex Henning whose credits include *Shutter Island*, *The Amazing Spiderman*, and *Star Trek Into Darkness*, among others. Seymour weighs in on Magnopus's chances of success:

The team have worked both sides of the fence, supervisor and supplier, they know all the top studio production executives and many extremely influential directors. In other words, if anyone can pull it off these guys can.

Given the fact the MAGNOPUS has already had success working on projects using this model, **a solution to the financial pitfalls of the VFX industry may finally be at hand.**

November 25th
The Best Film Visual Effects Through the Years

Take a trip down memory lane with this compilation of the Oscar winners for Best Visual Effects.

This video montage by independent filmmaker and editor Nelson Carvajal has been making the rounds over the 'net, and is a real treat for filmmakers and movie buffs. Nelson has compiled a montage of the winners of **The Academy Award for Best Visual Effects** since 1977, the first year this award began to appear as a regular category by the Academy.

It's amazing to see how VFX have improved so much since then, and also interesting to note how many films that were "way ahead of their time" in regards to their special effects work. Do you recognize each of the films in the montage? Check out the full list below.

Academy Award for Best Visual Effects

1977: Star Wars
1978: Superman (Special Achievement Award)
1979: Alien
1980: The Empire Strikes Back (Special Achievement Award)
1981: Raiders of the Lost Ark
1982: E.T. the Extra-Terrestrial
1983: Return of the Jedi (Special Achievement Award)
1984: Indiana Jones and the Temple of Doom
1985: Cocoon
1986: Aliens
1987: Innerspace
1988: Who Framed Roger Rabbit
1989: The Abyss

1990: Total Recall (Special Achievement Award)
1991: Terminator 2: Judgement Day
1992: Death Becomes Her
1993: Jurassic Park
1994: Forrest Gump
1995: Babe
1996: Independence Day
1997: Titanic
1998: What Dreams May Come
1999: The Matrix
2000: Gladiator
2001: The Lord of the Rings: Fellowship of the Ring
2002: The Lord of the Rings: The Two Towers
2003: The Lord of the Rings: The Return of the King
2004: Spider-Man 2
2005: King Kong
2006: Pirates of the Caribbean: Dead Man's Chest
2007: The Golden Compass
2008: The Curious Case of Benjamin Button
2009: Avatar
2010: Inception
2011: Hugo
2012: Life of Pi

November 26th
Top 10 Best and Worst Practical Effects in Movie History

Are practical effects making a comeback? Let's take a look at some of the amazing highs and laughable lows from the history of practical effects.

Practical effects have been around since the dawn of cinema. Legendary French filmmaker Georges Méliès, considered by some to be the father of special effects, was one of the first visionary artists **to create cinema sorcery with tactile objects.** Can you imagine how mind-blowing it must have been to see the mechanically operated scenery and stop tricks of A Trip to the Moon in 1902?

(Sorta) Gone but (Mostly) Not Forgotten

Practical effects reached an early apex with films such as 2001 A Space Odyssey and The Empire Strikes Back. These days, filmgoers are seeing fewer **practical effects** make their way into the final cuts of films. Long gone are the days of successfully **blending practical and digital** like in Jurassic Park and Lord of the Rings. Instead, the studios are opting to augment (and in many cases completely replace) **practical effect shots** with **digitally composited CGI effects**. But there is hope for fans of **practical effects.**
The new Star Wars trilogy will be showcasing far more practical effects than the Prequels. And George Miller is employing **traditional practical effects** and stunts in Mad Max: Fury Road, as he spoke about in this piece with Entertainment Weekly:
You want to have that sort of almost, I'm not going to say documentary experience, but you want to feel it like you're really immersed, like it's really happening. So we decided to literally do every car that's smashed is smashed, every stunt is a real human being, even the actors do a lot of their own stunts, and so on.
So, it looks like we could be entering a new Golden Age of **blending practical and digital effects**. In order to understand what manner of movie magic we might encounter in the years ahead, let's take a look at WatchMojo's **Top 10 Best and Worst Practical Effects in Film History.**

Top 10 Best Practical Effects

Top 10 Worst Practical Effects

Why Do Filmmakers Shy Away Away from Practical Effects in the First Place?

Amalgamated Dynamics, Inc has a long **history of practical effects** work, having won the **Academy Award for best visual effects** on the film Death Becomes Her. In this video, founders (and Stan Winston alumni) Tom Woodruff Jr. and Alec Gillis discuss the reasoning behind Hollywood's habit of replacing **practical effects in current films.**

November 27th
Turn Your Timelapse Videos into Moving Paintings

These stunning timelapse videos are true works of art. See how they were made — and learn how you can make your own.

Check out these two different approaches to creating a moving painting. Whether using apps or the provided source code, you'll be creating artistic **timelapse videos** in no time.

Prisma Timelapse

Drew Geraci and the crew at District 7 Media are behind plenty of well-known **timelapse videos**, like the intro to *House of Cards*. District 7's latest video is a fantastic look at China through the artistic app Prisma, which is available now for Android and iPhone. Prisma uses artificial intelligence to **transform still photos into works of art**, done is the style of artists like Van Gogh, Picasso, and Levitan. Using footage of a recent trip to China, Geraci pulled individual frames from a sequence and then sent every image through the Prisma app for processing. In the end, **2500 individual frames** were uploaded to the app.

Each frame of the 1 minute and 20 second video had to be processed via the Prisma App which took almost 80 hours to complete. The processing/rendering was at the mercy of the servers. Most of the project had to be completed between 11pm and 4am EST because the app would freeze or shutdown due to overloaded serves or too many users on at the same time.

The project required a tremendous amount of repetitive work — enough to drive Geraci mad.

The easiest way for me to create the video was to physically take a picture of the video (on a 4k monitor) using an iPad and save each photo directly to the iPad. Once all of the photos were taken, I used my PC workstation to directly pull the images off the iPad and onto a local harddrive to continue the processing.

The worst part was the constant repetition of taking the photo, processing the photo, moving 1 frame forward, and then saving the image. Sometimes I would forget to do a step and have to start over completely. It was mind-numbing work to say the least!

Computer Algorithm Timelapse

VFX artist and art director Danil Krivoruchko took a different approach to create his Van Gogh-style moving painting of New York. Krivoruchko skipped the Prisma app in favor of a computer algorithm developed at Cornell. Using footage of New York, and with the assistance of artificial neural networks, the final video is beautiful.

Krivoruchko used an open source code from Manuel Ruder, Alexey Dosovitskiy, and Thomas Brox.

If you want to **download the code to use it yourself**, Ruder has put the open source utility online. You will need Ubuntu and a pretty serious computer to handle the workflow. After export, you'll need to use **After Effects** for some compositing, color correction, motion blur, and to tweak any glitches.

November 28th
VFX Scenes You Thought Were Real

You can't always believe your eyes. VFX isn't always made-up monsters and otherworldly landscapes. Sometimes the best VFX executions are subtle enough to be invisible.

You'd be surprised at some of the films that frequently rely on **VFX**. While they are now applied to almost every feature film for minor touch-ups, many movies rely on **VFX** to create objects, moods, or even entire locations that would otherwise be expensive, difficult, or even impossible to depict. They also make filmmaking much more forgiving by allowing production mistakes to be solved in post-production, rather than with a reshoot. Here are a few truly astounding breakdowns of what goes into the modern Hollywood picture.

Nightcrawler

We'll start with the more subtle examples of what capabilities computers have provided us with. The 2014 film *Nightcrawler*, while grounded in reality and not overly-stylistic, still benefitted from a plethora of minor adjustments that individually may seem pointless, but come together to create a perfect image as opposed to a slightly flawed one.

This breakdown of the car chase in the film's last act demonstrates some impressive digital compositing skills that are applied to everything from changing the color of a traffic light to replacing Jake Gyllenhaal's ponytail.

Rotoscoping, the art of cutting out on-screen elements frame-by-frame to hide or move them elsewhere, is a painstakingly tedious process that is used to great effect here. Also note the use of selective **color correction** to remove shadows and lighten underexposed areas. **This breakdown is a perfect example of how forgiving filmmaking has become.**

American Hustle

Next up, we have the 2013 crime-drama, *American Hustle*. This is another movie that at first glance appears to be untouched by visual effects artists, save for some color grading. However, this breakdown reveals the problems the film's production faced involving timing and set location, with unattractive construction equipment cluttering the building facade in the background.

Obviously, the removal of this equipment was not essential to the aesthetic of the shot, nor the audience's suspension of disbelief. However, **it did result in a much cleaner image that was much closer to the director's original vision.**

This showcases some more impressive rotoscoping, especially around the characters' hair, which is one of the most difficult surfaces to deal with. Additionally, this breakdown shows the importance of good 3D motion-tracking. **3D motion-tracking** is the process by which a program analyzes hundreds of high-contrast, consistent points within the shot, and using these points, calculates the placement of the camera within the scene based on how they move in relation to one another.

This fundamental process is what allows artists to convincingly place any element they want into a shot that involves a moving camera. **Even if all other aspects of a visual effect are flawless, the entire effort will fall flat if the motion tracking points aren't accurate.**

Zodiac

David Fincher is known for using **VFX** to aid the visual style and story of his films. Arguably the most impressive of these is the largely virtual crime scene featured in his 2007 film, *Zodiac*. This again prompts the question of whether or not digitally creating a simple neighborhood intersection is necessary. Regardless, the resulting scene featured a distinct lighting aesthetic and an imaginary environment that likely could not have been shot the traditional way.

Among the most prominent techniques shown here are the placement and digital removal of the blue screen. Despite the consistently uneven lighting of the blue screens on set, there is not the slightest evidence of them in the final product, thanks to some expert-level **chroma keying** (removal of a color from an image). Like motion tracking, **precise chroma keying is a key part of creating a photo-real scene.** Additionally, the use of detailed **3D models** and the seamless implementation of them are really inspiring.

The human eye is very good at detecting fake light, and getting digital lights and textures to trick it is extremely hard to do. While not necessarily the most important element of CGI, **accurate lighting is often the finishing touch that will take something fake from being *impressive* to being *unnoticeable*.**

Children of Men

The 2007 masterpiece, *Children of Men*, is conceptually a bit more far-fetched than the previously mentioned films, and contains many sequences that, while realistic, are still clearly a product of CGI. However, the most impressive of the many effects throughout the film is **the digital recreation of a newborn infant.**

While it makes sense that acquiring a real human newborn might be difficult for a scene like this, it's still surprising that the baby shown on screen was *completely* computer generated. An older baby could certainly have been used with some adjustments to the cinematography and editing, but director Alfonso Cuaron was able to commit to his vision with the assistance of CGI. This impressive feat was accomplished with all of the aforementioned techniques and more. **One of the most challenging aspects of VFX is the depiction of physics.** Like lighting, **physics are** an integral part of our visual perception of the world, and **we tend to quickly notice when a familiar object doesn't move the way it should.** Every tiny movement the baby makes is entirely convincing, and despite Clive Owen's hands being empty, it still appears to be resting within them.

Texturing is one of the most difficult aspects of recreating human flesh, as it's one of the most common surfaces we see on a day-to-day basis. While the infant's textures were certainly top-notch, **any flaws in them could be hidden with the low-key lighting and heavy shadows.** This is a prevalent technique within the visual effects industry, seeing as **darker lighting is more forgiving than say, daytime,** which exposes every detail of its subjects.

The Wolf of Wall Street

This drug-fueled roller coaster ride of a movie was full of excess, and its utilization of **VFX** is no exception. Many of the set pieces of this film may have still been possible to shoot on location or without alteration, but Martin Scorcese clearly wanted to take everything above and beyond by creating extravagant settings beyond what even exists — though they aren't necessarily far-fetched, either.

One of the most fascinating **VFX** breakdowns of recent years, **this mind-boggling highlight reel brings to light how far computer-driven filmmaking has come** and will likely make you begin to question everything you see on screen.

Matte painting (the blending of elements, both real and not, to create one landscape — based on set extension using actual paintings) is the most notable of the skills applied to create these sequences — though the use of 3D models, textures, lighting, 3D motion tracking, rotoscoping, green screen chroma keying, and more, are not to be taken lightly.

The potential of being able to expand on the mise-en-scène of any given shot is endless, and *The Wolf of Wall Street* makes great use of this potential without the viewer ever realizing that they aren't looking at a real place.

In a time where Hollywood has become cluttered with a surplus of over-the-top CGI, it's easy to view it as overused and even harmful to the industry's creativity. However, if you can look past the shameless, invasive visual noise of many modern blockbusters, you'll find that **VFX**, when used sparingly, can be a wonderful and inspirational tool in bringing even the most modest story to life.

November 29th
What Does a VFX Editor Do?

What is it like to work as a visual effects editor on an animated or feature film? Discover a real-world perspective from industry pros!

Judith Allen was VFX Editor on the recent Aardman animation *Pirates!* (you may recognize Aardman as creators of the popular Wallace and Grommit series). I watched *Pirates!* on the plane from SFO to JFK and I thoroughly intend on buying as soon as I can as it was delightfully hilarious in a very British fashion. But I digress…let's get down to talking about **working in visual effects**!

If you've ever wondered what a minute by minute **view into a VFX Editors world** might look like Judith has kindly written up an extremely detailed account of a typical day on an animated feature film. This will give anyone interested in **a career in animation, film editing or visual effects** a realistic view of the day-to-day nitty gritty:

0930 – The working day begins. My assistant begins negotiations with the floor to make sure that VFX get our 10am time in the viewing theatre for our shot approvals. I update some spreadsheets on the network to reflect the shots which I loaded into the Baselight earlier, with any notes which came through from the floor at the time they were published about take choices (sometimes they film options to decide on at a later date, sometimes two versions are needed for international purposes, action can be split across several plates on greenscreen – there are many possibilities).

For a fascinating peek into what it's like to **have a career in visual effects** read all of Judith's Day In The Life of a Visual Effects Editor.

How to get started in Visual Effects

Atomic Fiction, the visual effects team behind work on films such as *Looper*, *Flight* and *Transformers: Dark of the Moon*, have kindly written up blog post with a ton of great advice for those seeking to **break into the visual effects industry**. The advice from Atomic Fiction to those **looking to get a job in the VFX industry** is in part intensely practical:

In this industry, attention to detail makes a world of difference. Get all your applications in order. Print up some snazzy business cards and hand them out to every industry contact you meet. If you have a website or demo reel make sure that everything is polished.

And also very grounded in the reality of the current state of the visual effects industry:

you may have to settle at some point. Whether it's a crappy job at an awesome company or a decent job at a company that is less than ideal, you'll find that some less desirable jobs are a lot easier to land and they will look good on your resume.

All in all, it's a great post with a lot of sound advice from a visual effects team who really do know what they're talking about. **If you really want to make it, persevere until you do!**

Assistant on a Hollywood Feature

Anthony Snitzer worked for five weeks as a VFX PA on *The Avengers* and he shares his experiences in an entertaining and detailed online journal. For yet another peek into the real world of working on a blockbuster then check out Anthony's blog. His account gives great insight into what a **visual effects editor** does (much of it as not near as glamorous as you might think!).

August 1st, first day.
paperwork. tour of offices.

Got in empty office. Made sure things were set up according to diagram.

Vacuumed, cleaned.

August 17th

slow day in the office, so Peter Sjolander invited me out to the splinter unit that was shooting a crowd of people running out of a building which explodes.

watched Peter type in all the data that's needed by VFX into his iPad. all the camera data, such as lens, f-stop, height, angle, and distance from cam to subject.

I got to hold the spheres in front of the 3 cameras after the explosion for reference.

November 30th
Where are the Major VFX Houses Located?

Learn the exact location of all the major VFX houses in the world using the VFX World Map.

It is definitely an understatement to say that the domestic VFX industry is hurting right now. Many studios have shuttered in recent years and there's been a major outcry from US based VFX artists that their jobs are getting sent overseas, due to foreign subsidies and cheaper labor costs.

In the past, US based VFX houses were mostly centralized in NYC and LA, but in recent years there has been a wider geographic spread of these types of businesses. For aspiring VFX artists and those looking for work, the choice on where to live has become more complicated.

Thankfully there is an online tool that makes finding VFX houses incredibly easy, VFXWorldMap.com. On the VFX World Map users can view every major VFX house and their location.
The map is designed to help VFX artists, animators, and anyone else figure out the exact location of biggest VFX and post production facilities in the world. Users can sort their search by Animation, Feature Film, Games, and even Schools.

The map gives out the actual address of the production companies listed, as well as links to their websites (which usually have detailed information regarding the software they use and their respective job requirements).

Additionally, VFX World Map features a super awesome job board with dozens of jobs, from animators to developers. The job board also features a few Twitter resources that are entirely dedicated to tweeting out new jobs.

If you work for a production company that isn't listed in the map you can easily add your company to the list. VFX World Map has also introduced a new bookmark features that allows users to save production companies to their login so they can easily reference them in the future.

December 1st
Working in the Visual Effects Industry

If you are considering a career in the visual effects industry, here are a few things to know.

If you're interested in **building a career in the visual effects industry**, hearing how others who have gone before you have worked their way up the ladder is a great way to **pick up some tips on how to do it for yourself.** Studio Daily recently posted a great interview with Industrial Light and Magic VFX Supervisor Russell Earl – whose most recent film is *Captain America: Winter Soldier*. It seems like having the guts to wing it, and the work ethic to pull it off, is a helpful combination.

"Because Earl had run the laser camera, the producer's assistant believed he could do digital compositing. "He said, 'Hey, you know Unix, don't you?'" Earl says. "I said I did, which I didn't. He said, 'Can you start today? At 7?' I said, 'Yeah, I can do that. I thought I could figure it out. I packed my car, went to the bookstore, bought a book on Unix, hid it in my bag, and drove up there. I had these little Post-Its. When they would ask me to do something, I would write it down on my Post-It, go back to my desk, and look in the book."

Starting a Career in Visual Effects

So what does it take to build a career in the visual effects industry, especially if you're considering going to a university to acquire the skills you need? Interestingly *The Mill*'s co-founder and chief creative officer Pat Joseph, believes that UK **higher-education in general is failing to equip students** with the skills or awareness of the VFX industry to create the supply of talent, needed to match the demand.

"I think that for a long time VFX had been seen as "trying to run a hobby as a business". My concern is that the British education system still isn't really laying out visual effects as a career option and so in turn, students aren't graduating with the right skills. Demand continues to grow, but universities that do train to industry standard, such as Bournemouth University, are struggling to meet it."

Things are probably quite different in the US with dedicated creative arts universities like the University of Southern California Film School and New York Film Academy. If you want a full list of film schools the Hollywood Reporter put together a list of the '**25 best film schools**' last year. But what if you don't want to spend $100k getting trained? UK based Escape Studios offers intensive training courses as well as plenty of **free training courses and advice** to help get your career in visual effects off to a flying start.

The UK ambassadors for up-skilling people is Skillset. In this series of videos partnering with the *The Mill, Double Negative* and others, they offer **plenty of good advice to anyone looking to build a career in VFX**. Get some **great tips on improving your vfx showreel**, shaping your CV and **what essential skills employers are looking for**.

Can I change careers into Visual Effects?

What animation software do you use or recommend?

"Pixar uses its own proprietary software built and maintained in-house. In general, we look for broad artistic and technical skills, rather than the ability to run one package over another. We concentrate on finding people with breadth, depth, communication skills, and the ability to collaborate. If you have those attributes, we can teach you the specific tools."

If you check out the first video above you'll quickly gather that **many people working in the VFX industry didn't originally train to do it** (at least not at degree level). And if you look on the Pixar careers FAQ you'll see that they are **looking for a broader range of skills and abilities** than just simply "being a _____ ninja." This should be an encouragement to anyone with a serious passion to apply their knowledge of particle physics, computer coding, lighting, fashion etc to the visual effects industry – that's **it is not just about being a geek, but being an artist first and foremost.**

One person who **switched careers to get started in the visual effects industry** is Chris Chadwick who moved from being a graphic designer, took a six week course at Escape Studios in Autodesk Maya and then landed a job at Prime Focus doing match move work for the film *Total Recall*. Starting as a match mover is the first step on the ladder, but at least you are on the ladder. Double Negative's 3D Artist Manager Dara McGarry shares how artists often develop in their careers at Double Negative. If you head over to this page, you'll also find **a ton of useful information about building a career in VFX too.**

"The most common entry point to begin a career in 3D is to start in the match move department, where they will be responsible for camera, object and body tracking. A very good understanding of Maya is helpful as well as knowing tracking software, even though we use some proprietary tools. Most people spend 12-18 months in tracking and will have the opportunity to pick up TD tasks along the way. This could include anything from running a pre-existing lighting set up on a new shot to creating small props or buildings. This experience gives our junior artists a complete understanding of the pipeline and the tools we use here at DNeg."

It's Not Just About Digital Skills

Stan Winston's School of Character Arts is a great place to start if you're **interested in a career in the physical side of the visual effects industry.** Their YouTube channel has over 200 videos on it, and you can purchase tutorials and webinars from top visual effects professionals on the techniques they use to create everything from the initial sculptures to final painted models. Legacy Effects (with founders from Stan Winston Studios) share how **new technologies like 3D printing are transforming their practical visual effects workflow.** It's just another example of how understanding new technologies and material's sciences can land you a job in the visual effects industry.

Life After Pi – The Economics of VFX

Lastly, it would feel a little remiss to be talking about working in the visual effects industry without highlighting some of the financial and economic realities that go with the industry. *Life After Pi*, the half hour documentary, examining the demise of Rhythm & Hues, the VFX company that created some of the miraculous visual delights of *Life of Pi* – and won an Oscar for it, while simultaneously going bankrupt. It is an eye-opening look into the current state of much of the big budget feature film visual effects industry.

December 2nd
3 Basic Tips for Creating Soft Light

Soft light can give you top-notch results when shooting talent, but many amateur DPs struggle with the basics. Use these illuminating tips to soften your shadows on set.

There's no exact science to lighting talent, although most often **soft lighting** will be preferable over hard lighting. The reason, of course, is because hard, undiffused lights will cast harsh shadows on faces, exaggerating imperfections and flaws. **Soft lights** on the other hand, do the exact opposite.

Many first-time DPs struggle to **understand differences in light quality.** As a result, they overlook some of the most basic fundamentals when on set for their first time. If this sounds like you, then read on! These three tips are essential to know when trying to create soft light.

1. Diffusion is everything.

This first point is probably the most obvious one on this list. **Diffusion is one of the simplest and easiest ways to soften your light source.** Whether you use a professional silk or simply clip some diffusion paper to your light, the quality of light you're producing will change immediately. Just remember, adding diffusion is a great start — but it's not the only way to affect the softness of your light.

2. Get your lights close to your talent.

The proximity of your lights to your talent has a huge impact on the softness of the shadows it produces. **The closer your lights are to your talent, the softer the shadows will be.** This is surprising for many first time DPs as they often assume that pulling the lights further back will soften the light. Though, in reality, that will only expose the talent less, while creating harsher shadows.

3. Make your source bigger.

The third main factor to consider about soft lighting is the size of your source. **A large light source will always be softer than a small source.** So whenever you can, use the biggest light source possible. This doesn't necessarily mean that you need huge lights, but rather that you create a huge source — these are two different things. For instance, you may point a small light at a large piece of diffusion, which effectively makes the diffusion your new source (not the light) and the overall softness will increase dramatically.

Hopefully these tips will help you out the next time you're lighting a shot. Now here are a couple of handy videos that delve a little deeper into the points above.

December 3rd
3 Pieces of Advice To Build Your Creative Business

Check out these quick videos on building your creative business in the fast changing digital frontier.

Even though many business tips may 'fit into a soundbite' **these ideas, insights and inspiration might contain a golden nugget that transforms the rest of your career.** Check out these three resources for many great pieces of advice…

#1. Eat Big Fish – Advice Collection

Eat Big Fish is a challenger brand consultancy with a great website with a ton of "3 pieces of advice" videos from marketing, brand, creative and business experts who pack a lifetime of learning into a short space.

In this 1 minute video Porter Gale, former VP of marketing at Virgin America and a marketing expert with over 2 decades worth of experience in branding, advertising and social media, packs 3 great pieces of advice on transparency, mobile and social media into just 60 seconds. *"96% of millienials are on social media…how's that going to impact your brand or service?"*

#2. Seth Godin – Guru of Gurus

Seth Godin is a social media 'guru' (in the nicest possible way) whose website is chock full of great free stuff as well as **daily thoughts on how to create more, do better and get recognized** Time reading or watching Seth is always time well spent. This classic and hugely entertaining TED talk from Seth will get you hooked on what he has to say.

#3. A piece of advice on how to make the most of social media.

Warren Cass lays out his **top tips for anyone entering into the social media frenzy.** Check out this simple, but foundational, wisdom on how and why you need to be making the most of Twitter, Linked In, Facebook and the rest.

December 4th
7 Reasons Why Your Creative Vision Isn't Translating to the Screen

Here's a few tips for translating your creative vision to the big screen.

Have you taken a film or video project from conception to completion…only to find yourself unsatisfied with the end result? Here's a few reasons your projects may be falling flat.

1. You Focusing on the Details, Not the Big Picture

When it comes to filmmaking there is a lot to remember and we are afforded the opportunity to learn something new every time we shoot. In a way, creating a film is a lot like a flexible checklist. While you would never say it out loud, the thought that's probably going through your head on-set is something to the effect of:

- **Composition, Check.**
- **Depth of Field, Check.**
- **Continuity, Check.**
- **Stabilization, Check.**
- **Focus, Check.**
- **Actor's Delivery, Check.**
- **Motivation, Check.**

- **Etc, Etc, Etc, Check, Check, Check**

    It can be easy to compartmentalize the production process and fall into a series of checklists, but this can be extremely harmful to your end result. The beauty is not in the details, it's in the finished project. If you're busy focusing on small stuff like script formatting, and not the script itself, you're going to be disappointed.

2. You're Putting to Much Emphasis on the Craft Instead of the Story

We talk a lot about gear and rightfully so, it's fun to follow gear. New cameras, lenses, and equipment releases are exciting. But one rut that new filmmakers tend to fall into is focusing way to heavily on the gear and not the story at hand.

Sure having an impressive 2 minute long tracking shot is cool, but how does it fit into your narrative structure? Have you spent more time focusing on the gear than the characters in the film?

Having cinematic quality footage *is* important for keeping your audience engaged, especially if you are trying to prove your legitimacy, but we live in an age of progressing technology. If you want your film to have real staying power, focus more on the story. It's easy to forgive a film with average cinematography if the story is solid.

3. It Wasn't Feasible Given Your Constraints

In a perfect world you can simply come up with any idea and have the tools available to see that idea through. Realistically there are many limitations to an indie-film budget. Recognizing these limitations, and creatively working around them, is vital for creating a believable film.

Don't bite off more than you can chew. Sure, you **should** push your creative limits every time you make a film, but have reason when considering a new idea. This is a tough pill to swallow **especially if you are a passionate filmmaker**, but setting unrealistic expectations will only leave you disappointed.

4. You're Not Hiring the Right Crew

Having a solid crew is vital for creating a good film. If you are forced to pick up the slack from other crew members it's going to show in your end result. One of the biggest things to look for when choosing a crew is **attitude**.

It's not uncommon in this industry to work with people with pride issues. Avoid them like the plague! Ultimately poor crew members will distract you from the story at hand.

5. You're Not Communicating Well

Communication is your most powerful tool as a filmmaker. How well your creative vision comes to life depends in large part with how well it is communicated to your talent and crew before, during and after production. Spend the time before the camera rolls to make sure that everyone involved is 'in-the-know'….and this isn't just limited to just the story and how you invision the final product. Communication around the logistics of production can make or break your project. Use a call sheet, use a camera log, and stay organized.

6. You're Skipping Over Pre-Production

There's nothing sexy about pre-production – except storyboarding (I love a good storyboard!). It can be easy for filmmakers to skip over this aspect of the filmmaking process and into production. Create a detailed shot list, storyboard scenes if necessary, set realistic production timelines and finalize your budget.

Take the time to personally visit all the locations you're planning on shooting. Did you obtain any necessary permits or forms to shoot at that location? What is the lighting situation? Where is power located? You *must* know these things well in advance of your proposed shoot date to allow time for change of location if necessary.

7. Your Creative Vision is Muddy

Is your idea fully baked? It's easy to fall in love with a story idea, but you need to validate it early.

How well vetted is your script? Is the story confusing in any way? If you're too close to the project and story you may not recognize it's weaknesses. Seek brutally honest feedback.

Successful filmmaking is collaborative filmmaking....nobody wants to work with a dictator. Settle on a vision early and then have others poke holes in it, finding flaws with the story, the production plan and the overall vision. Revise the plan and repeat. Your creative vision may not be the same as it was when you started, but you'll be the better for it.

December 5th
3 Ways to Improve Your Marketing Campaigns

If you're like most marketers, the past 12 months were filled with their fair share of victories, as well as near-misses, and maybe even a total flop. Step up your game in 2015 by setting (and sticking to!) these three simple resolutions.

Create monthly content calendars, and actually follow them

Whether you create content calendars weekly, monthly, or even quarterly, having a documented plan in place is critical. A well-crafted content calendar provides the high-octane fuel to keep social, SEO, and email channels running effectively. By taking the time to make a calendar ahead of time, you ensure that messaging and promotions are synced across channels, presenting a consistent interaction with your audience.

New to the content-calendar game? It's a versatile tool that is actually very simple to create. At its most basic, a content calendar can be a spreadsheet that serves to document:

– Dates and times that you'll publish your content

– Content format (photo, video, infographic, etc.)

– Key messaging to use

– Distribution channel(s) (Facebook, email, blog, etc.)

Putting together your first content calendar can feel onerous and time-consuming, but you'll be astounded at how much time it saves throughout the month.

Track each and every campaign metric

With a strategic content calendar in place, you can sit back and watch the impressive metrics roll in. (Wait, you are tracking your campaign metrics, right?)

Making the effort to establish Key Performance Indicators (KPIs) and set up tracking against those metrics is what will ultimately make the difference between a successful campaign and a failure. When you're tracking properly, you can make better marketing decisions in future campaigns, but you also look like a rock star when you can quantify the impact of your efforts on the bottom line.

Many marketing platforms have built-in reporting, but a third-party tool like Google Analytics will enable you to track traffic across multiple campaigns and channels. When you're determining which metrics to track, think beyond instantaneous results (for example: the open rate of an email campaign) to bigger goals, like click-through rates, and even bigger goals, like purchases.

Never use the same stock photo twice

As a marketer myself, I cringe every time I see the same well-groomed, average-looking guy smiling on the home pages of doctor's offices, dentists, and B2B websites. Let's face it: we're all tired of seeing the same John Doe.

This year, make a pact to pass over all the images you've used time and time again, and dig a little deeper to find a real gem. With more than 40 million images on Shutterstock alone, there's bound to be something fresh to accompany your best content.

December 6th
7 Things Filmmakers Can Learn from Incredible Aerial Footage

There's a lot to learn from this collection of visually spectacular aerial footage.

We live in the golden years of **drone filmmaking**. Everyday there's a new inspiring aerial reel released online, so it's not hard to stay in a perpetual state of drone inspiration.
Now that we're inspired, what are we to do with all of this information? Well, there are a few takeaways that can help both **aerial cinematographers** and filmmakers alike.

1. Great Footage Parallaxes

When shooting (not just **aerial footage**) you need to examine the foreground, subject, and background to determine if your frame is well-composed. When it comes to drone footage, it can be easy to simply view your footage as a flat surface. **This is a mistake.** Take this clip for example:
Sure, the subject is interesting. You have the Manhattan skyline with good colors, but the movement is incredibly limited. This is fine for certain circumstances, but as filmmakers you want each clip to have the **greatest cinematic potential.**
For a better example, take a look at this next clip.

Notice how cinematic it looks when you **have a foreground moving at a faster rate than the background.** You have the bridge, cars, and skyscrapers in the background, all featuring interesting movement across the frame.

2. Dynamic Range is Incredibly Important

In a nutshell, dynamic range is the key difference between a cinematic image and a "video-like" image. Essentially, dynamic range deals with **the number of stops your camera can handle.** A quick way to know how great you camera's dynamic range is: look at the sky. Is it blown out? Or can you see sky detail? If it's blown out or almost completely white, you might want to get a better camera or shoot at a better time of day.
This footage was shot with an ARRI Alexa, which has 13.5 stops of dynamic range. Notice how much detail is in the bright sky and the dark ground.

If you don't have thousands of dollars to spend on an Alexa, check out the Blackmagic Micro Cinema Camera. With 13 stops of dynamic range and the ability to record in RAW, the camera is a dream for aerial filmmakers.

3. Unique Perspectives Create Incredible Footage

As with most cinematography, unique camera angles help separate good and **bad aerial cinematography**. Instead of doing the usual fly-by, try thinking of unique perspectives. This video is a great example of looking at a scene from a unique angle.

Instead of shooting from a traditional angle, the cinematographer let the camera look straight down toward the ground. Take this same approach. Drone footage of all kinds is cool right now, but soon the market will get so saturated that you'll need to **separate your footage from the rest**. Unique perspectives can help.

4. Composition is Key

Composition applies on the ground and the same is true in the air. Instead of simply having your subject in the center of the frame while circling, try thinking of ways in which you can **lead the audience's eye toward your subject**.

When an audience is viewing piece of video, there's a fight for attention going on. Good composition will guide their eyes where you want them to be. Composition is not something that can be learned overnight, it takes years of practice to **become a compositional master**. A quick way to make your compositions better is to treat every frame as a still photograph. At no point should your audience be able to pause your film and not be impressed.

5. Color Grading Puts it Over the Top

Color grading is essential for separating **professional cinematic drone footage** from amateur footage. Unfortunately, many filmmakers simply apply presets to their footage or, even worse, skip the process entirely in post-production. **This is a huge mistake.**

Take this clip for example. You'll notice that while the subject is cool, the real thing that sets this clip apart is the **color grading**. The artist/filmmaker took special consideration into the color palette of the footage instead of letting it remain flat.

All cinematic footage deserves to be color graded by hand, but when it comes to aerial footage this is especially true. In order to have greater control over your colors in post, you will need to **make sure your footage has a high dynamic range** like we talked about in point two. One of the best color grading tools on the market right now is **DaVinci Resolve**, which just so happens to have have a free version. You can have great control over your grades using DaVinci Resolve and it's regularly updated interface is making the grading process easier with each update.

6. Patterns and Lines

Aerial footage gives you a unique chance to shoot perspectives that can't be found in everyday life. **Great aerial footage** utilizes patterns and lines to increase visual interest. For example, the following footage showcases a seemingly average suburban neighborhood, and yet it's visually stunning because of the incredible design patterns created by the houses.

Here's another great example. Check out this breathtaking footage of Thailand. While the footage would certainly be amazing without the river flowing through, the river actually helps guide the viewers eye throughout the composition.

Next time you're **filming aerial footage** (or regular footage for that matter) make Stanely Kubrick proud and take time to look for lines and patterns.

7. Movement = Cinematic

If you wanted to shoot incredible footage on the ground, you wouldn't simply stick your camera on a tripod. You'd try using a slider or glidecam or even a crane. The same is true in the air. Movement can do wonders for boring footage. Instead of keeping your camera still, try playing around with complex camera movements in the air. It takes practice, but once you're able to **maneuver your drone** as needed, you can achieve incredible results.

This clip is a great example of movement:

Sure a simple stagnant **aerial shot** would have been cool, but the real visual impact came from the camera movement in combination with the **parallaxing effect**.

One particular drone you might want to look at is 3DR's Solo Smart Drone. The drone was designed to help with camera movements by automating complex movements. Users can set virtual cable cam lines and orbit points while monitoring the footage on their phone.

December 7th
A Trick for Driving Repeat Business & Client Satisfaction

Whether you're a motion designer, video editor or professional photographer, this plan for nurturing repeat business will keep you more organized and your clients more satisfied.

Ever gone to deliver a project for a repeat client and were unable to remember their preferred delivery specifications? What frame size to export a video out, or what file type they typically need? Maybe you couldn't recall who is supposed to be copied in on all of the client correspondence?

Don't rack your brain trying to remember these small details, or worse, having to ask for a reminder. Instead, **take notes on every project you complete** and your client will not only be amazed you "remembered" their preferences, but you'll also save time in the process. Let's break it down…

What Details Should I Be Logging?

I've had many repeat video editing clients over the years, and although minor things change each time, I've been shocked at how many **things stay consistent from project to project.** A few things beneficial for remembering:

- Knowing what **file formats** a client prefers for production and delivery. Is there a particular delivery codec or file format they usually want?
- **How do they prefer to receive the final product** – DVD, online delivery, tape, etc?

- What are their **consistent brand style guidelines**? Are there specific fonts that should always be used?
- **The names of parties involved** in the production process (producers, marketing employees, designers, etc.). Nothing is more embarrassing than someone showing up to an edit session that you've worked with before and not being able to remember his or her name.
- **Do they prefer a shooting or editing style?**
- **ANYTHING quirky!** Video editors may want to note if the client was picky about things like keying, text position, graphic design, etc. Photographers may want to jot down a client's retouching and photo editing preferences. Every client has the one thing that they tend to zero in on. It's worth noting so you're better prepared to address that pinpoint in the next project.
- If you're working with a client that often comes in for a creative session (video editing, photo shoot, etc.) log what they **preferred to eat and drink** (this may seem trivial but you'll get major points for making sure you have this available for the next session).

You may be wondering, **is it really worth logging this info for EACH project**? Well, if you've ever had to dig through old emails to find file specifics or open up old projects to determine project specs you'll likely see the tremendous benefit of having all of this information in one place. **A little time on the front end may result in huge time savings on the back end.**

The Best Way to Log Specs & Preferences

You may find that you can quickly **log this info in a spreadsheet** after completion of a project. This is the way I did it for years and it's certainly effective. **Create a spreadsheet in Google Documents** and you'll have access to it from any edit bay or computing device. If you're looking for a more robust alternative for this type of note logging **check out the free app, Evernote.** Evernote is a feature-filled note taking application that is available for, and syncs between, all popular computer and mobile devices – PC, MAC, Android, iOS, Blackberry and more.

Evernote excels in its rich toolset and ease of use. Did you use a client's logo for a project? It's simple to attach it to your Evernote to use for future projects. **Create tags for notes**, so you can quickly parse all notes by client name or project type. Each note is labeled with the day it was created, so sorting by date is also a breeze. **Visit the Evernote site** for more information and download links.

Repeat clientele is what any business professional hopes for. Using a simple strategy for **remembering client preferences and project details** is important in any creative field. It will save you time and most importantly, keep your clients coming back for more.

December 8th

An Inside Look at Facebook Marketing

Used correctly, Facebook can be a great tool for promoting your creative business. There's a lot to consider — whether to launch advertisements, if you should watermark your work, even choosing the right resolutions and sizes for uploading. But today we're going to look at something more fundamental: the distinction between profiles and pages on the social network.

Let's zoom out and look at Facebook's network broadly. It consists of two things: profiles, meant for people, and pages, meant for businesses. You, as an individual on Facebook, have a profile — it consists of your personal information, your friend connections, and anything you've elected to like and share. Brands like Coca-Cola have a Facebook page.

Though the presentation is similar, Facebook pages don't have friends. Instead, they accumulate likes from Facebook users. Once people like a page on Facebook, updates from that page will start to show up in their news feeds. Businesses can also advertise to reach the friends of people who have liked the page, or to get more distribution within the news feed.

For the majority of businesses, marketing on Facebook is straightforward: create a page, get people to like it, and start posting updates. But for photographers or other creative types, things aren't so simple, particularly if you're running your business as an individual. If I want to sell my services as a photographer, do I use my Dan Fletcher profile, or do I need to create a Dan Fletcher Facebook page? Let's look at the benefits of each individually.

Facebook Profiles

Facebook profiles used to be a poor solution for any sort of marketing — unless you were comfortable adding business leads as Facebook friends, there was no real way to connect with them. This changed with the launch of Facebook's "Follow" functionality in the winter of 2011. People could now allow other users to follow their profile, which enabled them to see any public updates without needing to be their friend.

That's a complicated sort of social relationship, so I'm going to pause on it for a second. In the early days, people on Facebook could only connect by becoming friends with each other, which required one person to send a friend request and the other person to accept. With Follow, Facebook gave a second option. Now people don't need to become friends at all. If you want to connect with me, all you have to do is go to Facebook.com/DanFletcher and click on the "Follow" button. I won't get any notification or anything to approve, but you'll be subscribed to my updates.

This is slightly different than a friend connection. First, it's a one-way street: You'll see my updates, but I won't see yours unless I subscribe to you in return. Second, you'll only see updates that I post publicly. Whenever you post on Facebook, there's an option to choose the audience. Something set to "Friends Only" just goes to people you're Facebook friends with, not to subscribers. Updates that are set to "Public" are sent to everyone, subscribers included.

As an individual running a creative business, this can be a valuable marketing tool to enable. Facebook even includes a "Follow" button that you can embed on your personal homepage to help build your numbers. Marketing via your Facebook profile also lets you handle all your Facebook activity in a single place: there's no additional property like a Page to manage or keep fresh.

But there are a few shortcomings to using a Facebook profile for marketing:

– Anything you post publicly is also visible to all your friends, as Facebook doesn't include an audience setting for "Public minus your friends." Consider whether it'll be jarring for your friends to see your marketing messages popping up in their news feeds.

– There are limited tools for paid promotion. Unlike Pages, which can run ads to accumulate more likes, there is no ad unit to get more followers. You can pay to promote an individual post, which broadens your distribution in the news feed, but there also isn't access to the fine-tuned targeting data that Pages have to manage ad campaigns. If you ever plan on dabbling in Facebook advertising, a profile isn't the solution.

– There's no ability to add additional administrators. Only you can run your Facebook profile, so if you have someone to help out with your marketing, there's no way to give them access.

Facebook Pages

Facebook Pages solve for a lot of these problems. Unlike profiles, they're backed by a robust advertising system, you can have multiple admins, they can be named anything you like, and they're separated from your personal profile so you don't have to worry about bugging any of your friends. And, just as with the follow functionality, Facebook lets you embed a "Like" button on your site to help convert website visitors into Facebook fans. But pages come with a few drawbacks as well:

– A page gives you a second thing to manage. Think of your Facebook page as a completely separate Facebook account. Nothing you do on your personal profile will be reflected automatically on your page, so you'll need additional content to keep your page fresh and engaging or you'll risk losing your audience.

– Though there are exceptions to this rule, it's tougher for a branded page to be engaging on Facebook to the degree that a person can. If you opt to go the page route, keep in mind that your page needs some life to it, too. Your posts should seem like they're coming from a person, rather than a brand page.

– They may be tougher to find in search. This is particularly true if you're running your business as an individual. Someone's first instinct will be to seek out your personal Facebook profile, not necessarily your page. It's a good idea to include your page's URL on your business cards and the Like button on your website to help people get to the right place. (Facebook helps with this too. You can choose a friendlier URL — something like Facebook.com/YourNameHere — through this link.)

Keep in mind that pages and profiles aren't mutually exclusive — you can have a Facebook page and also enable followers on your profile, although you run the risk of redundancy and splitting your audience. But in general, marketing via a Facebook profile is a great solution for someone just starting out and wanting to share their work to a broader audience beyond their friends. As your business grows and becomes more robust, it's a good idea to switch over to a Facebook page, giving you more tools and resources to help you grow.

December 9th
Are We Too Obsessed with Camera Specs?

With the rapid advancement of motion picture technology, many of us have placed an emphasis on camera specs over art. Is that mindset a mistake?

While writing various articles on cameras recently, it dawned on me that I had become a little too **obsessed with camera specs**. Instead of looking at how the camera performs under real production conditions and the imagery it creates, I was looking first and only at the **specs** from the manufacturer.

While **specs** are an important factor that can help you achieve what you want for your production, they really shouldn't be the reason why we make a purchase. They also really shouldn't be the overriding factor as to why we choose one specific camera over another. So what should we be looking at? Well that's a pretty easy answer. But first let's look at why we like to make purchases based on **specs** and then why we should be focused on something other than **specs**.

Spec Obsession Disorder

David Pogue from the New York Times wrote about this disorder in his blog post back in 2012, and while he was specifically speaking about smartphones, this logic holds true for any advancing technology. I also think this logic is even more true today than it was three years ago when he wrote the piece.

We've been wired through marketing and advertising to search and look for these specs. Yet for cameras, the **specs** alone don't make the image. You need the quality lenses to funnel and capture those images. Still, we tend to place **camera specs** over the lens more often than not. This has a lot to do with being conditioned to look and make **decisions based on specifications.**

It's All About the Final Image

In the end it's all about the image. We should instead focus all of our attention on the end product or the final untouched image that comes from the camera. Remember that what your doing, in the end, is an art. So, while some **specs** are needed for specific reasons, we shouldn't completely dwell on them to the point that we lose our focus on the end product.
Many different cameras with vastly different specs can work seamlessly together. For a great example of how well a multi-camera, multi-spec setup can work together, cinematographer

December 10th
Average Video Editor Salary – How to Make More Than Your Competition

The future outlook of the video post-production market might keep you up at night…or cause you to create your best work.

The Bureau of Labor Statistics' most recent report shows that film and video editing positions are projected to grow only **5 percent from 2010 to 2020, slower than the average for most occupations.** The Bureau states that the consolidation of video related positions is partially responsible for this slow growth, as producers and reporters are becoming increasingly more responsible for editing their own work. No doubt, tighter production budgets have led to this merging of what were traditionally separate positions.

Applications and hardware continue to drop significantly in price (note: DaVinci Resolve and Autodesk Smoke). Low cost access to video editing tools will without question continue to drive up the number of individuals who claim themselves as "video editors", further increasing competition.

Let's take a look at the numbers. **In 2010…**

20,600 video editors were salaried.

11,000 video editors were self-employed.

$50,930 was the average video editor salary.

The type of post-production work encompassed in the term "video and film industry" is wide ranging. This is one factor that leads to a significant disparity between the highest paid editors and the lowest. In 2010, **the bottom 10% earned less than $25k, while the highest paid video editors (top 10%) made over $110k.**
So, in an industry with slow job growth and declining barriers to entry how can you stay competitive, keep moving forward AND be one of the top earners? **Be better.**

- **Stay knowledgeable about industry happenings.** Know what's happening online, offline, with cameras, technology and other industry news. Read blogs, magazines, and press releases.
- **Network.** It's been said 1000's of times before and it's true. Reach out, make connections and you'll get more work. (Tip: freelancers go to local ad and marketing meet-ups, not just creative user groups)
- **Diversify your skill-set.** It's no longer enough to know one editing application (FCP is case-in-point). Be able to work with motion design, photography, audio, video editing and web applications. That last one's huge. As video moves increasingly more online, it's imperative to know about encoding and putting video online, as well as the basics of building and maintaining sites.
- **Market the heck out of yourself.** Be a productive member of your local film and video community. Post your work online Develop your own personal brand and push it.
- **Don't get stuck.** This is very much a ladder-based industry. You work your way up, taking on better projects, better clients and better money. Drive forward creatively and take calculated job risks. You're never going to be a top-earner by running in place.

The future outlook of the post-production industry may be a bit flat according to the Bureau's report, but it doesn't have to be FOR YOU. **Work hard and separate yourself creatively from the rest of the pack.** The cream of the crop always rises to the top.

December 11th

Cutting Trailers – Understanding How To Create One That Works

How do you edit a compelling film trailer that will tell your story and sell your film?

A film trailer is what can make a film live or die. It can help escalate anticipation, word of mouth, intrique and "I've just got to see that film" feelings. Similarly, it has the power to turn turn viewers off completely if they feel like they've seen all the best bits with nothing left to surprise.

Stephen Garrett runs a 'trailer house' called Jump Cut that has for the last 10 years specialized in promoting documentary, foreign and independent films. He's also been in Filmmaker Magazine and the New York Times. In the following resources he shares some brilliant insights on what makes for a great trailer.

Personally I would love to break into the business of editing trailers as it requires a bit of art, part marketing science and part awesome creativity. **If you feel the same then check out these great trailer making resources.**

Dissecting a Film Trailer – What Makes The Cut

This is a brilliant piece of infographical insight from the New York Times which is also great fun to play with. **They have dissected the trailers for five of the nine Best Picture Nominees for the 2013 Oscars.** As you scrub along the timeline of the trailer, the video window updates with that particular shot, so you can see where each shot has originally come from in the order of the actual film. As well, you'll pick up great insights from trailer experts Bill Woolery and Stephen Garrett. Click here to enjoy the interactive trailer timelines for *Silver Linings Playbook, Argo, Lincoln, Amour and Beasts of the Southern Wild.*

How To Craft A Winning Trailer

In this post for Filmmaker Magazine, Stephen Garrett talks through **how best to create and craft a trailer that will win your audience over** and get them to turn out to watch the film. The whole article is pretty much **a masterclass in how to make a trailer from scratch** – from how to create timelines of great dialogue and shots as the building blocks to setting the right tone and selecting the right music.

The humble movie trailer, once a delightful distraction seen only by punctual film goers exclusively in movie houses, is now the principal way most movies get exposure and remain in the public conscience. And as long as there is a computer and an Internet connection, it can be watched anytime, anywhere, indefinitely. Along with the movie poster, it is arguably the most important marketing tool available to a filmmaker.

At the bottom of the post are some extra goodies from Dan Schoenbrun on the realities of trailer marketing and explanations of a few common trailer terms (although nothing anyone in post wouldn't understand already).

December 12th
Freelance Video: Managing Client Expectations

Freelance video pros need to set clear client expectations around timelines, budgets, and production value... and then get it all in writing.

Most of your clients will not have an intimate knowledge of video production **or what it takes to create the images in their heads.**
Now that the tools for capturing video are more accessible than ever, non-professionals are **making a lot of assumptions about your work based on their ability to pull out their iPhone.**
Whether you're working with an aspiring artist wanting a music video or a large corporate client needing a video training series, to some degree, **you'll need to educate them on the process and the resources needed to get them to their desired goal** — and that's usually not a cell phone video.

Creative Plan

When you go in to talk to them about their project, **be prepared to ask a lot of questions so you can understand their vision and advise accordingly.** They need to tell you where will the video go, what the desired length is, and who the target audience is. You'll also want to ask what the goals of the video are (to educate, entertain, excite?), the tone of the video, and what the core messaging needs to be.

Kimbe MacMaster, with Vidyard, notes that all the stakeholders in any given project need to be on the same page if they want to be successful and even supplies a template for questions. *Lay everything out ahead of time in a creative brief, send it to everyone who will be involved in the project and allow at least one meeting for walking through the brief and answering any related questions.*

Service Agreement: What is It?

The point in the process in which most of the expectation management takes place is in the **crafting of the service agreement.** After the client agrees to move forward with you on the project, you'll want to create a service agreement that, among other things, outlines the **scope of the project**, an **engagement summary**, and all the **defined deliverables.** Video marketplace, Nimia, offers an example of a standard video production agreement (partially pictured above) that you can use as a resource for creating your own.

Service Agreement: What's Covered?

1. Project Scope

Project scope will include **hiring talent, music selection or production, and a tentative production schedule.** Examples of deadlines to include in this phase are **script delivery, shoot date(s), and delivery of first and final drafts.** To emphasize that the agreed-to deadlines **are dependent on both you, the producer, and them, the client,** you can use language like this: Any delays caused by the client including cancelled meetings, delays on creative feedback or direction, and especially delays from the final decision-makers, will cause delays to the final deliverable. Changes to the estimated project schedule may affect pricing.

Here's a quick tutorial/reminder about all the things to consider **when managing the scope of your project:**

2. Engagement Summary

The **engagement summary** should state both what you're going to do and what they're going to do. This is where you protect yourself with limits on changes and revisions. For example:

This proposal includes two rounds of revisions for the concept and script and two rounds of revisions for the final draft of the video.

3. Defined Deliverables

Defined deliverables will be items like a storyboard, a script and, of course, the video. Include the formats expected for each deliverable and how it will be provided to them.

4. The Fee

Of course, note the **fee** for the project and when you'll expect payment. For example: Client will be invoiced 50% of the project total at the start of the engagement. The remaining 50% will be invoiced when the final video is approved.

Look at examples online and talk to your friends in the industry about what they put in their service agreements. Yours doesn't need to look like it was written by an attorney, **but it does need outline clear expectations on both sides.** Don't do any further work on the project **until you get a signed copy back from them.** No matter how well you know or trust the client, you don't want to find yourself in a situation where you wish you had something in writing and you don't.

Post-Production

The part of the process clients seem to have the hardest time wrapping their head around is post-production. They know the footage has been shot, **but they don't understand the bandwidth needed to process that footage, cut it, color it, add effects, and render it.**

I tell clients that for every hour we shoot on set, we'll need 10 hours to process it (give or take). This isn't always the case, and you can use your best judgement on what that number will be for your project. Just know that providing that expectation can help you **get the time you need to get the footage where it needs to be for client approval.**

Chris Potter, co-founder of ScreenLight, reinforces that open communication and setting expectations will save time during video review. He also notes in *9 Ways to Improve Client*

Communication During Video Review that **using your agreed-upon deadlines is another tool to help keep client revision under control.**

Creative review is a form of negotiation, and one thing that helps keep a negotiation moving forward is a deadline. A deadline can help force prioritization decisions. Anything can be done with enough time. But chances are, neither you nor your client has that luxury.

Assuming you've talked to them about their vision in the creative planning phrase, and received concept and script approval from them, there shouldn't be too many surprises at this point. Doing more on the front-end will allow you to shoot for the edit and save time (and stress) in post. Above all else, **try to be transparent about the process and stay in contact throughout.** As you reach milestones in the production timeline, reach out and let them know what's going on. **Your client will enjoy seeing what happens "behind-the-scenes"** and you can demonstrate your expertise.

December 13th
How to Find the Right Subject for Your Documentary

It's not easy to find the right subject for your documentary. Nonetheless, there are a few qualities you can look for in subjects to ensure they'll be great.

To find a story worth telling (and a story worth spending copious amounts of time, money, and energy on in every stage of production), ask yourself these questions about your potential documentary subject.

Are they challenging what is the norm?

If your subject is challenging the norm, it's typically a great sign that they will encounter **trials**, **conflicts**, and **unexpected turns** throughout the filming process. Also, if they're challenging societal norms, this will give them something to work towards and a goal to accomplish. If they have a goal to accomplish, this will make crafting a natural **three-act structure** in the edit much more feasible.

Can they progress?

It took me a year to find the subject for my last **documentary**. The reason I had such a tough time finding the right subject was that when I started, I was only researching and talking to multiple **world champions in their field**. I just couldn't see where their story may go because they had already achieved the pinnacle of their craft. I just kept asking myself **where could they go from here?**

After months of not being able to answer that question, I finally decided to start looking at more people who were just starting in their field. Granted, the more experienced subjects will be great **supporting characters,** but I just couldn't envision where the film could go with them as the **main characters.**

Once I stopped talking to world champions, and started talking to people who were starting out and **challenging the status quo,** that's when I finally realized that we had a story. What will they overcome and what have they overcome?

One of my favorite documentary series right now is Chef's Table. It's such a fascinating exploration of character for **documentary filmmaking.** Most of the chefs they feature on the show had overcome something drastic — something that helped them achieve the success that they're currently enjoying. The **narrative arc** for each episode is typically structured around a trial they overcame in the past.

When **researching or interviewing subjects for a documentary film**, don't be afraid to ask them what big trials they overcame to reach the point they are now.

Are they likable and relatable?

Everyone wants to root for the underdog. There's just something about the "can do, against all odds" attitude of an underdog that makes people cheer them on. Ask yourself if your subjects have personality traits that appeal to a broad audience. If so, this will **keep your audience entertained** and rooting for your character throughout the entire piece.

December 14th
How to Make Event Footage More Cinematic

Most of us are capable of capturing cinematic looks on narrative productions. But what about event footage? Here's how to get great results at your next videographer gig.

Shooting events like **weddings, bar mitzvahs, and corporate functions** may be not always be the most exciting type of work, but many filmmakers moonlight as event videographers to pay the bills. Naturally, they still want their work to shine. That said, many of these same individuals run into issues when shooting on the fly, as their usual approach to working on set doesn't always translate well to a live environment.

Compared to capturing narrative material, **event coverage is a very different beast.** Things move extremely quickly, quantity is often preferred over quality (by the client at least), and the shooting schedule can be much less predictable. Unfortunately, many shooters with a narrative background try to directly translate over their style of shooting. They end up missing shots, not getting enough coverage, and ultimately delivering a poor end result.

The good news is that there are ways to still capture beautiful footage even when working in less than optimal shooting conditions. Many of the tips and techniques that will help you accomplish this will likely go against what you're used to doing for narrative work. But that's all part of the process. As long as you as you are well-prepared and still bring your creative A-Game to the table, **you'll end up with a solid final product.**

1. Shoot on Fast Zooms

Like many DPs, I prefer **shooting on prime lenses** for many reasons. They're usually faster, sharper, and more detailed than their zoom lens counterparts, and in a narrative environment you always want the best of the best.

When shooting events, however, everything changes. Depending on your circumstances, you may be able to get away with shooting on primes (and if you can, you really should), but in most cases they simply aren't practical.

Ideally, you will want to have some relatively fast zoom lenses in your kit, like the **Sigma 18 – 35 F1.8** or the **Canon 24 – 70 F 2.8**. These lenses will still deliver beautiful results while allowing you to work on your feet more quickly and swap your lenses far less often.

2. Get a Low-Light Camera

Usually with event coverage you have little or no control over the lighting. This is obviously problematic for a number of reasons — the worst of them being under-lit shooting situations.

It is very common to walk into a wedding, corporate event, etc. and realize that even at 800 ISO and F1.4 you don't have bright enough exposure. For this reason, low-light cameras are a must. I would suggest looking into cameras like the Canon C100, a7S, or other DSLRs that can record cleanly at ISO 3200 or above. You don't necessarily need the best low-light camera on the market, but you definitely need one that can produce great results above ISO 800 or 1600, which is where many cameras top out.

3. Bring a Second Shooter or Assistant

One of the most common mistakes that first-time event shooters make is going at it alone. 99% of the time, **you absolutely need another shooter or at least an assistant to help you capture live events.** This matters for a few reasons... Firstly, you can't be two places at once. There will be at least one time during any event that you need to be covering two things simultaneously (let's say a speech and crowd reaction) and have to choose between the two.

Secondly, and most importantly, **a huge part of being an effective event shooter involves moving very quickly.** With an assistant, you can pack up gear, change lenses, ask for assistance, and move around far more quickly and efficiently.

4. Rethink Your Audio

We all know that **audio quality is just as important as video quality**, and this notion applies to events just as much as narrative projects. That said, the way in which you capture the audio will vary significantly between those two types of productions. Unlike narrative films where you have the luxury of working with a boom operator and likely also have lav mics on your talent, during an event that will not typically be possible.

You will want to look for other ways to get great audio without being too invasive by asking guests to put on a lav mic to be interviewed, or have a boom op walking around with lots of gear. I always suggest only using lavs on guests that you know you will be featuring throughout the video (for example someone doing a main speech at a corporate event), but then also looking for alternate solutions.

You may be able to plant a Zoom recorder on a podium, record a live feed off of the house mixer, or have your assistant hold a mic during interviews. This approach will change drastically depending on the event you are shooting, **but always be prepared for any type of situation.**

5. Avoid Event-Style Lighting

One of the most obvious signs of event videography is flat lighting. Typically, videographers will have a small LED light mounted directly on top of their camera which does help with exposure, but also can diminish the overall aesthetic. The reason? Placing a light directly in front of a person's face is going to really flatten them and make the shot look very synthetic.

I would highly advise anyone that needs to use LED lighting for event coverage to **find a way to offset it to one side.** You're going to get more useable results if your light is set up on a 45 degree angle (as opposed to straight on), so do whatever you can to make that happen. You might need to rig up your LED on a light stand, magic arm, or even have your assistant hold it in place.
As long as it isn't directly in front, **you'll be lightyears ahead of most other event shooters.**

December 15th
How to Supercharge Your Content Marketing

Content marketing was 2014's biggest buzzword, but 2015 will be all about how brands can make that content strategic and make it start working for them.

As you look at your content strategy this year, take a look at these 5 tips and learn about some of the tools and ideas that will help you supercharge your content in 2015.

1. Identify Your Brand Values

Every piece of content you create doesn't have to (and shouldn't) be about you. By creating a content mission statement, list of brand values, or editorial guideline, you'll have a solid foundation for which topics fit with your brand.

From there, you can expand beyond just talking about your brand, and start to explore stories that resonate with your audience and show what your company or organization is all about. (To learn more about the brands that are doing this well, check out the "Stop Talking About Yourself" webcast we hosted with Ad Age and Contently.)

2. Start Planning

If you've started playing around with content marketing but don't really know where to go next, the best way to kick your content into gear is by establishing an editorial calendar.

In Trello, you can create "cards" that are viewable either by category or in a calendar view, allowing you to plan everything in advance.

We use Trello at Shutterstock to organize and collaborate on upcoming blog posts, and I use Wunderlist to organize my content ideas (and every other aspect of my life). Other options like Google Calendar, Opal, WordPress plugins, or even a basic spreadsheet will work just as well — the idea is just to plan out a few ideas and start to put thought and organization into the work you're creating.

Wunderlist allows you to make simple lists, assign due dates and priority, tag categories, collaborate and even share files.

Once you have a set strategy, you'll find that planning and regularly creating content comes much easier, and the final product is often stronger and more thought-out.

3. Look at the Data

As you begin writing and publishing content in 2015, it's important to keep an eye on the data, and let the numbers show you what your audience is thinking.

Insights, a tool by Contently, focuses more on engaged users than simply on traffic. It allows you to sort stories by "attention time," a combination of time on page and number of viewers.

Some key metrics to look at are average session duration and average time on page, both of which let you see how long readers are staying on a story and on your site as a whole.

If you're getting a lot of traffic to one type of story, but the time on page is low, you may be drawing readers in with an inaccurate headline, or the content might not be strong enough to keep them interested. On the flip side, if your traffic isn't so high but the time on page is far above average, you may want to tweak your headline or try more social promotion to draw more readers in to what might be your best content.

Sorting by traffic source in Google Analytics lets you see how much traffic comes from where, and also see behavior patterns based on where the reader came from.
Another valuable area to look in your analytics software is the traffic referral or source/medium section (in Google Analytics), which allows you to see where traffic is coming from. In the example above, we were able to see that most of the views on our 2015 Color Trends infographic were coming from direct traffic, but almost 15% came in from social media. This will help you determine which traffic sources are worth investing your time in, and which could use a little more work. It can also help you see which type of posts perform best with readers coming in from Google, from email, from banner ads, etc.

4. Make It More Visual

Copy is great, but it doesn't always tell the whole story. With the Internet getting more and more crowded by the minute, you need more than words to make your content really stand out. This year, try making your content more visual with photos, infographics, data visualizations, and even video. Whether or not we writers want to accept it — it's the visuals that draw a reader into a post, and (hopefully) the copy that makes them stay.

5. Give Distribution a Try

If 2014 was the year of content, 2015 will be the year of content distribution. As more and more companies look to profit from their content marketing, they'll need to reach audiences and create new opportunities for ROI, many of which will come from investing in their content and different types of distribution. Whether you're testing advertorials, distribution through a platform like Taboola or Outbrain, or sponsored content, it's likely that your company will want to explore paid content in the coming months.

December 16th

Is Prosumer Video Gear Threatening to Professionals?

Is the line between pro and prosumer gear becoming so blurred that it could threaten high-end professionals?

For the last decade, the **gear needed to make quality films** has gone down dramatically. Most indie short films traveling the festival circuit are being shot on **inexpensive cameras** that the director or cinematographer own themselves. Because of this, one has to think about how this is effecting the industry professionals. So let's look at each major component of video production and filmmaking, and then try and determine if they are in fact threatening the industry professionals.

The Price of 4K is Dropping Rapidly

A few years ago, you could tell a major difference between what was shot on **high-end studio gear** and what was shot on **prosumer gear**. However, that distinction isn't so crystal clear these days. With camera manufactures like Sony,Canon, and Blackmagic Design, independent filmmakers and video pros are able to get their hands on **great gear that can shoot in 4K** for a very favorable entry price. Are these cameras being used on big-budget film sets? Yes, but usually as crash cams or B cameras for cutaways or coverage. In fact, the majority of the films we see on the big screen are still using the ARRI ALEXA.

Another factor that we should talk about is lenses. This line has blurred as well, up to a certain point. If you take the prosumer line of **prime lenses** and judge them against the next level of lenses, **the cine prime**, you're going to find it hard to tell a difference.
In fact, see if you can tell a difference between a $5-,7oo lens compared to a $12-15,000.

Quality Sound Can Be Had for Little Money

Sound is another area of **film and video production** that is absolutely crucial, and it's one that's dropping in price. Now you can buy a quality shotgun mic and wireless lapel mic for very little money and record that audio to an inexpensive field recorder like a Zoom H6. Because of these advancements in audio capture, you can realistically get **high-end level audio** for a much lower price point. In fact, let's check out this comparison between a $200 Blue Spark and a $3200 Neuman U 87 Ai condenser mic. The results are quite impressive.

Lower Cost of NLE

Non-linear editing software has also seen a drop in price. You can pick up DaVinci Resolve Lite for free or you can buy it outright for $995. Then there is Adobe Premiere Pro CC, which comes with the Creative Cloud for $29.99 a month. You can also purchase Final Cut Pro X for a reasonable price of $299 or, for just a little over $100 more, you can buy Lightworks. The one **NLE** that was still a bit pricey was the industry standard Avid Media Composer, but now Avid is available for a modest $49.99 a month.

Where You Can't Replace a Professional

As you can see, there are plenty of reasons that **prosumer gear and software** are getting tougher to disregard or simply dismiss. Will we see this prosumer gear showing up as the A camera on big budget film sets? Not likely. Studio productions will still use the big guns like the ARRI ALEXA camera with Cooke lenses and, really, that makes sense. I have yet to see a camera, other than maybe RED, that can rival the ARRI Alexa in terms of getting so **close to film without being film**. This is one area I just don't see prosumer gear overtaking pro-level gear. But what about micro-budget or mid-level-budget films? I actually see that happening now. There are many independent films, as I said before, that are opting for cameras that are $15,000 and lower. With so many options out there on this front, you can grab a **quality camera that produces a great image** and rent the high-level lenses you need and you're set. So, in this arena of filmmaking, I see it making a difference.

December 17th

Recent grads discuss breaking into the video production and post-production industry

Breaking into the video production industry is hard to do...

Remember what it was like to be freshly graduated from college, navigating the murky sea of the production and post-post industry? Now, imagine that you're trying to break into it in today's economic climate.

I was curious, so I asked several of my former students what it was like getting a job after graduation. (These are students that graduated from Columbia College Chicago within the last two years. About half of them moved to LA to find jobs; the rest stayed in Chicago.)

How easy was it to find a job in the industry?

The market seems to just want freelance workers, but nothing salary or full time. Persistence has always landed me the job in the end however. *–Rob*

Depends on what you want and how little you'd be willing to pay. Out in LA there are bunches of PA listings for short shoots that are $50-200 for a day or two. I've found it incredibly hard to find anything semi-permanent or worth my time. It's highly competitive out here. *-Caitlin*

I don't have a job in production. I did freelance work for some time, but went into retail to pay my bills and haven't re-emerged since. I go out of my way to accommodate the freelance work over my day job, but I can't do that in every case, however. *–Ivan*

It seemed fairly easy only because I was hired by the company I was interning for at the time. I would probably be in a very different place right now had it not been for my internship. The timing really helped. *-Megan*

It was easy for me straight out of college to get a job—I began working at a post house for $400 dollars a week non-taxed. So you can imagine I was working almost 60 hours a week for crap pay. *-Mallory*

What were the greatest challenges in finding work?

Morale! It's so hard to continually send out resumes into that abyss everyday. Sending your resume out here is like that LOST station where they send in the composition notebooks of research and they end up in that pile out in the jungle. -*Caitlin*

The greatest challenge in finding work is that every place seems to promote within. I have had 4 internships, but now I am beyond interning and finding an assistant editor position is almost impossible. My only hope is that I eventually become promoted to assistant editor and to full time. -*Mallory*

Money. Not having a steady gig in production has made me resort to working a regular job, and I can't always fit in a freelancing opportunity. -*Ivan*

Knowing people. It's hard when you move somewhere new and have to re-make all your contacts. -*Vinnie*

I find people are intimidated by the younger crowds. I was told many times that I was too qualified for the position, which I thought was silly, but after being hired in a few of them I found I actually was. Columbia trains their students extremely well! -*Chelsea*

The biggest challenge in finding work was finding a job with not much "real world" experience and marketing myself as a qualified professional against people with more experience. Many of the jobs I applied for were looking for candidates that had two years or more of professional experience. -*Brittnee*

Making good connections... making sure to have the right dose of 'being in their face' while 'staying out of their face'. –*Matt*

My biggest challenge with finding work is putting the time into applications and hunting the "right" job for me. Also getting in contact with some employers can be frustrating while working part time. –*Rob*

When I was looking for a job I used the only resource that was available besides personal connections: the internet. And so was/is EVERYONE else. It was challenging because entry level jobs, like the ones I was applying to, had hundreds of resumes/cover letters sent to them. You have to see the job posting asap or else your resume/cover letter will get lost in a see of applicants. -*Anne*

What aspect of college prepared you the best?

The honest talk about the industry. Everything I've encountered so far, I expected. Also, knowing a little of everything about the business surprises people. Like how I'm a writer, but I can edit. It blows people's minds sometimes. -*Caitlin*

Great teaching. Collaborative projects. Classes that focused on post-production fundamentals. Also, any encouragement/help provided for internships. -*Megan*

Deadlines in college as well as competing with my fellow classmates prepared me most for the real world. Also working with the newest gear and software gave me a leg up. –*Rob*

The hands-on work, or the availability of resources were always invaluable to me. The instruction taught me a great deal, but the ability to mess around with stuff on my free time gave me an understanding that I otherwise wouldn't have had—of production equipment, of the facilities, etc. –*Ivan*

I think I was really prepared for the working world because I took advantage of the instructors around me and networked like crazy! I also feel the opportunity to intern and freelance was huge at Columbia. -*Chelsea*

Learning how to interact with all different kinds of people. Trust me, if people don't want to be around you then you won't last long! -*Vinnie*

One aspect of college that prepared me greatly was the variety of classes I was required to take. Even as a production major, I was required to take writing, post production and a variety of other classes. This made me well versed on a variety of subjects. I felt confidence in having a strong foundation in multiple facets of production. -*Brittnee*

Frequency TV [college TV station]; I can't imagine doing college without doing Frequency. It taught me how to deal with producers that didn't know what they were doing. I hope to translate that into how to deal with clients someday. -*Mallory*

I would say just the social evolution that occurred within myself during [college]. And, of course I found that my Film specific classes prepared me the best by giving me on set experience, as well as professional knowledge of the equipment that is used currently in the industry. –*Matt*

What aspect of college prepared you the least?

When I was hired… it was as a tape-op. This involves a lot of capturing/dubbing/exporting etc. Things of that nature. It also involves a lot of troubleshooting when it comes to decks, software issues, and file conversions. This is an entry-level position, yet based on my college experience in terms of curriculum, nothing actually prepared me for that role. -*Megan*

The worst preparation I had were talking too many classes that had pretty much nothing to do with post. I think producing, directing, and writing are important to know, but when you're a post major, you shouldn't have to take a million classes that don't concentrate on post. -*Anne*

TAPE types, VTRs, the post production world is still tape. Turning in every assignment on a DVD *never* happens in the industry. -*Mallory*

Some of my non major classes prepared me the least in college. I wish I could have spent that time focusing only on my desired career path, or something similar. I understand they want you to be a well rounded character when graduating, but I didn't pay all that money to squander my time. –*Rob*

I never got a sense of what something was worth monetarily. From work, equipment, and other aspects, I never developed a sense for the business part of the business. –*Ivan*

I don't know if I can think of any aspects of my college career that I can look back on and say weren't beneficial in some way. For example, dealing with classes or people I wasn't interested in just prepared me for dealing with projects and clients I have no choice but to deal with these days. Every day was a learning experience whether I knew it or not. -*Brittnee*

Nothing. You can learn something new every day in college. Embrace it. -*Vinnie*

What else can you share about your job-seeking experience?

I think your work speaks for itself. Finding a job is a lot easier if your good at what you do, and passionate. Those who are working towards their career every day in college will find the transition easy. Good work gets noticed. Also, don't take unpaid internships that have you doing nothing but office work and running coffee. I think you need to fight for good internships that are willing to teach you the ropes and give you real experience. –*Rob*

I think a big part of job seeking for fresh graduates is patience. Another big part of job seeking for a young graduate is being a good communicator. Even with no professional experience, if you can communicate to an employer that you have a set of skills that can benefit their company, you've got a shot. –*Brittnee*

I've worked regular jobs since leaving college, and they don't leave a whole lot of time to pursue too many interests. I'd advise anyone in my situation to gun for production work hard, and not depend too much on a steady paycheck if they can help it. –*Ivan*

December 18th
Secrets to Facebook Advertising: Where Image Is Everything

As I've mentioned before, images are consistently the most engaging content on Facebook. No other type of post gets as many likes and shares, meaning those with images usually receive the widest distribution. This is particularly important to keep in mind when constructing an ad campaign on Facebook. You might have a great offer and crisp copy, but without a compelling image, you won't be nearly as successful.

For this post, I'm going to set aside introducing Facebook's ad types and formats and focus instead on the types of images that will perform well in a campaign. Generally, though, this advice applies to nearly any type of advertisement you'd run on Facebook, from the smaller marketplace ads that appear in a user's sidebar to the larger sponsored stories that appear directly in the news feed.

Consider the competition

Before creating a campaign, it's worth taking a step back to think about the competition you're up against. You're hoping users will notice your ad amid a perpetually updating feed of status updates, photos, videos, news stories, page updates, and music recommendations.

That's a daunting proposition, particularly considering this might be the first introduction someone has to your brand. Making a good first impression is important. Fortunately, Facebook allows you to create multiple ads as part of the same campaign, as a way of testing different variations. Before burning through your entire budget, it's worth experimenting with different image and copy combinations to learn what performs best.

Find the right image

Remember that your image has to catch the attention of users, even when they view it at a small size. (Facebook requires a minimum resolution of 154 x 154px.) Images that are horizontal generally look better in Facebook's ad sizes, so I've chosen examples here with a bias toward those. *Faces* People tend to click on photos of other people's faces. The tighter the cropping on the face, the better; bonus points if the person's smiling. But avoid images that feel too posed — the goal should be something that feels like a really nice photo a friend might have taken.

Simplicity Images with a lot of clutter won't display well, particularly at a smaller size. Choose images with one subject that dominates the frame. The goal is to be immediately comprehensible, even at a glance.\

Contrast Bright colors perform really well. Remember that most of Facebook's interface is largely blue, so images with blue tones will tend to blend in. Images with white backgrounds tend to get lost, as well. Reds, oranges, and yellows make for a nice contrast.

Humor/Quirk Images that prompt a double-take can be really powerful, provided they're not too cheesy.

Of course, no matter which image you choose, it's important to be authentic. Users aren't dumb — they'll know if you're trying to game the system by attaching an image unrelated to your brand or offer. It's an unnecessary risk that can damage your campaign.

It's worth noting, too, that Facebook approves all advertisements before they go live. So, as tempting as it might be to show some skin in your ads, they still have to abide by Facebook's content guidelines.

Gather inspiration

There are a few places you can go to gather more ideas for your Facebook ad campaign. The Facebook Ad Board is a good start, as it will show you a collection of advertisements targeted to you personally at the moment. (No promises as to the quality.) Facebook also maintains a site called Facebook Studio, which highlights some of the best examples of marketing on the platform, as selected by Facebook's creative team.

December 19th
Tax Deductions for Filmmakers and Videographers

Make tax season a little less painful with these tax deductions for filmmakers and videographers. It will likely save you money!

Before we begin: We're not Certified Public Accountants, so be sure to consult a CPA to find out exactly what tax write-offs work best for you. Let's kick this off with two pieces of very important advice...

Keep Immaculate Records

Keep your records in order and set aside a percentage of every dollar you earn for self-employment tax. I've found that utilizing assets such as Square to send invoices and run credit cards really helps me keep my records tight. Then I tie Quickbooks to my bank account to **consolidate all of my records into one place**. At the end of the year, all I have to do it send the QuickBooks documentation to my CPA so she can prepare my taxes for filing. Speaking of CPAs...

Hire a Certified Public Accountant

You're going to need help navigating the ins and outs of what can be deducted and what can't. **Hiring a CPA** *will* help you save some money in the long run.

Deductions for Filmmakers and Videographers

As we explore these possible tax deductions for filmmakers and videographers, keep in mind that you could end up audited. Be sure that you can **justify your deductions.** That point is going to come up a lot as we move forward. Now let's look at some easy ways that deductions can save you some money.

1. Small Items

Any small item that you spend money on for daily production tasks is something you can deduct. Tool kits, dry erase boards and markers, gaffer tape, etc. These are all things you can deduct. You just have to be able to **justify the purchase and its use** in your daily business.

2. All Computer Related Items

If you purchased a new computer this year, it's deductible – with some conditions. If you use that new computer solely for work, **then you can claim the entire purchase price**, but only by using a Section 179 Deduction. If you're using the computer for business *and* personal, that changes how much of the purchase price you can deduct. Your CPA will be able to give you a more concrete idea of what those numbers are.

It's not just hardware that can be deducted; software is eligible too. Your Adobe Creative Cloud subscription is a great example of software that's deductible. Just make sure you give your transaction invoices to your CPA in Quickbooks or physical form.

3. Film & Video Production Equipment

Every piece of equipment that you purchase for your work is a deduction during tax season. Did you purchase a new camera this year? That's a deduction. Did you go to B&H Photo and purchase new lenses for that camera? Maybe a penguin case? ND filters? Those are deductions. Or maybe you purchased new sound equipment from Sweetwater? Deduction. Even batteries, memory cards, tripods, sliders, and stabilizers are deductible as long as they are being justifiably used for your business.

4. Digital and Print Research

As filmmakers and videographers, we are **constantly consuming content** in order to stay on top of what is going on in our industry. Because of this you might be justified in deducting the whole cost or a portion of the cost of Netflix, Hulu Plus, Amazon Prime, cable service, movie tickets, industry books, periodicals, and smart phone apps. Again, you have to be able to justify these expenses as something you need for your work. Your CPA will be able to give you a concrete answer on whether you can apply these expenses as deductions.

5. Dining and Entertainment

To deduct dining and entertainment expenses, you need to be able to justify **how they relate to your business**. More than likely you wont be able to claim the entire amount. When dining with clients or colleagues, I usually **claim around 50% of the cost**. I'll also deduct the cost of a wrap party for my crew after filming has concluded. Screenings and premiere costs are also deductible. All of these things can be seen as the cost of doing business.

6. Online Presence

All of us need some sort of online presence in order to build our business. Because building this **online presence is so crucial to earning a living**, you should look at deducting the cost of this presence. Things that could apply here are cloud storage costs (Onedrive, Google Drive, Dropbox), yearly website domain and hosting costs, and online membership costs such as IMDB Pro. Even the costs of website design and development are deductible.

7. Travel Expenses and Conferences

Expenses you incur while doing business outside of your home might fall into the travel expenses category. Whether you're driving for five hours or your taking a flight across the country for a film shoot, these are all deductible expenses. Be sure and **keep records of everything** including rental cars, taxi rides, and hotels. **If you paid for the travel of your crew, add that cost as well.** Additionally, if you're attending a conference like NAB or SXSW, you can deduct the attendance costs, as they directly pertain to your work. For more information on travel expense and conference deductions head over to the IRS Website.

8. Business Startup Expenses

Keep track of all the **costs that you pay out to start your business** such as incorporation fees, lawyer fees, and copyright/trademark filing fees. You can even deduct the payments made to your CPA or financial advisor. Also check out Caron Beesley's Startup Cost Tax Deductions article on the SBA.gov blog.

9. Printed Self Marketing

In addition to your online marketing, you'll likely want to **purchase printed media** like business cards, flyers, or brochures. These costs are deductible as well. In fact, business cards were #4 on the Bloomberg Business list of 25 Unsung Tax Deductions.

10. Home Office Expenses

Home offices and editing rooms are loaded with potential deductions, including the actual space you use. Other likely deductions: desks, chairs, lamps, pens, printers, printer paper, ink cartridges, staples, etc. You get the idea. These may seem like small insignificant purchases, **but they add up quickly.** The IRS has an entire page dedicated to the ins and outs of home office deductions.

What We've Learned About Tax Deductions

Deductions aren't too hard to decipher, as long as they are legal and pertain to your business. With that in mind, the most important take-aways are: **Keep immaculate records and hire a CPA.** Talk to other filmmakers that you know – chances are one of them has a CPA that they can recommend.

December 20th
The 4 Unsung Pioneers of Film Editing

The original cutters of film. The 4 women who predated the term "film editor" and whose names dominated the Academy Awards for decades.

The Birth of a Nation (1915), *Stagecoach* (1939), *The Wizard of Oz* (1939), *Singin' in the Rain* (1952), *The Ten Commandments* (1956), *Lawrence of Arabia* (1962), *Bonnie and*

Clyde (1967), *Jaws* (1975), *Star Wars* (1977), *Apocalypse Now* (1979), *Raging Bull* (1980), *Pulp Fiction* (1994), *Memento* (2000), *The Avengers* (2012), *Star Wars: Episode VII* (2015) Each of these films made cinematic history, but many people don't realize one thing. **All of these films were edited by women.** But who are the original pioneers of film editing? Who paved the way for females in film? Before we go in depth, it should be stated that the following is a list of incredible editors. Not "female editors" or "women editors." No. These are some of the best damn editors who have ever worked in the industry.

Women working as editors dates back to the early days of cinema. In fact, the term "editor" was not even used as a job title. When working with actual film reels, editing a film required you to **literally cut and splice scenes together.** This gave rise to the term **cutter**. In the early days of film, cutting was seen as unskilled labor. Practically anyone could be hired for the job, and it actually became a common position for women. The reason most people don't know this comes from the fact that **all of those cutting positions went uncredited in the films.**

Margaret Booth

In 1910, actor Elmer Booth frequently starred in the early works of director D.W. Griffith. Elmer was set to have a large role in the Griffith film *Intolerance*, but he died in a car crash in 1915. Griffith actually gave the eulogy at the funeral. After his death, Griffith hired Booth's sister, Margaret, as a "patcher." This low-end editing job provided her with a living. She immediately got to work on Griffith's film *The Birth of a Nation*.
The Orpheum Theatre in Haverhill, Massachusetts bought the exclusive rights to show *The Birth of a Nation* in the New England area. The owner of that theater was none other than Louis B. Mayer. In 1924, Mayer would form the Metro-Goldywn-Mayer company, widely known as MGM. Mayer hired Margaret Booth as a director's assistant, where she would eventually rise to cut films like *The Mysterious Lady* and *Camille*, starring Greta Garbo. It was actually MGM's head of production, Irving Thalberg, that would coin the term **film editor** when describing Margaret's skill.
In 1936 came the release of *Mutiny on the Bounty*. The film was a massive success, and Booth received an **Oscar Nomination for Best Film Editing**. The film had a total of 8 nominations, and won the **Oscar for Best Picture**. Her talents would not go unnoticed, as Booth soon became the studio's editor-in-chief in 1939. She immediately became the supervising editor

behind *The Wizard of OZ*, which was edited by Blanche Sewell. Booth did not receive editing credit for working on other major MGM films like *The Red Badge of Courage* and *Ben-Hur*. She remained the editor-in-chief at MGM until 1968.

Throughout the 70s and 80s, Booth would supervise a variety of films. The last film she supervised was the 1982 hit *Annie*. She received an **Honorary Oscar** in 1978 for her contributions to the art of film making. She passed away in 2002 at the age of 104.

Anne Bauchens

One of the most notorious names associated with early directors is that of Cecil B. DeMille. One of the little known facts about DeMille is that he collaborated with the same editor for over 40 years, Anne Bauchens. Bauchens was personally trained by DeMille as an editor, receiving her first credit on the film *Carmen* in 1915. DeMille had directed and edited all his previous films himself, but by 1918 he had entrusted all his edits to Anne. The two worked together on nearly every project.

The **Oscar for Best Film Editing** was first introduced in 1934. Anne Bauchens received **one of the original 3 nominations** for her work on *Cleopatra*. In the most shocking revelation, Bauchens is not even credited as the editor of the film. Neither is most of the production crew nor some of the cast. She lost the award in 1934, but would soon return. Bauchens **won the Oscar for Best Film Editing** in 1941 for *North West Mounted Police*, the first time a woman had won the award. Anne received 2 more **Oscar Nominations** for *The Greatest Show on Earth* and *The Ten Commandments*. (She actually edited both versions of DeMille's Ten Commandment in 1923 and 1956.)

Despite her success, Bauchens was often criticized for her technique. In 1965, Margaret Booth had this to say of Anne Bauchens.

Anne Bauchens is the oldest editor in the business. She was editing for years before I came into the business. DeMille was a bad editor, I thought, and made her look like a bad editor. I think Anne really would have been a good editor, but she had to put up with him — which was something. – ***Editors Guild Magazine***

Barbara McLean

In 1924, Barbara McLean married J. Gordon McLean, a film projectionist and cameraman. Soon after, she found a job as an assistant editor in Los Angeles, California. Her talents were quickly noticed. She received her first film credit in 1933. That same year, film producer and head of production at Warner Bros., Darryl F. Zanuck, decided to leave the company following a salary dispute. Immediately after his resignation, he created 20th Century Pictures. Two years later his company merged with the Fox Film Corporation. In 1935, Zanuck became the head of 20th Century Fox and named Barbara his editor-in-chief.

1935 also saw the release of *Les Misérables* in theaters. The film was a hit and garnered McLean her first **Oscar Nomination for Best Film Editing**. She lost, but was again **nominated the next year** for *Lloyd's of London*. Once again she lost, but would soon be back. She was nominated five more times for *Alexander's Ragtime Band* in 1939, *The Rains Came* in 1940, *The Song of Bernadette* in 1944, *Wilson* in 1945, and *All About Eve* in 1951. She only **won the Oscar for Best Film Editing** once, for *Wilson*.

McLean remained with 20th Century Fox until her retirement in 1969. In that time, she was granted full authority over the studio's film edits. In that era, film directors were not nearly as involved with editing, if they were involved at all. Director's contracts had them working on their next production while editing had just started on their last project. McLean supervised all those edits. A 1940 issue of the Los Angeles Times declared,

"Barbara McLean, one of Hollywood's three women film editors, can make stars — or leave their faces on the cutting room floor."

Dorothy Spencer

Dorothy Spencer began working as an assistant editor in 1924. By the late 1930s, she found herself employed at 20th Century Fox. In 1937 Spencer began co-editing with Otho Lovering. Together they collaborated on several features, most famously known for the work on John Ford's 1939 western *Stagecoach*. The film was also John Ford's first collaboration with John Wayne. It was a massive success, garnering seven Oscar nominations, including Dorothy Spencer's first **Oscar Nomination for Best Film Editing**. The film won Best Music and Best Supporting Actor. She would later collaborate with John Ford again on *My Darling Clementine*, which is still regarded as John Ford's best western.

In the 1940s, Spencer took on a solo editing role. It was then she first worked with director Alfred Hitchcock on *Foreign Correspondent* and *Lifeboat*. She then worked on four films with director Ernst Lubitsch, including his hit film *To Be or Not to Be*. In 1945 she edited *A Tree Grows in Brooklyn*, the feature film debut of legendary director Elia Kazan. As the 1950s rolled around, Spencer was quick to grab her **second Oscar Nomination** for *Decision Before Dawn*.

By the 1960s, Spencer had already worked on 60 films. Her experience and skill would come to a test with the 1963 version of *Cleopatra*. The film was the most expensive movie ever made, and the director's cut ran a whopping 320 minutes. When released in theaters, the film ran for just over 4 hours. Her work paid off, as Spencer received her **third Oscar Nomination**. She would continue editing an average of one film a year for the rest of her career. One of her final credits was the 1974 epic *Earthquake*. It was her seventh collaboration with director Mark Robson, which earned her a **fourth and final Oscar Nomination**. It was fitting that her last nomination reflected her first, a tremendous skill for editing action and suspense.

December 21st
15 Online Marketing Trends to Watch

Online marketing is no longer optional for brands who are serious about pushing their businesses forward. Digital marketing often feels like a moving target that's impossible to hit, yet despite the frequent guesswork, there are some clear trends that will be defining the industry in 2015. Whether you're a seasoned pro or a digital novice, these 15 key trends should be on your radar over the next year.

1. More User-Generated Content

If 2014 was the year "Content Is King" became a reality, 2015 will be all about sourcing content from the kingdom at large. The onus will always be on publishers to produce high-quality (and expensive) content, but brand followers are willing, and expecting, to contribute to the conversation. Whether you tap a small handful of ambassadors to create meaningful posts on a corporate blog or promote a branded hashtag that allows the public to share content on your site, take advantage of this engagement opportunity early and often.

2. Death of Free Social Reach

Over the course of the last 12 months, rumors of brands being slighted on social media whipped marketers into a frenzy. While some companies appear to be unscathed, retaining their organic reach, others are forced to increase their social ad spends. Whatever may, or may not, have happened in 2014, Facebook has confirmed that it will be cracking down on overly "promotional" posts from brands in its newsfeed.

3. Advancements in Social Advertising

With organic social reach potentially in peril, brands are increasing their social advertising efforts to maintain their presence. Luckily for advertisers, social ad platforms are also improving their offerings. In 2013, Facebook took on some of the ad-creation legwork for its advertisers. Over the next year, Facebook will continue to innovate on its ad platform with a stronger emphasis on auto play video ads.

Twitter is also rolling out new features that will allow advertisers to tailor ads based on mobile app data. New players to the social ad space, including Instagram and Snapchat, stand to gain the most ground in 2015 as they unlock access to rapidly growing audiences.

4. Make-or-Break Native Advertising

Few marketing trends stirred as much debate and controversy in 2014 as native advertising. Following this year's big splash, native ads will face their reckoning in 2015 and either rise to the occasion, or flounder into the archives. While the benefits and potential of native ads are obvious to marketers, they're also up against some stiff threats. Most notably, possible interference from the Federal Trade Commission could stop native advertising in its tracks if the industry doesn't self-regulate before a ruling comes down.

5. Mobile Optimization

2014 was the first time that mobile web traffic outnumbered desktop traffic, shattering any last doubts that smartphones and tablets are the go-to browsing device for most users. In the marketing sphere, this also cements the notion of mobile-first products, designed and produced for an optimal experience on smaller screens. However, with the lightening-fast release schedule for new devices, marketers (and developers for that matter) will behoove themselves to invest in a responsive design that won't render the website obsolete as soon as the next big thing comes out.

6. Focus on Content Marketing

BuzzFeed VP of Agency Strategy Jonathan Perelman was the first to coin the phrase, "Content is king, but distribution is queen, and she wears the pants." While some marketers still have their pants on backwards when it comes to content marketing, 2015 is a prime time to refocus efforts in this area. With so much quality being created by big brands, finding new, quality distribution methods will be the key to success. Most notably, brands (yes, even the small ones) will need to embrace paid content distribution to bolster the reach of their owned channels.

7. Intelligent Marketing Automation

Until recently, marketing automation was reserved for enterprise-size companies who could afford hefty software licensing fees and had substantial volumes of traffic. With rapid innovations in the space, new marketing automation vendors are offering similar features at prices that won't scare off small B2B companies. Over the next year, advancements in marketing-automation algorithms will become more complex, as software interfaces become more intuitive. Ultimately, this means greater performance for a greater number of marketers — big and small.

8. In-Store Mobile Campaigns

A 2013 study from the Google Shopper Marketing Agency Council and M/A/R/C Research revealed that 84% of smartphone owners use their phones while shopping in a physical store. Over the course of the last year, many retailers, including Macy's and Urban Outfitters, launched significant initiatives aimed at in-store mobile users. With advancements in beacon technology, the potential to create meaningful in-store experiences is ripe for the taking. In 2015, more marketers will start latching on to the idea of in-store mobile campaigns, taking advantage of the opportunity to use mobile as a sale-closer instead of a distraction.

9. Micro-Targeting

Traditionally, marketers have been tasked with developing programs that convert customers, and delivering those programs at-scale to a mass audience. However, with the rise in big data, 2015 will be all about segmenting those mass audiences down to the individual components and speaking to consumers using messaging that resonates. Micro-targeted campaigns can be implemented most easily across email and paid-content distribution channels, where access is controlled. Finding ways to replicate this intimate, targeted conversation on social and owned content channels will be the challenge facing marketers in the next year.

10. SEO Becomes Even Harder

It's been a good many years since SEO was "easy," and the challenge in gaining and maintaining online positioning will continue to be an uphill battle in 2015. Sites that aren't optimized for mobile in the upcoming year may face ranking hits across the board, and the cloud of link-building protocol (Should I guest post? Should I nofollow?) will become even murkier. With the end of the Google+ Authorship pilot, social signals from Facebook and Twitter are likely to carry even more ranking weight. The most significant move in 2015 will be the shift away from dedicated SEO resources (or outsourced firms) to broader marketing efforts that blend SEO with social media, content marketing, and more.

11. Increase in Video Production

Study after study has revealed that online videos are the key to driving brand awareness, audience engagement, and even purchases. 2015 will be the year that companies, beyond the big players, finally dedicate resources to integrate video into their ongoing marketing strategies. But while smaller brands are taking their first leap into video efforts, big brands will be advancing video usage, working video into their marketing automation, paid campaigns, and mobile promotions.

12. Actionable Analytics

The idea of "Big Data" has been floating around for some time now, but 2015 may be the first time that most marketers are able to actually harness the power of this data and put it to use. Early steps forward for most companies will include creating re-marketing and customized paid campaigns based on user data they've captured and analyzed. More sophisticated brands will begin merging their vast online data with offline data for the first time, presenting a 360-degree look at their customers' behavior.

13. Emphasis on A/B Testing

With all of the data available, it's simply silly for any marketer to make a decision based on intuition. Marketing winners in 2015 will be those who set out with a structured approach to A/B or multivariate testing, and are relentless in finding new ways to gain more traction from existing assets. The availability of A/B testing tools is making it easier and more accessible for marketers to tackle this work with minimal investment needed from design or development resources.

14. Wearable Technology

One of the hottest markets to be in right now is wearable tech: Internet-connected devices strapped to our arms, legs, and eyes. This space will continue to see explosive growth in 2015, and marketers who are ready to pounce on early promotion opportunities are poised for massive reach and impact.

15. Embracing the Top of the Funnel

With so much effort placed on closing sales, deals, and contracts, it's easy for marketers to forget that these decisions have an initiation point that occurred hours, weeks, or months earlier. While advancements in A/B testing and in-store mobile campaigns solidify the bottom of the funnel purchasing decision, and marketing automation pushes users through the middle of the funnel consideration phase, it's critical for marketers to optimize how the actual conversation begins. Attracting new audiences with the right messaging and content provides more fuel for a well-oiled marketing machine to churn into a hefty bottom line for your business.

December 22nd
Shooting Tips: How to Remove Glare From Reflective Objects

Hot spots. Accidental cameraman cameos. These are just a couple of the problems caused by shiny objects on set. Here are a few ways to remove the glare from reflective surfaces.

Reflective surfaces can be one of the biggest burdens to a DP, not only because of the possibility of reflections from the crew, but because a **highly reflective surface or object** can cause **hot spots**. A **hot spot** is a region of clipped whites which cannot, by most means, be recovered.

If a surface or object is spherical or curved, you have a higher chance of **clipping the highlights** within this object when it has been lit. Usually, objects with a chrome finish are the biggest offenders: Door handles, drawer knobs, chair/stool legs, metallic light switches, glasses, and so forth. I'm sure I don't need to list every metallic object you'll likely find within a scene.

In the still above, there's a **clipped hotspot on the chrome handle of the kettle**. In this particular instance, it's not all that detrimental to the shot, although it would be better without it. Yet, if this shot had an actor in the foreground talking to someone, and the **hot spot was glimmering in the background**, it would become an eyesore and distraction to the viewer. Before we start spraying objects or coating them with something to **kill the glare**, let's have a look at a few methods for stopping that reflective surface from bouncing so much light in the first place.

1. Cut the Light

We have recently discussed how you could stop light hitting parts of the set using a variety of different flags. If your composition has one particular **hot spot** which cannot be removed — perhaps a vertical stack of drawers has chrome knobs, and the 2k you have outside is kicking the highlights into overdrive — set up a **small vertical finger flag** between the light and the chrome object to kill that reflective light.
If established properly, the flag might just look like a window fixture. However, this isn't going to help when you have several reflective surfaces such as stools or chairs.

2. Soften the Light

In the circumstance of having several reflective non-removable objects, it is appropriate to look at possibly **changing your lighting source**. If you're lighting your scene with a set of **hard fresnels** that aren't being diffused or bounced, then your reflective surfaces will all have a glaring hotspot.
However, if you switch your lights to a **soft source** — or at least diffuse the hard light — the light reflected will be a shapeless highlight, which is a lot less intrusive than a glaring hotspot. There is, however, creative leeway for chrome objects.
A sun glint shining off a vintage car's chrome bumper is going to be off the charts by any scale of measurement. That's not a highlight worth preserving because chances are the camera that shot the scene recorded next to no discernible image data within that highlight. This is a highlight that you should have no problem sacrificing to the broadcast-safe clipper of your color correction application to lighten more important parts of the image.

But what about when (along with distinct reflective highlights) the **crew and camera also appear** within the reflections of shiny objects? This is where dulling spray will come into play.

3. Use Dulling Spray

A dulling spray is a spray that **applies a matte layer to a reflective surface** to stop the incident light hitting the reflective surface or element. You can purchase dulling spray in a variety of different colors and matte strengths. For example, you can acquire a semi-matte, which is perfect for **applying to wine glasses**, as it doesn't *entirely* remove the transparency, but it does **stop the glare** it would have if directly being lit by a light.

Two important notes for dulling spray. As with almost anything, there's always an option to buy a cheaper alternative, or perhaps purchase a spray which isn't dulling spray but may do the same job. Be wary — it's important to make sure the spray is free of chlorofluorocarbons, and that the spray is **easily removable** when dampened and wiped.

Dulling sprays are also ideal for hiding the reflection of crew members, especially if you're tracking toward an actor where there is a curved metallic object, such as a lamp — the closer you move in, the more exaggerated and apparent the reflection will be.

There's one manufacturer of dulling sprays called Dirty Down, who also produce spray used by costume and art departments to dirty and age materials. They say that, "Dulling spray can also be used to make a natural grime or dirt look and can be smudged with a damp sponge."

This leads me to this point. Sometimes it may be more suitable to **dirty an item** rather than just to remove its reflective glare. In the scene above, we required a close-up of an old kettle reaching boiling point and needed to capture the steam coming through the nozzle.

Unfortunately, **the camera was obviously visible within the reflection.** Using dulling spray so close to the kettle didn't work. It looked incredibly artificial. Nonetheless, we still had the problem of the camera in the reflection.

To get rid of this, we simply used the end of a candle to **slightly smudge the kettle**, which added to the grime which had already built up. In the final result, **the camera is not visible**.

There are countless options available for applying dulling spray and having more control over your image. In the video below from Grip Tips, Dave Donaldson runs through a variety of different sprays that can be used to **diffuse light bulbs** and **remove lens flares**.

December 23rd

Best Video Drones Under $1000

Here are some of the best drones that can capture amazing footage without breaking the bank.

From capturing over-the-head aerials, amazing dolly shots, or even some traditional camera moves, these **drones** offer great video options with prices that won't bust your budget. All of the **drones** on this list have a price tag **under $1000**.

DJI Mavic ($749 drone only, $999 with controller)

The DJI Mavic is the **newest drone** on this list. The Mavic was so popular on launch, there are currently shipping delays — but everything should arrive in time for the holidays, if you're looking to treat yourself. The **drone** is exciting because it collapses into a small and easy-to-carry mode. This is the first **true drone** for those shooters on the go. It can be controlled by a smart phone and hand gestures or with a dedicated controller. Here is a look at **DJI Mavic footage** from Bokeh DigitalRev TV

DJI Mavic Specs:
- Max flight time – **27 minutes**
- Max speed – **40 mph** (65 kph) in Sport mode
- Max distance – **8 miles** (13 km, 0 wind)
- Weight – **1.62 lbs** (734 g)
- Forward and downward vision systems
- Intelligent flight modes
- Camera
  - 1/2.3" CMOS sensor
  - FOV 78.8° 28 mm (35 mm format equivalent) f/2.2 lens
  - ISO 100-3200 (video)
  - Micro SD (max capacity of 64 GB)
- Video Recording Modes
  - **C4K:** 4096×2160 24fps
  - **4K:** 3840×2160 24/25/30fps

- **2.7K:** 2704×1520 24/25/30fps
- **FHD:** 1920×1080 24/25/30/48/50/60/96fps
- **HD:** 1280×720 24/25/30/48/50/60/120fps

GoPro Karma ($799 without camera, $999 with Hero4 Black)

The GoPro Karma is great for shooters that already have a **GoPro Hero4**, since they can save on the initial costs. The **drone** is also compatible with the new **Hero5** and **Hero5 Session**. It's built for athletes and travelers, coming with a backpack the also doubles as a mount. The camera gimbal is removable, so you can attach it to the included handheld stabilizer. **footage** from Brent Rose.

GoPro Karma Specs:
- Max flight time ~ **20 minutes**
- Max speed – **35 mph**
- Max distance – **1.86 miles** (3 km)
- Weight – **2.22 lbs** (1006 g)
- Auto shot paths
- Camera
  - Requires GoPro Hero4, GoPro Hero5, or GoPro Hero5 Session
- Removable gimbal
- Handheld stabilizer
- Backpack case with stabilizer attachment

Yuneec Typhoon 4K ($697, $899 with SteadyGrip)

If the appeal of GoPro's Karma system is the included handheld stabilizer, consider the Yuneec Typhoon 4K. The **drone** has a package that includes a SteadyGrip that works with the **drone's** built-in camera and gimbal. Even with the camera, the Typhoon comes in cheaper than buying a GoPro Karma and Hero4 bundle.

Here's is a look at some **Yuneec Typhoon 4K** sample footage from Digital Trends.

Yuneec Typhoon 4K Specs:
- Max flight time ~ **25 minutes**
- Max speed – **17.9 mph** (8m/s)
- Max distance – **0.5 miles** (800m)
- Weight – **3.74 lbs** (1700 g)
- Smart flight modes
- Camera
  - 1/2.3" CMOS sensor
  - Micro SD (up to 128 GB)
- Video Recording Modes
  - **UHD 4K** at 30fps
  - **2.7K** at 30fps
  - **2.5K** at 30fps
  - **1080p** at 24/25/30/48/50/60/120fps
- Removable gimbal
- Handheld stabilizer

DJI Phantom 3 ($499 Standard, $799 Advanced, $999 Professional)

Just because the Phantom 4 ($1199) is out doesn't mean the DJI Phantom 3 is outdated by any means. From the 2.7K capabilities of the Standard, to the 4K capture of the Professional — the Phantom 3 line is bound to have everything you need.

December 24th
Favorite Focal Lengths of Famous Directors

From Orson Welles to Ridley Scott, great filmmakers have developed signature styles that we know and recognize. Let's look at the favorite focal lengths of famous directors and how they made them their own.

Disclaimer: We acknowledge that all film directors use a wide variety of lenses and focal lengths in their films and throughout their careers. We are merely looking more in-depth at the focal lengths which may pop up time and time again in famous shots and films which we relate to famous directors' legacies. Enjoy!

When creating a film, the director is usually considered the one person with the **vision to tell the story**. All parts of production feed off the director in concert to bring that vision to life. One of the many, many decisions that a director must make going into each and every shot is on the **focal length**. If you look back through the cinematic histories of some of the most famous directors, you can uncover **patterns and rules** to how these directors have made systematic use of **different focal lengths to elicit different feelings**, themes and motifs to tell their story. Sareesh Sudhakaran at Wolfcrow.com put together a comprehensive breakdown of how **nineteen famous director**s have used specific **focal lengths in their films** and which ones are most representative of their work.

Orson Welles: 18mm and 25mm

Orson Welles in Touch of Evil via Universal

Orson Welles, like many directors of his era, mostly shot scenes with **wide focal lengths** and little movement. Instead, the characters moved within the frames between the composed fore and backgrounds. Sudhakaran points out that the **two prominent focal lengths** Welles used in his most famous films were **18mm** (*Touch of Evil*) and **25mm** (*Citizen Kane*). The wideness, while not too wide, allowed Welles to "get that **deep focus and majestic blocking** over long takes." Other directors who often favored wide angles like 18mm and 25mm were Jean-Pierre Jeunet in *Delicatessen* and Roman Polanski in *Rosemary's Baby*.

Steven Spielberg: 21mm

According to Sudhakaran, "Spielberg reportedly sees the world through 21mm," which can be traced throughout his **vast filmography**. The Oscar-award-winning director makes heavy use of his **preferred wide angle lens,** letting the characters of his films move throughout their frames. His style is **similar to Orson Welles**, Sudhakaran argues, as he uses blocking within his shots better than anyone.

Other directors who make predominant use of the **21mm wide angle** are Tim Burton and Martin Scorsese.

The Coen Brothers: 27mm

The Coen Brothers join the long line of filmmakers who **prefer the wide-angle approach.** Although they vary film to film, Sudhakaran makes the case that **27mm is their true favorite focal length**. Sudhakaran points out that David Fincher, like the Coen Brothers, is another director who **varies his lenses** but makes the most use of the **27mm.**
Directors like Wes Anderson have made heavy use of **wide lenses like the 27mm** but in a different format. Wes Anderson likes to use anamorphic lenses, which, while wider, creates the same **compression as a non-anamorphic lens.**

Alfred Hitchcock: 50mm

Ever the perfectionist, Alfred Hitchcock preferred the **50mm for the majority of his films,** as it was the closest to the **"natural field of view"** according to Sudhakaran. He even went as far as to have his film sets built to best accommodate the framing he would need for the **50mm field of view.**
Famous **international filmmakers** like Robert Bresson and Yasujiro Ozu also **preferred the 50mm** and would make adjustments to their sets to accommodate the lens.

Ridley Scott: 75mm+ Ridley Scott is one of the rare directors who **prefers to use long lenses.** For 1979's *Alien,* he used **anamorphic 75mm and above.** Sudhakaran also notes Scott's affection for using **zoom lenses and shooting spherical and cropped for widescreen**. His shots are well-composed but **lose some of the depth** that accompanies wide focal length shots.

Sudhakaran points out that **one of the most famous directors** in film history, Akira Kurosawa, is often believed to have used **long zoom lenses** as well, but actually worked mostly in the **35mm to 50mm range**. Only occasionally would Kurosawa use **telephoto for its extreme compression**.

If you're interested, Sudhakaran has charted **the preferred focal lengths of nineteen of his favorite directors** which you can view below. You can also watch his **video on the subject** to get the full experience.

December 25th
How to Frame a Long Shot Like a Master Cinematographer

Learn how to frame a Long Shot the Conrad L. Hall way. Break down the work of a ten-time Oscar nominee by learning the difference between a Long Shot and Extreme Long Shot.

Conrad L. Hall, ASC is a **ten-time nominee for the Best Cinematography Academy Award**, winning three times for *Butch Cassidy and the Sundance Kid*, *American Beauty*, and posthumously for *Road to Perdition* — also winning three **Best Cinematography BAFTA awards** for the same films. He earned four **Outstanding Achievement in Cinematography in Theatrical Releases** from the American Society of Cinematographers, who also honored him with an ASC **Lifetime Achievement Award**.

The long shot (not to be confused with a long take) is the widest of all the standard camera shots. They are often used as establishing shots to **set up the context and space of a scene**. The long shot is **also called a full shot or a wide shot**.

Long Shot (AKA: Wide Shot, Full Shot)

Long shots often **show the scale, distance, and location of a scene.** They don't always feature characters, but if they do — the **subjects traditionally should be framed from head to toe.** That is a rule that Conrad L Hall frequently breaks, which is why he is the focus of this breakdown.

People think you're a genius for planning something like that, when in reality you were just smart enough to notice it and exploit it. — Conrad L Hall, ASC

Robert Richardson's wide shots, many of his characters were portrayed as heroes standing tall in frame. In Conrad L. Hall's long shots, we often find that **many of the characters featured are either broken down emotionally or are overwhelmed by their situation.** That means the way the shots are framed are completely different, as Hall often uses empty space to make his subjects feel smaller.

Take the above example from *American Beauty*, in which Lester Burnham (played by Kevin Spacey) sits slump-shouldered in the middle of a boring room. If he was standing, he'd have a much larger presence in the frame — yet the purpose of this long shot is to make him feel insignificant.

I chose this frame for several reasons. It's possibly one of the most "Conrad Hall" examples to further explain the DP's style. When Hall uses long shots, **we often find that characters are seated.** Another **one of his trademarks is cutting off the feet of the subject.** He often frames from just above the ankles — whether the character is seated or standing. Also, note the door in the corner. Conrad L Hall **uses doors and door frames** to either add value to another characters entrance, or as a frame within a frame.

Long Shot: Frame Within a Frame

Conrad Hall's long shots tend to **focus more on individual characters**, rather than the location itself. He uses locations and sets to **draw attention to a character's emotional state**, often framing his characters within a door frame. Below you can see Michael Sullivan (played by Tom Hanks) in *Road to Perdition* standing at the foot of his bed.

Sullivan is perfectly framed between the door frame and the door itself. There are also **leading lines** all over this shot. Leading lines are the **subliminal lines and paths that point a viewer's**

eyes towards a subject. It's a cinematography tool that gets the audience to look where you want them to. In this shot, notice on the trim on the walls direct your eyes towards the door frame, and the lines on the open door direct you right towards the main character. There is even the much more direct leading line of the bed post pointing directly at Hank's head.
It's a great shot, and one of many from *Road to Perdition* I will reference — which truly is one of my favorite films of all time. Not only is the cinematography top notch, but the film on the whole is just tremendous.

Another great example of a **long shot frame within a frame** is this one Hall shot for *In Cold Blood*. Once again leading lines direct you straight to the character in the door frame. The film is an adaptation of the Truman Capote true-crime novel, and this shot brings the entire eerie story to life.

Here is another **well-composed long shot** from *Marathon Man*. Multiple frames balance the character in the center. You have the main vault doorway center, with a balanced frame of the door on the left and a trash can on the right. Then behind we have another rectangular door frame with bars, then *another* frame in the metallic circle. Beautiful.
While Conrad Hall does frequently use doors to create a frame within a frame (or a frame within a frame within a frame within a frame), the concept can be created in a variety of other ways. Another one of my favorites from *Road to Perdition* is this interrogation scene below. We see two characters in a warehouse **framed by the silhouette of Michael Sullivan's legs**. It's a voyeuristic view, as Sullivan's son is peeking in on the scene. With the frame drawing our direction center, and with the overhead light pointing straight down onto the interrogation, we can't help but be captivated by the conversation.

Here's a great frame within a frame from *Cool Hand Luke*. **Is this a long shot, or a close-up?** Well it's a close-up, but it's also a frame within a frame reflection of a long shot. It's a really unique way to frame the prisoners.
Beauty comes from contrast. I love contrast, either the lack of it or the abundance of it. – Conrad L Hall

Long Shot: Conversations

Long shots are great for capturing conversations. Most long shots tend to be intercut with two medium shots or two close-ups of each character speaking. **Hall uses them to put the audience in the location.** The above silhouette is a play on the title *Tequila Sunrise*, where Mel Gibson and Kurt Russell sit on a swing set.

They are **beautifully framed within the A-frame of the swing set**, but you should also note how their silhouettes are also framed by the mountains and water. It adds an epic scale to the space, while also using some stellar background lighting from the sun.

The cinematographer was frequently asked how many nights he needed to get the shot just right; he revealed that he shot the sequence like a commercial, using a portable swing set that could be moved so that the setting sun was always in the ideal spot. "Contrast is what makes photography interesting," he maintained, "and there is more than one way to create it. I used all of those techniques on Tequila Sunrise." – American Cinematographer

You'll quickly realize that Hall often has characters seated in long shots. In another example, here is a look at two young chess players competing in the Conrad Hall-lensed film *Searching for Bobby Fischer*. The added headroom may seem a bit excessive, but were the characters adults — this would seem like a traditional shot. The emphasis is on the youth of the characters. Also, once again notice all the leading lines. The table legs stand **center frame pointing straight up** to the chess game, and an added emphasis comes from the arms of the chairs.

Another note worth taking is the **close proximity of characters sharing the screen**. Whether he has two characters talking in the scene, or dozens sitting around — Hall is not afraid of stacking people on top of each other. In *Butch Cassidy and the Sundance Kid*, you will often see the titular characters attached at the hip. They are never too far removed from each other.

Long Shot: Character Entrances

When it comes to bringing other characters into a scene, Conrad Hall will often have **a well-lit door** on stand-by. Above, you'll see a double frame within a frame, as the **doorway on the right frames Michael Sullivan Jr** awaiting the return of his father. Once the elder Michael returns, he is perfectly **framed by the hallway on the left**. Also note that he leaves the door open, and **a nice light spills into the scene**.

Hall has done a similar setup in *American Beauty*. This long shot places **two characters well off to the right side of frame**, with a single door **balancing the composition** on the left. There is **a beautiful contrast in the scene once the door opens** and a tungsten light dominates the color spectrum. The door itself also adds a beautiful leading line shadow to the characters on the right.

Now this shot is borderline **between an extreme long shot and long shot**, but for the sake of this article we'll call it a long shot — as the character will walk into frame. Like before, notice the frame within a frame using the bridge supports, and all of the leading lines directing you center frame. This is our first introduction to Jude Law's character Maguire, an oddball photographer obsessed with death. His presence is unsettling, and through his entrance on screen — the audience is already made uneasy by the way he walks into the scene.

Long Shot: Multiple Characters

Conrad L Hall is also a master of **framing multiple characters in a long shot at once**. Perhaps the culmination of everything he learned over the years was the shootout in *Road to Perdition*. I could write an entire piece just breaking down this one scene. We see **six silhouettes majestically lit in the pouring rain**. The street curbs perfectly frame the action, and the street lamps in the rear add some depth and definition to the end of the street. This image might be the most iconic shot from the film, and one of the most remembered of Conrad Hall's career.

It's certainly a long shot he has had experience with, here's another silhouette dating back to his work on *In Cold Blood*, this one featuring five silhouettes walking through the prison yard. A **strong light source adds some stunning shadows to the characters** as they walk, lining up nicely with the **leading lines in the bleachers**.

Extreme Long Shot: Establishing Locations

When long shots are used from a farther distance, or when the characters are much more minuscule in size — the framing is referred to as an **extreme long shot**. These are used **almost exclusively as establishing shots, transitions, and finales.**

Above you'll see an extreme long shot from *Butch Cassidy and the Sundance Kid*, where we see the heroes (still joined at the hip) riding right down the **center of the frame**. You attention is **immediately drawn to the signature mountain shot** from western films, as the landscape itself is practically its own character.

In a similar fashion, below you will see another extreme long shot — this one from *In Cold Blood*. Once again the **mountains play a huge role in establishing the scene**. The characters are once again **side by side**, framed by the two railroad crossing signs. There is the added beauty of the railroad tracks cutting through the pavement and then turning directly towards the mountain range.

Now that you have a glimpse at the amazing work of Conrad L Hall, and a better understanding of framing long shots — like me, you can now stare off into the vast void and question how you could ever compare to such greatness.

Filmmaking is about finding things out, it's about examining, it's about discovering. You should approach your work in the same way that a child discovers new aspects of the world. I draw inspiration from absolutely everything around me, and what I observe from life. When you get to be a visual storyteller, you learn to watch how people behave and to see things – to study the light, to watch a field as you're driving by it in a car. It's like making movies 24 hours a day.
– *Conrad L Hall, ASC*

December 26th
2 Ways to Add Digital Distortion to Your Video Projects

Get glitchy with your next project with these digital distortion video packs from around the web.

Whether you're going for a *Mr. Robot* feel or a *Black Mirror* vibe, tweaking your project out with **digital distortion** is a goal well within reach, thanks to these video element packs. Featuring overlays, tutorials, backgrounds, and more, these assets are the key to retro-cool effects.

1. Red Giant

Price: Free

Red Giant's stacked collection of distortion tutorials is priceless. They're **fast, free, and invaluable for building your arsenal of skills**. Even though you have to create the effects from scratch, the **customization aspect** can't be beat.

2. DOD MEDIA Featuring Twitch

Price: $45

This route does require you to pick up Twitch from Video Copilot, but it's a great resource to have at your disposal. The tutorial is just under twenty minutes, and it covers everything you need to know to apply a **basic video glitch effect.**

December 27th
Cinematographers Who Establish an Instantly Recognizable Look

Follow in the footsteps of today's top cinematographers by creating and maintaining your own unique vision.

When you think of your favorite working **filmmakers,** be they **directors** or **cinematographers,** what's the first aspect of their work that comes to mind? A specific scene in one of their films? The music from their films? Maybe the feeling you had when watching their work for the first time?

One thing **masterful filmmakers** have is the ability to **create a believable world**, one that invites audiences in while telling an enthralling story worth revisiting. Directors often have cinematographers they prefer to collaborate with — think the Coen Brothers and Roger Deakins. Christopher Nolan and Wally Pfister. Paul Thomas Anderson and Robert Elswit.

Some pretty amazing things can happen when a **director** and **cinematographer** click. In my opinion, a film and a film's director are only as good as the **director of photography** working on the film.

Some cinematographers have an **instantly recognizable look** for each of their films. Some focus on character before atmosphere and vise versa, but every cinematographer sees the world in a different way and they allow us to step into their head for a few hours.

Let's take a look at some working DPs who excel at **establishing their look** with each new film they shoot.

Hoyte Van Hoytema

Most notable for his work on *Interstellar*, **Hoyte Van Hoytema** has achieved mainstream success in the past few years. With recent credits like *Spectre, Her,* and *Tinker Tailor Soldier Spy*, Hoytema made a name for himself shooting *Let the Right One In*. With David O'Russell taking notice soon after, he enlisted the young cinematographer for *The Fighter*.

He doesn't overexpose character faces like most cinematographers; his backgrounds are almost always the same light levels as their faces. As for **focal lengths**, his favorite for close-ups and mid-shots is **35mm**, which, if you were shooting on a DSLR, would be a **50mm lens**. He often shoots very wide with a **shallow depth of field**. This technique (plus minimal backlighting) isolates his characters from their surroundings, calling attention to emotion and action rather than the background. Watch out for Hoytema's upcoming work on next year's *Dunkirk*.

Roger Deakins

Working behind the lens since the late 1970s, **Roger Deakins** has established himself as one of the **greatest cinematographers of all time**. With thirteen Oscar nominations under his belt, he shows no sign of slowing down anytime soon. Deakins has proven to audiences to be a dependable artist and a top tier DP, a trend likely to continue with the upcoming *Blade Runner* sequel.

As seen in the still above, Deakins **overexposes** the lit side of his subject's face by a few stops. Unlike **Hoytema**, a trademark of his is to have the background lit oppositely of the talent, giving spacial separation while remaining in close proximity. Employing lighting in unheard of ways, Deakins finds endlessly inventive ways to light his subjects and fill the frame with **visually arresting** images.

For **exterior shots**, Deakins often makes sure to keep the subjects as the focus of the frame while wowing us with expansive backdrops. Some of his best work in this department was on last years excellent *Sicario*. He's expressed his deep love for **shooting digital** and his favorite lenses are **ARRI master primes** on an ALEXA body. Roger Deakins' own website is a reliable source of information, providing insight into his past and current projects. The forums cover areas like lighting, cameras, and post-production. He even responds to questions posted on the site, so it's definitely worth a visit.

Reed Morano

Over the past few years, **Reed Morano** has evolved into a force to be reckoned with. Working as a full-on director as well as DP, her projects are those of passion and depth. Working with Martin Scorsese on the recent HBO show Vinyl, her style is **warm and intimate,** as she prefers a shallow depth of field.

Though *Vinyl* had Morano working with cranes, dollies, etc., she prefers to shoot handheld, giving her films a sense of intimacy. That intimacy is apparent in her 2015 directorial debut (in which she also served as DP) *Meadowland*, where Morano puts the viewer right in the actors' faces, allowing us to feel like we're there in that moment in time with the main characters.

When you're handheld, it's the least restricted way. If you move a few steps in one direction, then an amazing flare could happen or you catch the right look from an actor from a not so typical angle. You can emotionally enable the audience and bring them deeper into the story and perspective of the characters — Reed Morano

Robert Richardson

Another frequent Scorsese collaborator, Robert Richardson's work is most often associated Quentin Tarantinos. Richardson makes use of **hot backlighting** for his characters. This strong backlight allows a soft light to be bounced onto the front of the characters' faces. His consistent collaboration with heavyweight directors has afforded him the comfort and trust to experiment and test the reaches of his craft. His most recent daring endeavor, *The Hateful Eight*, brought back shooting Ultra Panavision 70mm earning him an Oscar nomination.

With each film containing a new and expansive canvas, the DP specializes in **shooting on film,** giving his pictures an aged, timeless feel. Crafting beautiful wide shots like nobody else in the field, Richardson continues to put his skills to full effect with each new daunting project he takes on.

Bradford Young

In high demand after his stellar work on Ava DuVernay's *Selma* and JC Chandor's *A Most Violent Year*, Young's next hit, *Arrival,* will be landing in theaters soon. Compared to others on this list, Young is just kicking his career off — but he's already showing a consistently strong visual palette. One of his first projects — *Pariah* — garnered much praise and got him noticed by some big leaguers like **DuVernay** and David Lowery.

By positioning his characters towards the edge of the frame, Young gives his projects a sense of scope and a classic feel. While shooting digitally to portray New York in the 80s and Alabama in the 60s, Young found a way to give the images a **lived-in feel** that the stories needed. A prominent theme in his work is **underexposed images**. This preferred method of choice gives his work a distinct feeling, and the subject matter he chooses to take on and the **spacial awareness** combined with the **dimly lit characters** establishes Young's vision as unique.

Robert Elswit

His crowning achievement to date, *There Will Be Blood*, won him the oscar for Cinematography in 2007 and things are only going up for Elswit. His work is an inspiration for anybody interested in long, wide camera work that paints a picture with each frame.
For his frequent collaborations with **Paul Thomas Anderson**, Elswit shoots with film using anamorphic lenses. This move has produced some of the best looking movies to date. Elswit shoots his subject with 3/4 top light just in between soft and hard, while keeping the key side **overexposed**.

Having recently worked on *Nightcrawler* and *The Night Of* using the ALEXA, Elswit has expressed warm feelings for shooting digitally, especially at night. This is a big shift from his usual work method of shooting only on film.
ALEXA was a great way to go because it's a little faster. The exposure index is twice as high as the fastest Kodak film stock, and you can get away with murder. By shooting in places that had a lot of street and business lighting, I didn't have to light backgrounds. — Robert Elswit

Benoit Debie

Working with **rich colors** and **abstract landscapes**, nobody makes images pop on screen like Benoit Debie. Working with Directors like Gaspar Noe, Wim Wenders, and Harmony Korine, Debie often lights the sides of characters and experiments with **offbeat gels**. **Colors are pushed to the limits** as his traditionalist style and methods blend perfectly with the weird subject tones of his films. Having just completed his next film with Wim Wenders, Debie is an excellent addition to your watchlist. Side note: He only shoots on film, making his technique and work that much more difficult.

When you shoot, you think in visual terms of light, contrast, and color. And then as the editing is getting closer to the end, you see things getting better together. Sometimes you can change your mind about color or contrast. You might have a very *sad* or *intense* sequence, and after you see it, it may seem too *bright*. Then, as you see an almost-finished movie, you might decide to change the intensity of the light, or make the colors deeper. It might not be a big change, but I would sometimes change a sequence when I feel that it will make the movie better. — Benoit Debie

Emmanuel Lubezki

An obvious inclusion to this list is three-time Oscar winner Emmanuel Lubezki. Collaborating with prolific directors such as **Terrence Malick**, Alfonso Cuaron, and Alejandro G. Innaritu, Lubezki is the most **unpredictable** and **groundbreaking** artist working right now. Crafting long-takes with sweeping camera motions, working with natural and artificial light, no matter what the subject is, Lubezki seems to find a way to blow your mind and plug you into the world right from the first frame (see *Gravity*).

Working exclusively with digital now, Lubezki's experimental endeavors with the ARRI 65 broke new grounds on what lighting and camerawork mean for productions. The subjects are close and unavoidable in front of his lens, establishing a brand just from a single frame. His past three Oscar-winning films couldn't be more different in tone and subject, but they still have the feel of Lubezki — alive and profound.

Establishing Your Own Look

Even though these big time cinematographers have (occasionally) unlimited resources, they've made a name for themselves by having a good reputation with **producers**, **directors**, and anyone they came into contact with along the way. They know **visuals** and **aesthetics** as they apply for the story and find a way to put themselves in the work. This recognition and appreciation for the craft has gotten them a long way.

Whether you like the films or not, a cinematographer's work should always be deconstructed for intricacies and the care that has gone into the process. As long as you remain consistent/persistent with your work and strive to do better, people will notice and spread the word.

This doesn't just apply for films as well — **commercial, corporate, music videos**, and **video production** in general requires a dedication unlike any other. A podcast I've recently started listening to is Cinematography Database with Matt Workman. Talking to real DPs working in the industry, **Cinematography Database** is not only motivational but super informative, providing excellent advice and insight into how the industry works and why establishing your own brand is important.

Episode Recommendation: Ryan Booth on Career, Life & Instagram

For more in-depth looks into the minds of cinematographers, Wolfcrow has an outstanding YouTube series that focuses on individual DPs and what makes their work great. A few other cinematographers with masterful style to check out are: Natasha Braier, Jeff Cronenweth, Wally Pfister, Janusz Kaminski, Robert D. Yeoman, and Benoit Delhomme.

December 28th
The Influence of Paintings on Filmmakers

See the art of painting and the art of filmmaking meet in beautifully composed shots.

Top image: The Blue Boy via Wikipedia and Django Unchained via Columbia Pictures

Artists have always **influenced** other artists, and many artists steal from each other. Whether it's the influence of legendary painters on filmmakers, or a single painting helping a writer tell their story, there are countless examples of **filmmakers finding inspiration in other works**.

Here are a few examples of paintings being recreated in films (and paintings showing up in films) to get your creative juices flowing.

Paintings Recreated in Film

To see the influence paintings have had on filmmakers, start with the great **video essay series *Film Meets Art*** by Vugar Efendi.
In this first video, you will see how **paintings come to life in film** — as artwork like the *Birth of Venus* by Sandro Botticelli was recreated in the film *The Adventures of Baron Munchausen* by Terry Gilliam. Other inspirations include Thomas Gainsborough's *The Blue Boy* in the Quentin Tarantino western *Django Unchained,* and Edward Hopper's *House by the Railroad* being built as Mother's home in Alfred Hitchcock's *Psycho.*
The second installment has even more stunning recreations — including the actual recreation of Jean-Auguste-Dominique Ingres' *La petite baigneuse, dit aussi Intérieur de harem* in Jean-Luc Godard's *Passion.* You will also see the classic *Freedom from Fear* by Norman Rockwell in Steven Spielberg's *Empire of the Sun,* and Jacques-Louis David's *La Mort de Marat* in Alexander Payne's *About Schmidt.*

Paintings in Film

From characters visiting museums, famous works of art hanging in a protagonist's home, to subtle storytelling cues — paintings have appeared in many different ways.

The James Bond epic *Skyfall* used the famous British painting *The Fighting Temeraire* by J.M.W. Turner as a talking point, as Q asked Bond about his interpretation of the piece.
Q*: It always makes me feel a little melancholy. Grand old war ship, being ignominiously hauled away to scrap... The inevitability of time, don't you think? What do you see?*
James Bond*: A bloody big ship.*
This particular question was a **meta reference** to the aging James Bond franchise, and whether or not a fun-loving spy from the 60s had any place in this current generation.

Skyfall certainly wasn't the first James Bond film to use paintings to influence the story, as the very first Bond film, *Dr. No,* featured Francisco Goya's *Portrait of The Duke of Wellington.* That **painting was famously stolen** from the National Gallery in London on August 2nd 1961. A replica of the painting was used in the 1962 film, hanging in Dr. No's lair — suggesting he was the one who stole it.

Those two examples alone show **how drastically paintings can be used** in completely different manners. For more examples, I highly recommend diving through the archive of Paintings in Movies. The website is full of film stills with paintings — which you can sort through by styles of art (like **impressionism** or **surrealism**), as well as sorting by **colors**, **artists**, and topics like **landscapes** or **portraits**.

Paintings and **art theory** certainly have plenty to offer **filmmakers**. For more inspiration, be sure to take a look at the basics of color theory, applying a film's color palette to your own projects, and even turning your films into moving paintings.

December 29th
The Art of Lens Whacking

Lens whacking can elevate your shot in seemingly magical ways, from adding light leaks to creating a vintage look. Here's everything you need to know about the technique.

Lens whacking. It sounds like something that will cost you a night in jail. However, it is indeed a very creative use of the camera and lens which can help produce a gorgeous in-camera effect which can never be replicated as organic in post.

What Is Lens Whacking?
All images are captured after the light has passed **through the lens** and hit the sensor (or film). The light passes through many elements within the lens that have been engineered in a very specific way. A **20mm** has different elements than an **85mm**. Nonetheless, the light passes through in an orderly fashion.

Lens whacking is where you **remove the lens** and physically hold it in front of the sensor. Light then passes through both the lens and the gap between the lens and the camera body. This essentially causes a **light leak**.

As you are partially pushing one part of the lens forward to let in the light, it also will cause a section of the image to fall out of focus, and, to some extent, produce a slight **tilt-shift** effect.

This is entirely done by hand, and as a result of this, no two takes are going to look remotely the same — it's wildly unpredictable, and as a result, it's **great fun.**

How To Do It

The **lens choice** is the first important step to undertake. **Lens whacking** a 200mm, well, it's not going to happen. Not successfully, anyway. Lenses that have a short focal length are ideal for **lens whacking,** as you want the focus window to be as wide as possible. If you were to use a lens such as an 85mm, you might find yourself trying to find the subject in the viewfinder more than **perfecting the light leak.** Older lenses with manual aperture and focus are preferred, as it can be quite a pain to have to keep reconnecting your lens to the camera if you wish to change the aperture.

You want to set your lens to have the **smallest aperture** available to you. Again, this is to stop the extremity of your subject falling too much out of focus.

Set up your framing, start recording, and then **remove the lens from the camera.** You only want your lens to be detached from the camera like the **cover image above.** If you open the gap *too much,* you'll flood the sensor with light and wash out the image. (Although, that in itself can work very well for a creative transition.) The best method for lens whacking is not to keep the lens fully removed from the camera at all times, but to bring it **in and out** every so often. The shot can become very distracting if there's a constant light-leak focus-loss throughout the entire shot.

For the best results, try removing your lens to the side where light is hitting the camera. You'll have a much more powerful flare. Alternatively, if you find that the **light leak** is too strong, **place a finger over the gap** you've created. The light will still find its way to the sensor, but your finger will **diffuse** most of it, creating a **softer light leak.**

Many **lens whacking** examples often have the camera free in the hands of the operator, which in most cases, causes shaky footage. I would recommend locking the camera down onto a tripod for a smoother shot. You can then delegate panning/tilting to another person while you take the sole focus of the **lens whacking.**

If needed, you can also take **lens whacking** to the extreme, and cause mass blur and washout. Just remove both sides of the lens away from the body. I recently used this method to put emphasis on how dazed and confused a character was. He's awoken after watching himself die, enough to cause confusion to anyone, I would imagine. The character is going to be in a state of confusion, and he's not going to understand why he is alive. To emphasize this, I removed the lens **quite far away** to completely **wash out** the image at points to add to his hysteria while he was coming around.

Why Do It?

The most important aspect of any **filmmaking** choice is asking, "Will this further the story?" Or, "Will this enhance the emotional impact?"

If the answer is **no,** then at most times it's probably best to ditch that idea. While **lens whacking** is extremely popular with music and fashion videos, it's also ideal for many creative storytelling elements. Here's a small list of scenarios where you can creatively implement the technique.

- The character has been poisoned.
- The character is under the influence of drugs.
- The character is disoriented.
- The character is dying.
- A dream sequence.
- A scene involving magic.
- A flashback.

The list is almost endless; I'm sure there are many other creative applications to **lens whacking** that haven't even crossed my mind. In the still below from *Killing Them Softly* by Andrew Dominik, the character is under the influence of drugs, and **lens whacking** (along with several other in-camera effects) has been applied to help portray his state. There are some considerations to take into account. This effect is, of course, in camera, and there's no removing or "fixing" it if you change your mind later on. Test and practice the effect within your free time. If you have an important job coming up and think the **lens whack effect** may look great on a few shots, but you're not 100% confident, have a look at a few digital elements you can use to help mimic the effect in post.

December 30th
How To Create Realistic Old VHS Footage

Here's how to use After Effects to capture the distorted retro vibes of authentic VHS footage.

There's always been an affinity for the old, for the **retro,** for the look of yesterday. While technology pushes forward and picture quality is increasingly improved, we often see companies offering services and tools to make that incredibly sharp image look, well, less sharp. You can acquire film grain, light leaks, film burns, color washes, interference layers, static noise, and so forth. The list goes on.
As we move forward toward the end of the 2010s, the **VHS/camcorder look of the 80s and 90s** is starting to become a lost relic of time. I bet that made some of you feel old, right? You can download all kinds of templates and plugins to make your footage look like the **VHS tape** has distorted it, but nothing beats using the real source material.
A lot of people tend just to throw an **overlay** onto their footage and call it a day, but there are a few **fundamental elements** that also need to be included.

After looking at the **amateur VHS footage** above, it's important to note that while there is some visible **VHS interference** in the shape of **white lines** running across the screen, the prime characteristic is the **skewed distortion** of the footage itself.
To some extent, **it wobbles like jelly.** The displacement of the picture itself is often missed and is key in making footage look like it's come from an old **VHS tape.**
How to Give Your Footage an Authentic VHS Look in After Effects
Many kind people on the internet have uploaded real captured **VHS** noise. I like to use these two, which are both free to download: Heavy VHS interference, and Light VHS Bad Tracking.

Step 1: Get Your Distortion

When you've downloaded them, rename the first file **Heavy VHS** and the second file **Light VHS**, as their interference difference is very apparent. When you've acquired your noise, open up **After Effects** and **create a new composition** based on your footage size. If the **VHS footage** is smaller, just **increase the scale**.

Import your footage and the two VHS layers into After Effects and place them within the composition in the following order.

1. Light VHS
2. Footage
3. Heavy VHS

Then change the blend mode of Layer 1 to **Add**. Your sequence should now look something like this:

You have the classic **VHS** stripes running across the footage, but it still doesn't look very convincing. Don't worry... It will soon.

Step 2: Displacement Map

In the Effects panel, type in **Displacement Map** and drag that onto your actual footage layer. You may need to realign your footage and increase the scale to 105%, so it fills the entire composition.

In the Effects control panel, set the following settings.

- Displacement Map Layer: 3. Heavy Noise
- Use for Horizontal Displacement: Luminance
- Max Horizontal Displacement: 20
- Use for Vertical Displacement: Luminance
- Max Vertical Displacement: 20

You can increase the **displacement values** by increasing the numerical values. Or decrease the **VHS glitching** by lowering those values. This is the result of using the **Displacement Map**. You can see in the image above that the shot now looks a lot more like it's part of the **VHS footage**. However, it's still too sharp. Therefore, insert an **Adjustment Layer** and add a **Gaussian Blur** of **7.5**.

Step 3: Color Fringe

There's one final step to take. The **VHS format** ages poorly, and if the footage has been passed from camcorder to VHS, you can expect some **color fringing** — not much, but some. To do this:

- Duplicate your video footage three times
- Add the Set Channels effect to each layer
- On the first footage layer, **Set Red to Source 1's: Red**
- On the second footage layer, **Set Green to Source 2's: Green**
- On the third footage layer, **Set Blue to Source 3's: Blue**

Your **Set Channels** should look something like this:

Your footage will likely look like it's just come from a Tarantino scene in *Kill Bill*. To fix this, set the blend mode for the first two footage layers to **Screen**. To get the **color fringing,** you need to slightly offset the two layers.

Do this by rotating the first layer by 0.7 (**R** on the Keyboard), and move the second layer over to the right with one nudge of the **right arrow** on the keyboard. **This will give you a very subtle color fringe.**

December 31st
The 7 Best Films About Filmmaking

Skip film school and watch these seven films about the art of filmmaking. They're entertaining, educational, and essential.

If you're interested in becoming a **filmmaker,** you've got to surround yourself with the culture. You've got to create. You've got to spend time on set. You can also watch how other filmmakers do their job. These seven movies are perfect for that. Let's explore **how filmmakers making films about filmmaking** can teach you how to **make your own films.**

1. **Man With a Movie Camera (1929)**

What to Watch For: Basics of cinematography and the beginning of self-aware filmmaking. The original **film-within-a-film film**, this Russian classic is a film-school textbook staple for its **montage and mise en scène innovations** in the late 1920s.

Filmed over a three year period, the film was an experimental look into **daily urban life inside a typical Russian city**. Of its many groundbreaking techniques (including **double exposure, slow motion and split screens**), its self-aware narrative gave **iconic insight** into the mind of a filmmaker.

2. David Holzman's Diary (1967)

What to Watch For: Introspectiveness within yourself and innovation within your film. It could be argued that, when **filming a film about yourself making a film**, you're really just **filming a film about yourself**. David Holzman (played by L.M. Kit Carson) explores as much when he **films a film about himself making himself into a film**. The lines of **reality and fiction are blurred** (along with the lines of documentary and docu-fiction) as David Holzman struggles and **searches for meaning in his film's existence** (see his quote below).

"*As soon as you start filming something, what happens in front of the camera is not reality anymore, it becomes part of something else, it becomes a movie. You start becoming very self-conscious about everything you do. Should I put my hand here, should I put my hand here? Should I place myself in this part of the frame, should I place myself in this side of the frame? And your decisions stop being moral decisions and start being aesthetical decisions. And your whole life stops being your life and starts being a work of art — a very bad work of art.*"

3. Day for Night (1973)

What to Watch For: The compromises a filmmaker must make on a film set and with him or herself.

François Truffaut's look into his filmmaking process is one part **behind-the-scenes featurette** and two parts **introspective review of who he is and why he's a filmmaker**. The film features the frustrations faced by a filmmaker as they must deal with everything from **actor relationships to uncooperative animals on set**. The **facade of control is withdrawn** as Truffaut shows how the filmmaking process is a series of compromises to **simply get a film finished**.

The film's ramshackle-style was **homaged by the Truffaut devotee** Wes Anderson for an **American Express commercial** that shows how the process is pretty much the same for everyone.

4. Hearts of Darkness (1993)

What to Watch For: How battle through the madness of filmmaking and being a filmmaker. Technically speaking, *Hearts of Darkness* is the **behind-the-scenes documentary** about the making of Francis Ford Coppola's universally acclaimed *Apocalypse Now*. However, viewed within itself, *Hearts of Darkness* is considered **one of the greatest films about filmmaking**, as it shows the sheer madness behind the filmmakers making the film.

Filmed on location in the Philippines, where a typhoon closed down production and **everything that could have gone wrong went wrong**, it's amazing that the filmmakers were able to just stay alive, **much less make a film about it**.

5. American Movie (1999)

What to Watch For: Tribulations of low-budget filmmaking and determination to never give up.

The story of *American Movie* is a perfect allegory for the **American filmmaking dream**. Making films can be difficult, **making films about making films can be arduous**. The main subject in *American Movie*, aspiring filmmaker Mark Borchardt, **embodies the filmmaking** spirit with pure passion, joy, and a resolute stubbornness **to never let any set-back big or small** get him down.

6. Best Worst Movie (2009)

What to Watch For: How to embrace both failure and success.

Best Worst Movie is perhaps the **best film made about the worst filmmaking ever**. The film tells the story of *Troll 2*, which is widely considered in contention for **the worst film of all time**. However, **the film about the film** picks up two decades later and follows how the film's makers have coped with their failures and, ironically, **learned to embrace its success** as fans find joy in its awfulness.

7. Side by Side (2012)

What to Watch For: The future of film as told by filmmakers.

From noted filmmaker Keanu Reeves, *Side by Side* is an exploration into the budding divide between **digital filmmaking and classic film filmmaking**. With interviews featuring everyone from David Lynch to James Cameron to Martin Scorsese, the film's behind-the-scenes peeks into **the minds of filmmakers** offer terrific insight and inspiration for **how filmmakers see the future of film** — all through a film.

Made in the USA
Charleston, SC
20 November 2016